RAY MAN
Modern True Tales of Aggressive Living

S. Ray Jackson

Copyright © 2012 Stan R. Jackson

All rights reserved.

ISBN:1484811070
ISBN-13:9781484811078

DEDICATION

"Not everyone who wanders is necessarily lost"-unknown

"Son... always be aware of your surroundings"- Uncle Bill Jackson

For Tee, who once said "Just do it"

Cover design: Casey McCarthy

CONTENTS

The Tales

3 Sunday in the PM

8 Hollywood

14 A Crawfish Boil

22 Tuesday Morning

44 4 O'clock

54 Wednesday in the AM

59 A hard rains gonna fall

66 A Lack of Lunch

80 And then came Jacksonville

92 Three O'clock in the PM

131 5 O'clock, quitting time…

142 Summertime and the Livin's Easy

178 The Era of Mexican George

183 When your super heroes can't fly

186 The Circus Witch

188 Gone Fishin…

193 Uncle Buddy

199 Ghosts of Viet Nam

206 The Big Move

249 Kid Stuff

256 Saturday Last

262 Matt and Marty

265 Hard Day's Night

279 The Volunteer

281 Letters from Tee

284 Snowed in with Russ

290 Thursday PM

292 A dangerous fellow

297 Lost Weekend

306 The Cat Dude

312 The Vietnamese Hick

317 The River

318 New Year's Eve

323 "OWN"

328 Fear

333 Trade Unionism

337 The Cushion

340 Facebook

345 Renos

349 Do NOT serve Paul

353 The Wind

357 An Outing

361 Drunk Driving

364 Trust

368 The Stalker

372 A Bad Idea

377 Endgame

383 Fear and Loathing Revisited

RAY MAN

ACKNOWLEDGMENTS

I would like to acknowledge all of the persons, living and dead, who touched my life in some way and contributed to this journey.

"Yellow Truck"

SUNDAY IN THE PM:

    This fine Sunday I find myself browsing in our local modest but very top quality Modern Art museum. The Arkansas Arts Center to be exact. This is usually a relatively pleasant way to lose some time but today this is not the case. One of the most annoying things in the world is to be shadowed by a pair of pre-thirty something sophisticated "want-a-bees" in matching muted cords, Ill fitting driving caps, one green, the other a sort of pale almost maze color. The couple looked like a combination of golfer and Irish pub patron, both options not uncommon to this southwest region in this land of ours. Each trying to best the other on where they have been or what they have seen. How Chicago is mediocre. New York Metropolitan is not as important as Los Angeles. How red is striking as a predominate color. Blah...Blah...Whatever.

    Sunday afternoon in the local Art scene. You're here looking for something to fulfill your lame ass day, or perhaps you're striving for an insight? Or more important a shred of truth possibly unknown to satellite TV and Barnes and Noble. It's organic and cerebral. It's only you and the work. Preferably and hopefully with no opinions to sway and try and sell you an item or concept. The explanatory card at work left... era, region, etc. is all and almost more than you need to know. And these two rat bastards are up your ass on your every turn.

I try not to let these types of things bother me so much and as a part of my new life philosophy I have begun to internalize things more and not act out. Ordinarily it would be in my nature to sharply turn on the pair and confront them concerning the details or flaws in their conversation.

That's not me now, no sir. One of my biggest flaws at this moment is the fact that I do have opinions about things. By and large they are not always politically correct and for that I am sorry. Well now that I think about it I'm not that sorry.

It would be politically correct to be sorry so you might say I'm unconventional. That's a good word. Unconventional. That's a word that kind of sums me up without being pretentious and/ or overbearing. I have a roadmap in my head with a moral overlay. All is flexible. Yes, I like unconventional. I think it empowers me to be off the grid when I desire. It almost becomes a private joke ; that I can see things for what they are without the predetermined accompanying rhetoric. Thirty minutes into this mental trauma and I'm ready for another cold beverage as was abused to excess the night before. I know I shouldn't, Sunday is for recovery and mental strengthening before the new work week. Perhaps there is truth to be gained however at the corner saloon. At least they have peanuts.

The parking lot at the pool hall is all but deserted but I push on and enter upon my own risk. There is hardly anyone here this day as most regular folks have lives at home with laundry and dogs and grilled cheese sandwiches. (Man that sounds good... the sandwich part). I don't recognize the two black guys at the corner tables and the bartender is that new chick with the weird shaped ass. I think she might be a man.

I really am not into this tonight so I slam two and hit the door. I didn't even want to mess around with the new "intra-web" connected juke box that is advertising over a million songs. That is really cool except the fact that each song costs two dollars. Hell, I can download a song from Wal-Mart for a dollar and keep it. But only if it is absent of derogatory language or suggestive themes. Its store policy.

As I pulled tight against the wind my mind shifted to the right and I considered calling my mom. The thought reminded me of something Tyrone Power said one time in a black and white film about every boy has a dog and a gray haired mom waiting for him at home.

My mom just got out of the hospital where she spent the Christmas holiday. To fully appreciate my mom you have to understand a few things. First, she and I learned how to drive together when I was fifteen and she was forty oneish. Second, she just got her first job three years ago when she was in her late sixties. Third, she cannot taste salt. She could be considered a little bit of a late bloomer who tried Chinese food for the first time two years ago and Mexican this year. She really doesn't understand me and my friends and I don't know that she is terribly concerned about it. She refers to most of them, even if she has known them forever as "hey you". Her solution to any problem is a meal.

I am perpetually too thin for her tastes even when I have additional holiday poundage. My face is too thin. My beard is too long. I need to dye my grey hair black, like hers. My being prematurely gray has been a real problem and she always felt awkward around her friends having a son much older than she was. I never hear "hello" and I guess I never will. I'm struck with a slight pain in my neck as I ponder the question as to whether to go for a visit and sit among the menagerie of aged and affirmed animals in the overstuffed chair and talk of urine flow *or* the dark safety of some other cavernous pool hall. Dollar beer or good son? I had a sudden flash of the recent chum incident. My mom's medicinal concoctions had over the course of time greatly limited her sense of smell and taste. As an "old school" cook who had no idea the gravity of the written recipe, it was an extreme hit and miss proposition as to the quality and palatability on any given day.

Mom had been on me quite some time with the invitation of a home cooked meal. She suspected I probably lived in my van and was most likely on my way with a case of rickets and scurvy and was convinced that beef liver was the cure-all contributing loads to my mental and physical well being.

After two months of dodging the issue I finally relented and a Wednesday night date was set. 5:30 PMish, which was the customary week night serving time I recalled thirty plus years ago. My one and only little sister, Linda, through her exceptional mental intuitive powers, (ordinarily used for potential evil), had heard the culinary plan and applied the classic guilt maneuver of "why are you cooking for him and not me too?" As a quick result of this question she was consulted as to what type of dish was required of mom for such a momentous occasion. We, the four of us, had not sat together alone for a week night meal in at least twenty-five years and we were very uncertain of the outcome. Sis chose the classic southern favorite "chicken and dumplings". On the surface this seemed like an exceptional compliment to the possible dryness of fried beef liver and a well rounded meal was anticipated. The time arrived and the punctuality of all involved demonstrated the electric excitement.

One very important element unknown to us which would affect the outcome of the soirée would be the fact that mom had not attempted to construct a scratch meal in over three years. All was well as beverages were dispensed and quiet conversation ensued. The table was finalized with a large tray of hardened beef liver, which was in season, and a gargantuan sized mixing bowl of steaming dumplings with generous meaty clumps of pollo (chicken). Smiles were the order of the day all around as this little jaunt down memory lane was presented in all its majesty. I helped myself to a generous portion of the charred entrails and proceeded to gather an overflowing bowl of the soupy concoction.

I salivated so hard in anticipation I almost started to believe the earlier propaganda concerning my living arrangements and I dug my over sized spoon nearly to the bottom of the Kroger brand chinette bowl. As I lifted the goo toward my gaping pie hole I was suddenly overcome with a very strange, sickly aroma.

This was not expected and I began to study the clumps, inspecting for the source of the wafting scent. Upon further scrutiny of the bowl and its contents I encountered a series of color combinations not common to the dish. A hush overtook the festivities as my eyes and my sisters locked across the table. She had not been as fortunate as myself. Her olfactory alarm had failed and she now had a large mouthful of the disaster. Tears of terror filled her brown orbs as she mechanically chewed on the gum like substance. I had been spared and bit my lip avoiding comment for almost eight minutes before I could hold my tongue no longer.

"This smells funny?" All action stopped as if a shroud had been tossed over the table and us in turn. "Maybe, I can't tell" was moms reply. "I haven't cooked in so long". Apparently, the lack of ability to smell had allowed a rancid chicken to be partially boiled as the first element of the formula. Everything after this development seemed in sync until the heat was turned to a danger level on the boiling pot. This created a dumpling and sauce dish which was consistent with burnt popcorn. The charcoal fragrance could not quite overcome the strange sweetness of spoiled yard fowl and the entire attempt spiraled seriously toward madness.

Sweat popped up and motioned toward me from my sissies forehead as she completed the unthinkable spoonful of bacteria soup. "What a gal," I thought as I pushed the bowl out of nose range and dug into my desired food order. "Want some to go?" Mom asked with ladle in hand. "No thanks" was repeated in unison by all as I pondered if I could freeze the balance, cube and sell as catfish bait.

Two beers at the house is about all the interest I can muster and I soon take an early retirement toward my chair and possibly some type of rerun before bed. There usually is something fairly decent on the History Channel although they have been on a hard left turn almost exclusively toward UFO's and all related items and locales. These are strange shows, no matter where you fall on the subject, because you watch hour after hour expecting some sort of revelation or new data confirming something and in the end there you sit, head up your ass.

Bedtime.

Hollywood

Monday morning came much earlier than expected today. Within the first two minutes of my work week I had at least ten solid, legitimate reasons for my non participation. As soon as I was prepared to make the call, a voice seeped in to halt the advance. It was my dad in his all too familiar tone extolling me in the virtues of honest work and how do I know I feel bad if I didn't get up, shower and see. This spirit haunts my very marrow. At that point, thirty minutes later into his theory, what is the value of warm covers. My entire escape fantasy, guilt and punishment all take place within a minute and forty three seconds and I hit the bricks to meet the day. The windows of the yellow truck are frosty with the remnants of the night.

This is awkward based of the fact my defroster is less than effective, my scraper is MIA and I'm a little short of time. This will make me three minutes late with standard traffic and I sit back, rev the engine and hopefully expedite the process. Damn, I forgot my XM radio faceplate so it will be NPR morning edition. If I hear one more Baghdad or hurricane victim story I think I'll shit right here on my waterproof neoprene all weather seat covers. I took a deep swig from an extra chilled diet coke can and watched the slow, yet consistent melting action creep north up the windshield.

It was going to be a good day after all, but I really can't wait for lunch. My day drags on and my mind starts to wander. I consider if some day it might be feasible to live in Los Angeles. I had one project there several years ago for a famous British mercenary. He flew me out for several site visits, with the main event, a benefit for the World War Two war memorial in DC. The

Queen Mary event park in Long Beach was the back drop and I think I may have taken the ship ghost tour five or six times based on ticket stubs I found later stuffed in the pocket of my favorite leather satchel. That tour is awesome after fifteen to twenty beers are consumed.

Timing is essential however as there are no restroom breaks below ship tour decks. It was odd to me how my client had housed me at the Sunset Marquis Villas, at fourteen hundred dollars per night, and where we would party like Joseph March for two days, after which he would vanish every third for at least thirty six hours. I didn't want to be too far from the room since I was on his dime, therefore I watched lots of TV and observed the elite at the pool deck from the balcony in my room. The client, well known on the streets was great friends with the owners of several clubs on Sunset and bragged as being the road manager of a famous rock band in the sixties and seventies between Foreign Service mercenary gigs. One night we met a photographer acquaintance of his who I gather was looking for a free-lance project. We had beers near the street at the Rainbow Room until my lazy, beer soaked tongue allowed my southern dialect to parade out in front of two bikers who had recently joined our party.

All that saved me from tasting cool California pavement was the pair's intense love and interest of all things Bill Clinton, of which I was very familiar. Once my attention shifted solely back to the buxom, all natural photo journalist, my benefactor and the object of his attention quickly excused themselves for what I assumed was part two of the interview. With his wife in England this would be the private portion. There I was, three or four miles from my hotel, or maybe ten blocks...after dark it's hard to tell distance. No transportation in a no-cab town, you know, much like Memphis after ten pm, with two huge drunk bikers wanting to talk Lewinski with me. I did not like the look in their black shark like eyes. I felt the best course of action at the moment was another shot and a beer as I nurtured the idiotic notion that the client would be back by for me. That first hour flew by.

I decided it best at this point to hoof it with two quick detours. One to see where River Phoenix departed this world outside the Viper Room and later a quick tour of the Hustler superstore. No male can pass that store without at least a quick peruse. I never understood how they can screen-print such fine lettering on black sheer thongs. After several nervous street encounters and the loss of one of my huarache sandals near Tower Records I think, I made it to the hotel. The lodging is also, beyond celebrities, the home of a notorious whiskey bar like those made immortal by Lizard King Jim with its late night velvet rope and line of under twenty ones, feather boa wraps and plasticized hair spikes. As I limp past the line in an attempt to enter the lobby, I am hit with the realization that I have never met the three am door thugs during my stay. I have one shoe and no apparent door key to prove my legitimacy. I also am remiss in mentioning the small pink hustler store bag I lamely attempt to hide behind my back.

I was too drunk to be belligerent, for once in my favor, and after dropping all the days' employees names I could muster, everyone was convinced my words rang true even if I slurred to the point of speaking Chinese. Twenty dollars American gained me room entry from the hotel security and a sleep on the floor sounded good, my head spinning.

Next morning early I was summoned by a light rapping on the door, much like a coin tapping…a dime maybe. Light as not to be heard but somehow urgent. I maneuvered up on all fours and halfway across the room toward the portal as I realized I was expelling urine into my Dockers at an alarming rate. The beacon became more consistent as I pondered how the mauve rug might stain. After what seemed like twenty minutes, I pulled myself to the peep hole and realized my one left shoe was on the right. I focused on the figure with dark glasses looking up and down the hall and realized it was the photog queen of last evening. I opened the door for what I thought was a thank you/glad to meet you when at the slightest door crack I was shoved back onto my rug bed in the dark abyss of room 324 with the door slammed violently behind.

"It smells like piss" she whispered. "I did not know that" I whispered back not understanding the meaning of the muted vocal levels. I collected myself as I realized a haze of fear hanging just slightly at thigh level. Electric light seemed inappropriate so I opted to crack the trilateral floral pattern curtains and allow a level of solar illumination on the situation.

"Sit down… do you want some water?" seemed a reasonable statement, so I offered. I couldn't believe what was before me cowering on the multitude of pillows decorating the pretentious sofa. She removed her Beretta style oversized sunglasses and revealed two huge black and blue splotches in place of the pair of green pools I noticed the night before. She looked down and to the left, much like Kennedy and I noticed a good sized dry drip of blood flat against her delicate ear. Earrings were also missing as if violently removed in haste. "You need a doctor…or a cop…or both?" "What happened?" She wouldn't and would never say. What she did want was me to shut up, walk her to the elevator and out to the adjacent lot to her environmentally friendly Saab. It was amazing to me how a night can go so far left as I looked at a natural beauty who just twelve hours before would never need the slightest amount of traditional makeup. She had glowed under the neon of Sunset Boulevard like she was radioactive. Now she was half life.

As par, the elevator stopped on the second floor down and a very attractive elderly couple gathered two small alligator bags and clambered aboard. At least it wasn't the client and we both drew a collective breath. The man looked of old Hollywood and I was amazed at how a mustache could be cut that thin. What tool could possibly? Perhaps wax. The lip art was only surpassed by the exquisitely high, yet inconsistent arch of the women's eyebrows. While admiring the pristine grooming, I realized the pair's eyes were widening in our general direction. This snapped me out of my trance as I reviewed our collective look. Horror swept me as I once again considered my left-right one shoe look and my two gallon of urine soaked khaki pants. In the fluorescent I also determined a heavy grass stain on my right knee and a spattering of dried blood in a ring around the base of my bicep showing through my white Cuban style "daddy" shirt. The kind your dad mows the lawn in while wearing Bermudas, black socks and slippers. I surmised the plasma was coming from the fresh arm ring tattoo of which I was quite unfamiliar. Thank god it wasn't connected.

In disgust at my own look I retreated to admire my charge. She was bruised in ways I had never seen and it seemed she had somehow lost several inches in height. If we wanted to make the lot without a bypass to county I would have to address the couple's concerns. I smiled a wide sweeping grin, which hurt my face, I believe from dried vomit and extolled "we are in a rock band". The smiles returned to the pairs stretched and stitch lifted faces. They understood totally. "You rockers…" one of the ancients contributed. "I never understood how on earth a man can smash perfectly good pumpkins?". I felt as if I was totally naked at my grandma's birthday party, and holding the cake.

The doors couldn't open fast enough as we squeezed through and out the automatic, eco-friendly tinted glass front doors. As I pulled her to the car, she pulled me close to her in order to hear. Apparently the damage was in and outside and her larynx was not allowing strong speech. The force of her breath was stronger than her words as she strained "he's a very bad man, your client...go home". I asked once again if she wanted a doctor and I offered to drive. She said she just wanted to go back to the valley and I sent her forth. It was eight am now and the whiskey bar was closing. I felt like a drink and knew if I advanced the rock theme I just might get served. The unconventionally low light was perfect to hide the color discrepancies of my wardrobe. I pushed deep under the padded bar and without hesitation ordered a white Russian.

The short glass was in perfect layers and almost sinful to dismantle. "Eighteen dollars dude" "Fuck", I whispered to myself as I dug out a crumpled twenty from deep in my pocket among the damp lint, Queen Mary ghost tour tickets and loose change. "Keep it" I snarled as I tossed the green ball in the bastard's direction. I drank deep and hard and wondered how quick I could pack. My client had the room and incidentals in his name so stealth and speed were essential. From the look of his party guest he had had a long night and should sleep in. LAX by about ten thirty, flight at noon. Possible beer at Chili's. I loved the weather here but CST was on my mind. "Adios dude, can you call me a cab....?" "I'll be back in ten bro" I shouted at the haggard bar keep as I hit the lobby elevator door. "Fuck you" he growled back. Go figure.

Back at work... Ten thirty in the am with lunch only thirty clicks away. I was still a little peeved about our ancient part time delivery guy Merle's weekly trivia question last week and I contemplated a revisit on the issue. Usually it's something along the lines of fur bearing mammals, chart of elements or the occasional noir movie star (always men). But for this one it was a religious, philosophical puzzle that you could tell he had gotten off the Seven Hundred Club, although I was unconvinced he could stay awake past eight pm on a school night. His query was if God intends his subjects to be holy or something like that, I really wasn't listening as one of my friends had just walked by outside. I have to suspect the motives of a man who starts smoking when he is seventy five. He also had almost backed over me with a pick up at least six times... by accident?

It's not that I'm not religious. Both my grown children went to a very strict Catholic school as non-practicing Catholics for their own good. I think when you put it all in historical perspective you can gain a true sense of where you are in the food chain. Did I mention they both flirted briefly with Buddhism upon graduation? Nothing is more complicating to a young man or women than to be exposed at home to a party spirit that would make Keith Richards weep like a school girl and the plaid skirt and khaki world during the day. It was my unsavory friends and the fringes of radio and rock business that created the sticky environment. Late eighties, early nineties. I think my children turned out so good because of the "son of a preacher man" syndrome. You know . . . opposites. Whatever.

I do wear a medal of a saint and have for many years. I chose, after careful reflection to don Saint Frances de Sale. Supposedly the patron of authors, poets and sailors lost at sea. I like to fancy myself all of these things, particularly in my slumber. Last year I decided to grow a Hemmingway beard. This took little effort over many months as I find it quite easy to not do things. One morning I woke up and discovered my Saint Francis metal was off the chain. In panic, I searched frantically the bed and immediate floor area. No luck after twenty minutes. I gave up alarmed that I had somehow lost it prior to retiring. As I entered the shower, depressed, to begin the day I began to lather and I heard a hard metallic peck on the shower floor. My medal I had searched frantically for had been lodged in my Hemmingway beard and had fallen to freedom. "What the hell?' I pinned it to the floor with my toes to avoid possible escape in the drain. In traditional fashion I took this miracle as a sign and promptly bush hogged my growth to acceptable levels.

A Crawfish Boil

Lunch at last!

I have a regular rotation of eating establishments designed to allow me to have the familiarity of a regular coupled with the variety of a tourist. Monday is a challenge however as there is no clear order of sequence to begin or end the cycle. Everything is geared off the initial TBD selection. I'm a bit of a maverick so I do what I least expect myself to do as I opt for two bags of microwave flavored oatmeal and chapter ten of my Civil War adventure book. I can still surprise myself sometimes. The rain was a factor I'm sure but I have never shied away from weather. I am drawn to the uncertainty of storms and often find a clear day boring. My buddy Casey enters the break room and flips on the history channel with the remote.

He knows instinctively I won't mind. Today there is a show on about the explosion and disaster at Texas City, 1947. I can hardly pay attention to my faux strawberry and cream mush and literary crutch with the pixel drama unfolding. Casey and I have been acquainted for several years, it seems maybe longer. When I first met him I was at my new day job, a result of 9-11, and he was the only person brave enough to approach me with small talk. I had a terrible rep as an absolute prick and was written off totally without even an interview by the general new job population.

He was a Nazarene youth minister which neither impressed nor frightened me as I was raised Nazarene. Both my feet were firmly planted in evil at that time. After several bullshit attempts at real conversation, the young man, of Irish pedigree and slight stature became a challenge. "Do you drink beer?" I cut to the chase. He seemed puzzled, torn and genuinely affected as he answered "I guess so". "Well alright, we'll grab a beer after work." It took little effort to draw him to the dark side in totem where he has resided consistently since. All that being said Casey's true value over the years has shown most brightly in his ability to pull me and my mouth out of tense and or potentially dangerous situations. As reported, he might on a good day, if he's proud, push the tape to five foot six or maybe seven, but he has pulled giants off of me. Call it adrenaline. Call it moxie. I don't know but I swear by it. I was born with the curse of a quick wit and tongue, and when drunken to stages of six to ten I seem to relish in the sport of antagonizing others to the point of distraction. I think I do this just to say I have been there. Playing with fire may excite me. However, my eyebrows often get singed. My best case in point is my last great bar fight, if you can call it that.

My friend Henry Lee owns Vinos, a pizza and microbrew joint up the street where my kid picks up charity shifts when in town. Henry is part Cajun and hosts each year one of the most outstanding crawfish boils, free flowing extravaganzas on terra firma and that year was no exception. Four or five of us thought it a great idea to hole up and pre-party at our new summer hangout and gain the proper attitude to deal with the anticipated parking issues and multitudes that would surely attend. Casey was dating my sister at the time and they opted for the short lived certainty of seating, food and beverage the bar would offer. This option allowed me to float. That was fine by me as it gave me the flexibility and freedom to interact with the party dynamic to whatever end would develop. At the party I ran into many old and new friends, some for good and some for ill. Almost as I crossed the threshold of the outer party portion held in the back yard I was jerked violently from behind. It was Shawn, or that was his Anglo name. He is a really funny guy of Iranian origin and had married in the early eighties for a green card. To his horror he had been held to this day tightly in the grip of his benefactor.

Shawn had a great love for all types of tequila and mescal derivatives and this could not be good for me. The bottle he carried and the bag of limes was exactly what I needed to overlook his broken English and backward attempts at humor. Man, I had really missed this guy. The gathering was very quickly too mundane for our way of thinking and we decided to hit the high adventure and uncertainty of the streets. In our excitement and zeal for a Saturday night we decided that a cross town trek to force Casey and my sister out of their nest to join us was in order. Frankly, I required some additional input of western influence as I can only take Shawn in small doses. I had forgotten this fact. We had a two song loop going at maximum volume on the stereo with the Foo Fighters wailing and the retro 80's "Safety Dance". Awesome choice. I and the sandman, on the return with hostages in tow, decided a liquor emporium stop was a necessity. This particular outlet, in this part of town, at this time of night was extremely packed at all parking spots as well as the drive through. This caused us to make the poor judgment call of double parking my bright yellow Xterra at mid space behind two Cadillac's.

We were a little obvious as we were the only white and near white guys within three miles as we entered the store. Shawn was really out there and walked past several banger types and Saturday night hedgehogs and directly to the counter for service. I would imagine the clerks and patrons alike expected these crazy pricks to pull guns and commence to robbing but were surprised at the gall as Shawn screams "if they were too busy to sell to a sand-N word". I stood there and thought of all the things that I wished I had done in my life and hadn't as I waited for the thump or loud pop I knew was just a moment away. After what seemed like five minutes and as I looked out the window at Casey and sis catching their breath locked in the backseat I heard an unexpected sound. A chuckle. And then another. They seemed to think we were both the craziest or stupidest sons of bitches they had ever seen and either way it was ok with them.

They cleared a path for service; I think to see what was next on the program. After this quick and dangerous liquor store spree in the hood which netted us another ketchup style bottle of two worm mescal and a Cuervo decorative shot glass set we were ready to head back to the sure comfort and wait service of "Phil Goods". As we swaggered in we noticed C and sis had charged on ahead in a feeble attempt at distance from us and had barstools pulled and waiting. To my right there was a very wide yet well dressed young man in a business suit staring into a bourbon and coke. Apparently his fiancée was attending a bar exam passing party on the upstairs mezzanine and he was either uninterested or had been coerced into attendance. Not a happy camper. This, a tactic not uncommon to females, and there he sat. In my typical, tactful, approach I struck up a conversation with the mysterious stranger. On the barstools we were almost eye to eye which seemed to give me the confidence to test the boundaries of taste. Shawn was no help in this matter. After several civil attempts I posed an important question to my new reluctant friend. One of Casey's values is he has learned through trial and error what certain voice inflections or pitch can mean in regard to present or future events and he can act accordingly. As he eased forward on his high stool, I asked the ex football player "How tall are you anyway"? "Six foot eight and a half, why"? My new Amigo hissed to himself. "I didn't know they could stack shit that high" I extolled so pleased that I had not stumbled on the punch line. I hadn't blinked before a huge trunk of an arm scraped me off of the stool and through the air, tangling and wrenching my knee in the legs of my perch. As I lay on the ground, the giant over me kicked me several feet off the floor and laughed "Didn't see that coming did you?" Tears flooded my eyes and I could barely make out a strange apparition in the haze, a slight figure leaping to my rescue. It was Casey, firmly attached to both the giants' earlobes and lifting him back almost like a pup who had overstepped its playful bounds. After the submission we bought each other rounds and all was right. The owner of the bar finally came out of his hiding hole and joined in the banter. Casey had saved me once again from certain annihilation and as usual I was grateful. I was lame but grateful. This would become Casey's quest and I his worthy patron. This seemed like something he really enjoyed (saving me). I didn't walk upright for several weeks but somehow felt lucky. But I pretty much always am lucky like that.

   Zack dropped by out of the blue today. I guess it's been four or five years, but it's like he never left. It's like the other of my close amigos and amigettes float in and out at various intervals with never a question of motive or regret. Most time, "Catching up" can take all of five minutes. This phenomenon is based on an understanding… this Kerouac principle of life. Alcohol is a major component but the base is understanding truth in relation to the road. My life is a journey. Sometimes I travel with others, sometimes alone. There are exits which I may choose to take and there are often wonderful people and exploits which I may choose or not. These exits may take a night to fully experience or they make take years. The trick is to understand that it's all for the sake of your journey, and know when you should move forward. Most humanity would consider this shiftless and sad and would only see a person they would consider unable or willing to commit. This is judgmental on many levels and judgment is something not recognized on the road. The sun comes up and the sun sets and if you can still see it, then it's a good day.

This network includes many, and we are never strangers to each other. Sort of like "fight club". Uncle Gaylen was one of the first and Zack certainly is one. Zack, when last around worked for me at the day job and at shows. He was in his late teens and was from a prominent yet very broken home. His grandparents were very fine people, a compliment I don't bestow lightly and came from very old money. A mantle they wore without pretence. They were some of the good ones. They say that goodness skips a generation, whoever they are, and this group is a case in point. He is a pretty big guy who you never feel uncomfortable around. Most important he went along for the ride with Casey and me the insane summer of the downtown apartment and the El Barrio days. This was basically a five to six month period of the most intense drunken revelry which left all who came in contact broken in finances and spirit. Nothing can turn a boy inside out like truly seeing the other side, and tasting its salt and sand.

Our summer hangout goal was always to seek out a comfortable, often dark and flexible drinking establishment to call our home. This is very important as a base of operations on a personal and business level. Geography is important, and a certain strata must be attained in the level and quality of banter. Character trumps all. El Barrio was a new venture by a pair of amateur restaurateurs and was their first experiment into a bar as a focus. It was three blocks from the new digs, ten from our day job and one block from the Amphitheatre. There is a God. Just the fact that our two, with a usual four to five more faces in tow, were almost daily barreled up made us the joint's new best buddies. We produced shows, knew lots of people and bands, drank enormous amounts of draft beer and paid cash on occasion. Our patronage however came with some demands of our own standard design. Fifty cent happy hour draft was the initial grand opening draw which we demanded would stay in force for us at all times. Our party guests would pay full retail. We determined early on, that if we were not ready at closing time, generally Thursday through Saturday night, they would let us close with a loose, blurry accounting of the damage. The deal maker or breaker at all our haunts is total use on demand of the TV remote control. Cheese dip is also a plus with points deducted for flagrant use of Velveeta. Zack, being under age slightly had to hang back for this selection process to complete. He learned quickly that all doors open when he was in our adventure club and all he had to do was provide physical backup in an altercation and occasionally laugh at our stories.

There was a multitude of interesting people we came in contact with at our small corner of nightlife. Next door there was a florist shop which supplied a steady stream of young, party types who were so pleased to talk with anyone without a lisp. One in particular had become very chummy with us, which was not a problem with her downtown based, live in boyfriend. He seemed like a pretty good guy for a drug dealer and we could tell she was more drawn to our collective charm and wit than the day to day shit at the house. She was on a pretty stable beer schedule with us for about a month when we noticed she was uncharacteristically missing from her stool and from the job. We didn't think a lot of it until we picked up the paper on the bar and spotted the police beat section. There in black and white was the boyfriend, who had answered the door in the night to be shot square in the face. He was alive but as a vegetable. That nice little girl, I understand, was somehow responsible and was later arrested. I'm not sure what bullet we dodged but that is how things work sometimes. Most of the time actually. Right up until the time it doesn't.

The wait staff was something as well. There was one particular waitress who had gone to high school with Casey and would hang back whenever she had an afternoon shift. She could do things with a shot glass like I've never seen before or since. Kind of a bitch but we all have our faults. The afterhours music of choice was Nine Inch Nails and Rob Zombie at full tilt on the house system and I can only imagine what the typical River Market tourist who could or would not gain entry thought.

The weird thing is El Barrio faded in the sunset in perfect timing to the end of our summer party. My house, again by virtue of geography was often the crash local after we would run the room of fun and frolic. One of the fuzzy times, you know the times when you don't know where to go now that you've gone too far, we hoofed it on to nighty night. I would cook eggs for the boys on occasion and it was not uncommon to go through three to four dozen eggs in a weekend. I was way past chef duties tonight and I collapsed into my overdone mess of a bed.

Toonses, my Pet Smart stray cat named after the driving cat and my only true friend at the time had created a perfect fur collar around my neck and blended exquisitely with my frosted salt and pepper beard. AM light flooded the blinds and it was time to take a count of the remaining guests and what may or may not have transpired. When I reached in the fridge for my morning d-coke, I did recall I hadn't cooked for the masses upon return but there was something amiss. I had grown quite fond of preparing a potent dish of late comprised of canned Wolf brand chili poured over whole wheat pasta and subsequently flooded with multiple slices of American cheese. This recipe does not translate at any level to a single serving and I usually will fill one of my mom's old Tupperware bowls with the excess for later microwave consumption. I had been on an out of town excursion the weekend or two before and the leftovers on last inspection had developed a thick moss of growth. It might have been a month. I'm not sure. The empty container was in the sink. This didn't look good. I inspected the slumber party for clues and it was Zack, on the floor between couch and ottoman, with a faint orange wolf brand mustache. He was still breathing so the unprocessed penicillin taken orally was not fatal. I don't think we ever told him. I think upon reflection only the cat and I had the laugh. Every one dealt with that summer differently. I had to hustle some new clients to keep the plates spinning. Casey had taken a vow of silence....temporarily, I think just for reflection and Zack had joined the marine reserve. Iraq was just a rumor and the independence of room, board, tech training and school money was worth the risks of future deployment. I think things at home weren't rosy either but we never discussed such matters. Everyone had those types of issues at some level and that was not to enter our circle of jerks. His military command was based in New Orleans and in a strange twist the Katrina hurricane had scattered his group orders to the proverbial winds. *He came back.* He had been back around for two months in town, gotten engaged, and most important, after much speculation and delay, gotten his orders. Front line infantry, Iraq. Summer in Iraq. As he described his deal and his upsides of the cash and travel I saw a slight wetness in his eye. This boy of twenty three or four was just a kid and I saw the fear of a kid. I believe his organized, planned, predictable world was rotating slightly out of sync and he needed a taste of our chaos. To see if he had changed, possibly settled in and became normal like everyone else. He had convinced himself this should be his goal. He was looking for the summer when there was no fiancée and no Baghdad. It was hot outside and beer was cold. I had taught him how much fun it is to catch rides and not worry about the destination. Leave your watch on the dresser with the cat on guard. I once went five years without owning a car which is impossible in these parts and was only better for it. A lesson for putting a Porsche into my neighbor's house in less than spectacular circumstances. I used my pain in these matters to teach this boy lessons he might never have known, and with much less expense. He needed these things at this time. We are all going to our new hangout Friday night for happy hour. Casey and I tell him the single rule there is cash only but we do have the remote. We will give him all we have because that's the road and that's what we do. He won't be disappointed. I decided to try and chill a little and let traffic west clear out so I decided to stop by the pool hall and see what the Monday gang was up to. That is the unique thing about the pool hall. There is a group of daily regulars who come in about eleven in the morning and play for cash until about three or four. Dollar happy hour starts about four thirty and that group leaves to be replaced by a rotating different daily group. I'm considered a floater because I refuse to conform to the structure of an organized group. The Monday crowd is a little slow on the uptake with its co-chairmen being a feed dock hand and a disabled railroad brakeman. You never know exactly what is going to confront you when you hit the door and today was no exception. Today's topic of heated debate was "how would you know if you saw the ghost of Chester A. Arthur?" After muscling myself up to my near-regular stool and slamming two quick Lites I could take no more and bolted back into the early night.

Sleep comes a little harder than usual tonight for me. After suffering through two late night Law and Order episodes which I've seen at least twice I attempt a CSI. I decided to cut it short but that stupid "It's a sin" song by The Pet Shop Boys is for some reason bouncing around the inside of my skull. Damn the eighties. Damn them to hell I says.

TUESDAY MORNING:

Tuesday is my favorite day. This is reinforced by the fact "Welcome to the Boomtown" by David and David is playing on the new XM radio I got for Christmas. The last two Christmases were pretty shitty for me as I was in flux, but my kids who live in New York, and Chicago respectively pitched in and got me the mobile and stationary set up. I'm a tried and true NPR man and it would never have occurred to me to get satellite radio but I have to say it's been good for me. Deep tracks have brought back so many of my youthful ideas it's almost scary. I may be a little out of touch with my channel selections but how many news reports can you hear about the Middle East or Dr. Martin Luther the King in your lifetime.

Business is a little brisk today and I'm thinking maybe the holiday slump, which was a little longer than usual this year may finally be ending. Bob Dylan's radio show just came on and it fails to disappoint, as usual. The one quote about musical instruments which catches me is "A violin sings, and a fiddle dances, and a viola burns longer". I've worked with him a few times and I've seen him good and bad. Either way he was and is my hero. That sounds goofy but he enticed me to shed my kid veneer so long ago I can't remember and begin my trek. You know, the road less traveled. He seemed to reveal hints about the path, but would never divulge too much information. He allowed you to develop at your own pace and in your own direction. These things I know after forty plus years of one foot ahead of the next.

When I first became aware of his work, I think was right after the Johnny Cash Folsom prison album came out. My dad was a huge country music fan and it seemed like a natural transition for me to folk music at the time. When I was young we would often vacation in Maryland and Delaware at the shore in an annual reunion with my borderline mental case cousins from Philadelphia. 1969 was no exception and I was quite taken with the throngs of bohemians that camped along the turnpikes basically all over the Northeast. Later I would know they were in route to Woodstock and I would curse the fact my age would not allow me to join them. (A situation my son and I would rectify in 1999.) I saw the freedom and the joy and I never saw people laugh that way before or since. LSD? Perhaps, but I like to think it was more basic than just chemical. Maybe that's what freedom looks like…I'm still not sure.

As the world outside my mom's kitchen and the small collection of latch key friends became less important these outside influences grew in stature and screamed at me in the night. Levi jackets and black lace up boots were the norm and probably made we all look like miniature hobos in the Guthrie style but that was our desire. We knew whatever there was out there was not here and Bob Dylan was a window to this fact. An attitude of rebellion was ripe in us, and at 14 my bud Gary Smith and I decided to strike out.

I'm not sure about the logic of winter as an escape season, and I can't remember exactly the school consequences but we had decided the best experience to gain would be to work in a logging camp. This proposition was driven by the fact that my friends grandfather owned a sawmill in the Southeast part of the state, a part not uncommon to the black bear and the cougar. In addition, his entire family in the region were strict Mormons, many were elders in the church. It is a religion which I had had limited contact with to date. Our arrangement was based on a room/board exchange predicated by the fact we had virtually no experience and the limited strength of our years. But we were determined and I told my dad I'd be in touch, and off we went. I'm not sure if my dad was crazy or confident. He had forged his own enlistment papers at fourteen and went to the South Pacific in the big War, so that may have been a factor with his apparent flippancy. Or maybe he thought it was funny. I can't know because we have never spoken and will never speak of it. The room we slept in had an electric blanket as the sole heat source and sleep was not to come except from sheer exhaustion. I remember being able to see my breath in the light from the street through the blinds. I had begun to drink beer almost a year before and in this environment, that was a rare treat, but one we aspired to.

 The work as I recall was brutal and I think it was the goal of our keepers to break us and they were intent. What they didn't know was our fuel. Every time we dragged in dirty and hungry, we felt alive. We talked endlessly about our long range goal of working for the railroad like my asshole uncle had done for many years until his legs failed him. This entire drama made us strong. At some point, there was an intervention, I think in relation to formal education and the party ended. Gary's grandfather had received money from my dad for a one way bus ticket and my departure was set. I had my Levi jacket and my boots and two small colossuses on each hand that were worth a million dollars to me. They were my badge and ticket to move forward. I hadn't died and beyond meeting the girl up the street who smoked cigars, I was virtually unscathed. The best thing about this whole experience is Gary through persistence and guts stayed true to our dream and retired after thirty years with the railroad. I think he lives somewhere near Kankakee with his family. He did it... that lucky son of a bitch. That trip was what Bob Dylan first did for me, but don't think twice, it's alright. What I got from the deal was invincibility and a strong dislike for long bus rides.

 I called my mom today to check in and see how she was after her recent hospital stay. She related exactly what it was to be stir crazy as she had only been up and down the hall two million times in nine days. She also reported my dad had been plagued by a stiff neck and had gone to the doctor. The physician had not found anything but surmised it was infected. "Anytime a doctor doesn't have a clue, it's an infection." She volunteered. I listened intently as she trailed off.

It was starting to drizzle a little as the sky began to close with the approach of a low pressure system from the Southwest. I really didn't mind except the delivery drivers at my work, which are all over seventy, and very opinionated, will be up my ass all afternoon for rain bags. Rain bags come in one size and I know I will be asked at least ten times about larger bags. Do they exist? How big would they be if they did? Do we have anything bigger than these? After the first hour of this tango I either don't make eye contact or if I'm in a really good or bad mood, I make a barking sound like a dog in response. Not a large dog, but more of the terrier or larger toy variety which is very effective. Through practice I have perfected this technique to the point where only my subject and myself are aware of the sounds I am emitting. I don't want to look foolish to my fellow cast a ways.

Aside from this annoyance, and my lack of a clear view window to the outside, I really do like the rain. Rain always makes me think of New York, first and foremost. NYC has a feeling that can only be truly realized in a steady pour. It's as if all the restless, living and not are allowed to venture out and share a collective moment. My son Dylan and I were there on a trip to visit schools, some years ago and this tapestry was woven most tightly for me. We had walked many miles north and south on Broadway with jaunts right and left for the occasional side adventure throughout the day. Our hotel was on the edge of Chinatown and heading in that general direction, we opted for an Italian meal at a mom and pop in the village. The village is the perfect spot to blend as there is no norm. The street names and Washington Square stand as monuments to change and ideas but somehow manage to remain a constant. Like old friends you can visit and are always welcome. The "beats" are very dear to me and their bodies of work illuminate these heavens. This is where their spirits reside. Every corner and stoop. We enjoyed a dessert beer as the rain began to work its way through the obstructions and down to earth. Most people would bail, cab it, and call it a night at this point, but my rule had always been slow down and enjoys things.

Another beer or two would suit this purpose at which point we opted for the ten or fifteen block hike. We cinched our gear and pushed off into the abyss. Of the colors of the street…late is the best. Black with the occasional red umbrella bouncing, slick and shiny with God's tears. Faceless travelers… avoiding eye contact running from awning to awning. This is the life. Earlier in the day, I had purchased a new Yankees cap over on Forty-second, and it was coming in really handy. This wash was a perfect baptism for a new lid and would allow, when dry, for a perfect soft shaping of the bill. Along our way, we opted for a coffee, restroom opportunity and a respite from the damp and now noticeable cold. All-nighter, NYU students crammed into almost all available seats at the Starbucks save for two which was all we needed. Just to take off the edge. Lap top illumination sent an eerie science fiction glow to the inside of the windows of the corner space. A bum was asked to leave. These times are more interesting to me sometimes than the most intense. These times have depth of levels. All depends on how deep you stick your toe in. About half way through my mocha Grande I notice my son looking past me, a trick with which I have some experience.

In the reflection of the glass, I also notice the smile of a really cute undergrad with a black turtle neck sweater and loose drawn hair taking a break from her term. After ten or fifteen minutes of this envious enamor and I think we are ready to head out. "You ready?" I enquired. "I think I'll stay, another coffee sounds good…I'll see you at the hotel later and we can have some of that good Chinese off the lobby for breakfast." "You sure?" I quizzed as I was a little unsure about basically leaving him on the streets alone at that hour in a city of this one's reputation. He looked me dead in the eye, glanced past me again and said "I'm sure."

I slyly passed him a folded twenty and gathered my bag and coat. Be careful, I whispered, as I slid out and toward the door. The late night counter girl smiled at me seemingly aware of the chess game unfolding into its third move and nodded approval. The rain had eased somewhat and I stopped to adjust my collar, got my bearings and looked up. Rain pellets glowed in the gala of lights and I thought of my boy at the coffee shop. He was living my dream there in the dark as he officially joined a world of which I could never. All my heroes were smiling down on me and I could feel it in every drop that struck my face. I never worried about him again and I awoke with calm about dawn when I heard his key turn the lock tumbler. It would be one of many very good days.

Near lunch:

I'm not really sure about all the attributes of flavored instant oatmeal. Don't get me wrong, there are some really fantastic flavors. Considering the fact that in my home growing up we ate Quaker oatmeal in the true Quaker style every work day for almost seventeen years consisting of raw oats ran through the deflavorizing machine, spoon after spoonful of unprocessed sugar, some whole milk. and a half stick of processed butter per bowl- (5000+ calories per breakfast serving). Modern product flavors did not exist with such delicacies as "strawberries and cream", "peaches and cream" "yaw yaw and cream" " blah blah and cream". I think cream must be a common and important element in each and every flavor. I really enjoy the convenience factor and the fact that if I have errands or want to get in some reading at lunch I can have a hot, microwave, nutritious meal prepared in under three minutes. Regardless, the main by-product for me currently is one of the richest and most satisfying bowel movements it's ever been my pleasure to enjoy. Important to men my age.

It's much how when a man is under forty all he wants to talk about is sex. After forty all he and his friends want to talk about is pie. My friends and I once talked, in a bar, for forty five minutes about which pie was better, pecan or banana cream. I think pecan won. It's a southern thing.

I'm really struggling now for the last fifteen minutes before my anticipated break. All that can quickly go to shit if one of my customers comes in with a brain teaser emergency, one of my specialties, but I don't feel that happening today. It's just not in the wind. Instead I decide to occupy my time a little more constructively by making a list of some facts about myself. This is an adequate plan and should be good for at least five minutes if I don't get to introspective;

1. I'm a relatively white guy.
2. I prefer dogs over cats but I can appreciate the ease of operation associated with cat ownership.
3. I hate children. Not all but most.
4. I hate Fleetwood Mac but mostly Stevie Nicks. I was a little offended by all the drama within the band that led to several breakups and the loss of artistic direction. (Much like the Mommas and the Poppas). Make a note: Never, ever shit where you eat.
5. I like maps.
6. I like atlases even more because it's a combination map and book. There are some wonderful atlases at the book store but I prefer mine. It's a little out of date but has served me well and that is worth a measure of dedication.
7. I might have a hula girl tattoo on my chest which I can make dance for a dollar. Not 25 cents, not 50 cents… a whole dollar.
8. I am the only person in my city of 250k that has been banned from riding the electric trolley car in over 85 years.
9. I don't like drugs or the abuse of.
10. I am well liked by police because I don't lie to them.
11. I like anything by Sly Stone but I care little for the family.

That exercise was fun and as expected it took me right up against the door for lunch. Today will begin my rotation cycle and I think the lightness of a Catfish sandwich and fries at Doe's Eat Place will more than fit the bill. Catfish sandwiches are a very delicate item of lunch fare (much like blowfish) and can be done very well or very badly. No amount of fries can overshadow a poorly done dish. I think the secret is the right cut of filet as well as the appropriate hot frying oil temperature. If the meat is too thick and the oil too cool then you end up with a limp, soggy dripping mess (much like most Hooters sandwiches) and its all you can do to suffer through the stimulus assault.

The perfect creation should be a light and flaky work that fits firmly in the palm and has an edge throughout that snaps in the mouth. You have probably surmised I am over forty and am probably overweight. You are one for two. I just appreciate when things are done properly or at least at some level of standard. Doe's Eat Place is as usual perfecto as my new Mexican running buddies and helpers (amigos), Chaps, Hernando and Roberto would say and after several glasses of exquisite unsweetened tea I settled in for some light historical reading.

This is political season and the one huge inconvenience about Doe's is all the darn legislators and their minions. You thought I was going to say vampires and perhaps I was thinking it. These often overblown, pontificators descend on this location like swallows to Capistrano for three main reasons.

1) Proximity to the capitol of my state.

2) Tradition.

3) Old Bill Clinton hangout.

When I worked a lot in politics it was very cool to meet in the Huey Long room in the back. This private dining room (complete with a H. Long portrait on the wall) has a claustrophobic feel because of the extra thick rough wood paneled walls and lack of décor. It is a strange place. One way in and one way out, much as you would expect these days. I never venture past my corner table and I think I'm much better for it. The food is great and I think they really are honestly glad to see me each week, in their turn of rotation. I got a little engrossed in a story I was reading. It concerned the Civil War battle of Cold Harbor and as a result I will be a couple of minutes late getting back. That should be fine in light of the light workload. Once back and settled in I decide to flip the radio over to the early rock classics and see what's up for the afternoon. There is some really great, obscure stuff on air that I would never own again after 8-tracks, but is none the less wonderful to hear. Today does not disappoint as the Beatles, a band I have grown to distrust and question, is belting out one of their over produced numbers "I want you". This reminds me of how that horrible movie "Sergeant Pepper" single handedly ruined the bad-boy image and career of Peter Frampton. More important was that first time my parents left me at home while they went on vacation for a week and this song was high on our communal play list.

I'm not sure exactly what the reason was for my abandonment but there I was, a young man with a home, no bills, a full refrigerator and a song in his heart. First order of business was to get some of my shiftless acquaintances from the neighborhood and 65th street to come over and assess the situation with me. I was a little unfamiliar with these waters and felt the opportunity could not be allowed to be short changed. This may never happen again. Once my crack team of advisors were assembled we proceeded to create a list of optimal expectations and outcomes. This design process took most of fifteen minutes before we were off to the races. The first order of business was completely rearranging the furniture.

With five excited and strapping boys it was no great task to change complete rooms leaving nothing untouched with the exception of the bedrooms of my sister and parents, both of which being aromatically sealed. The primary move here was the relocation of the nine-hundred pound console high fidelity stereo with the turntable and eight track into the living room as a centerpiece. The first casualty of our plan, which should have been a sign of the prevailing winds of fate, was the tearing of the thick velour speaker cover on the starboard side. This was not good, but also not of primary concern at this time.

Once everything was in order, taking several rewrites, it was time to plot what types of activities were worthy of such accommodations. Beer would be a very important element and would contribute loads toward our legitimacy with ourselves and potential future guests. I was forbidden explicitly from having a party and would never stoop to something as predictable and mundane as a teenage house party. This was my opportunity to be an adult and have all the trappings that I felt should accompany that mantle. We all had been able to grow wisps of mustaches from early on. My own had the accompanying Frank Zappa style soul patch, which had grown to an impressive length. This meant beer could be purchased quite easily at Sullivan's on the other side of the neighborhood. Miller ponies were the rage although the long time favorite was the pre-formula change Schlitz. The occasion would require both as well as Old Milwaukee tall boys which were on sale for one dollar per six pack. The forty dollars we had collected and extorted from all we knew would go far. The next issue would be what refreshments would be suitable for the ladies who would potentially throng to our new arrangement. Obviously Boones

Farm was the answer as we had and would never waste beer on a female for any reason. This was an unwritten rule but one highly understood and recognized. If I had a nickel for every date of mine who had puked beer I'd be eating nickel soup.

With all the low key details for the week set in stone it was time to shift to the third phase of the operation. Who to call? My first thought obviously would be forbidden fruit. You know, the one opportunity which would never arise unless your folks were at least three states away. Several situations came to mind, so in my customary style I chose at least three options. I felt that the possibility of one materializing was excellent and the hopes of two of the three scenarios was better than average.

The most improbable and appealing was to attempt and contact my old (stupid bitch) girlfriend from the northern part of the state and request a sit down. We had an extremely torrid and volatile relationship which had ended very badly several months before. She at one point was the one. Loni Anderson from WKRP, pre Burt Reynolds, could have been her twin and I was willing to do all including commute every weekend the two hundred miles just to bask in her glow. I believe I was engaged to her when the shit hit the fan. One weekend on my customary trip I learned she was no longer in town. Seems all along she had been seeing an older (25 year old), Hispanic karate instructor in town and the pair had taken the opportunity to pawn my ring for cash and headed back to Vera Cruz or somewhere. I couldn't hear or think clear over my sobbing. That deal apparently didn't gel and she was left by the outlaw pendajo (I think that means ass hole to you anglos) in San Angelo with a one way bus ticket back to town and an empty purse. She was very sorry but I was broken, which I'm sure contributes greatly to my intense distrust of anything with a Y chromosome. Don't get me wrong, I like all types of people but I just get an occasional pang behind my left eye in certain company and only the ageing process has helped. My dad and mom, rightly so, viewed this vixen as a cross between the antichrist and Easter Bunny (with large, real breasts)and any type of conversation which remotely appeared like reconciliation would not turn favorably for me. This would be perfect and the call was made… collect. Next on the list, at the urging of my best friend, would be the Henderson twins from south of town. Way south of town.

My friends and I attended an all black Junior and High school and were always somewhat intrigued by the cultural differences particularly in the area of party likes and dislikes of our black brothers and sisters. The Henderson twins would fit this bill and for purely research purposes the call was made. Again excepted, but with some trepidation based on my past history of school boy pranks and the related mass violence.

The third call seemed irrelevant at this point as we were two for two with the prevailing winds smiling at us. The next big issue was the relocation of all the refrigerator contents to the storage room fridge to make room for the beverages. This was a chore as most of the food and staples were not suited to a freezer environment for a week and the meticulous screening and selection process was creeping into valuable living time. Luck winked again when in the exchange our group ran across three round steaks which had been to this point hidden in the crisper. In all of five minutes the grill was fired, myself and my three closest co-conspirators were ready to cook on the patio with a cold brew and survey all we had created. Time and temp were in the positive column and we were kings all the way to the Interstate and perhaps beyond. It felt like Christmas Eve and sleep was a nonexistent concept.

I slept on the couch, mainly because no one could tell me I couldn't. It seemed an eloquent and appropriate act of defiance and would set the stage for the weekend activities. My friend John was obsessed with the Beatles and woke me early that Saturday with level eight volume on the console of Mr. Kite or Mr. Mustard or some such shit. I just know it wasn't Deep Purple or Tull, which was more to my liking. My "north country" girl was to be hitting town at about noon and, having not seen her for about six months, I was really intent on showing her exactly what she had blown off. I'm not sure exactly what I could have done to prepare or alter my meager appearance at this stage of the game but I'm sure a valiant effort was made. High Karate cologne perhaps.

I doused myself with my dads' cologne and my shortest cutoff jeans (being the 70's) so I was good to go. She showed up right on time and I felt the first order of business was to sit at the park in Wakefield and discuss all that had transpired and got us to that point. She looked great and was everything I remembered. She was tall, curvy and every young boy's dream.

The only addition was the hurt, sorrowful look in her eyes. She seemed truly sorry and I think she leaned toward wanting to rekindle and go back to our plans. Just right where things were before the proverbial truck slid into the fucking ditch and over turned. After this exchange it was time to rejoin the group. That first night I created the fatal error in a progression that would begin a spiral beyond my control or concept.

For some stupid reason, at that point, I had the misconception that you could trust your extended family. Call it blind zeal or the excitement of the moment but I decided it was a good idea to take my prize to my aunt's house in Jacksonville to hang out and have a beer. For some reason I didn't consider the fact that they were aware of the situation and subsequent disaster of our previous ill fated relationship. I also hadn't considered the possibility that my parents had asked them to check in on me and make sure I behaved. These facts would serve later to cause me great discomfort upon the parents return, at which time I would learn a valuable lesson. Of course the Jacksonville crew couldn't wait to spill their guts all over me and the floor.

At the time I didn't realize the gravity of my actions, but I figured out quickly that the least amount of information to the folks, on any given subject, is always the best tact. This is a practice I observe to this day. The next day seemed bright, like after a rain, and I decided whatever was going to come of this between us it was time to get the rest of the team together for the continuing plan of action. The reunion was, as you would expect, a luke warm reception.

My buddies had heard it all and thought she was the most vile piece of punch bowl turd on the planet and were not really sure what had drawn her to me. That was part one of the plan. Plausible deniability.

The local university at the time had a very loose fraternity structure and students with an even looser set of morals and ideals. It was the disco era. Somehow, even though we were a year and a half shy of a high school diploma, we had convinced one of the frat houses we were enrolled at UALR (our local University) as freshmen. Our goal at the time was to play intramural football and have all the house beer and chicks that were afforded casual student athletes of our caliber. Everything had worked perfectly. Anytime the subject of classes, professors or grades came up we just avoided or changed the subject. It was actually quite sad. That night there was a big frat party and my best friend David and I decided that the gathering would be perfect for us to attend with my ex. She, as you can imagine was extremely popular with the upperclassmen, who grilled her concerning each and every possible topic of discussion. After the proper amount of beer and baiting it was time for phase three.

Upon our arrival I had strategically parked my Trans Am in the side drive just underneath the bathroom window. The party had become increasingly nasty and the guys thought it funny to try and belittle me and David in front of our guest. This was a weak attempt to sway her in their direction and away from the less than adequate freshman. It was near impossible to hold my tongue but after a point I did notice several sideways glances that my out of town lady friend had directed at the club president. He was one of those career students in his early thirties and I had grown a very strong dislike for him and his feathered hairstyle and puka shell necklace.

The stage was set and any remorse I might have had evaporated quickly in light of the arrogance and deceit that was so thick in the air I wanted to gag. I gave Dave the high sign and he went out to the car to look for a tape. It had become a common practice for us, when leaving these gatherings to go to the back screened porch of the frat house and ever so gingerly help ourselves to a six pack or two for the road. We knew exactly where the party stash was stored and the diversion of the blonde bombshell made this phase of the operation even more easily accomplished. In keeping with the overall treachery of our actions we would go well beyond our usual score and go for all the beer available. This turned out to be six and a half cases of fine premium lager which we borrowed and stashed in the back seat and trunk. Once discovered that the entire night's beer was missing it was sure to be a very disturbing development. All hands were jockeying on the sofa for who the lucky bastard would be, which is kinda shitty since I, her date was still on the property.

The car was loaded and ready. David was in the passenger seat with the motor running. He had "Radar Love" by Golden Earring jamming on the 8 track and was starting to grind his teeth. We were ready. In a last attempt to check and see if there was a future with these new friends, or "frat brothers" as they like to be called, and this woman who I gave all to, I went in the living room to check the action. "Maybe we should leave soon, Marsha" I threw out in the room to see where it might land. The collective room looked in my direction like I had horns coming out of my ass and I knew I should slink away to phase four of the operation.

I excused myself to the restroom with no one noticing or caring what or where. As planned I locked the double lock on the door and propped the sawed off broom handle in a wedge against the knob. The shower curtain rod in this older home would just support my weight and I lifted up just enough to kick both of my boots through and out the bathroom window. Plate glass flew all over the hood of the waiting getaway car and I was out and standing on the gas meter in no time as adrenaline took over and my heart pounded heavy. This heightened state would come in handy in a minute. None of the preoccupied "brothers" and guest heard any of the commotion and we proceeded to ease out of the drive and onto 22nd street. Slowly we directed our vehicle and its bounty back toward the University proper.

Phase five. We headed straight for the University Security office, woke the night supervisor and proceeded with our tale. The best defense is a good offense. It was important he not look in the car so we charged up in a panic. "There's an underage girl drunk and being molested at the SIG Blah house on 22nd. "I think she's 15 or 16 and you better hurry". His feet hit the floor and his thumb the patrol mic almost in unison and the troops were in route. He shouted thanks as he slammed the door running past and that was our queue to head toward Duckville and the relative safety of the southwest part of town. We never saw any of them again.

I did hear "my brothers" were looking for us for about ten months. They would never venture to our side of town, so there was no immediate danger. I also heard that the University released my ex into the custody of her grandmother, who had to drive down from Harrison. As my dad told me, at least three thousand times, "be aware of your surroundings". As long as that advice was heeded we would be fine. Things would blow over. I think it was all worth missing the football playoffs even. Oh well.

The Henderson twins, they were another story.

In a really stupid "kid" move and after some deliberation the group determined that a total neighborhood product liquidation was in order. There was way more beer than we could ever consume in a month on hand and certainly impossible before my folks return in three days time. If we could recover our cost plus a little for future endeavors that would be smashing.

The concept worked too well and within about six hours we were looking at a pile of about $200.00 dollars. We were terrified. Fear however soon subsided as I determined through close calculation that the $200.00 dollars split one way was very close to $200.00 dollars. Steak was sounding very good again. I could offer to purchase some Churches chicken for the guys or maybe some twenty five cent raw half shells at the back door of the oyster bar. Even then I'm out ten bucks at best.

They were well pleased at the offer and with the involvement of the entire crew, our goal, met within the six hours was in reality hardly even an blemish on our otherwise lackadaisical day. Once word got out about the total liquidation we had to literally run to avoid the herd of late comers. The lucky ones in almost the entire neighborhood, under twenty, were feeling no pain and thinking I'm the coolest son of a bitch on the planet. Not a bad place to be at this moment of my young career.

The Henderson's had lost all driving privileges due to a misunderstanding with an auntie and were going to be dropped off by the fire station within the hour. I'm not sure exactly what the return plan was but the one thing for sure was that they could not be seen anywhere near my moms. This would definitely have to be an after dark, covert operation. After some quick deliberation it was determined that we would just have enough time to head over to 7-11 on 65th street and get a couple of large slurpees (strawberry) and possibly a half dozen radar range pizzas. I hoped Zane and his group of asshole friends weren't there because we were on a schedule and didn't have time for any of his shit.

Ever since I beaned him the last Halloween with one of Gary Smith's rotten goose eggs from about a quarter mile we had all been on his "list". We didn't know exactly what that was supposed to mean but it sounded ominous. "Do your worst" I always thought about yelling at him but never seemed to get the opportunity. Apparently he had just left so we were golden, made our purchase and high tailed it on back south.

Once we made it back up the steep hill and past the fire station we had just about ten minutes till show time. The sun had set, so we were in a perfect position to spirit our contraband guests into the relative safety of our newly decorated party pad. I had pulled all the R and B "8" track tapes I could find and had them positioned, titles showing out, so that my perceived musical tastes would be apparent. I had the lime green and orange throw pillows strategically placed in classic "playboy" style. There was no such thing as adjustable dimmer switches on lights and in the style of the time so a scarf (usually red) was draped over the lamps. This effect is much more personal and can be quite striking in the proper circumstances. The mood was set and the spiders waited for, in this case, the two horse flies.

At this point I felt it in my best interest to excuse my forlorn friends. It was going to be awkward enough to just make small talk much less with an audience. This was coupled with the fact that both of my compatriots had a red ring around their mouths due to the slurpees. We were absolutely too old for that sort of thing and it would certainly set the wrong tone for the evening. This would be a solo errand. They would just have to trust me and get whatever details later.

The proper time of arrival came and went. Sweat was a shimmering glow on my forehead as the door knock I had painstakingly anticipated came. What do I do? Do I just sit quietly and hope they go away? Do I run out the back sliding glass patio doors and into the woods? What the fuck am I saying? I got up and answered the door. There they were. The twins. They were dressed in probably the ugliest knit outfits I had ever seen on a human but the low cut of their jib drew all my attention away from the K-Mart blue light special fashions. Stunning.

This could get interesting. First order of business was drinks all around. As you may recall my leanings concerning beer and girls, I was momentarily torn as I considered my options, beer and more beer being all I had left. I made inquiry into which type of beer would be appropriate based on my vast selection. After brief deliberation, we were all sipping slyly at our plastic, semi faux frosted tumblers.

After at least four drinks I had pretty much exhausted my entire repertoire of inter-racial, x-y, southern Baptist beer conversation and I nearly choked as I caught myself eyeing that sliding door and possible freedom. The stillness of the moment was broken when one of my guests inquired" why are you talking so damn much?". In stunned silence I sat and stared in disbelief. This was the one direct question I had not prepared for in my monologue. "We gonna make out or what"? I had never before or since had that type of pressure put to me, and if I hadn't been currently seated I'm sure I would have hit the floor. I was able to make my escape with the fail safe method of the emergency phone call.

My buddies knew that if the advance signal was not given at the appropriate time urging them to wait then the call would be placed. As I sat there obviously no signal was made. The story went that my mom and dad came home early and were calling from up the street. I quickly led my party to the car and took them to the mall parking lot where they could wait at Denny's for their cousin or auntie or whatever. Getting close to danger and the unexplored was enough for me and I caught my breath after some time. I chickened out and really didn't explain this fact to my friends. They knew I didn't have to.

After I cast off the twins I decided to scan the groups of cars at the Mall area I had dropped them and see what kind of action might transpire with my new found freedom. Right off the bat I ran into one of the finest looking, yet dangerous women, I have ever known before or since. Later she would become the first women to ever shoot at me. We had a brief stint where we dated one summer, leading up to the attempted murder, and I wouldn't trade the experience for anything. Donna was one of those rare breeds who developed very early in shape and stature as she pushed six feet tall with zero body fat, and if there is such an animal...dips and dives like a California coastal highway.

The only problem with the entire package was the loose spring just slightly under the hairline. She had a very bad habit of doing whatever chemical was available and then demanding your complete and utter attention. (This was not always unreasonable when she wore a low cut top or the two size too small wife beater T). The beginning of the end came one night when I had turned in a little early and would not return her call. I had just dozed off when my slumber was shattered, along with my window, in my parents' home. Apparently, when I wouldn't respond to the coaxing she found it appropriate to hurl a brick into my room in an attempt to see if I'd come out and play. This approach worked perfectly as the disturbance also summoned the folks and all the family pets. After picking the shards of non-safety glass out of my bed clothes my dad encouraged me to go out and see what the emergency was. The answer would determine if police involvement would be necessary. As I approached the car I could smell her state of mind, at which point she floored it in reverse and darted into the night. As she rounded the corner I could just make out some sort of cursing (foreign in nature) barely audible over a fully cranked heavy metal tape. Even in this situation she was extremely hot in her Chevelle Super Sport with the side pipes her brother had installed for her. As I headed back to the house I could feel a collective sigh as the crisis had obviously passed. At this point I had a very irate father, probably intensified by the fact it was a Tuesday and the delicate family schedule had been destroyed, along with the glass. He tersely instructed me in the proper technique of taping plastic over the hole, where it would hopefully stay until morning.

At that point our homeowner's insurance would be contacted and a report of vandalism would be filed. I'm positive her name would have appeared in bold letters on a police report if she had stuck around to attempt and explain. The window was eventually repaired and several days went by with no contact by either party. I thought that surely all had passed. I hoped. That Saturday I and a good friend were almost ready to hit the streets when I heard the Super Sports thumping exhaust.

"Oh shit" we exclaimed in unison, and for once I was really glad the folks were out for their weekly grocery store run as she was sitting in our drive way, blocking our escape. We determined, after some debate, that a face-to-face was in order. I took the lead but made sure that my buddy John was in tow as a possible witness to whatever might occur. She appeared extremely lucid and apologetic and even offered to pay for the window. An acquaintance of mine was in the front seat, my old friend Charles's little sister, Rhonda. Charles had been my best friend in the 7th grade and was possibly the most extreme example of a latch key kid I had ever seen. He had been a wiz, at an early age in the art of preparing instant iced tea, and cooking various breakfast meats, out of necessity I'm sure. The most interesting thing about this time was the entertainer Glen Campbell's sister lived next door to him and we would often see him pull up late at night in his limo for a visit.

The last time I saw Charles or Rhonda he was shipping off to the Army at age 15. He had been interrupted attempting sex with a same age girl in a house near our 2nd bus stop by a fanatical Pentecostal mother who demanded a rape charge. There is no way her very plain and upright daughter would be interested in sex otherwise so the charges were filed. The compromise would be the military and no charges. I think sparing the girl from testimony on the stand was the motivation. As a result, this pal of mine, who wasn't shaving yet, was suddenly a man with a fort and a Texas address. All over a very mediocre clandestine, awkward sexual encounter. His sister was also a total fuck up who we all suspected as being a little mentally off- balance. She would often gleefully show us the huge scar that ran across her entire belly. The result of a boiling pot of spaghetti water hurled by an overworked, drunk mother who had recently misplaced her upper bridgework. Attractive.

All of these images flooded over me as I saw her smiling that idiotic grin of hers. "Get in, we need to talk." Donna whispered in my general direction as I ventured just slightly into the open driver's side window. I felt John kick me on the heel and say "no fuckin way." His presence did help reassure me that we could handle whatever might be in the making, so I began to consider our options. I think it was at about this time that I looked down and began to survey her evening attire. She was wearing a cut off football jersey sliced raggedly too short for a girl of her stature. With her every breath, skin was noticeably peeking out from just underneath. Now she had gained my undivided attention. This was all the encouragement I needed, the brick incident quickly became a distant memory. John and I excused ourselves to confer. "Come on man, there are two of them". "I'm sure Rhonda will look just fine in the dark", "we'll just see what's up. What can happen?" after several long whines, John agreed. We eased back to the idling gas hog and I leaned in to make the deal. "Just talk, maybe a beer, right?" "That's all" she said as she fluttered her long black lashes in my direction. Rhonda climbed into the back seat and was summarily joined by John. I took the "shotgun" position and we advanced slowly out of the yard.

We had not quite hit the pavement when she floored the ride. Away we went. "Where we going?" I asked a little concerned. But the enjoyment of the bouncing bosom as a result of the high rate of speed made my vantage point fantastic. This overrode all anxiety. "Bauxite pits off Ironton Road... I know a place". We sped off into the night and reached our destination within about fifteen minutes. Not hard to do at sixty to seventy miles per hour.

The area of our destination was a series of abandoned mines honeycombed by deserted gravel roads and unauthorized trash dumps. Not a pretty place, and no one around for at least ten miles. She hit one gravel road at the end of a lane and eased down quickly to an appropriate speed. Almost as quickly as the conversation void trip had begun she braked to a complete stop and there we sat. Everything seemed in slow motion as my attention was shifted from the bottom of her pride peaking out and to her hand turning down the volume of the tape deck. "Don't Fear the Reaper" by Blue Oyster Cult had been blasting and the quiet hum of the engine was almost as disturbing.

I followed the arm up and in the glow of the dash board I noticed a strange flash in her eyes. Dread welled up in me. "Hand me my gun, Rhonda, it's under the seat". John and I both thought it was a joke until I saw the blue steel. They had obviously rehearsed the movements, and before I knew what was happening Donna had drawn down on me. Instinct took over and just as I grabbed hard on both her wrists and thrust up she let a round go through the car roof. I remember two very odd things at the time. One, I couldn't hear from the report so close to my head and two, the smoke escaping through the new hole.

I held her arms tight and, in turn, the 38. In one motion I kicked open my door with both feet, breaking the door lock. "Get out John!" I screamed as he bolted out the back door and off into the pitch dark. She seemed as dazed as I did. I knew this situation was beyond reason and if I wanted another sunrise I would hang on. After I collected a slight amount of composure I decided to bang her arms on the steering wheel in an effort to release the weapon. I would have broken her tan and resolved arms if necessary as fear was replaced rapidly with rage. "You crazy bitch" I shouted as I slammed her arms at the forearm and wrist. In one motion, the hand cannon hit the floorboard. I had my chance. "This is it" I thought unsure of Rhonda's ability to fight me for the prize. The gun was hot to the touch as I grabbed the barrel and hurled the chunk of metal out the door. I was right behind as I followed into the roadside ditch.

Luckily, the ditch on either side of the road ran the entire length of the road and was very deep and dark. I had no idea where John was but I knew we couldn't risk detection at this point. I didn't know what the girls' plan B was. I assumed it was to get a flashlight and finish the job. I worked my way toward the road until I stumbled over my panting and terrified companion. "Come on, If they pull a light out we're toast". After about 300 feet in the ditch we stopped to survey the current situation. The car sat lifeless in the exact position we had abandoned and we figured they were either freaking out or developing a plan. I felt confident the gun was lost but we didn't know if they were prepared for its loss or not. As two shadows emerged we heard a sad cry, "we're sorry, come out and we'll take you home".

That concept was of no interest to me at this time and a better idea was to keep working toward the main road where we could thumb a ride. After what seemed like 30 minutes they got back in the car and eased past us down the road. As they crept by I noticed that the door I had broken was secured by a piece of rope or duct tape. I couldn't be sure and really didn't care. Once they hit the pavement of the state highway, they floored it and were gone. We walked and breathed and shared an uneasy laugh or two. That was all we could do. We had come very close and home had never looked better.

After whatever deranged high had subsided, and the realization that her future rested on my next phone call she came by around midnight to apologize. John had gone home with the comment that he might call me sometime. Apparently Rhonda had been relieved of duty. The condition for me to go near her was she had to stand very still in my yard so I could check for weapons. Once satisfied, we talked. What I saw was a very confused and frightened person who couldn't control herself. She knew I would have her arrested but she didn't know me as well as she thought. I held her on that warm and muggy night and eventually joined her in her haphazard state of dress. The damp and soft blanket of clover underneath my sister's window in the shadows made a great stage for our dance. We fought and clawed each other and our collective young blood boiled. I will never forget her. When you go through some crazy shit like this when you're young it somehow empowers you with a confidence which doesn't easily leave you. Other things seem a little less complicated. Maybe even simple.

I'm sure there's a lesson here somewhere but I really can't say exactly what it is. Years later Donna married a much older man and had a multitude of stair stepped kids. I heard she died last month of some kind of cancer. I hope she found what she was looking for.

4 O' CLOCK

The afternoon was a little slow and that gave us a chance to catch up and bull shit around about sports and upcoming spring projects. Even though I've played sports all my life, and even had a college football scholarship offer when I was in high school, I pretty much have no interest in the subject. I think It was a gradual thing to lose but none the less it was well gone. The sad thing is I really don't have any idea who all of the current pro football teams even are. If my friends were privy to that fact I probably would be ostracized to an existence outside the circle so I just avoid the subject and go about my business.

The main topic is usually college sports. Our state's main University is a political mess and has devolved, over the last thirty years into a hapless wonder, with a complex against success. We have never been able to win the big one and will, almost on cue, give the victory over to whomever. This was the focus of today's discussion. I nod and pretend to express interest, my mind wanders to sailing and laundry.

The end of the day comes and I think that after a quick visit to the gym, tonight would be a good night to play some electronic trivia. There is a decent little bar near the University in a strip center that has a pretty good set up. Tonight is also the night they have the revolving poker for point's game. This is also entertaining considering the total freak show that accompanies it. They recently rebuilt the bar area so that from almost any angle you can play your game and have a total vantage point above the gaming area. It's similar to the poker on Television but with a slightly bent, redneck twist. I'm talking mirror sunglasses. Big cigars. Dogs playing poker dress shirts over sansibelt slacks.

Every combination of silly shit you can imagine. The beauty of this sublime parade is that all the participants are totally serious. It is their edge. A style you might say. When beer is added it is almost better than HBO.

My other favorite thing about this bar is I am totally anonymous. I go in there just about every other week and they act like they don't know me from Adam. I really don't want to know anyone there and that works out fine. Everyone there that plays trivia operates with player code names which keep running score totals. I, in an effort to confound my fellow players, will alternately switch player names and sometimes list the same name as a current regular player followed by a numerical digit. This really pisses the victim off which is exactly the intent. The only player exempt from this taunting is my former lawyer who goes by the code name "Lester". This is for several reasons least of which he is a master of the game. He can shit answers for 1000 points consistently that no human being would ever reasonably know. I admire a guy who can name all of the countries created after the soviet breakup, or element number eleven of the periodic table. That is style. To hell with those poser poker playing jerk offs.

I decide to log in tonight as *GUEST6*. The other players hate that because they don't understand exactly what the fuck that is supposed to mean. That gives you the edge when you attack them with their own intellect. The first game topic is movies, which I can rule if not under the influence. The difference in reaction time is amazing between two and six beers. That can sometimes mean the difference between 980 points and a shitty 234. Once I get situated and see the player board I realize that I forgot to log off last week when I was *g-master-p*. Oh well, little late now. It is amusing though to see that name on the board every answer with a 0 beside it. My own private joke. I do ok but come in second behind *UK Navy*, who is a bitch on basic topics. He tends the bar at a joint down the street. After an hour or three I decide that enough is enough and I log off all my entries in the middle of a game. This pisses them off too because they assume it is just too easy so why bother. Maybe I am a prick like everyone keeps telling me.

I'm really overtired now and although the scene at the trivia bar is exhausting I'm still not quite ready to put a lid on the day. I think maybe that checking in at the pool hall may be at least worth the drive over the river so tunes are popped into the CD and off I go. The selection for the ride is the ever popular "Man Music" which is a compilation of 22 songs which are relatively anti-female. This was put together during a low period where I needed some alone time. The first track plunges directly into "Young Lust" by Pink Floyd and follows quickly with "Cocaine Blues" by Johnny Cash. At our concerts the last couple of years during band change over or during set up or tear down I use this as the house music. It has become very popular with my guys and I have burned several copies for friends.

After about 15 minutes I hit the door to a surprisingly crowded room. I guess by this either a tournament is running long or maybe great minds think alike? The former rings true which is of no consequence and I pop onto my favorite barstool. Usually the empty one. A big smile shines at me from Keith and a frozen mug materializes in front of me. One of the most gratifying things in the world, aside from a good slice of pie, is to be able to walk in a joint and get what you want without ordering. This implies a level of trust and a bond between client and business that is uncommon in this day and age.

Sitting next to me is Tatum, probably my closest Afro-American friend. Tatum is a survivor. We struck up a conversation about two years ago based on the fact I had played football in school with some of his cousins of the same name and we had been fast friends since. He works up the street at a feed mill and processing plant and on the way home, wherever that is, he stops here to unwind. I don't think he has cable and he likes most of the shows I choose to view. His thoughts on drug use and death help reinforce my own but greatly overshadow what meager contact I may have ever had with either subject. Tatum is a recovered addict.

He's not a large man but you can tell he has the power of will, and a back developed of hard work. He is a year or two younger than me and twenty years older, all at once. You can tell by counting the rings under his eyes. It's like the local police dept says, "we work hard and we play hard". His favorite thing is to buy me my first two drinks, I always oblige him. I suppose this is some type of insurance that I won't turn and run from his conversation or not give him the measure of respect he is entitled to. Whenever the subject of women comes up in the conversation, which is daily, he always relays the story to me of the lying, cheating bitch ex-wife of his and we get to reexamine the healed through- and- through bullet hole in his upper shoulder. This is his survival badge, and I never act annoyed at the explanation. It seems that she is also the person who hooked him on the crack and in the process stole and sold basically all of his personal belongings to feed their habit.

The laundry list included items such as his deceased father's gold retirement watch from the railroad and pretty much everything else that could fetch a dollar at one of the many pawn shops near the river's edge. In his stupor this was of no mind. It was just stuff in his sock drawer. He always says the best thing that ever happened to him was the argument that led to the shooting. The wound was not life threatening but the intent was. The positive results of the trauma were two- fold. First, she went to jail for several months which would allow the addiction and enabler cycle to be broken. Two, the extended hospital stay because of nerve damage allowed him the opportunity to be freed from the chemicals and gain new perspective. Oh yes, he was proud of that little 9mm hole! That was his new life just under the surface. Another result of the hospital stay was his current job of eight years as dock foreman at the mill. It seems that during his visit there had been a shortage of private rooms and he had been joined by the feed mill owner who had been admitted for an emergency hernia operation. As you would expect a conversation ensued and before too long an opportunity was on the table, based on the potentially being clean aspect. Drinking was not of as much consequence to the owner, who believed everybody deserved a good belt occasionally. Drugs and gunplay, however, were another matter.

His other favorite topic is how bad he used to be about all night smoking binges leveled by multiple 40's. All this before he went to work that day in his landscaping job. Thank god no heavy machinery. Just a shovel. He was a backfill man. But now he was just a regular man. He had a job. He had people that were as close to regular friends as he had ever known. He was out of the negative column. His taste in music was not as you would expect and leaned more toward classic southern rock. This was not totally unreasonable considering the time and place from whence he came. The internet jukebox was a different matter for him and was not easily mastered. He would often prepare a list of what he would like to hear and then when things were slow he would get Jeri, the day bartender to plug in his selections before she left the building. This arrangement worked quite well and he always asks if I want anything special. My reply most times is "the usual". He always smiles that wide grin of his and plugs in "This Ole Cowboy" by the Marshall Tucker Band. He knows that makes me very happy.(Not the live version but the studio). I really do admire this guy and enjoy his company although I can't say our relationship would be the same outside of the context of these walls. That's just how things are. Adapting to your surroundings has always been easy for me and the group of friends that comes with that ability is wide and varied. It always confounded my family that I was just as comfortable drinking quarts of beer behind the Shell station downtown as with the president's staff at the DC Occidental Grill. I'm lucky that way. "Human beings are the best people I know". I think Abraham Lincoln said that.

    I decide that all this reflection can only mean one thing… restroom break. I gingerly test the knob and thank the lord it is fixed and turns tightly. Last Saturday we went to an afternoon funeral for a local strip club owner friend and came back to this bar to meet about an upcoming event. Apparently, the night before a patron with an extreme bathroom emergency had rushed the door and broke the lock. The bathroom, although clean and bright is basically a one hole-r. Even though there are two wall urinals there is only one toilet basically in the middle of the room without dividers or cover. Sort of like a state prison or county lock up. There was a tournament that day and many new faces. After the meeting and several cold beers in our friend's honor, I decided to break the seal. The knob was turning oddly and with a slight push there I am making eye contact with an elderly man doing his business. There is no creepier feeling than making eye contact with a total stranger at his most vulnerable. Especially when it happens two more times before you leave. Once I did get in I saw something very bizarre that I have had to think a lot about. As you may or may not be aware, urinals are not set up to dispose of anything except liquid. This is widely known among most all males so what I experienced had to be a deliberate act. In the urinal, someone or something had placed probably fifteen of the bubble gum jokes from double bubble packs, folded origami style into funny shapes. Just the act of this would have taken an enormous amount of time, not to mention reasoning. Was it a test of some kind? This required more thought.

It's getting a little late now and I'm a little blue. The two coolest people in the world I know are 1000 miles away each and I miss them very much. They are funny and alive and I am so blessed to have touched them in some way and they me. I wish there was more I could do with them because text and email is a little impersonal. But we all seem to function well with that type of contact. They were my adventure buddies for a long time and I hope for a long time to come. They are my children.

My next possible great road trip is being planned now to help relocate my daughter from Chicago to San Diego. She is currently a third year design student in Chicago and will finish her degree in California while residing with her boyfriend. I really like this guy and I think he has good intentions and may be good for her. That's a big deal considering I usually am a harsh judge of character, because of entertainment dealings and I can spot bull shit as soon as I smell it. We met last Christmas for the first time and had a wonderfully fun time with my son and his now defunct gal pal. I would come to find out later I was totally wrong with my first impression and he is somewhere in the wind now.

Casey, who is expecting his first with his wife, would theoretically join me in early July. Load all her heavy and cumbersome gear and haul cross-country to SoCal. We would loop the trip on western routes I haven't traveled in almost five years, and stop to visit and stay with many of my old friends along the way. This is the kind of trip that heals the soul. If the soul doesn't need healing then it builds the blood. The trip includes stops in Mesa, Vegas, LA, Tijuana, and Denver and where ever else time will allow. It will take about ten days. I need it badly and not because I'm unhappy here but I just need to feel it again right now. Trips that were every other week are now further and further apart and my taste for traveling alone is not as sweet. I would rather experience things with someone than try and relay. You can't really describe smells and colors accurately to people, so you keep them and in a way it's sad you can't pass things on. It's like pushing hard ahead of a snow storm at 3am near Tucumcari New Mexico when a meteor crosses right across the front of me in heavy fog striking the field to my left with sparks and flame. You have to be there for that. My children were lucky enough to get some of this but they are on their own roads now and I'm not quite finished. If Casey doesn't work out his stand in is my nephew who needs this kind of trip as much as me. I hope he does. This would also turn out to be a misjudgment.

Last time I drove out west was just after 9-11. I had a gig in Vegas for Clark County doing the children's portion of a county festival. I really needed the money as I was hemorrhaging funds due to the fact that no entertainers would fly. I had about six shows cancel the first thirty days. The common agent response even though I had a signed contract was "sue me; My guy and or girl is not getting on a plane". I didn't blame them and no suits were ever filed. The gig included the erection of an outdoor rear projection movie system and I decided to maximize my profit I would rent the gear from myself and haul it out west. I could use the trip and needed to stop and see a guy in Phoenix anyway. I knew I might have a little problem along the way, based on the look and condition of my gear. I had a wide array of electronic devises, mini truss and detonator looking shit with wires sticking out. All of this was packed into green military duffel bags from my local surplus store and tossed onto my general load of clean and dirty clothing, ball caps, and bootleg CD's. This did not look good. Money was a motivating factor I think pushing me to make the journey under these conditions.

The first sign of trouble was the exit at Kingman, AZ and a military check point on the road to Hoover Dam. I was directed over to the shoulder and ordered out of the vehicle. After presenting all the proper ID and papers to the stone faced National guardsmen with M-16's I stood back and awaited the battery of questions I knew were hanging in the air. In anticipation of whatever, I had produced an extra copy of the invoices and contact information for my project and handed it over to the officer in charge. This seemed to ease the level of tension in the air and we all breathed a collective sigh. I was one of them. After about thirty minutes researching my social security number and seeing until recently I had received a decent level of White House Secret Service clearance I was allowed to proceed. Before my departure I was cautioned that about two hours ahead there was no guarantee I would be allowed to cross the dam. The rumors were flying everywhere about terrorist plots to blow the dam or at least poison the drinking water it afforded and the alert was high. It was explained that the command in that area was very old school and hardnosed and no bull- shit of any kind would get through the filter. I thanked them and explained that I had to give it a shot, and assume I would have the same problem at the smaller dam at Laughlin, California on the southern route.

The view was spectacular as usual as I maneuvered the switchbacks on the approach to the Colorado River. Traffic was a little heavier than I expected or had experienced to this point in the trip. Most people were fearful of further attacks and stayed close to home. The traffic I found later was a result of miles of backed up tourists at the pre-dam approach check point. Every third car and anything remotely suspicious was completely searched, meaning that everything was taken out of the vehicle and poured over with dogs and explosive experts. Consider how much gear a family of five might pack on a cross country trip and do the math.

It was a good thing I had allowed an extra day. As I got closer I could see I was not the third car but none the less suspicious. Everyone frowned at me as I was directed way further off the road than most and three armed soldiers peered into the windows of the yellow Xterra. "What the fuck do we have here?" an officer with a clip board shouted as I handed over my SS card, drivers license and registration. I started to try and explain in the same manner that had worked in Kingman but he would have none of it. "Son, there is no way in hell your takin that load of shit across my dam. . .you'd be easier getting kittens to walk in a parade. . . my god damn advice to you is turn this fuckin banana bus south son. . . you turn it around or we'll unload you takin about five hours and then we still not let you cross. So save us all sometime shit head!" I thanked the man for his candor and wished them all well and good luck. I told them I knew they had a tough job and we all, as a nation, appreciated all they were doing. "Fuck you... hippy" I think I heard him shout as I eased into a u-turn at the behest of the guards and headed back south on the two lane. I'm still not sure what he was getting at with that statement.

Now, three hours late and two hours back to where I started. I was thankful but I knew I didn't want to have to dip into old Mexico just to get past the river. I could only imagine trying to get my load back across the border. That would not be cool. At Kingman I wave at the officer from earlier who was the polar opposite from that pile of shit at the dam.

A cold beverage was exactly what I needed and a suitable biker bar was located. In no time I was sinking teeth into a huge burger with frosty beer on the side. This made everything better before it was westward ho. As I approached Laughlin there was nowhere near the congestion as the other route and I made a stop to enquire about the security measures. "What security?" was the standard reply at the RV camps and a beer was passed my way for the road by a man who looked exactly like Hank Hill on cartoons.

As advertised, the dam approach was free and clear and after a quick stop at the casino on the river I was ready to roll. I had a morbid curiosity and wanted to see the casino gaming floor where the recent Hell's Angel vs. Banditos fight had occurred a little earlier, killing two. It was smaller than I expected.

Vegas was achieved about dark and after checking into my county provided hotel room I took a long sleep until morning. It was definitely the longest trip I had been on in relation to miles versus time. I was toast and a big few days were ahead. The return would take care of itself.

(Present time) Sleep time here as well.

The Road to Vegas

S. RAY JACKSON

WEDNESDAY IN THE AM:

Today should be a good day. This morning we are having a little bit of a warm spell and there is a premature hint of spring in the air. That's the weather here. They say if you don't like it wait ten minutes and it will change. I cracked open a diet coke and the passenger side window and busted out onto University Avenue to begin my day. I'm quickly ground to a halt by the third red light before the freeway on-ramp but, from there it's a straight shot downtown.

While I daydream just a tad and attempt to tune out an NPR story about the ramifications of English as a worldwide second language I noticed a bread delivery truck just adjacent. A bread truck is an unusual sight that late in the morning and reminds me of just one thing, my old friend Mike C.

I've mentioned the collective of latch key kids that congregated at my mom's house, and Mike was the only one ever asked to leave. Mike was a little pushy you might say. Looking back I think he came by it honestly. He never had a lot of things we took for granted, namely security and all that that word implies.

Saturday breakfast was a huge thing at our house and at least six or more of my friends were counted present at any one time. Mike was late one morning and walked in unannounced, went straight to the fridge and helped himself to milk. I think not saying hello didn't sit well with my dad. He was told come back when he had some manners. That meant never because he didn't need any shit from us; even if it had gravy and biscuits attached. That was his style and I understand it now. Back then it just pissed me off. It was never enough with him. Somehow though it all he had a personality that was infectious. You had to like him. Loyalty was very important to him and he gave as much as he received. He was just a fucking ass- hole.

His mom worked nights as a cashier at a 24 hour grocery and his jerk- off older brother served as assistant manager during the day. His brother was abruptly fired when it was discovered he was lifting cash from the safe nightly, doing drug deals, and then returning the capital before it would be discovered. His own private bank for illicit gain. This apparently worked great right up until he got fired and eventually sentenced to two years in state. This had been his father figure. A fat assed, pimple faced drug dealer. Good riddance.

And mom? I spent a lot of time at their trailer and I think I saw her twice. He cooked his own TV dinners and made his own rules. His neediness first became apparent to me when a girl named Pat moved to our school. Pat was an eleven. She was a little older than us and was in our grade based on her birthday being in late September. She was flush with womanhood. The whole deck. She just made the mistake one day of saying "hi" and being nice to him.

This act said everything Mike wanted to hear and he fell deeply in love. What he didn't hear was that she had a serious boyfriend. A fiancée in fact in the person of an older man. She had been dating for some time a very nice, yet impatient, bearded man of 25 years. He would tolerate a lot of things, least of which a pair of whore mongers with love struck eyes. We were not welcome. I could give a shit and knew straight up we weren't even in the same ballpark much less league as her.

Mike didn't get it and somehow they became friends at school with him taking the role of third wheel at some dates including prom. It was really quite disturbing. At the time he had a decent brown Chevy Malibu much faster than my ride. I enjoyed tending bar much more than driving so our temporary roles were established. The big drink at the time had been tagged "pink G-D it" and we were on a first name basis. The formula included 100 proof Southern Comfort liqueur mixed with red grape malt duck poured over crushed ice from 7-11. The name was derived from the fact that if a line was crossed and too many consumed you may be seen later puking up pink stuff and moaning "oh G-D it".

We were nearing that line of demarcation when Mike came up with one of his many bad ideas. I was riding shotgun, tending bar and working the radio so I was in no position to argue. He wanted to drive out to the country and see if Pat was home. She lived with her parents basically in the middle of a corn field and any approaching car could be seen from nearly a mile and a half. A drive by look-see would not be regarded as happenstance. You only would go there on purpose. It was what it was. As fate would have it here "HE" was waiting. As we rounded the corner on the gravel, her boyfriend and father were blocking our path, aluminum baseball bats in hand. What Mike had neglected to inform me of was this wasn't his first trip down this road. Time before this he had crept in, jumped out and sprayed black paint on the side of the boyfriend's really nice GTO in the yard. Also left out was the fact that the Grant County sheriff was a close friend of the father and the equivalent of a "good-ole-boy" restraining order was in place. My absent minded buddy had royally fucked me. He was now officially a stalker and I, a very unaware and unwilling accomplice.

I think both of us froze, thinking the silver bats might be shot guns; that we were going to die and the only reasonable reaction was to slam on the brakes and size up the situation. It measured about two feet deep in shit. I somehow felt unprepared as I sat there with a pitcher of whisky punch in one hand and my proverbial you know what in the other. I felt like a midget at a barn dance and I didn't like it. The thought of my last breath on earth being taken in the presence of this real live ass hole was just too much reality.

We sat what seemed like ten minutes. All I could hear was my own heart beat and Mike's ZZ-Top tape. I noticed the exhaust thump was increasing so I knew the gas pedal was being slightly pushed toward the floor. This was about to go down one way or another. I took a deep drink from the pitcher, which seemed like the right move, and glanced at the tall corn to the left and right of us. "Turn it up" Mike yelled in a low guttural shout as "La Grange" came up and I responded accordingly.

He floored it and fishtailed sending a spray of pea sized projectiles into the gatekeepers as well as a bevy of old and new vehicles. Bad move. Luckily the ditch adjacent was only a slight bottom out and we hit the corn. We were cutting out a diagonal swath across and actually began to pick up speed. We had screwed ourselves and there was no going back. Not unless we wanted to be buried there in the soft black soil. I noticed the speedometer was kicking around 60 and I knew if we came across gravel or god forbid, pavement, it was not going to be pretty.

No lights could be detected trailing us and that was the one good thing. We may make it yet. That's when something strange caught my eye. There was something ahead in the high beams, moving fast counter to us. I realized quickly as I saw an eight foot high logo flash by at a high rate of speed what was blocking our path to freedom. "*Santa Fe!!!*" There was a train track through the middle of the corn field and Mike was zeroing in at break neck. "Train"! I screamed like a school girl, whisky pitcher flying through the air and drowning me in sticky goo. Mike had seen it too and hit the brakes with both feet. The vegetation gave no traction at all and we slid closer and closer finally wedging against the gravel shoulder just at the tracks. "Fuck me" we both gasped in unison and sat for a quick moment to reflect. "You ok?" I asked as I wiped the punch from my eyes and looked for the fifth, a straight up shot for me to get my heart restarted.

The embankment would be way too steep to cross over so we decided it might be wise to follow once the train had passed. (A terribly lucid thought under the circumstances). The track would supersede any other obstructions like irrigation canals or anything else lurking in the shadows. At that, we eased up and put two wheels in the center. The thump of the ties was tough but not as bad as a bat to the face would have been. It was slow going but finally we hit a cross road and raced from the County and back to familiarity.

I drank deep and breathed out the open window. I finally forgave him the details he'd omitted. All charges were dropped on the condition we never visit again. This was not a request. This is the reason I am to this day most possibly banned for life from entering that county. All terrible misunderstandings... many thanks to professor Dick weed.

The last time I hung out with him we were kicked back having some beers at his mom's. She was working, as usual, and we had just eaten some cold watermelon slices we found in the fridge. It was about two AM and the small black and white TV they called "entertainment" was airing the local cheap version of Championship Wrestling. I was sitting on the ratty green sofa directly in front of the unit when I noticed Mike was absent. He had a strong dislike for anything Texan and the wrestler being interviewed was a very vocal "Big D" resident.

I figured he was in the bathroom and didn't think much of it. About then was when I saw the metal lower at the end opposite me about three to four feet away. I just sat wondering what the hell when I saw the flash. That stupid son-of-bitch had shot out his own television with a shotgun. As I pulled myself up off the deck my ears rang and I threw a full beer can square into his fat face.

I hit the door and walked the three miles to the house and that was it. What else was there to say? What I knew at that moment was that some people's anger burns so hot you have to get away or you'll be consumed yourself. It's what's important that you should gravitate to, not this bullshit. It's a sad fact that some people can't be saved. It's as simple as that.

Years later he was a bouncer at a real shithole bar and was made a proposition. The paranoid owner decided it would be good business to burn out some of his stiff competition with a series of "accidents". Mike was enlisted in this effort and was successful in taking down five other bars in total or near total losses. He got away with it until his boss turned him in as a deranged arsonist and denied all involvement.

He got ten years and was out in seven. I saw him much later at a school reunion and after gathering up the sand I asked him how much he had earned for the crimes. He looked down, counting floor tiles and replied "two hundred". I walked away and thought about that... he drives a bread truck now in the southern part of the state. $200?. That's $28.57 a year I think.

A Hard Rains gonna Fall...

Most all morning is consumed with the fact that I have a funeral to attend at lunch. The email I received concerning the event, listed the location as the state veterans' cemetery. I'm not exactly familiar with where that may be, but I'm sure if I guess wrong I can call my steady and true navigator dad with his litany of maps and general information. That's what my dad does these days, runs the local City Visitors Center on weekends. This is the perfect job for a road worn retiree. No matter how I disguise my voice on Saturday mornings and call for some obscure directions just to mess with him he always is quick to answer "you can't get there from here". I hope he knows it's really just me.

I had only known the deceased for maybe a year or two. He died from some complication during routine surgery, due in part to his age of seventy eight years. I am and he was a member of an American Civil War ancestor group honoring military service on the side of the Southern States. Terms of membership require a National Archive search and a linage verification study proving a direct link between you and the target subject. This is much like the sons or daughters of the American Revolution. Our group was established in 1901 by actual Civil War veterans who wanted to pass on, to their sons and future descendents, a sense of pride concerning their sacrifice. There is also another group that was established for descendents of officers and I am a member of this also. My primary ancestor was a veteran of the southern US Indian wars serving under Andrew Jackson, who I am also a descendent of, and Zackary Taylor. Captain James Jonathan Jackson enlisted as a Captain out of North Carolina and served at many prominent battles such as Gettysburg under Robert E. Lee. He finished his career as a judge advocate and surrendered with Lee at Appomattox. His son also served as second Lieutenant out of Tennessee and was gut shot and killed many years after the war by a drunk while serving as a town marshal in Arkansas. A second younger son was killed as a private at the Battle of the Wilderness which had also claimed General Stonewall Jackson with friendly fire.

I am very proud and interested in my heritage and although I am probably twenty years junior to the other club members I really enjoy my historical link to these men. We are linked by fate. The funeral did require some guidance to find. Dad rose to the occasion and I was only five minutes late. Not bad considering the driving rain storm that was flooding the roads and fogging my windshield. The ceremony was well attended and apparently on hold waiting for a lost sister that was being guided feverishly via cell phone. After about twenty minutes the decision was made to proceed in light of the large crowd and the weather. She never showed.

It was a military funeral based on his World War Two service and was a little haunting by the faint report of weapons at a nearby National Guard firing range. It was creepy and seemed almost staged with the billowing flags.

I have attended many funerals, some with the deceased more familiar than others. Death is an occurrence. It happens. I try to appreciate and enjoy life every single day in all its simple and complicated things. I think I can say I don't fear or worry about death. I just feel like there is so much I have and want to do so I'm not ready just yet. My epiphany about death came at the hands of a very hated and despised first cousin, when I was eleven or twelve. He lived on a remote farm near Kansas City Missouri and we were out one day messing around an irrigation ditch. We were startled as we walked up on a large and unhappy rattle snake coiled and ready to strike. My cousin came up from the side, snatched the snake by the tail and in one swoop cut the serpent in half with a large knife he had stuffed in his belt. I was shocked and could only utter "aren't you afraid of dying?" he laughed and said "there's nothing I can do about it, when it's my time I'll go." (as a side note he recently died of organ failure at a weight of over 500lbs...my father still counted him as a great success).

That made sense to me although I do like to try and preserve the option of another earth day as much as I can. Funerals that stick out with me are usually ones that involve the young. It's the music selection that strikes a chord or answers a question for people seeking answers.

One of those was Carl. A really good guy, a little out there but a generally a good guy, Carl was the older brother of a close friend of mine and our junior high school independent ride to school. He became an execution style murder victim on the fourth of July one year. He was forced to lie face down in the back of his van and accept a .38 slug to the back of his head. The slug traveled through the skull and van floor and was recovered by police in the pavement below. The body was not discovered in the parking lot of the busy street for several days as neighbors thought the gunshot was fireworks in relation to the holiday.

Carl was gone. The murder was at the hands we surmised of a newly released parolee from state prison but never conclusively proven. Carl had made the mistake of making company with the depressed, middle aged wife of the parolee and was frequently seen carrying her groceries for her. All while the dude was safely in the stir. I don't think they ever even had sex but I can't be sure. I think he just needed a friend in this neighbor as did she. We were just out of high school maybe two years and this was one of the first of many of our close group to be lost.

The affair was a large Catholic event, with all the pomp and ceremony attached, and was well attended by the many friends and extended family. The interesting thing is we, his buddies, were asked by the family to select his music. As it turned out, when quizzed as to what he liked or didn't like as the bereaved parents had no clue. They had spent the entire life of this beloved son, the oldest of several, in total ignorance of what music he liked or didn't like. It was just background noise to life and I think they were a little sad and embarrassed by this fact.

It was at this time that they struggled and searched for some grain of truth about who their 23 year old son had been and had become. This was an eye opener for me. That one thing taught me to pay attention to people you care about. Be connected if you can. Know them. In the end that may be all you have.

The music selection for the main song was a no brainer as his favorite was the Moody Blues song "Nights in White Satin". This seemed very appropriate to the occasion and was played over the cathedral sound system to the crowd in its entirety. After the service his dad walked up to me and firmly grasped my hand. He leaned close and with shaking voice he whispered "thank you". He shared further that he had heard that song many times in the past. He explained he had never taken the time to listen and consider the beauty hidden in the words. It wasn't just juvenile background static. Somehow his sense of loss was filled a little. He now understood something about his son's heart. He and his family would get through this. They would be ok. I can never hear that song today without remembering that conversation.

I personally want a funeral much like that great pioneer of life, Hunter Thompson. I want a huge party that insures guests free beer. My cremated ashes will be packed in and launched in the nose cone of a large TBD color firework. The launch would be at the stroke of midnight and accompanied by a song played over the party's sound system .I am still considering which Dylan song. If the family requires a marker of some kind they can place it at a location of their choosing.

My most unusual funeral to attend was the one where no one came. It being for another close junior high acquaintance who had succumbed to hepatitis and liver failure a few years ago. I remember him as a good kid who was turned bad by sports. He was a reasonable football player and had played since the age of six in the local "pee wee" league at the insistence of his underachiever father and wall flower mother. I remember spending many nights at his house where he would be punished for not doing as well in a game as was expected.

I think it was tenth grade when he said "no". I went home with him after our Saturday morning sophomore football game and his dad knocked him to the ground in the hallway. I excused myself and went home but I knew things would not be the same for Danny, and they weren't. He quit all sports the following Monday and had flunked out and quit school entirely by month's end. He had been turned.

It wasn't long before he would join our neighborhood beer parties high and shoot up heroin in front of us. I didn't like it and I saw him whither and lose all the life he had ever had in his eyes. It was a daily change. Eventually boredom and the need for a fix led to firearms and robbery. Danny's once bright and articulate mind had grown desperate and ridiculous.

There was a television show on at the time called "The Gong Show" which featured a performer who wore a grocery bag on his head with eye holes known as the unknown comic. Danny, on one of his binges, started a spree of restaurant armed robberies wearing a similar disguise and was dubbed quickly by the press as the unknown robber. His undoing was when he entered a local steak house on Cantrell Road in the bag mask and stood patiently in line to gain access to the cashier.

Of course, there was plenty of time for the police to be summoned and he was arrested without a struggle. That stunt gained him fifteen years and he was out in six. After his release it wasn't long before he fell back in with another group of acquaintance crime geniuses I had gone to school with. The plan involved insurance fraud with the staged drowning death of one of the three gang members and a split of the proceeds. The victim had access to a cabin near a lake and made ready for a lengthy stay until the cash could be dispersed. All was working according to plan, complete with the surviving sister cut in to complete the transaction.

After about a month with no recovered body, a death certificate was issued and insurance was processed. All looked good, then the vast intellect of the group came into play. Danny, in his infinite wisdom, discussed with one fourth of the enterprise, the fact that, according to all involved, the victim was drowned. If he really was dead that was one less cut. They had already even had a funeral and shed some tears. No great loss.

After some discussion and a few beers the decision was made. On the weekly Saturday grocery delivery they came with only beer and offered to stay a while and visit. They all sat, drank, laughed and swapped stories about what they were each going to do with all that money. As the sun started on the decline all had a good buzz and Danny went to piss on the path by the wood pile. Upon his return he had the addition of the newly sharpened axe that had been buried into a nearby tree stump.

They said it was one whack that split Westmoreland's skull in two. So much rage. Now just a threesome and soon to be a two way split. They waited until morning and after cooking the last of Westmoreland's bacon and eggs and the two remaining Miller beers they buried him off the path toward the creek. Next issue was the sister. She would have to remain in place at least until after the check came and cleared. That is where things went south.

Danny's partner had the conversation with the newly departed's sister about the latest development in an effort to possibly leave with her and cut Danny out from the proceeds. At the least he might expose some new options. This freaked her out and although no love was lost between her and her brother she could feel in a great feat of female intuition that she was next. As soon as the check cleared she would be toast. She knew this for a certainty. Her next conversation was with the police. The entire plot was exposed and after arrests were made it was no great act of police work to find the shallow grave and the weapon. One fact that did not play in Danny or his friends favor was they had buried the weekend's trash and beer cans with the body complete with store receipts. Store surveillance tapes confirmed the transaction. They may be robbers and murderers but they were not going to liter. The trial went quickly and it wasn't long before he was back at the only home he knew those days. Fewer privileges but happy none the less. Prior to this disaster he had also managed to shoot another friend of mine's spleen out in a drug filled card game as well as other multiple robberies.

After the trial and subsequent publicity, his parents moved away and were never heard from again. Shortly after, he was joined in prison by his only brother, three years his junior. This little bastard became famous for running a two year long bootleg liquor business while in incarceration. He would take orders from inmates which he would in turn have delivered UPS from an outside associate. I understand at that time all packages were x-rayed and as there was no metal to alert guards nothing was questioned.

What did he have to lose? It was great for him until he got caught.

While Danny was serving his sentence he started back to sharing needles and quietly developed hepatitis. This was undiagnosed or maybe just ignored and liver failure was the result. I had not had contact with him beyond an occasional unanswerable letter every few years and when I noticed the small blurb of an obituary I debated on whether to attend. Someone with the family, I assume the mom, had petitioned the court to allow burial in the family plot north of town.

This request had been granted and a time and date for interment had been set. I decided out of respect as he had been a friend in another life to attend. After the 45 minute drive I began to be concerned that I had bad information as there were no cars in the cemetery. I drove around to make sure and saw the fresh turned earth of a new grave in the corner with a waiting backhoe and driver. A lone, bible carrying figure stood at the head with a confused and uncertain look.

Relief seemed to wash over his face as I parked and exited the car near him and the plot. I had been there about a minute when he made the statement he would now begin. It was as if I was his point of reference for the rehearsed dissertation. The machine operator smoked, disinterested and glanced several times at his cheap Timex. The service took all of ten minutes. After multiple bible references concerning the wages of sin the two of us had heads bowed in prayer. It had never occurred to me that he really had no one. He had either attacked or fucked over everyone and thing he had ever known and this was his reward. When it was over and I was driving back to town I could only think of one glaring fact:

All this was because of one dropped pass in a 10th grade, Saturday morning football game... "Good game, Danny... good game ass hole."

A LACK OF LUNCH

I had decided to skip lunch for important reasons. Basically I couldn't decide which fast food bullshit on the way back looked least crowded so I was late getting back to work. This seemed reasonable, I left it to fate. Our office manager was smiling today and as I walked in and shook off the inclement weather, I sensed the wafting odor of cooked fruit. There is a very nice older man at the office that bakes as a hobby and he is often more than pleased to bring by his latest creation for comment, always with whipped cream. Today it was a banana and pineapple pie.

The lack of food quickly became a non-issue and the abundance of fruit in the dish erased the guilt factor. It had to be good for me. I had a large piece and considered how much I liked tropical fruit, and the tropics as well for that matter. All my life I have considered the Continental US my personal playground but I think based on my southern nature I have always gravitated toward the warmer latitudes. The little ones if you will. I have always ventured to the beaches and cities of the gulf and lower Atlantic coast. I have puked in many a New Orleans dumpster and chased a skirt or two from Cape Fear to Cape Canaveral, always having totally different groups of friends up and down the coast. Always welcome. When they see me they know I've hit their exit and it's all good.

Several years ago I had the great opportunity to go a little further south than I'm normally accustomed to. I was in between concert and racing gigs one spring staring out the window of my office when the phone rang. It was my old friend Lynette from St. Louis who I had met through her Ticket Master auditing job. She was a real sweetheart and we had always worked well together. A very detail oriented and good event person who had one very valuable trait, she always knew when she was in over her head or needed an extra hand.

She knew my forte was large scale projects and she had been there first hand. Once I brought her into D.C. as part of my team on an inaugural event and I think she was impressed. She also appreciated my small company's design skills that complimented the productions when needed. I recognized her immediately when she whispered in a shy tone "I need you". It was great to hear from her and it was perfect timing considering I had sat still for about fifteen minutes and was looking for my next move.

"I've landed this gig out of the country and I need some help. . . I've already been to the site for a month, changes are killing me and I'm running out of time". "Whatcha got and where?" I cut her off wanting to cut to the chase. "I moved to New York about six months ago and landed an event and PR gig for an ad agency. They are handling the Latin American introduction of the American Express card at a private big wig party in Old San Juan. You want in? I really need you there . . . My Spanish is weak. . . I'm a woman... a white woman . . . I can't get shit done!" "Get the fuck out!" I replied in earnest "You're a white woman? I had no idea!"

After getting details I was on a plane by the end of the week, head phones on and watching that movie about the old man riding a lawn mower across country. After the movie I cracked open the file folder full of faxes to get the who, what, where, and why. The wire transfer of funds and plane ticket had arrived just in time so I had no reason to doubt the sincerity. And . . . it was Puerto Rico for god sakes, birth place of the Pinacolada and home to me for ten days to two weeks.

I really could have given a shit about the assignment. I could smell adventure and it smelled sweet. When I hit the ground it was in the wrong part of town. Old San Juan and specifically Ponce De Leon's yard (the courtyard museum at his ancestral home) was our site and a long cab ride away. The location had an incredible garden of huge palms basically in the shadow of El Moro and two blocks or so from the governors' mansion. The first odd occurrence was at the airport. The airport, for those who haven't been, looks like something from the seventies and is about the size of a low "B" or even "C" market in the US. Very third world. It does however have self serve free daiquiris in all lobby and concourse areas. I guess the theory is this will make up for the overall shit- hole nature of the place.

The baggage claim was the weird part. As fate would dictate my bag was the very last to appear. I always try and travel light which may have made it suspect to the handlers. I'm not sure. The carousel, which was short by any standards, had one lone disturbing unclaimed item. This item made the rotation circuit about every three minutes. It was a crushed and badly broken car baby carrier. The carrier was covered in what looked like blood spatter and had a ribbon of what looked like crime scene tape holding the arms to the back. It was creepy to say the least. As the only item, in addition to my absent bag, it came around with more questions than answers. Why don't they get it off and to a lab. . . or a dumpster . . . or whatever? I did not know the answer. I just know it mocked me so another frozen beverage was in order.

I did have cell service and let Lynn know that "the eagle had landed". She gave me the address to alert the cab to and off I went. The original plan, or lack thereof, was for me to meet at her state funded apartment near the site and the ocean. She said I could stay on her state funded couch and save a nickel or whatever. This seemed reasonable at the time. The first two things outside her place I noticed were the five thousand cats and the black coble stone streets. Both, I understand were products of the Spanish.

In that part of the city cats ran rampant for rat patrol and the road color because of iron ore accidentally used in the brick firing process creating a strange dark metallic color. The roads are quaint and cool to look at in certain light. The cats created a perpetual urine smell. Maybe it's all bull shit and the cats are really responsible for the street color. I'm not sure upon further reflection.

Her place was really neat, until I got inside. The entire back half of the flat including the open shower were open to the sky. Floor drains accommodate this design element. It rains a lot, which explained the moldy smell from all the furniture in the covered portions. Remember, like my bed on the sofa. I still toured and reserved judgment. Maybe there was more. And there was. The stove had two burners and was powered by propane. Tropical campout? Can't wait to see the women! I stuck my hand in my pocket and forced a smile.

I could tell she really wanted the company but my hand was fingering the wad of cash I had brought for just such a situation. "I could never impose . . . you only have one towel" was the only weak reason I could muster and I pressed to speed the tour and get to a cold beer.

She was game as we both were sweating like teenagers and we hit the bricks. Every other corner near the governor's mansion had an Uzi carrying guard. We strolled by and smiled with no response. "They won't fuck with you, just keep going". Only a few beers to cut the rum edge would suffice and we ducked into a cantina. After a few, she paid and I felt like a wicked restroom break was just down the pike. After inquiring about any nearby accommodations I settled on a reclaimed convent turned hotel called El Convento.

It was on a small square and about six blocks from our site and about the same from the ocean. There is no beach at El Moro and it is mainly rocks and cliffs with no access to the water. There is only a windy tourist path that is not to be traveled by anglos after dark. If you don't have cash they will kill you for the silver in your teeth so stay in town amigo!

The hotel was interesting as it had actually been a convent with the architecture reflecting this. The rooms were all open to the outside and into a central courtyard. The rooms, in a former life, had been the living quarters of a single nun. They were very well equipped and spacious compared to my moldy sofa option. Also interesting was there was nothing below the ground floor after dark. Check in, room service, everything basically was on the second floor.

First floor was just an elevator with a guard needed for access, with the exception of a courtyard restaurant and bar at certain times. This was all either good or bad. I did like the ocean breeze in the room, which more than made up for all the Spanish speaking television. The rooftop hot tub and pool were cool too. Each floor had an honor bar which featured a fully stocked hard liquor selection. You would write down on a slip of provided paper what you got and room number and then place in a basket. Whatever.

I asked a guard once about 3am what time the pool closed to which he laughed and replied "what?. . . never" I was home! It was hard to get any real work done but we pressed on. I saw immediately what Lyn had spoke of in regard to a lack of cooperation, particularly to females. She was all but ignored and cash was not necessarily king.

What was effective was barter. At home if we needed something we pick up the phone and buy or rent. Here, there are two companies who supply or rent gear and both don't want us here. We are getting in their pockets and they don't like it. Therefore barter. In one transaction I needed to trade a fifth of rum to a city employee for the use of a twenty foot extension ladder. Rum was the best trade good. Beer was worthless. The tourist trade had allowed Miller Beer to pretty much overrun all the available Mexican and Puerto Rican beers and eventually polluted the market. I picked all of this information up in the course of an hour.

About my third day there I was sitting for a moment after lunch in the square outside my hotel. Not thinking about much. Just being quiet and enjoying the shade of the lush ancient trees. Cats chased pigeons and for some reason I thought that a little funny. I guess the flying rat analogy. Out of the corner of my eye I saw two very attractive and scared looking girls making way down the sidewalk. What I noticed first was the bright pastel colored linen dresses followed closely by the smeared eye makeup from crying. One also had a limp due to a broken heel.

This was not my first rodeo and I was not going to get sucked into some kind of scam but I was intrigued. I was correct as they zeroed in on me and started to whisper in Spanish. *"No habla"* I responded to which they began in very broken English. The story was they were hookers. They had grown up about an hour away in farm country where their extended families still resided. They generally worked near the cruise ship docks. They were sisters and one of the pair had gotten sick the night before with cramps. The pimp manager of theirs had beaten the shit out of them with their lives only being spared by a jammed gun. They were marked to be crab food on the rocks.

I sat and listened and sized them up. After watching the rapid eye movements with over the shoulder emphasis I was convinced it wasn't bullshit. I had rented through a chummy guard at the hotel a .32 to hold while I was in country so I wasn't particularly concerned with robbery. Based on the skimpy dresses they had no concealed weapons. My cash was in the hotel safe so what the hell. What they did want was sanctuary and to be off the streets where they would certainly not make it through the night. They needed a day . . . two tops until an uncle could get there from the country and take them away, back home. The big city had been a mistake for them.

My first response was we needed a drink to consider the up or downside of this. After about six, and as many missed cell phone calls things sounded acceptable. At the least it would be interesting, and ultimately that's why I was here. I loaded in. I would smuggle them to my room, where they would hang. I told them I would hide them but I wanted all the cash they had on them which came to about $120.00. That made me feel even better about it and I assured them I would only use the cash for their food and drinks. What was left when they were ready to leave I'd give back. It was just good faith insurance.

I went out for a while with Lyn and her friends and returned early to offer them t-shirts and old boxer shorts to wear. The other clothes were a little ripe and one girl had a good amount of dried blood if closely inspected. I wasn't throwing a dance and the dresses made me feel a little awkward and uncomfortable. I had nothing of real value in the room so leaving them was no big deal. I knew they weren't going anywhere with anything. After they showered with the door open they slipped into bed on either side of me and lay down to sleep. I sipped at some two worm mescal and watched a really bad game show on Telemondo until I heard them snoring. They looked like they had never slept before and I really was glad at that particular moment I could help. I've seen most every scam and heard every bullshit story under the sun and it was nice to hear something that could possibly be true.

I remember stirring at first light and hearing the sounds of the waking city and the crash of the ocean below. The color of their naked skin in that new light was like nothing I've ever seen. They were calm and dangerous all at once and I knew I could pay a great price for interfering in local business. This was very evident by the substantial bruising. As far as the hotel was concerned I had partied all night with the pair and all was well so no foul. I had a Del Negro beer and a banana for breakfast and waited for what next. I sat on the small porch three stories up in the tower, a porch that would only accommodate one chair. A very uncomfortable straight back with a broken slat aligned perfectly with the crotch.

Next came about ten AM when Maria got her cell call. Her cousin was just outside and waiting. I told them to keep the T shirts and shorts I had loaned them to expedite the escape. After two kisses I wish I had stolen the night before they were gone. I stood on my balcony and saw them dart into the backseat of the idling heap. One rolled down the window, looked up and waived. As I walked back in the room I noticed an item left behind, my souvenir of the night being the broken shoe. They would be just fine now. And it was time to get back to business.

Lyn and I met and had some eggs at her place. Aside from the heat I really think with the proper training I could get to like this place. When the event day arrived everything went fantastic. We were able to create some great special effects and the entire affair had a strange, other worldly feel to it. There was an incredible jazz band that spoke absolutely no English. We managed to communicate pretty much through hand signals. Latin jazz is generally not my favorite as I lean more toward Charlie Parker and Miles Davis and the 50's New York scene but they were entertaining in light of the atmosphere. The actual site was a courtyard with somewhat neglected gardens populated with enormous palms in the 30 to 50 foot range. I know this because a sail backdrop for video effects required me to scale one to the extent of the 20 plus foot barter extension ladder, a little scary as it moved in the breeze but a great photo op.

The band members were all in their late fifties or early sixties and had a real passion for the gig work. In my business I often experience the burned out and dull eyes of road weary musicians and this was a pleasant change. They had fire. After about fifteen minutes I noticed the accelerant to their fire as I saw the hidden pints of nameless rum in paper bags behind the bandstand. Cups with ice all around. The pint bottle is one of those inventions which has allowed the social advancement of man into many different areas. It is no accident that there is a slight curve to the back of most bottles which allows comfortable concealment as a back pocket carry on. The first set was exactly what I needed to take the edge off the somber spirit that had been left by the sisters. I was in party mode again and reached back to adjust the hunk of metal that was sticking into the curve of my back. My insurance was in force. When the event wrapped it was broad Latin smiles all around. Hands were shook. Pictures were taken. All was well. We had pulled off a fantastic feat in adverse conditions while making Lyn's New York employers look great, in addition to a shit load of money.

Next stop was a cantina around the corner for some more back slapping and photos. Red Stripe beer all around . . . and around . . . and around. The highlight of this impromptu party was the announcement of a potential sister gig based on the night's success. The clients were interested in a similar soiree to be held the next month in Argentina. After about eight minutes of quiet consideration I knew I would have to pass. I was already under contract with an ex Boston Red Sox player to do a gig in Vermont for his wife and for him at a fantasy camp in Ft. Meyers Florida.

I kept this information to myself at this point. Nothing is ever totally impossible. Everybody was jerking each other about how great and beautiful it was but my mind was elsewhere. I had seen earlier from my room the approach and docking of several cruise ships at the end of old town. I knew an infusion of new blood; even tourist from Cleveland or wherever, would be interesting and always good for some free drinks. Tourists always assume that an anglo that is not in their party or not a tourist in general for that matter is either on the lam or at least an interesting conversation piece.

The additional funds for my contract back half had hit my bank so the immediate next stop was the ATM at American Express. I stopped at the shopping district on the way to the dock area and picked up a duty free R. Lauren button up and I was all good. I felt like a fresh shirt would be needed and could replace the two T's I had awarded to the sisters. First thing I picked up was a white one in just my size. A sign? I plucked down the ten bucks and tied my purchase around my waist for safe keeping. Night awaited me. The streets near the governors' mansion were a little quiet but I could sense the buzz of activity, twelve or so blocks to the north. The *tourista* were all clad in almost identical plaid, or linen mix and match with golf hats or the standard panamas. It was quite depressing and reinforced the need for the shirt purchase. I was fashionably middle of the road and that was an acceptable place. Dangerous if necessary but not extremely. Sun had set and the neon of the various clubs set a tone which my ear recognized in perfect pitch.

Night was my music and I jumped in with both feet. It was about nine or ten and I spotted a very posh cigar bar maybe two doors down from the Pinacolata birthplace bar. I knew that to be true based on the tile mosaic attached to the outside bar wall, I think the date was 1932 and Hemmingway may have been mentioned. I wasn't paying that close of attention. The names just cried out to me.

The cigar bar front was open to the street as most, and very healthy palms waved violently at the street traffic. It was very minimalist in design with clean white stucco walls accented by rich black or dark brown leather furniture throughout. Each a sofa or love seat, (there were no single chairs), had a single print hanging center. I sat below a Lichtenstein print which I noticed was signed.

Whoever owned this joint did it right. It was a hard contrast from the junked up Caribbean themed cantinas and tourist traps surrounding this oasis. This was for locals and their high roller friends from the mainland. Cigars started at twelve bucks and each purchase came with a trim and light by one of the most exotic and stunning women I had ever been near. Thin red lips and legs that went all the way down to the floor. "I'll take two" I stammered "one for later". She smiled and I melted.

As I settled back and sipped on a frozen drink I felt just fine. The New York boys (our gig bosses) had bought us maybe eight or ten Red Stripe beers and I needed something a little sweet to take off the beer edge, especially with the heavy, dark tint of this cigar. I settled for a banana banshee. Not the TGI Friday version; but one blended with real bananas and flavored liquor. Tasty. I got a shot of mescal for the side as a neutralizing agent in case of emergency.

I had been there probably fifteen minutes when I'll be fucked if my jazz band from the gig wasn't coming in the door with instruments in hand. In a strange twist they had finished my event, went to eat and then made way to their standing house engagement. This was great. They recognized me right away as the crazy gringo who had fucked with them all afternoon. There were smiles wall to wall. The stand up bass player came directly over and gave me a huge drunken bear hug. Instant credibility with the club.

After this public display, my cover was somewhat blown with the patrons who had assumed, and were correct, that I was some sort of producer or something. The evenings start would not be quiet after these complications. I much prefer to observe from a corner and decide on a plan of action. Not to be thrust into unwanted conversations or situations.

I was enjoying the music and starting to get a little hammered so I decided to eat a bite. For some weird reason the house specialty was *huevos* so I said what the hell and loaded in. They were indeed special as they were almost poached, perched high on a flat tortilla with some type of sweet salsa on the side. Perfect enough to not greatly affect my buzz but insurance that I would last the evening with some faculties.

Settling deep in the leather I watched the street traffic as it started and stopped. Always off balance but alive. It was about this time that this brunette chick and her friends rounded the corner. You could tell as the cruise patrons slinked by that there weren't enough recognizable logos in our place to warrant attention. No golden arches. No Miller or Bud. This was not for them. Plastic is not accepted and *touristas* don't carry cash. I think that was part of the plan. She and her girlfriends had cash. Lots of cash. They slowed and started to pass when I overheard one of the group proclaim she loved cigars. The collective giggle was a little unnerving but I would leave well enough alone for now. You could tell they were a little young, very intrigued and starting to settle into a pit group. Within minutes they were palming cigars much too big for their tiny hands and sipping boat drinks. There is something really interesting about watching a group of young women toke on big stogies in a hot tropical environment. The band also approved and poured on layers upon layers of bull shit heavy with indecipherable dedications and banter. To ease this process an English speaking bus boy translated the load of crap into eloquent prose.

Everyone was pleased. At least the band drowned out the constant snickers from the girl's table. Within an hour or maybe ten minutes I had joined the party. They were a group from Chicago in their early thirties who had won a sales competition with their company. After that info I pretty much just shut down and didn't hear any more of the story except that they were off one of the cruise ships that had docked that morning.

I did also get the fact each sported a large diamond ring and they flashed mischief in their eyes. This was all true and they were on a ticking clock. The bands winks and nods were starting to get a little annoying so I suggested we explore a little and work our way back around to the relative comfort of the cigar bar. I decided to take a pee break first and suggested they do the same.

I had all but forgotten the small, black .32 protruding out of the back of my pants creating a very slight bulge in my shirt. I was questioned upon my return. "You gonna kill us?" the red head quizzed with a playful look. "Well hell no. . . You're the only friends I got here . . . but it IS early". That seemed to please them and we hit the street. The exotic beauty winked at me as I flipped a twenty on the table and told me to be safe. They would still be open to about six or sunrise. That was good to know.

We hit several spots and the girls were tossing back margaritas like ice water. I started to be a little concerned because I didn't want to and couldn't carry four drunken bitches around all night. Then I remembered they were from Chicago-land. Not a problem. My personal routine was an alternating program of mescal and then beer only at the next stop. This created functionality or at least perceived functionality as I felt a responsibility for my new charges.

After a couple of hours they had a bad idea. They wanted to see the cliffs near El Moro. This was near where I was staying and I was familiar but had also heard the many warnings. It was not to be done after dark. It was always at your own risk even in daylight and very dangerous. The daytime tourist path and park at dusk became the domain of the silent and invisible roaming thugs. They were a lot like the cats. You couldn't always see them but you caught the smell. They were the street people and they waited patiently for dumb asses like us to come see the beach at night.

I was just drunk enough to go along and in a misguided attempt to impress I agreed. It took about fifteen minutes to get to the base, and the full moon gave great detail to the rocks just below the stone walkway. That's about when something caught my eye. It appeared to be a flag or a marker of some kind and I climbed the rail to investigate. It was a cane made of dark wood and broke three quarters of the way down and shoved among the boulders. The ornamental top was a metallic monkey head and it had a torn yellow bikini top tied to it like a flag standard. I stood there and pissed into the wind wondering what the fuck it all meant when one of the girls behind me whispered to me strangely. "Hey. . ." I zippered and turned away from my find in the sand and noticed the row of dark silhouettes framing our party. My heart jumped and I wondered what type of flowers I would have at my funeral when I felt the jab of steel into my lower back as I crossed back over the railing.

I had never heard of bums being armed and I always operate on the assumption that the best defense is a good offense, so out it came. The ground they had gained on us was quickly recovered and I shouted loud over the surf to "vamoose". The girls held close to each other and backed out and up the path back toward the street. I took the position between them and drew down on the shadows; easing backward and begging not to stumble.

Much to my surprise no shadow on the shore made any moves as we neared the street lights and I began to breathe again. We had been extremely lucky to not become a statistic and the island was beginning to look good again to me. Back on the street I stashed our dark metal savior and we eased quickly toward the life and sounds of the main strip, looking often over my left shoulder. "You guys owe me a shot". No one spoke as it sobered everyone in an instant. That type of reality jolt always leaves a person feeling damp and disoriented. Mainly damp at my age. They bought me about five shots of Malibu rum and soon I was human again, as were they. Three of the group however were still visibly shaken.

And they should have been. It was a really stupid thing to do and I knew better. That happens sometimes. The spirit of the party was damaged and could not be repaired. The three just wanted to get back to the ship and shower. It was bed time and tomorrow, another day. This one was lost. I told them I would show them the way, and so off we went. The cigar bar was on the way and on the hill just overlooking the harbor so I felt at that point I would take my leave.

They would be safe from there. The hostess was still in her place and the band in their third set. Even the love seat at the street side table was open. It was a sign. Three of the four gave me a hug and a kiss of thanks, and with that thick Chicago accent departed and off they went toward the gangplanks. The fourth wanted to sit a while and I said fine. When they thanked me they didn't realize I was saving my ass out there as much as theirs. I didn't volunteer that bit of information at this time. We talked, and drank, and smoked cigars. Sometime in the wee hours we feel asleep. I awoke way past first light with her asleep in my arms, both of us covered by a thick colorful woven blanket. In the back, the bartender was sweeping and, in broken English, informed us the hostess didn't want to wake us and gave us the cover. Apparently if you are spending money, or at least have a good personality, sleeping in is ok.

Once we became a little oriented she screamed "Oh Shit! . . . My boat!". I flipped another twenty at the table and we sprinted into the street and hailed a passing cab. After a quick ride there we were at the empty slip. She had missed the literal boat. I felt terrible for her but it really wasn't all my fault. Shit happens and all we could do was deal with it. I took her to the cruise line office and then to the American Express office near the docks. All we could do was to get her a flight on a small charter to meet the ship at the next port of call. This would run about four hundred dollars, which I offered to split with her. I'm not a total prick. My next thought was her explanation to her husband but that really wasn't my problem. I also agreed to ride with her to the airport at the other end of the island and provide whatever comfort I could. All the activity and the harsh mid-morning sun were starting to make both of us have a sweet, yet less than desirable smell. But there was little that could be done. She would finish her trip an adventurer and all would be fine. Her state room on board was as it had been. She would catch up just in time for dinner with the proper wind. When we reached the airport I gave her a hug and she kissed me on the cheek. As she walked away to catch her flight I realized something and shouted after her "I don't even know your name?". "I know" she smiled and waved as she ducked in the sliding door of the shabby terminal.

"Pendajo…" the waiting cab driver whispered under his breath toward me as I climbed in headed back to old town. The sun was bright and high overhead now and there were no clouds. Some lunch sounded good. Or maybe just some eggs.

AND THEN CAME JACKSONVILLE...

On most all of our teenage summer trips, which became longer and longer each year, Jacksonville, Florida became an important destination. These outings extended from the customary week to two or three months eventually. A lot depended on how much cash we had been able to squirrel away all winter with odd jobs or schemes.

We all worked *off* and *on* for my dad. I was mainly on. As a matter of fact I think I had been given no choice. I was in a work study program at school which allowed me the last two years of high school to work in the mornings, go to school and play football in the PM. I worked year round so I took my adventure trips very serious. For some reason Jacksonville Beach became very familiar. I think initially it was as far as we wanted to go. Probably because we would have run out of gas. You could always pick up an odd job or two wherever and if we were able or inclined to we could press on south, the short distance, to Daytona.

I had an aunt and alcoholic uncle from Cincinnati that had moved there several years before, to get away from the rest of the family. Also, my uncle's brother was one of the pioneers in the early sixties who had opened a dune buggy rental business one block off the beach on A1A. He was very well established as a fringe person and we were never allowed to meet. I never got that but never really worried too much about it either. Jacksonville Beach, prior to some lean years being overrun by drugs was a magnificent place. It is tropical and very redneck in ways that are not seen anywhere (except maybe the outer banks area), but with more palm trees. Beer was, and is, the regional drink of choice. And it was a great opportunity to try each and every brand available.

One summer trip we took my Pontiac Trans Am down and decided because of a short leash we would land there for the duration. I think we had to get back for some function and a week was all we could squeeze out. The gas station up the street had Old Milwaukee tall boy beer stacked up by the road and on sale for .95 cents per six pack. We calculated our budget and after the room charge we could swing two cases per day minimum and one mid-day McDonald's meal consisting of two quarter pounders with cheese and fries. This would allow us just enough fuel for the eighteen plus hour return. No odd jobs required. This worked well for us as we were already accustomed to "one meal-a-day" travel as I still am to this day. (Now that I think of it I have probably only actually once had three real meals in a day). It's a life choice I think. I think Abraham Lincoln really did say something like that. The hotel we'd settled on we had frequented before and was currently in the process of being sold. It was at one time the best Holiday Inn on the beach but had definitely fallen on hard times. The construction of a newer facility toward the interstate hadn't helped. It was heading fast toward Indian ownership, so it was our speed and price range. There was also a lot less security and a lack of tourist dads. There was however no lack of tourist daughters and locals who could appreciate the scant swimming pool controls. No lifeguards. . . no flotation devises. . .enter at your own risk. You get the drift. This was exactly the type of environment in which we flourished.

Then we met Sheila. That was an odd thing. She and her husband were there on their honeymoon and had the same schedule as us for the weeklong stay. We had all met late one afternoon in the pool when the perfect combination of party and sun were in their apex and conversation was sometimes freer than it should be. Bars are great but this time in a party day has got to be the most exhilarating. It's when you feel most alive. You realize you will never be here in this moment again and you survey and take in the people, light color, temperature, wind and water.

It's a moment and it's always good to have as many as you can, especially with this newlywed to look at. I may have failed to mention, T-back or "thong" bikinis are legal on these beaches and she sported a fine model of the latest fashion. It's sad when a group of young men just sit and wish for someone to have to get up and go to the bathroom. But there we were. She also had a short crop, bleached blonde hairstyle which was very uncommon at the time and that tan.

Not copper tone tan like on the commercial but a more natural primal tan. Almost farmer tan but not. More like a home swimming pool. That was probably it and as we found out later the situation. All that in itself is not weird but turns out she was the first trophy wife I had ever met in person. The groom was at least fifty years old and she was in her late twenties. Not naïve by any stretch, but still very fresh.

He was proud to have her and radiated happiness. He had somehow landed a "keeper". But in the immortal words of Sir Wilfred Brimley, "the worst thing that can happen to a man is to marry a beautiful woman". I'm not saying avoid them. By all means gravitate toward and enjoy all they have to offer. However, you must make sure your mind is right if you intend to sign anything. This is not a game for paranoids or insecure people. If you are not prepared and you lay with these women, insanity and death are sure to follow. He apparently was unaware or had somehow overlooked these pitfalls. I even was initially blinded by the venire and gloss of the relationship. It seemed right and I think they were genuinely happy. He had obviously not spent near as much time in the sun as his bride and after the second day we saw less and less of him. The big burn. I had certainly seen that before.

That was a shame as he rather enjoyed buying his new friends a "round" or three of boat drinks from the pool cabana. We gladly accepted as it would be rude to do otherwise. A sweet drink sometimes is just the ticket to gain balance after too many days of excessive beer, especially cheap beer from our daily bathtub stash at the hotel. Every day the maid would complain in Spanglish about her new Pakistani boss's kids and our excessive use of hotel ice. "Fuck her" we thought but kept it to ourselves.

Point is we really started to like this guy at the pool deck. His enthusiasm was contagious and we all started to buy into whatever he might be selling. We knew the young tigress to his left was who or what had brought it to him. I think on the fourth day of his stay he stayed totally in the shade near the pool bar. He had also shifted to shots of his favorite tequila which went down easier than I was accustomed to seeing with people of my generation. I think he had had enough of the sweet syrupy concoctions to last a lifetime. He was done. The big Tequila he sipped had worked its magic as well and he retired to his room for the night an hour or two before dark.

It wasn't ten minutes later that we noticed three overweight pricks from Ottawa circling like vultures around an exploded carcass. This wouldn't be a problem as we had seen her shut down unwanted advances, to the delight of her proud groom. I still thought this right up till she flipped over to receive suntan oil on her legs and ass for some late afternoon sun. Still no foul, but it smelled extremely funny. Around Tuesday or so we had bonded with the dude and we were feeling a little awkward, it was however; not our deal.

Surely it would go no further. We were a little better on our budget than we thought with two days left. With that in mind we decided to hike up the beach a mile or so and grab some drafts and half shell oysters at the shack off Atlantic Boulevard. We made the trek up and enjoyed the breeze as it picked up tossing sand and surf alike. Life was good, as it is most always. The plastic to-go cups from the room emptied on cue with our arrival at the bar. Once there it took about two seconds for us to park our white asses on the outdoor stools.

The oysters were fat, perfect, and at twenty five cents, just the right price. Two dozen was my limit and the small mug of brew was just enough. We were ready to head out as the strip action was heating up. The tourist up this way had all showered and changed and were seeking out the miniature golf courses and t-shirt emporiums before dinner. We did not need to participate in this ritual, however it was a little unnerving how they stared at us. We could have been suffering from alcohol induced paranoia though. . . I wasn't sure. I just knew we needed to hit the sand and get away from the neon and toward the north end. Home away from home. There had been a storm at sea the last couple of days and in the moonlight we could more than make out the deposit of dead and displaced jellyfish at the water's edge. These were not to be fucked with, even dead. A swollen foot was to be avoided at all cost. Especially with two days here and one to two road days left. Our path subsequently shifted more toward the sea wall and mid-beach where the sand was deep and harder to negotiate.

A broken bottle was a lot less of a risk than those slimy lumps on the hard sand. Birds would have them cleaned up by morning, but that wouldn't help us now. The hotel backsides were starting to be more familiar and we knew we were close to the pool deck and some more cold ones. Won't be long now . . . like the monkey said when he got his tail caught in the electric fan. That's when it happened. The wind at night and the sound of surf can mask most anything, just as it did the laughter.

My friend John was talking when he suddenly vanished in mid-sentence. He had stumbled over something hidden in the dark of the dunes. "What the hell!" was asked all around as our collective focused on the obstruction. It was Sheila. She was camped underneath one of the Canadian whales with the two others waiting patiently for turn two and three. None of us could believe what we were seeing. She looked at us and you could see, even in the shadow the wheels behind her eyes turning. Even in the dark.

She was about to lose everything. Everything she had gained in this union between her and her older guy. The house and pool. Everything. It was going to be a damn shame. I could have given a shit about her or any of it. What I did see was the smile on her man's face, his pride and happiness. His fucking honeymoon. A trip he and she planned and that he had most certainly paid for.

Everyone froze for an instant and held their breath. The fat boys weren't sure if fight or flight was in order, so no action seemed best. We had one more guy than they did and I think all of us were thinking the same thing. We liked the husband and nobody deserved this. But like Clint Eastwood said "deserves got nothing to do with it". John, who was also pissed over the fall grabbed the mounted one and tossed him a yard or more on pure adrenalin. "Get going you prick!" I shouted over the surf as his bare ass disappeared north in the dark. The other two joined him in a bee-line and were quickly out of sight.

She pulled her swimsuit on slowly and quietly inquired "what now?" "I suggest you go to your room and go to bed . . . maybe leave tomorrow." I replied. "You're not going to tell Ted?" I had never known him as anything other than "Dude" to this point. Angrily I answered "I wouldn't embarrass him with your stupid shit . . . you need to really be absent the rest of this trip." She thanked us, which felt odd, and slinked off to her beached, sleeping, so-called protector.

We got up the next morning about ten and hit the pool fresh breakfast beers in hand. The two sling back chairs they had commandeered all week were empty and sat staring at us. None of us spoke. Also, the Canadian flag that once decorated the fifth floor balcony was gone. We had done right I think but somehow it didn't feel that way. It actually felt wrong. We had an opportunity to meddle and maybe help an innocent and we didn't. Our disgust, however hypocritical it was, had guided our actions.

We had let everything lie and it was obviously eating at us, each in his own way. The question was; where do you draw the line on what you should or shouldn't do when it is not your business. Kinda like when kids at an adjoining restaurant table are throwing food at you. We just sat there. The sun rose and we sipped our beers. All I could think was "deserves got nothing to do with it". I do know I never looked at a beautiful woman the same again.

I lost touch with that town for many years after that. No particular reason. As my kids were growing up they much preferred the non-bar activities associated with Daytona, Orlando and Cocoa Beach to the south. J-ville pretty much became a stopping off point for gas.

Some years later I was retained to produce a very large scale music event there which would require many months of my time. A total re-visitation. It was a fantastic opportunity to get back, work with old friends and gain new ones. The project was a three day Celtic world music festival to be held at the City amphitheater across the street from the football stadium. It had been postured to be a benefit to raise funds and more importantly, awareness about the plight of a tributary of the St. Johns River. The St. Johns is one of the largest natural manatee habitats in the country and it was threatened by a cement plant that then Governor Jeb Bush had approved.

The client seemed to have an abundance of funds for the production so all seemed well. I was brought in to head the effort by one of my best friends, Dale, who was the lead guitar player for the classic rock band "The Guess Who". He felt it was drifting a little and needed a show producer to pull it tight. I was available so I was his boy. The event not only involved the live show but also a streaming web-cast, *as well as* video/ audio recording for possible later release.

I handled the live portions and Dale did the onsite audio recording live on the site with the aid of his brother from Canada. What intrigued me most, aside from being back in town on someone else's dime, was the complexity of the effort. The three days would feature almost seventy bands from thirteen countries, all Celtic based. This was everything from the Cowboy Junkies to a River dance type of act. I would be hiring French, Spanish and German interpreters and overseeing a ton of international travel. Great fun.

My first site visit was interesting as I showed up to my meeting and there before me was a large man in a kilt with his wife and twin step sons. Also in tow was a very thin, scowling female who I would find out later I, was replacing. She was now my local assistant and currently residing in the clients extra bedroom, where she had been for several months. This was not all that odd until, at dinner, in passing I learned she was a nymphomaniac and practicing witch.

I found this out after inquiring about the fertility ritual she performed at Chili's prior to her vegetable medley plate. I was wondering what my friend had got me into, but after a quick call to Nashville he assured me it would be OK. The money was good so away we went. The second big thing I found out was how much change can happen to an area in twenty years. Drugs were pretty much absent from the old beach area and the new beach front clubs and cafés were definitely drawing the tourists.

I insisted on staying at the beach on my site visits even if I had to pay, which I didn't. The trip from there to the client's house was about twenty minutes inland, which wasn't bad and oftentimes the witch would come out to get me. Joe's Crab Shack at sand's edge was around the corner so I was set. The client's pontifications could only be taken in small doses, and I didn't need a daily ass showing to get his vision. So far that had been the only downside and there was also the trip my sister (for fun and to combat boredom) went on where she informed me the client had nothing on under the ever present kilt. She learned this after an hour of deliberate flashing. It was horrible.

After a while, when he felt like he knew me pretty well, he let me go to one of his club "meetings". These were held on the North side near the beach causeway at a small bar. This location, I discovered was an IRA bar and one where if you didn't sport a weapon or an Irish accent you kept your fucking mouth shut. The beer was thick and dark and you better like it. Lots of it. "Drink up you little wanker". It wasn't a very relaxing environment, especially after the fourth fight of the evening but I got through it without puking so I was golden. I always found an excuse to go somewhere else after that.

Then there were the traps. After returning from one of my trips I noticed an article of women's underwear in my bag mixed with my dirties. This item was an extremely small bra which would expand into a great mystery. After this happened I noticed every trip would offer some item of contraband mixed with my own gear. Closer to the event I discovered what I could never have suspected. Apparently in the witches' religion, if you want to get close to a person you need but mingle an item of clothing with theirs while lifting an item to do same. She (the nympho)was attempting a spell of some kind.

I realized, upon reflection, that on her visits to pick me up she was making the switch without my knowledge. It didn't work but she did make a spectacular effort. I think she was the only ex-navy (on permanent disability), witch from Maine I have ever known before or since. As things progressed and even more additional bands were added I felt I needed some real backup.

This choice was easy and I was on the horn to my buddy Brian in Vegas within the hour. He was a first class stage manager who I had done several Vegas gigs for, and who had also worked with me in California and Arizona. This, I think, was his first trip east of the Mississippi in some time and he was all over it. He would free me up to deal with the more bull shit elements of the show like hotels, air and ground transportation for the small army of guests. It was coming together now. Things were looking ok but something smelled funny.

My first red flag was a collect call from Dublin inquiring about a dropped deposit. I had not been privy to the band negotiations and after a little scratching discovered that 10%, or in some cases, no deposit had been promised or delivered to anyone. I knew all the deposit cash I had required for gear had been met so nothing had flared up in my mind, but this was a little disturbing. In essence these people were coming from Ireland and France on the come in hopes of payment.

Some bands picked up their own air-fare and were to be reimbursed after the show. This is not how this works but I held my tongue, still assuming he had resources or at the least a plan.

Once you smell shit it's best to get a paper towel ready. About two weeks out I went into cover my ass mode and revised my contract to require a cash wire transfer, prior to my entering the state of Florida, to a bank in Arkansas. These funds would cover my back end fee, travel, all my friends from Vegas, Nashville and Canada as well as production costs.

I would not hold the bag and neither would my buddies if this blew up. I would be hauling gear and had waited as long as I could for the transfer, which never came. Finally, not wanting a gut check of a trip, I decided to leave. The client understood that I would not come without the transfer but I'm sure he thought I would be a little more reasonable. Reasonable, I am not. Not with contracts or promoters. I took my time and was in constant contact with my office and the bank concerning the funds but I wanted to get as close as possible to the Florida line.

That meant Valdosta, Georgia, which is just across the state line from my destination. I was a day later than he expected and was browsing in a Wal-Mart when the call came. The client was freaking as he was trying to answer the six thousand questions and calls addressed to me. Bands were starting to arrive and it all was collapsing around him.

In a meek voice all he said was" Are you coming"? "Have funds been transferred? If not I guess that's your answer and I hope you have a great show". The funds were secure within about twenty minutes and my compatriots and I were given the green light. That's how this business works. People often assume I want to invest in their dreams. Like they say "In god we trust, all others pay cash". I was on the site in about an hour and Brian was on the ground by ten pm. We were on our way, as was the weather. The rain set in after load in and the first day of the festival people stayed away in droves.

Bands got in and things were working. Then I got the reality check about the show funds, or lack of, as it were. The overall show budget was just a tad under half a million and to date I had seen just about $385k change hands. This, I found out, represented the holdings of the client including his kid's college funds. More important was the fact it included the assets from his new wife's deceased husband including a loan against her home in Nashville. It was a very expensive jerk-off with only about sixty percent of the potential debt covered by a total personal loss for he and his wife.

Not to mention hotel, food, and return travel to Europe for about a hundred of the three hundred musicians. This was fucked up. I had all of our money so we were whole but trying to keep the show going and steer the coming train wreck was a tough proposition. And the rain kept falling.

The second day, once I knew the score was very depressing, I went into "slash and burn" mode. He had assumed a walkup of 10k over three days and we were only in the hundreds, albeit in the midst of a freak cold snap and rain. It was not good. The thing to do was pull all the old hands into a room and try and minimize the damage. That was the only responsible thing to do.

I couldn't see this family who believed so blindly in the leader's vision, absolutely lose their own individual futures. Not over a show and not on my watch. After an hour of number crunching I determined if we pulled the plug at noon we would save the additional 40% of our expenses but I would have to sit the family down to discuss this. It was totally their call.

My friend Dale, would be my witness to the discussion. I had explained everything to him in detail and he would act as a good conduit between me and them. Reality is not always pretty. They still had a gleam of excitement in their eyes as they entered the production office and sat, much like a dog about to be put down. Something is about to happen . . . you're just not sure what. I laid it all out; The upside if we cancelled; The down side if we didn't. At best, they would keep the home in Florida and lose all the cash and college fund. At worst, if they continued, they would lose cash, both homes and still owe 125 to 150k. As I walked through the numbers I saw the light begin to dim. I'm usually very hard and pragmatic about these types of issues but on this I fought back the lump that was growing in my throat.

Dale knew I was having trouble and he put his hand on my shoulder. It was the wife and kids. I was just the messenger but it didn't feel that way. I didn't give a fuck about the dad. I didn't ask him to create this situation but I did feel an obligation to try and see him through a way out. He could have just as easily had ten thousand people, his money, and then some. It could have worked, but he lied. He was not prepared and worse yet . . . he believed his own bullshit. The bad thing is this woman and these two boys believed in him too. Sometimes it's like that.

After the gut wrenching details were all on the table I knew the thing to do was cancel and save the homes. It was obvious to everyone that I sat waiting for the word. Then came the unexpected. "I think they will come". He wanted to see it through. The boys both answered in agreement that "they" would come. I just sat for a minute and looked at Dale. The entire surreal comedy was something I couldn't wrap my mind around. I felt flushed and angry.

Not only was he dive bombing himself and the others around him but now I had to deal with the soon to be destitute and stranded bands. Groups I had hung with and gotten to know that week. And there was Carl Asch. Carl was a good friend of the witch and a minor star on the renaissance fair circuit. He looked a lot like Ian Anderson of Jethro Tull with the long mane and beard, even performed some of J.T.'s covers. In these types of events you always attract and bond with a person or two, often becoming fast friends.

They are usually the cream that rises to the occasion or maybe just someone you instantly trust. Carl was the one in this case. He had a duel role at the event as a performer and my local transportation coordinator. We are still great friends to this day and I've always been a little jealous of his Romany lifestyle. He is one of the only true gypsies I know. (He lives in a restored circus wagon near the shore in Tampa) He is also one of the only performers who got paid.

I have Irish ancestry but until that weekend I never really understood what it meant to be Irish. They took it . . . and they dealt with it. When it was darkest they sang, drank, joked, danced and counted their blessings. It was the most inspiring thing I have ever witnessed and the charge my spirit got from it lasted for many years.

I tried to stay in contact with as many as I could to try and keep that feeling, but it faded. Numbers and memories were lost. I am much better for having been there and it was no doubt an emotional roller coaster. I just wish I could have done more and given back just a touch of what they all gave me.

S. RAY JACKSON

THREE O' CLOCK IN THE PM

I had a little bit of a break and a thought occurred to me. Where is this generations Hemingway? I know they are out there because I've seen them. Just not on the bookshelf. They are in the world, moving, laughing, slapping backs of others like them. They are just silent in the plastic, plasma screen world. They are real and the world is not. So, as in most financial arrangements they are pushed to the rear of the line for payment or non-payment in this case. They are men of their time and are unaffected by their surroundings. No bullshit... on his own biological schedule. He may let others in on occasion but without rhyme or reason. Just because.

I think they are born of weather somehow. Weather and in particular storms. Storms, if you have felt a real one, can shape a person in look and character. It's a respect for things but also a confidence. You can smell it when it's thick. They like their whiskey, whores and dogs. Other types of them might opt for beer and sailboats, but whores are always a constant in the formula. Someday I hope to grow up and be one of these guys.

A new Irish Pub named <u>Creegan's</u> opened up around the corner from the pool hall last Friday. I will always in the future refer to the pool hall as the pool hall because the owner has changed the name based on his new power as sole owner and I'm not exactly comfortable with it. This new addition to my universe was the most exciting development we've seen in quite some time. This is due in part to my buddy Casey being full blown Irish and all of our groups' love of decent cold, draft beer. The interior is deep, rich wood and frosted glass which was constructed in Ireland, dismantled, shipped and reassembled. The best thing is the true pub style with seating broken into intimate venues with never more than ten to an area. This allows for actual conversations to take place and not the slaughterhouse atmosphere like at all the other new beer halls in the area. It will be our new home soon. I can feel it.

The most interesting thing is the manager. I haven't seen him in years but he was the co-owner of the bar we drank out of business that crazy summer long ago. And there was the stewardess he adored that hung there on layovers. The one I eventually had to call the cops on after a week, because she refused to leave the apartment near the bar. But I don't think he can hold that against me, statute of limitations and all. Those are just things.

Adventures don't always have to be a "jump through your ass" excited deal. Or trouble. Or imply danger of some kind. It can be the sky. How a dog looks you in the eye and you connect. Contentment can be an adventure; just, quieter.

The opposite of quiet is loud. And there's folks like big Al. Every time you start to feel a little decent about your immediate universe these guy's heads pop up on the National radar screen. If there was ever any larger, self serving bag of air as him ever on this rock they call earth I am unaware of them.

The band playing on the XM radio was "Morphine". "Sharks" the song I think. You know the one. . . "Sharks patrol these waters". It was ironic to me that earlier in the day yesterday my mom had been the victim of a home invasion robbery attempt. This little (5'7", 140lbs) black piece of dung short order cook at a 65th Street Diner saw his only option was to kick in the back carport door. Apparently he had been casing the joint for some time because once the deal went down my dad said he recognized the truck from other occasions near the house. On the day in question my pop had been asked on one of the rare occasions to work during the week. Thinking no one was home he backed his truck up into the carport, anticipating a haul, and proceeded to stomp the door into submission. The hero of the day was my folks little pup named "Lucky" (an orphan who once belonged to a deceased grandmother). This toy poodle mix had never proven much to me but this morning the scent of danger caused him to alarm just enough to wake my sleeping mom and could have quite well saved her life. She came down the hall, startled and scared the intruder as much as he scared her. After bolting from the botched attempt he was spotted by two neighbors walking their dog who were luckily alert enough to get a plate number. This led to his arrest shortly after and the rest is history. I hope? He got out on bail this morning.

The last time I heard that song "Sharks" it was blaring from the rattling, shitty speakers of an old Crown Vic driven by a pair of tweeking but not terrible looking strippers who had just got off work in Jacksonville. I'm not sure why I was there at 5AM, as that is unusual for me, but more important without transportation.

I can only assume I rode with someone who subsequently left. The older of the two had recently given birth to the product of a union between she and her mother's boyfriend. She would not shut up about how happy she was with this but glad to be back at work. The other younger, pretty one stared straight ahead, silent as stone. Before getting too far out of town, however she had the other pull into a church parking lot where she proceeded to take a piss in the headlights. She said because she was "afraid of snakes". She also explained that she couldn't wait to go before we hit the long stretch of no exits on the interstate highway between the proverbial here and there.

I guess the general appearance around me caused me to realize I was the only passenger the rear seat had seen in some time and the valleys in the faux leatherette upholstery were leaving dirt lines every three inches on my white, slightly bloody dress shirt. (The shirt caused me to suddenly remember more than I liked). Further examination in every overhead light revealed some puke remnants on the cuffs (not my own) and a strange sweet smell wafted from the floor below my feet. It was, however, a ride. Who am I to judge? I was a little troubled by the fact there were no door handles in the back. Retired police car I imagined. I wondered how many illicit sex acts this baby had cost? Not wanting them to know the location of my abode I opted to be let off in a central location downtown and they were fine with that. After indifferent goodbyes I gratefully flipped them a ten for gas and all were smiles. I headed home on foot and enjoyed the growing light and a quiet, broken only by the occasional drop of a dumpster by an insensitive and overworked driver.

The air was fresh and the birds were beginning to sing. That always reminded me of when I was young and lived with the folks and the fact that if I ever stayed out long enough to hear birds that meant I was in trouble. Today was an exception.

Despite the fact I had to be at work in less than two hours I felt exceptionally well. The positive spirit was rewarded with a quick pick up and lift on Markham Street by three westward party girls. I was home in less than ten minutes. Godspeed, all that.

For breakfast (which I never eat) I had two eggs with some wheat toast and a large glass of milk. I wasn't sure if I would see what was up that night but it was way too early to make that call. It's funny how sometimes your train of thought works. I was thinking about the strippers and how the ride seemed a little scary for a minute and I flashed straight to the chicks that had tried to kill me.

With that I thought about my other major brush with an unhappy woman and a firearm. I was seventeen I think, still in school and looking for all opportunities and any adventures perceived or otherwise. She was older, at least forty, which was awkward considering at the time my dad, was only forty two. When she would call I always raced to the phone with only a few misses for which I caught great steaming loads of shit from the folks.

She was a divorced woman who had acquired a car detailing business and two small independent motels on the interstate so money was not a problem. She was very demanding and after a time I realized I was just another thing she had acquired. You know this just had to have broken the heart of an impressionable lad such as myself. Our deal was very simple. She would keep the fridge in her big house stocked with my beer brand; I had a key and would come when she called. This worked exceptionally well, until it didn't.

One major complication I failed to mention was she had a daughter one year younger than me and we had been caught on occasion looking a little too long in each other's direction. I knew enough to never shit where I eat but it still was an intriguing thought. After a few months of playing houseboy I started to have wandering thoughts, (A new record for me). All my friends were just up the road most nights while I sat there drinking beer and entertaining this woman whose name now escapes me. It was time to go.

There was this fine redheaded preacher's daughter I had had my eye on for some time and already snuck around with a time or two. My previously mentioned benefactor I think could sense it, and it simply wouldn't do. I had purposely been busy and knew enough not to drive my car anywhere close for awhile and had even spotted her trolling for me several times "just to talk". After many calls and pleadings for the opportunity for a descent goodbye I agreed to stop by. I knew what she wanted and I was fine with it, as long as it was a clean break. It didn't take long to get from point A to B and soon I was firmly pressed into the mattress by her weight. I could get through it for sure with eyes closed, concentrating on the mission and subsequent goal.

It was then I heard an unfamiliar sound and with a start I noticed her reaching into the bed side table. She pulled out an extremely handsome, chrome plated handgun. "No one" she repeated in a low tone as she swung the weapon in the direction of my eye. Adrenaline kicked in and I continued the swing past me and on into the wall. Tossing her off the bed and pinning her between the bed and wall. I grabbed my pants (with wallet and keys) and hit the door at a gallop. I had no time for shoes, shirt or to get dressed at all as I raced through the living room and out the front door into the front yard. Her daughter and a friend were watching TV and were shocked at the spectacle. They got to the door in time to see me dive in the window of my Trans am, start up and " haul ass" as they said in the 70's.

"What the fuck?" the friend yelled while I heard the daughter shout after me "goodbye Ray!". I never saw them follow and after a mile or so I pulled over to put on my pants. Going home like that was not an option. Damn, that was my favorite pair of shoes.

I've always been lucky like that. Aside from the fact that a fortune teller at the state fair once told me when I was thirteen that I would be killed by a jealous husband. What the hell kind of thing is that to tell a kid.

It was also about this time in life in yet another clouded lapse in good judgment that we, as a collective and me by virtue of my fast car, decided to (inspired by the recent movie release "Smoky and the Bandit") look into the possible virtues of interstate commerce. Not a really serious enterprise but more for adventure and perhaps a small amount of pocket change. At the time it was against the law for Coors brand beer to be sold in our state which caused, through the concept of supply and demand, an extreme interest in the exotic nature of it. We didn't feel this was any big moral issue as the whole situation was the result of a stupid union labor dispute.

On a Saturday night an enterprising young man could get a ten-fold return on investment, which was not to be sneezed at. There was also a concrete element of danger based on the $500.00 per can fine levied on any found crossing state lines. The plan for this run was simple and familiar. First we would see who was game for the ride, which were the usual three suspects. The route was always back roads (reality was the interstate would have been much less conspicuous) which took us through mostly redneck country and to the state of beer origin which was Louisiana. There was also the pre-trip collection of investment capital with generally 10% taken off the top at lift off for road beer, or whisky as apropos.

This trip, there was a sale at Sullivan's on Miller ponies, the 7oz, clear glass bottle, which with adequate temperature could be downed with one, or for sure two, massive gulps. A case was obtained. With the remnants of a fifth of Southern Comfort from last Friday and two six packs of red grape malt duck for mixing. This sounded sufficient and after several stops to solicit females with no takers, off we went. The night air was crisp but we knew that the further south we traveled the more humid it would be. Just a matter of time before the windshield would be completely covered with bugs. The constant hum of the engine seemed in perfect harmony with whatever blared on the radio and the beer went quick. It was about an hour before the back floor board was up to the ankles with empties. Every time someone moved or shifted slightly the telltale clank signaled which direction. We were a lot of things but not prone to litter. We were on our way. The first major town across the border that wouldn't check us out for ID was Ruston. This armpit of an southern American town is only surpassed in shittiness by Shreveport. Even saying the name conjures up images of decay. I think it was about thirty minutes from our goal and we were long into the whisky and sufficiently full of shit and courage. I'm not sure who made the suggestion or maybe it was to be concrete proof of the trip but soon we were pulled over on a remote stretch, using my ratchet set to remove a 2ft x 2ft state highway road sign. In the truck it went, in about five minutes, and on we continued. At our rate down we should be back to town by 2amish to possibly unload the entire cargo in time for Saturday mornings chocolate gravy breakfast at my mom's house for me and my mates.

It seemed ambitious but it was certainly worth the try. Call it karma, or whatever, but it was soon after that things inconceivably went south. We had gotten to the package store just south of town and loaded as much as the trunk would hold (probably $25k worth in fines) and slowly eased back onto the four lane headed back into town. This part of the country closes very early and a silver Trans Am loaded with drunken ass-holes with Arkansas plates would show up like tits on a bull to anyone who cared to notice.

I think my friend riding shotgun first noticed the transmission seemed to be slipping. The engine would rev and slide back to appropriate levels without explanation. Over the next few minutes, which seemed like days, the slipping grew progressively worse. I pulled over at one point and turned off the engine to see if that would help. It was quickly apparent that was not the move as we realized that we were now stuck only with first and reverse gears due to an obvious lack of transmission fluid. On the approach we had seen the only gas station open within the last hour and felt like that might be the most practical goal. My "ass-hole" friends snored in the back seat oblivious to our potentially life threatening situation. The "situation" worsened by the moment as we realized we were on the wrong side of the four lane, engine overheating, and only able to travel about 5 to 10 miles per hour before pulling over to cool down.

To complicate things were the blue lights which had pulled up behind our lame duck asses, an obvious attempt of the officer to liven an otherwise dull as dirt evening. So here we are, drunk, out of state tags, sports car, and two guys asleep in the back seat knee deep in empties. Ten cases of potentially illegal beer in the trunk covered over by a stolen road sign.

We were in a tight spot.

Quick thinking led to the conclusion and the fact (as stated on numerous occasions) that a good offense was the best defense. I knew if I kept the officer from the car we had a chance. Some truth never hurts either and I knew some would be useful. As I pulled over I slammed into park and dashed out with my frantic face on, explaining about the transmission issues and the fact we were lost (a half truth) and only trying to reach an open gas station and fluid. Plus the fact we were afraid to stop because it might not restart and being near 200 miles from home that was not an option.

This pace of rapid fire information obviously overwhelmed the man and he was soon wishing me luck and sending us on. I think being white was to our benefit although hair length was not. Perhaps he wanted to avoid paperwork. Either way he seemed uninterested in obtaining any further answers. We eased our way the 5 or so miles to the station at 5 minute intervals.

After 30 minutes we arrived praying this was the answer. The attendant was the late man and less than helpful. He could sell us gas and canned fluids, but his boss always locked up the tools upon departure. This would include a handy thing such as a funnel. We knew time was of the essence before "Gomer" got bored and came to check our progress so we decided to improvise a funnel to pour the transmission fluid out; the Daily paper the boy had tossed earlier in his shift would have to do.

This worked great until the white hot engine ignited the paper causing two of the spark plug wires to melt to copper. At this point I was pissed. The dick weeds still snored in back and John was panic stricken in the front. Miraculously, the engine started. And aside from a rough idle, seemed to be functional. Outcome: the transmission damage had been done. I figured out through trial and error that reverse actually gave us better speed and distance. Based on the lack of traffic, population density, and the hour it wasn't a bad option. At this point in the ride I was as extremely sober and as nervous as a whore in church so I was ok with the attempt. What I was concerned with was the lack of guard rails, the deep ditches and lack of road shoulders plunging into the swamps and bottoms in light of my couple of years of driving experience.

I had never been as tired as I proceeded to back my way back into Arkansas. Even though it was a relatively straight road, my fatigue and general bad attitude made ten miles at a pop the maximum distance attainable. This caused the two plus hour trip to slide into eight and then ten. Not to mention the pull over every time headlights appeared to allow passage. It was the longest night of my relatively short life. Around 5AM my drunk ass passengers awoke, fresh as new daises and chatty. If I had had a gun I would be in jail as we speak. Once they realized what the night had held for us they were very apologetic but I still told them to "fuck off" and that my co-pilot and I would split all the cash, there would be no discussion on these points. My share would no doubt go toward the TBD engine repairs. That is assuming we returned to a familiar land and avoided jail time. Once we finally reached my friends grandmothers house about noon, I could go no farther. The engine was toast. The cargo was still on board and we couldn't think straight. After a few hours of sleep we limped over to John's house, unloaded in his garage and took the car on home.

My dad didn't want to talk much to me that afternoon and based on all the dried up left over fried eggs from the morning it was about wasted food more than car trouble. That was fine, I knew he'd get over it. The car however, was gone…total overhaul. I saw a trade in my future. But first we had some beer to move. Cold processed beer which can die quickly with heat. It would be close…

Spur of the moment trips are one thing that has always been a constant in my short time on this rock. It's never too late, too far or too much trouble. Vast amounts of alcohol always seems to lubricate the missions and potential missions. When we were young and based on the seven-ish hours it takes to complete, New Orleans was always the prime destination of choice, Mardi gras the preferable time. I can honestly say that after six or maybe eight starts for M.G. I never actually made it until much later in life. Not New Orleans mind you, which had been accomplished dozens of times, but never the big dance. It was a dream then and is still somewhat elusive, which makes it an all the more a whimsical notion. Especially post Katrina. (Aren't you really tired of hearing that . . . Post Katrina?)

Mexico is another matter. Border towns have a vast appeal to me. When I was shorter I had several cousins and an insane aunt and uncle living in El Paso which we visited on occasion. Juarez, while being one of the dirtiest (even shittier than Shreveport) destinations in the Northern hemisphere, was filled with tons of charm for a young man. Not least of which was my first bull fight and the dog races. Two of my cousins took up with Mex-gals and found life better on the south side where they married, started families and moved in with the in-laws. They were US citizens and worked in the north but returned below, daily to live the good life of sorts.

The first to take that step had three small children before he was twenty and developed a little drug and alcohol problem. Go figure. I never quite understood what his hurry was. It all looked and smelled very intoxicating but in the end I realized what a dumb ass he was and is and realized I really didn't give a shit. I think he lives in his mom's basement now in Midland, Texas. Must be in his mid-forties?

His older brother, a suspected mildly retarded fellow, fell even more into the depths through his use and sale of drugs. He also lived south for a time while he developed his contacts and trade, which from all appearances seemed a very lucrative one at one time. As these types of things go, it was just a matter of time until the locals decided the gringo had to as well. His money could stay, but he was done. To accomplish this he was taken out about a hundred or so miles into the desert, southwest of Juarez, on a moonlit night and left to die. I understand he was left with a small Boy Scout canteen of hot orange crush, to be sporting, with an attempt to balance that kindness he being left shoeless.

Authorities said he wandered for about three days and when found was very near death. Feet and throat both swollen and skin burned with 2nd and 3rd degree burns as a result of rocks and sun. His mother (my aunt) collected him, as the federales felt he had seen enough of this magical land. He was allowed safe passage back to Texas. Same with the border patrol. He never mentally recovered and is to this day confined to a psychiatric facility I believe is in or around El Paso.

Perhaps my most ill advised impulse trip to Mexico happened much later when I was working in Phoenix for about a month. We were primarily in the Queen Creek, Mesa, Apache Junction area off Superstition highway (60), where I was in charge of a regional mud bog four wheeler racing event for a very odd, eccentric client. Being desert, we had to dig the race course and flood it. This required us to be on site pretty much the entire trip in a heat unfamiliar to common southern boys. We would quit each day at four PM and haul ass to the first air conditioned bar with frozen draft mugs which happened to be Friday's in Mesa on Hwy 60 right behind an "On the Border" Tex-mex joint with equally cold beer at slightly higher prices.

The downside was there was no happy hour, for which Friday's is well known. That night, which I think was a Wednesday, was one of our site visits prior to the long stay. Jack Page and I had just driven in from Los Angeles the day before in our black, convertible Chrysler Sebring rental and chose the On The Border as our dinner stop. It may have been the Hispanic waitresses. It may have been the night. It was obviously, in part, the twenty plus beers . . . there was definitely madness in the air.

It was close to quitting time when the conversation turned toward foolishness. In this case, foolishness was personified by a busboy who was a terrible judge of distance. After much boasting and swearing Nogales was just over the border it became the target of the night's mission. The thought of the top down and the full moon as a beacon sealed the deal, especially with the promise of a 45 minute trip. Try two plus hours on a Wednesday leaving out from Mesa at 11 PM. Granted, it was interstate all the way and a beautiful night, but bullshit! After about an hour we were pretty sober and just over halfway somewhere. It became a quest. At that point, with us not having ever been there and no apparent plans other than to have at least one cervesa, look around and leave. It had never occurred to us that it would look odd for two white boys in a Hertz convertible with California plates to come cruising into town at 2 o'clock AM. (What were they looking for? What could they possibly want? Drugs? Sex?) We came across and saw immediately that we were alone; alone and unarmed. What I mean by alone is no others like us. The only Mexicans around were the sort that had obviously not been at church earlier in the evening with this being evidenced by the propositional sale of two of their thirteen year old sisters for you know. . . whatever. Then came the pharmacy. We parked the car close to where we thought it looked ok, "ok" being a cantina with effigies of the dead hanging from standards. This was it and we started for the doors, a swinging pair like in old western movies but painted a garish orange which seemed luminescent. It also had tiny skulls painted or maybe stamped on the trim. I couldn't be sure which in that light. In the course of a half block we were approached by five or six unsavory types who offered us every type of drug I had ever seen and several I had only heard rumor of.

Jack did a sample platter of something, but I, as you well know, abstained. One of us definitely had to function if we were to see the light of day. We gently pushed the doors, opening wide to an empty cavern of a room. It was totally empty and the three waiters, each having strange matching waxed mustaches, sat limply at the bar. One glanced in our direction slowly before returning to his paper, eventually we were served a luke warm pair of something's which we killed as soon as possible while trying to keep from gagging; a sign of weakness in these parts. The reality of this scene made us more and more concerned about our vehicle and, in what I considered a nick of time, we brushed some more hookers aside, easing the car onto the back street.

In the headlights as we backed out, flashed a polished machete dangling from the belt of a homeless guy. Very comforting that the homeless should be so well protected from the night. After several steady, but uncertain turns we ended up headed back up north on the main drag. Looking back, I think what saved us from peril was the absurdity of our visit. To a seasoned man of the streets, and its trades, for us to waltz in like that, they must have figured we were extremely connected or very dangerous, or both. No one tested the theory, for whatever reason, and after a very exhaustively long sojourn back we laid down to sleep around dawn. We never made it back that trip to beat the busboy's ass with the bad advice but it wasn't for lack of want.

It seems to always be just so you can say you did it. That seems to be all the trips in a nutshell. That's also one of the reasons I always prefer driving to flying unless its business that has the constraints of time or some emergency reason that would taint the spirit of adventure. It's who you meet and what they say. The smells. How simple things on most days make you stop. Afterthoughts mainly, become major things. One major advantage to my general geographical location in the US and its contribution to spontaneity is its central nature. I am pretty much most of the time in the center of the North American continent, and growing up next to a major Interstate highway (literally a stone's throw) I have always been struck by the notion of what lies down the road. What that means is I can reach a Great Lake in 9 hours, a Pacific or Atlantic location in two days tops and if I leave at 3AM, which is customary, the Gulf of Mexico by lunch.

The 3AM departure grew out of a tradition my father created on long trips which would allow the maximum amount of quiet drive time while kids slept. This time allowed the most available before breakfast, without being too early, and destroying the spirit with a sense of urgency. This always worked for us, so I fostered and passed on the tradition.

Vegas as well as New Orleans has always been a prime destination for many years. Anytime you are within five or six hours of Vegas it always demands a look-see. If the obvious reasons are not adequate just seeing what buildings have survived implosion from the last visit is somewhat entertaining. Again, nothing compares with driving in from LA, Phoenix, Albuquerque or Salt Lake City after dark. The laser beam from the point of Luxor is the perfect beacon for fun and frolic. You know you want it and fatigue, no matter how long on the road, is not a factor.

Except in the case of road construction cones. This was the last 3AM obstacle in one of my latest mad dashes between myself, my traveling companion, and the city.

Thinking the yellow short bus (Xterra) had one more good trip in her I took the opportunity and planned a quick one for points west once again. The Xterra has served me well for over ten years and has literally gotten me through deeps snows of Vermont, hurricane winds and rain of Florida, Mexico, Death Valley, and the high Sierras. She and I have done it all and the back cargo area can be very comfy for a nap anytime; day or night. The money you save on Motels doesn't quite make up for the fuel cost due to the shitty gas mileage, but it has its charm. Don't get me wrong, it has fucked me over on more than one occasion, like stranding me in Flagstaff with no cash for three days waiting for parts one time. That all goes out the window when she gets a good head of steam in her and the fact we've had more good times than bad. This trip was based on the fact that my little girl, who had lived in a fashionably young section of mid-town Chicago for three years had decided to move in with her fine example of a boyfriend in San Diego. You may be thinking at this moment that I'm being facetious but I'm not. I really liked him a lot and thought he was great for her. (I would find out later he was a cad and that was not the case and not at all as bona-fide as her current husband "Slaughter") Something I know my way around.

Most of her large personal items had been in storage in Arkansas, so I had the perfect opportunity to pack the short bus to the gills, fly the boy (her brother) in from New York and have a legitimate excuse to drive towards the sunset. It had been a good spring and cash was not an issue, plus the fact it had been two years since I had driven through and the many old and new friends I needed to bust in on. It made it a no brainer.

My son had been working on several projects in the City (NYC) pretty hard over the winter and aside from being stranded one Tuesday somewhere in Massachusetts by some crazy, vindictive bitch he welcomed the opportunity. So it was on. There was a pretty good load which filled and scrapped the ceiling of the SUV but that was irrelevant. It felt great to have Dylan as co-pilot again, weather looked great and obligations back home were minimal. So... with atlas in hand (even though we knew every step of the way except the California coast making it more ceremonial than essential) off we went into the early (3AM) hours. Dylan had come into town a couple of days earlier to visit friends and as I suspected pretty much refused sleep aside from the two hours prior to departure. He also smelled of stale beer, German variety I suspect, or possibly Pabst, so I demanded he shower before liftoff. With a very aggressive schedule and only a concept of hopeful destinations in our empty pockets we were extremely optimistic.

The vastness of the trip was driven by several factors not least of which were:

A. Wanting the maximum amount of distance in the allowable time.
B. A dread feeling that we both didn't want this perfect situation to ever end.
C. A deep sensation in me that every trip should be always treated as if it's your last.

This is not to be considered a morbid thought but more of a reality. These are thoughts that are inconceivable to someone under forty, but quite real and menacing to those of us who are. It's like realizing that steak can never and will never taste better. I think this may also be one of the factors behind binge drinking. (The next, next, next one may be better theory.)

The first leg of our journey was a long one. The area between Arkansas and New Mexico held little interest to us as we knew the meat of the matter to be beyond and into Arizona. This is not to say there are not great areas around Santa Fe where I am always welcome and well liked, but that's not important. We also knew enough to know that in the area of Albuquerque it would be near impossible to find a cheap motel room after dark. A beer or shot and a steak sounded good, so we started our search for lodging. Preferably in walking distance of one of those chain restaurant / fern bar kind of places. It was early in the trip and 700 to 900 miles was a good start right out of the box. What we didn't know, or in reality I didn't remember, was that the city was hosting the meeting of the Seven (American Indian) Nations that weekend. My friend in Little Rock who works as a food vendor for us at shows had told me about it earlier in the year and I had totally zoned out about the info. To people east of the Mississippi the meeting of the Nations is the annual gathering of the seven major Indian tribes so basically every roadside stop for a hundred miles was filled to capacity and beyond.

After a few false starts and a lot of no's we settled on a place near the airport; only moderately out of our price range. What sold us was the Applebee's across the street. We threw our pertinent shit in the room and had bellied up to the bar within no more than fifteen minutes.

A homemade margarita sounded awesome with possibly some queso and tortilla chips so it was all good... we loaded in. Being that I'm older there was no problem for me but Dylan on the other hand had several issues. New Mexico laws are pretty strict on underage drinking and anyone under thirty is immediately suspect and prone to interrogation and at the least I-D check. D, as a non-driver in New York had never seen the need to replace his still current (however badly water damaged) Arkansas driver's license with the curling off laminate and was subsequently denied service for sporting a forgery. Sucks to be him.

After an ok meal we felt we needed to turn in and get up early for the next leg which would be Albuquerque to Mesa, Arizona. We would accomplish this through a shortcut I knew at Socorro where we could cut through back country (straight through the middle of the US Line Array Telescope) and hook straight up with Hwy 60 passing near Superstition Mountain.

I had spent a great deal of time in this area and knew it better than I would have preferred. In a strange coincidence my old ex- business partner Jaqui, a wonderful lady and a great artist from San Antonio, had relocated here to the desert. Her husband was a commercial airline pilot flying out of Sky Harbor at Phoenix International and she had always preferred the solitude and nobility of the mysterious high desert. Also, Arkansas had become a little complicated and a fresh start was in order.

We had prearranged a visit to get caught up on events, get shit faced, and eventually get some shut eye. I, on the sofa and Dylan in the big chair near the combination private office and studio. The house was being remodeled but was a stunning example of the adobe style with a panoramic view of Superstition Mountain (home of the legendary and elusive Lost Dutchman mine) out the front picture window.

It was probably a huge culture shock for the boy from Brooklyn to be in a place where you could travel miles in any direction and not even see another human. It was almost perfect. Her husband David, in anticipation of our arrival had prepared a great spread of Bar-B-Que brisket, cowboy beans (beans, bacon, onions, and hot sauce in a frying pan on an open flame) and every other tasty snack of the southwest variety you could consider.

The drink of the day was again margaritas as we had secured a fresh gallon of Cuervo Gold a couple of towns back at a little Mexican grocery and found some mixer at the Quick Stop on Hwy 60. This gave us about a gallon and a half in our trip stores which was enough for us and our hosts. Especially when coupled with the ice chest filled with a plethora of beer varieties. This made it all work as we watched the colors change on the mountain from orange to purple and then to black. We laughed and told lies, all under the ever climbing moon. Around nine PM we realized we hadn't touched the feast, being caught up in the moment, so suddenly it was dinner time. All the animals had been secured well before dark because of predators. Upon arrival, I had noticed all her old animals (dogs) had been replaced by new stock and inquired the reason. "Owls" was the one word answer. She recounted how when they first settled in with the pair of wiener dogs from back home she had let them out back to explore the new yard. A short time later hearing shrill cries, she jumped up and out just in time to see a terrified pup being carried off in the clutches of an enormous raptor like bird.

It wasn't that long before a snake got the other so her new animals were selected to be more in tune with the region. This seemed appropriate. I loaded my plate with all I could hold and made my way out to the table that had been set just off the patio in the back yard. I had no sooner than sat down when I felt a searing pain in my heel which at first shot a hot needle image deep into my mind. I wear huarache sandals pretty much year round (at the time) and there is about an inch and a half of unprotected area which was the obvious target.

After jumping and brushing the wound I looked down just in time to see a large black scorpion skating back into the shadows. Its calling card heavy black stinger sat high in the center of a throbbing, pulsing spot about the size of a half dollar. "FUCK!" rang through the night air as I almost upset the table, hobbling in an effort to lose the sensation. Scorpion stings are a lot like bee stings and if you're allergic they can certainly mean bad trouble.(Like when you're in the middle of nowhere) I enquired from my drunken hosts if I should be concerned and they giggled "we'd know in a few minutes". In my case, I am not allergic as it turns out so after another beverage or two it all became more of a side note. The stinger however remained in the heal of my foot the remainder of the trip and several days after.

After a great meal, and mucho tequila, soon it was time to slumber. The next day would not be as long, and after a jog south; bypassing downtown Phoenix proper, we hoped to hit one of the southern, westward Interstates and head into San Diego. We had a map quest map my friends printed out of the specifics of where Amber was staying so we felt as prepared as possible. When cutting at a good clip in back country one of the disadvantages is the lack of toilet facilities between long stretches of civilization. This often requires drastic measures when it is suddenly imperative that you deal with the excesses of the night before. A cold sweat can often ensue.

Our savior in our particular time of need was "Pie Town". Pie Town is a very small place in the high country about seventy five miles in both directions from nowhere. I might also note that in the high country there are no road shoulders readily available if that was your thought. One thing Pie Town does have is a pie shop. This pie shop also has a restroom. This restroom is for pie eaters and pie buyers only and pie is expensive. This place is very rustic and sweet, with a pot bellied stove in the center to drive away the cold of the freak snows common to the area and owned and operated by a constantly smiling band of rapidly aging hippies. And why wouldn't they smile, with such an excellent shake down as this? They could be serving soap at ten dollars a slice to eat if you've got to go bad enough, and it would be just fine. You know they probably sit around after work, smoking dope and laughing about all the squirming pie eating sons-of-bitches that waddled through the ugly little clap board shitter door; the one with the butterflies and rainbows painted on it.

After a couple more hours, another different "non-pie" snack was in order and taken advantage of. We made good time after and arrived in San Diego, between three and four in the afternoon. After unloading the truck, we all piled into the Future man's Saab and the four of us headed for Mission Bay and the downtown waterfront for some pizza and beers.

The shoreline was very much like every other beach community I had ever visited. I was a little disappointed. I'm not sure what I expected, but this wasn't it. The entire City's architecture seemed to be a product of the seventies and I was not overly impressed. After getting a slight buzz and disturbing some sleeping seals (a dangerous proposition) it was time to head in.

We had decided at the onset to seek a nearby motel for accommodations, due to the dual facts we had not been invited to stay over, and the prospect of another sofa or chair bed was not appealing. There was also the enormous, 4 foot tall handmade doll house that populated Future man's mom's living room. We chose not to speak of this but it cemented the whole hotel idea. On an even more humorous but strange side note we had found a place around the corner and I was waited on at the desk by a slightly 50ish, Vietnamese woman who may have been a looker at one time, long, long ago (possibly during the war). This was not all that unusual except her hair extensions, slender body and enormous Pamela Anderson size plastic breasts which could certainly be a younger man's dream. The other even stranger element was her tight, off white dress slacks were buttoned but completely unzipped. Thus revealing a very attractive yet skimpy royal blue, see through thong front panel (One can only assume). It was a little scary but yet intriguing and impossible to ignore.

I was torn on whether to risk embarrassment to us both by mentioning it or letting it lie for the next victim to ponder. After my business was complete with the register I chose the high road and mentioned the dilemma. Prefaced by the fact I didn't want to embarrass her, but. . . Afterwards she seemed totally grateful and gave me a 10% discount for being so considerate. Sometimes things just work out.

The next day, after some brief deliberation, and having accomplished our primary objective, we decided to catch the 5 and head north to LA. If lucky, we might catch the Pacific Coast Highway and on to San Fran. This was only after we tried to convince Amby to come along and meet up with her guy in Vegas on the weekend where he could easily drive. That was a no go but I could see in her eyes there was interest. I had never been north of LA as most of my work there had been in Long Beach, south of town. I looked forward to the opportunity. After fighting the 100 mile commute north from San Diego we stopped and enjoyed our "load in" meal of the day. I think it was a Denny's, which sat across the drive from an In and Out Burger; more of a desirable target.

With this new found strength and the extended goal of Vegas on the return we felt Frisco was in the realm of possibility. Once we were well into the valley we found a spot to head hard west and soon found ourselves on the most spectacular stretch of road either of us had ever seen. The colors and the curvature of the earth were stunning. Not to mention the sense that we were following others. Others we had admired and in some odd way may have at one time tried to emulate. For us this was the proverbial road less traveled. The switchbacks and lack of shoulders make good or even decent time impossible but that was of no real matter to us. We were together in this place on the edge of our world, and no one could ever take that. Big Sur was next as the road meandered away from the shore and into the thick, primordial growth of some ancient fathers and sons.

Thinking more about the vastness left to cover and the lack of preparation for a late night San Francisco arrival I took the opportunity to buy a few gallons of gas at $5.53 per gallon from a grinning toothless "earth" chick (obviously smiling all the way to the bank) and call ahead to try and make some downtown hotel reservations.

This is usually not our style but based on the possible hour, the lack of urban knowledge of the bay area, and past experience it seemed a good course of action. No real need to put the trip in the ditch at this point. As darkness drew near and the novelty of the landscape began to wane, we felt the need to cut back over to some nearby four lane and cruse in at a more acceptable rate.

The downtown area was accomplished slightly after eleven o'clock. We were checking into a high rise near Fisherman's Wharf; someone, somewhere, sometime had made a comment to me about how small San Francisco was. They were out of their damn minds. As we rolled into unfamiliar territory in the dark we were overwhelmed by the complexity and enormity of it. It was beautiful and dangerous, and cities don't ever scare me. Once settled, we knew we had to move for some food and beer as we hadn't eaten in almost twelve hours, so into the night we went.

After a couple of false starts we met a benevolent bartender at Joe's Crab Shack who agreed to serve us after close. He said he had to clean up anyway and some company wouldn't be a bad deal so we were in. We kept it simple and killed as much draft beer as we could until the bum rush... all went away satisfied. With more exploring to do and no real destination in mind we headed on foot into the misty night. There was no idea, significant concern, or worry about the area as we barged our way forward in the direction of the Golden Gate. Around Madison Street we found a tiny hide-a-way Irish Pub by way of a patron being thrown out into the street through a closed plate glass door. Our kinda place. There was certainly enough false courage on our part to make ourselves at home. It became quickly apparent we were obviously in the void between the happy hour and the all-nighters. This allowed us to make friends with the two young

Irishmen who ran the joint and who seemed to enjoy our moxie. We were not afraid and we were armed with a decent repertoire of tasteless jokes.

Within two or three hours we were even allowed to pour drinks behind the bar as if we were there daily. The only other patron there at the time was an older man from Santa Barbara who worked inspecting oil rigs all over the state checking compliance issues. He said this essentially made him a bag man and allowed him much financial gain and travel as a joint employee of the Feds and the state of California. He had a lazy eye he said because of a golfing accident with a wayward slice. He played a lot of golf.

The bartenders also seemed to have a firm affection for blow as they would take turns retreating to the kitchen only to return sniffling and being ever slightly more aggressive each trip with the customers, few but with growing numbers as they were. They thought we were crazy based on where we were in our travels and the fact we firmly expected to be in Vegas by dark the next day. "You can't get to Vegas from here you dumb Arse". After much argument and the agreement of the lazy eye inspector that it could indeed be done a sense of satisfaction hit our end of the bar.

About this time a college kid on something slid in off the street up to the bar and whispered to the bigger bartender. In a rage he leaped over the bar like a ninja, grabbed the kids' hoodie and opened the door with his face, tumbling him into a parking meter just outside. As he stumbled off we decided it was time to shove off. Before we left we got some directions for future reference and were pleased to know that Madison, just outside, led to "City Lights Bookstore", Kerouac Alley and China Town. We also needed a good look at the bay and Alcatraz before our departure. Being about 3AM we turned in with the goal of being on the streets for a walk by 8, after throwing our shit in the truck and out of the room in case we were detained past noon. The early morning was marked by the traditional haze which soon burned off to a brilliant blue sky and cool temp. We had decided to head back the few blocks toward the bar as a good point of reference and were soon headed back up Madison away from the waterfront area. Passing several parks filled with exercise groups and dogs in various forms of dress, masters attentive, we started to get a totally different feel from the madness of the night before. It was a community that had a sense of history, but was not driven by it. It was more like a type of respect.

Even the homeless seemed to have a thoughtful look. They were in a place that strangely had some sort of dignity, even for their lot. After a short while of taking in the sights we reached the City Lights Bookstore. Dylan's day job at the time in Manhattan was at The Strand Bookstore which is billed as the largest used bookstore in the world with the C.L.B. being second. It's also well known as a publishing house and has the claim to fame of the controversial Ginsburg work "Howl". This was a definite stop and several souvenirs were acquired. It is also next door to the small stretch known as Kerouac Alley. This is a very interesting destination metaphorically and literally. You start on one end in the shadow of strip clubs and intellectual haunts and end up thrown into the edges of Chinatown.

Worlds seem to collide there in the distance of a short brick, graffiti covered passageway. We shuffled around another hour or so checking out The Beat Museum and decided to head back toward the bay and Fisherman's Wharf for some lunch of fresh seafood. After checking out the bay and opting to hit the road instead of the several hours required for the Alcatraz tour we settled in at "The Grotto" on the water and chowed. We took on a pretty good load based on the fact that that would be possibly and in fact was the meal for the day. Soon we grabbed our ride and within the hour we were buzzing across the Bay Bridge and into Oakland.

It was a little after noon and we had quite a haul to Vegas which we hoped to reach at a reasonable hour. A heavy task based on the fact we had been told there was no real way to get there from Frisco. This smacked of challenge so maps came out and a potential course was plotted. First we headed east at a clip to hit the 5 and travel south toward LA and into the desert light years away from the lushness of the farms of the valley. We hit several great small towns as we switched from one country road to another. Switchbacks one moment and then a high speed trot down vast straightaways. The truck was wonderfully on fire. After a few hours we were settling south and slid on down to the road change at Bakersfield and the jog over to sin city. I had called ahead to the Motel 6 on Industrial Boulevard across I-15 from the Strip that I always stay in and secured us a double for $49.00 per night. Late check in guaranteed. It is amazing to me that within eyeshot rooms are a minimum of $300.00 per night and who is there for the amenities (aside from high roller girlfriends) the room might offer anyway. It was dark and the beer and late hours of the last few nights were taking its toll on us so I eased over for 15 or 20 minutes of restful roadside sleep. We still had a good ways to go and it was about the Nevada line that we hit the construction, single lane, cones dangerously encroaching into the traffic. We did not need that at this juncture. Food sounded good but we decided to press on for whatever the city might hold for us two lonesome travelers. A little after midnight we saw the laser beam signal cutting a swath to heaven through the still, blackness. We were almost there and not a moment too soon. The motel was near the Tropicana exit just off the freeway and we settled in there quickly and hit the strip.

After a quick look, a Taco or something and a couple of beers we were good to go until morning and we retired. We had decided early on and based on the decent time made thus far we were going to blow two days here and then drive straight through the 22 or so hours back. That would give Dylan an almost whole day of rest before he had to catch his flight back to New York on Sunday. One food stop I and all my friends always make is the Harley Davidson Café on the strip. I know it's a chain but who gives a shit. There is one great meal there good at any time day or night and its called "southern fried chicken". Huge portions, lots of re-hydrating iced tea. It's exactly what you need as your meal of the day. A good load of comfort. The other great thing about this place is it has its own parking deck just behind for customers. The central location is perfect for leaving your vehicle in lock down while you trek out on foot.

After the meal it was 20oz brews from a street vendor and see what comes next around the corner. It was just now noon and Margaritas sounded like a good change of pace if for no other reason but the vitamin C. That meant a stop at another favorite being the open air sidewalk bar at Buffet's place. We caught it just at shift change and I don't mean bartenders. The all-nighters were releasing the hold on the prime spot overlooking the bustle of the street. This was a stark contrast to the fringe of Death Valley and the Mojave we had just crossed yesterday. We were in the middle of the shit, drinks were cold and tart and we soaked it all in. After a couple of hours on our perch it was time to dive in. Our spirits had regained whatever they may have lost the day before and off we went, full of vigor. It was starting to get a little toasty so we relegated ourselves to as much indoor travel as possible and navigated down the street by the many casino floors and malls with only the occasional street bridge bringing us into the light. It was on one of those mall jaunts that we saw the suit. Or to be correct, Dylan spotted the suit.

It was displayed in full form on a mannequin outside a magic shop and I had to admit it was stunning. In all its glory it was a man size white fur rabbit suit. "I've got to have that" tumbled out of him and splattered on the cold tile floor. After the laugh associated with the thought of him taking it home on the plane we moved on. We were not quite that drunk yet.

The next few hours were kind of a blur. Maybe it was the margaritas or the beer or both but here we were at near closing, eating mac and cheese at the Harley café and admiring the rabbit suit we had secured as it sat piled in the adjacent chair. It had been a great day and we were pleased with ourselves. With the truck reacquired we headed back to the hotel for some Law and Order on the tube but not before Dylan slipped on the head in the ride for some "Welcome to Vegas" photo ops. I thought I would puke I laughed so hard at the sight of the drunken rabbit waving at the chicks and Mexicans crowding the sidewalks.

The Rabbit Head

I'm not sure what we paid for it but it wasn't enough. It's probably stuffed in a drawer somewhere in Brooklyn … so full of potential, so little time. The next day we were awoken by someone yelling. One of the downsides of Industrial Blvd. is the whore and pimp trade. This morning's altercation was obviously concerning a financial shortfall which may or may not be rectified with someone's ass.

This was not exactly what I needed at this moment so we opted for a shower and a basic repeat of yesterday's activities. The only exception being a very short stint at the slots of one of the main gaming floors. Every time either one of us consider the rabbit head a low chuckle would escape to the surface.

I'm not sure why it was so amusing but it even eclipsed the fact that Zoltar, the fortune telling amusement game had labeled us collective losers. I think we spent about eight dollars to get that outcome. This was entertaining and quite possibly true. The next quest that evening now that our futures and the rabbit head was secure was the In and Out Burger. This establishment is not known in our world (the general south) and is seen primarily in the western United States. It is very famous due in part to its appearance in several popular mainstream movies such as Lebowski and others. We hadn't eaten in about thirteen hours if you don't count the salsa and chips at Margaritaville and I didn't. Something very plain, cheap and filling (almost comfort food but with many more additives) was exactly what was called for and "In and Out" filled the bill. We arrived there on the way back to Industrial, (actually on the Freeway) about 2am just as some of the lights were shut off.

The drive through still had some cars in it who had apparently already ordered but the sight of some others u-turning away from the order box was not encouraging. The best course of action in our state of aggressiveness was to barge in and either demand (not to the point of police intervention) or attempt to finesse our way into some remnants of the days and nights commerce. This was our current mission. This was our goal. As Dylan entered the door I sat in the short bus poised for escape if required. We had opted to not involve the rabbit head at this time concerned this would only confuse the youth behind the computer touch screen. More confusion was not required as I'm sure our lack of cohesiveness as a unit and the inability to complete whole sentences was certainly at full tilt. Perhaps this fact would help us? Would they feel sorry for us? I guess we'll never know.

As I stared intently at the window I knew things were not going well. Dylan was waving his arms wildly in some sort of animated explanation of some earlier event to a stone, yet pimply faced fat kid who seemed completely unmoved. Fuck, I thought and then quietly muttered underneath my breath. That's when my eyes cut away left from the downward spiral at the counter and caught the faint glimpse of a spirit apparition. It was the rock and roll icon from the sixties Grace Slick. Not the literal G.C. but Grace in 69. She was the first brunette I was ever moved by as a young teen and the result was a soul stirring which I'm sure contributed to my eventual move to the dark side (brunette).

They could have been twins. It was the dark hair, falling dangerously over one eye and the flash and fire emitting from the one remaining exposed eye. She was stunning. Until the first time I had seen the real Grace I was enamored with the blondes of the day such as Bardot, Dickenson and the like. But Grace was Grace. She was the shit. As quickly as she appeared, as phantoms will, she disappeared into the night of waning neon and thumping car radios with their cop killing bullshit message. Welcome to America. Dylan eventually hit the door with a dejected demeanor and onward we went to rest, one stop next door to the hotel for a quart of milk. 2%. Tomorrow we would sleep in some and hit the Harley one more time for early lunch. It was gonna be a burn home which with luck would be accomplished in about 22 to 24 hours, baring unknown construction. We would cut back south across the Hoover Dam and then on to the I-40 expressway, straight east across the U.S. my young friend. No holds barred. My heel was a little tender today from the scorpion attack but I really couldn't consider that right now. I would have to deal with that under different and better circumstances. The day was stunningly clear and after a quick discussion we opted out of another visit to the strip (I think deep inside we felt there was the capacity to be trapped one more day in the web which we could not risk). The new plan was to get right to the road while the general tourist still slept and pick up a buffet somewhere between town and Lake Meade.

In theory this was a sound proposal but after at least one botched food attempt at a lonely quaint, yet shitty roadside casino we pressed on to a small desert town diner. The food was acceptable however gravy was a must and I remember the service wear was wrapped in plastic. Strange. Was there a water shortage I was unaware of requiring prepackaged knives and forks? I'm not sure. This was obviously the town meeting point for the disbursement of news and information and a group of locals gathered around glued to CNN on an elevated 20 inch flat screen. The story escapes me but I remember a mild interest on my part. Very soon after several very welcome glasses of unsweetened ice tea and a restroom break, we were once again off into the now blustery day. Making good time we were confident in an arrival time allowing some sleep before the NY departure. The secret of a successful escape from Vegas is to make good time on the basically two lane blacktop south, over the dam and to the Interstate. If you dally or play the tourist you are pretty much screwed.

This can add hours and the fatigue that can ensue cannot be tolerated on the long stretches of I-40, not unless you want to wind up in the ditch literally. There are incredibly long stretches between shit towns with little more than the panoramic scenery you have seen for days to interest and delight. The saving grace is we would still be in New Mexico about dark which would plunge the most boring portion of the drive into total and absolute darkness. Perfect.

It seemed like about 10 PM or so when we caught gas at Tucumcari and I felt the need for some chocolate milk, which I secured just two days short of expiration. Just under the wire. I'm a lucky bitch sometimes. The fog common to this area this time of night failed to disappoint and on we went. It was about this area where I always remember driving through alone once when a fiery meteor slowly crossed my path ahead and crashed into a field on my driver's side, throwing dirt, flame and debris high into the air. That's the kind of shit you would like to share with someone. Otherwise you're not sure if its truth or delusion. That's how things work sometimes. We pressed on and crossed through Amarillo maybe around midnight and back into the dark, now cold Texas abyss. On into Oklahoma and I knew it was time for a little bit of shut eye. There is a roadside park there that is generally acceptable for this as it is pretty much open Plaines with no real opportunity for dangerous predatory behavior.

There was that one time though when my kids were younger and messing around in the playground while I visited the urinal. I was standing there in mid-stream when an enormous, shaved head, no shirt sleeves type of guy sauntered up to the urinal next and inquired in a nasal twang "want to see my new knife?" "Naw, that's cool" I whined as I hit the door and demanded the kids get immediately in the car. "We're late!" I explained at the protest. That was long ago and after scanning the horizon I determined he was long gone as well.

There can be no more restful or restless sleep than with your knees shoved against a steering wheel. Dylan had stretched out in back with his head on his bag as a pillow (a practice I had taught him many years ago by example) and we both sacked out for about an hour. The passing trucks, although most were actually exited in the same condition as us, were rhythmically whining and tossing us to the side with their violent wakes of wind and sand.

This helps sometimes to keep you just slightly aware of your situation which is not a bad thing. It was really cold now but we dared not risk the carbon monoxide associated with a running engine. We had come too far to risk the big sleep for something as trivial as creature comfort, and anyway we only needed an hour. We both seemed to awake about on queue and after taking one more leak and a quick walk around to get feeling back in my knees we were back on the "on" ramp.

Dawn was on the rise straight ahead of us and with it the dull, grey reality of the Oklahoma landscape. Our timing was great and in a couple of hours we would be in OK City and after a fill up I would let Dylan drive for awhile. I am old by the way and have nothing to prove. The farm folk were out in a big way at the diner attached to the truck stop we chose and we opted for donuts and soda at our leisure. We stank, looked road worn, crumpled and unshaven. We were obviously not from around here. Thus we did not intend to have a longer than normal stay, this due in large part to the groups of rednecks sitting just inside at breakfast who were eyeballing us and our suspected subversive behavior. We were possibly terrorists and at the least, god forbid, poets. We needed to leave. The saving grace was the Arkansas tags on the short bus which they had probably assumed we had stolen. As we eased out the twin doors Dylan got behind the wheel, I opened my diet coke; he turned the key and nothing. The motor was seized and as a tired parent will sometimes do I screamed "what the fuck did you do?" It was obviously a twist of fate but on the upside we were sitting in the parking lot of a busy truck stop on a Saturday morning, a Saturday morning when the mechanics are off. A Saturday morning where the little round face and ass pregnant girl at the counter is a replacement unfamiliar with the area and more concerned with the fact her boyfriend failed to return from the previous nights card game than what may or not be our fate.

She did however offer me the local phonebook where after several failed calls gleaned at least the address of where we were stranded. The breakfast diners were really looking us over now and Dylan expressed his concerned. We could at any time turn on the "aw shucks" vernacular which we were masters of but we would save that for unforeseen extreme conditions.

After sitting a few minutes and discussing our options I decided the 1-800-nissan roadside assistance call was best. It seemed totally reasonable to exclude the "barn folk" from the equation and rely on the calm and resources of others removed from the fear and emotion of the situation. This worked wonderfully and after a phone credit card transaction we waited for a tow. As fate would also have it after traveling almost 4500 miles in six days and having traversed remote areas for hours without cell phone service we had broken down at an Interstate truck stop six miles from one of the largest Nissan dealerships in the state of Oklahoma. It was absolutely divine intervention.

The tow came and soon we were sitting with the service manager hearing the good and bad news. Seems that the timing belt had broken the moment Dylan had hit the ignition. Based on the fact we were at a standstill and in park there was no significant engine damage. If we had been kicking it at high speed it could have been a total loss. It was just a bizarre coincidence that Dylan had just slid behind the wheel, weird but not for us to question. The downer side was that it could not be repaired until Monday. We were about five hours from home, it was now noon and Dylan had a flight out of Little Rock at 6 AM the next day. This would not work. The dealership again came to the rescue, got us to Enterprise and a rental mid-size and before 1PM we were back on the road. Once I got back to town and got secured then I could head back to OK City Monday or Tuesday after work and pick up the truck, making the rental swap at the lot. That was the longest five hours ever which all told, stretched our 22 to 24 hour burn to almost 36. Surprisingly I was very awake and alert due in part to the high abundance of alcohol in my system the previous week and the total sleep deprivation.

I was conditioned to it by this time being basically a functioning zombie. So this is what addiction is like? Dylan, being much younger and even more accustomed looked as if he had been badly beaten. I knew he wouldn't be worth a shit by the time he got back to NY if he didn't lie in a bed so I engaged the cruise and headed on in. I vaguely remember getting home but I do remember it was good to sit in my chair. Television even looked good as to this point it had only been background noise and color movement for over a week. This was the way trips are supposed to be. I think it was Steinbeck in "Travels with Charlie" who said something like "You don't take a trip, you become a trip". You have to allow for whatever happens. You have to remember things, colors, smells, catch phrases and even code names don't hurt. Code names allow you to have an alter ego or as young people say, an avatar. This can hopefully keep you immune from prosecution. Plausible deniability. You know the stuff.

My name on this particular trip was Jake Tunaman. Where did that come from? I don't exactly know but it served me well. The important thing is we went forward with no plan and we didn't stop. We became the journey and in turn it is now a part of us. It sometimes if you're lucky happens that way. Just always remember "you can't be dealt any cards if you're not sitting at the table". I think Abraham Lincoln possibly did say that. He was very prolific.

Not all trips are spontaneous and there is certainly nothing wrong with that. There are still highs and lows although there is just a framework or primary mission. It's when you make something intentionally historic to you and your party like a celebration of a major life change. One such situation with me was when I quit my day job of eighteen years with a world renowned Architectural firm to pursue my dream of concerts and events full time. This was a major leap of faith for me but I had just completed an out of town event where I had made more money in ten days than I did in a year filled with headaches and overtime. It was a huge step and this type of a move required something memorable and of serious note. I had just the thing and with a little coin in my pocket Dylan (who was sixteen at the time) and I opted to go on the trip of a lifetime to the Woodstock 99 festival in upstate New York. I remember vividly (and I really do care dearly for a lot of the folks I worked with those many years) how I felt when I walked out of that building for the last time at my at the time day job. The emotional rollercoaster was extreme and it had been a terrible drain on my confidence which I have found later is how they operate in these matters. I just remember the sky. I have never seen or noticed before or since a sky as bright and blue as that. I had to stop just outside to catch my breath. It was freedom, right or wrong, but it was freedom to succeed or fail and that is all anyone can ever dream of having. An opportunity…

Seems like I took a day or so to get us prepared but I can't be sure. The anticipation along with the fresh outlook and general excitement made it all a blur. I honestly couldn't tell you. I just remember leaving. We got in the jeep Cherokee I was driving at the time and we headed north. The one basic parameter we had decided on was to try and preserve a rock and roll theme to the journey. This meant we would travel up to Chicago, over to Cleveland (Rock and Roll Hall of Fame) and on through uncharted territory to upstate New York. The Hall of Fame was great and we really enjoyed seeing the Pink Floyd "Wall" stage props that were constructed in the main entry atrium. We took our time and spent the better part of a day checking it out top to bottom.

The festival, which was a total camping event, was to be held on the entire surface area of a retired Air Force Base. This was not a terrible concept except the locked in nature of the site and the terrible logistical layout when coupled with the unusual heat baked up a recipe for disaster. Not to mention the profiteering. Tickets were not cheap in the first place at a cost of several hundred each but the fact you were locked into the site miles from the nearest store with at least 350,000 people in the same position made us all very susceptible to being royally ripped off. Water for five dollars and up type stuff. The layout for some reason situated fresh water stations in close, pod like proximity with the portable toilets. There were no realistic access routes to pump and change out the quickly overflowing toilets which became massive raw sewage pits with the addition of the fresh water spewing from the recently vandalized drinking/ shower fountains. Health department officials would have certainly shut it down except what army would deal with the pissed off, drugged out, over heated mass of people waiting to be incited. Our survival and hopefully ultimate fun time would boil down to creating a routine.

   We determined based on the amount of cash needed and the heat, which was in the 100 and over range because of the concrete runways that crisscrossed the site, we would afford one meal a day and I would refrain from beer until the middle day. Beer like everything else was over five dollars per 12oz plastic bottle and Dylan, as a minor could not go into the beer garden. That was not acceptable for my piece of mind to leave him alone in the throng and to potentially get lost. Even though I had every confidence in him I couldn't risk his safety. When there are too many unknown factors to weigh you have to watch out. I knew this and he knew this so it was no big deal.

   Our campsite had ended up near the helipad area that was the transport area for all the artists in and out of the site. The limos or vans would pull up to the pad and we could catch glimpses of figures darting back and forth but no one we could recognize. The other thing of note concerning our camp was the animal that was burrowing under our dome tent. I like to think I'm relatively up to speed on my North American mammals and their habits but I've never been able to figure out what was trying to scratch through the lining directly under my head. At first it was a problem but after the first night it became just one more dramatic adversity in this zoo of an event. The site was divided into basically three separate stage areas with a hanger housing a 24 hour a day independent film festival and another with a non-stop techno rave with guest DJ's the likes of Moby. Not my type of deal but at night it was interesting to see the laser beams escaping out the open hanger doors. To set the tone for the overall adventure after we had settled in and made our way onto the grounds to scope things out we headed to the largest main stage. Based on our many years of experience we knew the quickest and easiest way near the front and a better view was to go stage far right or left and work down before pinching in to the center. The headliner for the opening night was Korn and there was a decent size mosh pit at center stage which we jumped into for a time. The crowd was really into the music as at the time the band was riding high and very hot. To get into the spirit of things and because of the heat us, along with everyone had gone shirtless. At several points I kept feeling something odd scraping my lower back. I just blew it off initially because it was so packed but after a time curiosity won over and I turned around. What was scraping me was the extremely perky breasts of a spirited young girl who was really into the band and the whole free love aspect. Better just walk away but only after 30 or 40 minutes to take full advantage of this "up front" view. This would set the stage for some crazy fucked up shit that never failed to amuse and delight. The next day was more of the same with more and more totally nude, and very unattractive people. Isn't it odd that the people who are quickest to disrobe in a public setting are the ugliest most misshapen people on the planet? By noon I really didn't care if I saw another naked woman the entire trip and I think Dylan concurred. The heat was getting pretty bad and based on necessity and the weak daytime lineup we figured the best thing to do is avoid everything by hiding in the dark of the film festival hanger. The hanger was floor seating only and there was a maze of people basically covering the slick, cool concrete floor. We also figured out that the sidewalls would be the best spots because we would be near the large, shop fans and have some sort of back support. This was the perfect opportunity for some restful sleep in a cool environment during the hottest part of the day and a great place to take meals, such as they were. The one meal would be taken at around two or so to break the day in half and based on the fact neither of us particularly ate breakfast. Meals consisted of personal pan pizzas (ten dollars each) with the stand being just outside the movie hanger.

As soon as shadows would lengthen then we would venture out fresh and make our way around the site and scope things out proper. The sewage at this point was unbelievable with people trying to bathe in the outer edges and throwing the hard caked, stinking filth in wads at each other's as well as passing strangers, every ten minutes or so someone who objected to this would get into a scuffle. This was great fun to watch and along with the various moshing injuries from the various pits at all the stages there was a ready stream of individuals at first aid. It was as if losing a tooth here was a badge of honor. There were also tattoo booths on the site which reinforced the notion considering the more unbelievable unsanitary conditions there were at every turn. At all main concert sites by this time trash from the last day and a half was piling up about ankle deep consisting mainly of plastic bottles. There were paths snaked throughout the site where people could get in / out and around.

The earlier headliner that night at the main stage was Limp Biscuit and the crowd was totally out of control. The front of house mix position, which had been protected with a formidable wall of 4x8 half inch plywood were being dismantled a panel at a time for the purpose of body surf boards. Each board would be elevated just over the crowd with three or more prone or standing riders and propelled down the bowl toward the stage, gaining speed and momentum. As they got near the pit area in front of the stage the riders would dive off just as the wood slammed into the jack legs of the staging. Security guards in the pit were barely getting clear as I'm sure it was difficult to spot a half inch tall board careening toward your face at high speed.

My injury of the day also happened that night at a restroom break. I was taking a piss in a port-a-toilet when I saw a shadow on the roof through the white plastic top. I had seen people earlier climbing on top for a better view of the stage and I remember thinking that was a really bad idea, based on the instability I knew was part of the usual construction of the units.

I had just enough time to punch with my fist as hard as I could to keep the chick crashing down on me from putting both feet and the sharp plastic into the top of my head. The edge of the roof at the center seam cut through two of my knuckles and soon I was covered with blood like I had been shot. Anywhere else this would have been alarming but here I went around virtually unnoticed. It was kind of surreal but in reality perfectly normal in this situation. To stop the blood flow and to give me a false sense of hygiene I took a few minutes and buried my hand into the side of my old Willis and Geiger ruck sack (this has always also been my pillow any time appropriate on the road) and strangely this worked perfectly and I was good to go. The large dark stains stayed on my bag for about three years as everyone knows it is terrible bad luck to wash them out... ever. It's a type of seasoning. People never understand that the character that a bag or a journal or any item that travels with one on a regular basis gathers is a dear part of the item and their owners. It's like wrinkles. I get so cracked up when I see men that go under the knife and have all their life experiences and character removed and for what? Getting laid, a younger piece of ass? What a waste. This being Saturday night the promoters had really gambled with the lineup. They pushed the envelope with some very serious, aggressive bands early in the evening only to finish with what they were billing as "The World's Greatest Rock Band". After participating in mosh pits for Limp Biscuit and Rage against the Machine we were pretty spent and after slamming a few beers with Dylan just outside the fence where we could communicate we were ready for some sleep. The last band I think wasn't going on until about midnight and as we walked by the Rave that had been in high gear now for about thirty hours we were more than convinced to move on. The before mentioned lack of trash pickup and the constant raw sewage overflow with subsequent mud bogs were at disaster levels at this point and management seemed to be ignoring the situation. Instead they marked up water a dollar more per bottle and food probably 30%. I believe this was because people had resorted to washing hair and sponge bathing with bottled water instead of attempting the ankle deep wade through urine and feces. An effort to get at the cascade of potable water flowing from the broken hose bibs. Trash, still consisting primarily of plastic bottles was now ankle and knee deep in most all areas of the concert venues. I never saw anyone in charge ever even looking at these situations. Not police or management. I guess they were too busy counting money out back. Speaking of which we were down to about 50 bucks in cash which might get us through the final day. There were a few ATM's on the site with I think a ten dollar minimum transaction fee for all business. This was irrelevant as they were out of cash the first day with no accessible route to get to the machines to replenish supply. The naked chicks were not getting any prettier either.

There was absolutely no air moving at night and the heat felt exactly as it did during the day. I'm sure this was the sea of concrete retaining heat and we hurried our way toward the tall grass of the camping area. After passing several more large groups of ugly, nude people doing whatever drugs we made it to our row and the rodent or small mammal that had been scratching the night before. The camp was full as many others had had the same idea and bedded down. For some stupid reason there was also a firework show scheduled for after the final main stage performance at probably two AM.

We had kept the top cover off the dome as there was no chance at all of rain and we needed the airflow through the open flap and up. The house lights shone brightly and illuminated the entire campsite and we could hear all of the stage announcements. We laid there and listened to the litany of sponsor mentions and waited patiently for exactly who the management considered to be the greatest band ever. There had been some very impressive (trendy not classic) talent up to this point so I was very intrigued. Finally after an obvious bull shit monologue stall the name "Metallica" was screamed over the PA. At that moment it seemed like almost a minute of silence (or so it seemed) which was immediately followed by giggles. You could hear them here and there throughout our section of camp and as giggles will do they became infectious. People began to contribute snide remarks with the laughter becoming almost the most entertaining part of the experience.

This lasted probably fifteen minutes after which calm descended eventually back down upon the area. Everyone was just tired. You could almost sleep to the uninteresting monotone thump of the band but then the fireworks started. After a few minutes of a thirty minute (eternity) show a lone, tired, drugged out voice in the camp mustered just enough courage and strength to scream out the plea "stooooooooop". His pitiful cracking voice hit the dark of the night with a primal desperation that was so sad it was hilarious. This caused an even bigger explosion of giggles and laughter than the band announcement and it was quite some time before things returned to normal. It seemed that all the commotion had also annoyed the under tent nocturnal visitor who started scratching more violently than ever.

The next day we got up a little early and basically repeated our routine of the days before. The only exception being a trip to the far end of the site (before the crowds) where we took some pictures, saw more nude people asleep all over the lawn and somehow found the only undamaged water station. Probably about thirty other people who had known of it or stumbled on it like us were in line for whatever use they had in mind. I was ready for a sponge bath and to wash my hair. Even though I had cut it very short in anticipation the constant perspiration had made it thick feeling and uncomfortable. Dylan concurred. We had been brushing our teeth each day with bottled water but we weren't about to pay twenty dollars or more to wash our hair. This worked out great and aside from the ugliest nude chicks yet we felt probably the freshest and most prepared we had been in days. Possibly even as far back as Cleveland.

The heat was back on as the sun reached about eleven o'clock and the temp hovered at around 105. We grabbed some pizza and headed to the shade of the film festival. The path we had developed worked perfectly and once again we found ourselves parked near one of the enormous shop fans, staying the better part of the day. The entertainment was pretty good that day, as it had been all along, with the main stage headliner being The Red Hot Chili Peppers. There had been rumors ever since we had arrived (I think to keep people spending until the last possible moment) that the final main stage performance would be a special secret guest. Everyone seemed to know that this group would be Pearl Jam who had been on hiatus for several years up to this point, making it perfectly believable.

I remember the sunset that night was without a doubt the most spectacular in color I had ever seen before or since and I have seen some great ones all over the country. I'm not sure what atmospheric conditions were contributing but I wasn't the only one to notice. The other thing I noticed at about that time was the strange smell of hostility in the air. People were pissed off. They had been screwed at every turn by the event, the vendors, the tee shirt guys, each other, and everything had been a big fuck around with rampant greed at levels before unseen at these types of events. It wasn't about the music. It wasn't about the happening. It wasn't about the community of man and his hopes and dreams for his and her world like the other original Woodstock had been. It was all about the cash money. How much you got and what have you done for me lately MF? They had had enough… all of them. I told Dylan that something was up and despite his protests I told him we were going to slowly work our way toward the exits in case there was a reason. I had seen crowd control issues on these scales of patrons and I knew that no amount of security can control the mob. Our truck had worked its way up the lot into territory I felt could be vulnerable to mob damage and I couldn't risk our ride home. Not 1500 miles from it. This could not happen. Even for Pearl Jam…

The other very troubling development was the destruction of the perimeter fence. The fence between the parking lot and the concert grounds was constructed of standard scaffolding and an outer barrier consisting of 4x8ft plywood panels. These panels had been painted with murals by local school children and had thick layers of possibly flammable substances. This, with the general bad attitude and the now knee deep very flammable empty plastic bottles everywhere made me very uncomfortable. Dylan knew I was genuinely concerned and quit arguing with me maybe twenty minutes before the first fire was set. Concert goers had piled several stacks of the plywood toward the back of the house (pretty much blocking the designated exits) in a crowd of at least two hundred thousand people and started them ablaze.

The fires were pretty modest at first but with the rampant addition of more wood and several thousand plastic bottles they were soon many feet up in the air, billowing thick black toxic smoke. My biggest fears at this time were that the entire yard of trash underneath the crowd might become ignited and panic the crowd. Being at least twenty miles or so from the nearest fire department this was not going to get better soon. The saving grace in my mind about the wall destruction was that with the wood panels gone it virtually opened up the concert grounds to the parking lot and with the exits blocked by flame that was a good thing.

And then came the song. The Chili Peppers, taking a queue on what they believed to be an innocent prank played a wild rendition of the Jimi Hendrix classic "Fire". That's when the shit hit the fan. I told Dylan it was time to go. Luckily we had earlier in the day broke camp and loaded everything into the Cherokee and were ready to head out as soon as possible to avoid the bulk of the crowd back to the nearest Interstate.

People danced naked around fires that were now ten to fifteen feet tall and totally out of control as it seeped small fingers of flame into the yard and through the trash. We picked up the pace a little when I counted the tenth new bonfire and when we saw people running through the fire barefoot and with smoldering clothes. I knew riots against the rapist vendors trapped in the site with the mob were just around the corner and the parking lot not long after.

We hit the truck, fired it up and eased out of the lot just as another fifty foot or so of fence came violently tumbling off and onto the mounds of leaping flames. Some of the fires had taken on a strange green color. More and more of the plastic succumbed to the heat and the dark sky began to take on some of the brilliant colors of the earlier sunset. Flame reflected on the unmoving thick fog of smoke hanging in the air.

The mob by now was in full attack mode. Artists had left the stage and I swear I saw absolutely no security personnel at any positions. They may have had a plan to fall back and protect the treasury at all cost but I can't be sure. I just know they were absent.

As we hit the main road off the base about forty New York state troopers at high speed passed us going the opposite way into the site and we knew once again we had been lucky. Or smart, or maybe both, either way we were off and back on the road. All we knew after that about the events of the night we saw on MTV once we got back. What we didn't know was all our relatives were back home watching it all live on television and fearing the worst for us. We found that out when after a few hours we hit the Interstate heading west and called back home to check in. I think we also had pancakes.

5 O'clock, quitting time...

It had been one of those day that you think will never end. Things were a little slow and that always makes you feel like it's time to get lost somewhere . . . anywhere. You know you have a lot to do and when things are slower in one area you feel like you need to shift your efforts to another area. You're wasting time. But once considered in rational terms you realize that you don't have to be going at 100 miles an hour at all times. It's ok to take it easy sometimes. Matter of fact it is a necessity. When I was younger I used to burn to the point that I would sleep for about two to three days every three months or so. This became my normal pattern throughout the early eighties until maybe 98 or so.

I'm a little troubled by some information I heard the other day. I thought about it for several weeks because I wasn't really sure how I felt about it. I was watching a documentary that I ordered from Barnes and Noble about the life and career of big Jack Kerouac. There was an interview with a woman that used to run with JK and others of his gang in the forties and fifties and she made a comment about how he was so shy and was more of an observer who liked to sit in the corner away from the crowd. He preferred to watch from a distance and not really interact. This was and is not exactly the popular image of this writer and his life. It has always been supposed that all or at least most of his documented exploits were pretty much based on the true acts of him and his collection of traveling companions. This would imply a fiction at many levels that I'm not sure I'm comfortable with. When you are young and take something as gospel and you are adamant in making fucking sure you live your life and report it as is you feel that others may have you feel short changed a tad. You actually go and do. You don't sit back, observe and try and imagine what and how things might have taken place.

But that is selfish. People are only responsible for themselves. Almost everyone I admire or have looked up to as iconic throughout my life has reinvented themselves in an image foreign to reality, some multiple times. This is like turning over a new leaf or changing what you want in life. Your direction. Sometimes this act requires a reinvention. I know these are the facts of things and I accept this. Like the old timers always said "when the legend is bigger than the truth, print the legend". It's just a little left of where you thought things were at. Sort of like when they decided the other day that Pluto was not a planet anymore. What's a boy gonna do if you can't even believe in Pluto? There are exceptions to the rule. These are people that are out of the mold. They are the ones that actually do live the life they preach. They almost always wear hats although I'm not sure why. Randy Murphy is one of these. He is a living, breathing hero for me. I have been thinking a lot about him lately after I found out that in the last two years he had beaten lung cancer and was in remission. I had no idea any of this was happening until it was done and I can't imagine what I would have thought if he had passed on without my knowledge.

I met Randy in 1983 when I first went to work for the largest architectural firm in the state. He started soon after I did and for some reason we took to each other. He was about ten or so years older than me and had just gone through a divorce. He had two children who he had limited contact with but not before he instilled in them the talent and bohemian spirit that would last them a lifetime and carry them all over the world. I think they call them "free thinkers". Not bums. There is a huge difference between being adventurers and being shiftless, even though

Randy Murphy —

you are in the book, not sure where?

Stan

BILLING WORK SHEET

☐ BILL ONLY   SEE ATTACHED ☐

Bill To: _____

Attention: _____

Billing Information: _____

QUANTITY	ITEM #	COMMENTS	PRICE (each)
_____	_____	_____	$ _____
_____	_____	_____	$ _____
_____	_____	_____	$ _____
_____	_____	_____	$ _____
_____	_____	_____	$ _____
_____	_____	_____	$ _____
_____	_____	_____	$ _____

☐ DELIVER   ☐ RUSH DELIVERY   ☐ WILL CALL   ☐ WAITING

☐ UPS   ☐ FED EX   CHARGES $ _____

REMARKS: _____ OPERATOR'S INITIALS _____

sometimes the veneer seems the same. Randy was and is without a doubt the most talented person I have ever met and I have met some incredible people. I had the extreme good fortune to work with some of the old time great architects from the thirties and forties by virtue of my father's business in their later years. This is always the best time to meet important people because you see the combination of what they were with an ease of living self assurance. There is a gentleness and aura to a man who is not at a point of being driven. You know greed, self absorption and the like. He was never like any of these phases. His difference is he doesn't wear it. He is a gentle sort who likes to dream. He is a man who credits his new (yet older) little dog, Corky, with saving his life through his ordeal. When a man has a purpose, someone or something that truly needs him to hang around it can serve as the strength of giants. That little fella needed his master.

And there is his life's work. Some of the buildings he has designed are great Doric structures with Classic scale and features, when you look him in the eye you can almost see their origin. He is also a very accomplished painter in classic and modern styles and I have acquired several of his larger works that I have owned for many years. Where I generally go they go.

We used to drink a lot of beer in the old days. My kids were young at the time and Randy, like the many other frequent houseguests was very close to them. We were a laughing, fun extended family of fractured and broken people drawn together by conversation and the joy of life. There were no limits to what one or all of us could achieve and it was infectious. We traveled when we wanted and we dreamed when we could. But we mostly stayed close to home. There was an old bottle style coke machine in my living room which would hold about four cases of long necks and would freeze them if desired. This was a very popular item with the group and was always in use. It was not uncommon at all for six to ten guys and or gals to be crammed around the kitchen table talking a multitude of topics from death penalty to religion and back to popular culture. We played board games back then too. There was RISK, Monopoly, Chess, Scrabble and on and on. Video games only existed in the game room at the bar "Slick Willie's" and as far as we were concerned that was where they could stay. We also used to stage bachelor parties in which our group would pick a day, designate a prospective groom, and pitch in ten bucks each and that was that. This would afford one quality or two substandard strippers, all the beer and or mescal one would want to drink and a roof for the night if safety became a factor. Kids would be gone to the baby sitter and this worked great for a very long time until one Saturday when the little woman found a size 5 stiletto pump under the kids' bed. Not cool. That was the end of my hosting duties but not of course the social atmosphere.

We were the home away from home and everyone (within reason) was always welcome. We sometimes had guests for months at a time and that was fine with all concerned. Randy was a major part of this world although not from his perspective. His strange shock of gray hair, overcoat and black fedora in winter and linen suits in summer made him a character and much older seeming than what he was in reality. He walked to his own beat and cared little for what anyone thought of him. He was slow to anger unless it involved his work or art. I wanted to be like him. He just never knew it. I always feel like he is these great times of my life incarnate and for that I am grateful…everyone needs a hero.

I drove around a little and just tried to collect my thoughts. I wasn't particularly hungry but a beer wouldn't offend me. I heard a joke from my buddy Carter the other day that is funny and I hope not applicable to me that goes; "Do you know the difference between an alcoholic and a drunk?" "A drunk doesn't have to go to all those damn meetings". I run into a lot of people in social drinking situations but I don't know that I've ever looked at anyone as a drunk or an alcoholic. There're just people. Some have better stories than others. Some are in bad moods. Some are in good moods. Some mirror whatever you're feeling. If you drink to relax you will attract like folks with the same goal. My biggest problem is I am inherently an asshole and it's not uncommon for me to say something I might find incredibly cute and funny in the most inappropriate situations.

I don't even realize it and I don't see myself in that light generally. I should have been suspicious however the time when I was about eleven or so when my dad said "son . . . you're one real live ass hole". I thought about what he said for about ten seconds but it registered in my subconscious and apparently stuck there. It didn't wound me per say but it seemed odd to me. Enough about that, such as it is… its show time. I drive by a couple of my haunts and I just really don't have the energy to do the same old shit today. Being Wednesday and in the south this would be known as church night.

On the surface this might not mean much to the casual observer but to the regular it means loads. That is when you have a strange collection of men who have this one night away from the church-going, fried chicken cooking loves of their lives. It's not that they are trolling for strange or anything, far from it, it's more to me about a level of tension and the uncomfortable air that follows a guy who is bound by rigid morals and schedule. His indiscretion cannot be discovered. He has a limited amount of time when the breath cleansing teeth brushing is taken into consideration, not to mention the potential smell of smoke on the clothing.

These people rarely have anything interesting to say and there is nothing more annoying than a novice attempting to create a string of coherent vulgarity. Vulgarity is our badge, and not just anyone can wear it. The pool hall is definitely out as I think I am about done with this place. They recently started to have a DJ on Friday and Saturday and for some reason they have opted to only play Rap music. Nothing is more unsettling than two straight hours without break with the volume turned up to twelve. This is not really for me, my friends, or our money. I'm sure it's socially relevant and all but maybe I'm just a little too old fashioned.

I think with all that in mind that I would head a little farther north and opt for a chain. At least that is the least offensive of the Wednesday options. TGI Fridays will do. It's not dark enough for the religious hypocrite and the bubble gum music never gets harder than the Stones. This would work and in just a few I'm sitting in front of a tall, relatively cold glass of Miller Lite beer. The first goes down smooth and leads to another which will be accompanied by the Jack Daniels Sampler appetizer platter. Nice. There's a newspaper nearby so I decide to do my bi-weekly scan of things and see where things are at. War, interest rates, another senseless robbery-murder gone wrong, war, more war, a new war. That was enough of that so I shift my attention to one of the hospital-like hanging televisions which are tuned to the nationwide trivia network. I opt to not take a box and get too involved because I'm still not sure how long or if I'm going to eat a real meal.

Just watching and keeping score on my own leaves me the option of the quick exit not to mention sparing me the possible humiliation of a shellacking by some young college grad upstart right there on five individual screens for all to see. It's happened before and it's a little unsettling. Not being beaten necessarily, although that is tough, but just the public nature of it. After scoring immediately on the first three questions (1000 points each) I begin to question my decision to not take a box and its legitimacy. That soon passes as my attention is drawn to the front area, the hostess stand and my consecutive miss of two questions due to inattention.

   I know it can't be prom night because it's the wrong time of year but there are about six to ten butter-heads in satin formal wear squealing like a herd of ravenous swine. This is mildly entertaining until the extremely drunk guy to my left injects himself into my line of vision, makes comment and knocks my fourth tall beer over and into my lap. Being in a very mellow and benevolent mood I didn't initially react as I would normally and opted for the more subtle approach of seeing what bounty my misfortune might lead to.

   This worked out great as the drunk guy had been there since noon (obviously being served past the point of inebriation implying some culpability on behalf of the restaurant) and had readily agreed to pay for all my drinks up to that point with the eatery picking up my appetizer and any drinks thereafter. That meant flat iron steak (medium) which I immediately ordered while the proverbial fire was hot. I waited for a little while before I broke the seal and went to the restroom so I wouldn't look like a total ass hole. My jeans are the light blue, acid washed variety so any slight liquid spot will show up like a sore thumb. Not to mention the spot created by a six or seven ounce spill. I was accustomed to looking as if I had had an accident, but the lights were really brighter than I was used to and me being alone I really didn't want to play the harmless old fool part tonight.

   The stain was getting dimmer and I took my leave only to return and find the party of sevenish seated near me in ear and eye shot. I had lost all interest in trivia or the ball games on the multiple tubes and even the drunks' incoherent ramblings were beginning to fade into the background of overly decorated wall coverings. I spent the next two beers trying to guess exactly what pastel colors were represented by the group. If you are at all familiar with the qualities of satin you know that different degrees of white light and shadow affect it certain ways, this when considering the actual hue.

This was my casual diversion for the day and about the time I thought I had it nailed my steak arrived. As did my steak so did the parties dirty martinis, thus identifying them as adult or at least sporting suitable fake ID's. I prefer the former. I'm just not a good judge of age. Must be a wedding party of some kind . . . but on a Wednesday? I couldn't be sure. I finished my meat and felt satisfied as I polished off the garlic mashed potatoes and ordered another beer. I was starting to get harsh looks from the bartenders as I believe they thought I was milking the kindness of the free offer based on my misfortune. They had no idea of what I was capable of. No fucking idea.

After a point the giggling of the drunken girls was getting a little annoying but not a total problem. Around eight or so the bartenders finally decided the guy (the spiller) to my left was ready for a cab ride the short distance to Sherwood and they hooked him up. I guess they were tipped off by the fact he had been sleeping with his head on the bar for about twenty minutes. He's a regular I guess. They got him out to the cab and before it left I realized he had left his cell phone on the bar so I rushed out and handed it to the driver. That little courtesy made me feel Teflon with good karma and I eased back in to my perch. Upon my arrival I was surprised to find another tall, brand new brew butted up next to my half full leftover. "What the hell, what gives?" I halfheartedly asked the clown behind the bar not really being one to look a gift horse, well you know. With an uninterested nod he acknowledged that it was from the butter-heads and with a quick over the right shoulder wink I accepted and went on to the beer for dessert. It took about ten minutes or so and I was firmly relocated in the center of the group. They were well on the way with only the occasional giggling fit as a distraction from the otherwise senseless banter.

From this totally different perspective I could now see that I was totally wrong and all the dresses were actually the same color, sort of shimmering lavender or maybe plum. I didn't really care enough to think about it any longer. Also sitting at the table I could get a really clear look at exactly the level of beauty associated with the party as I had not ventured out with my glasses. Not the up close pair or the faraway. Nothing, I was barefaced. From here I would rate them collectively at maybe a three, maybe. They were nice enough I suppose and I would hang as long as they were paying. The apparent leader of this party went on to explain to me that they were a wedding party at a church of scientology wedding and blah, blah, blah. I not sure the other details because I wasn't listening. What I was doing was paying attention to the ugliest one to my right who had proceeded to play some awkward game of footsy with me under the table.

Just the thought of that stumpy, freckly I'm sure, little foot groping under the table made everything not as appetizing. It was about then I had decided it was time to exit and I started the set up to gracefully "git". My first move was to flip open the cell phone and pretend that I had just received a text. I read intently and punch in some random reply and now I can do whatever, whenever, honorable request at the behest of some unknown caller or circumstance. You don't even need the BS third party call for the back story. Not to mention the fact that all of this James Bond shit was unnecessary as who cared anyway. This was not or would ever go anywhere. I guess it was out of some sort of respect for the drinks. They had enough problems without me throwing shit on them.

I mean, who the hell would wear matching satin dresses out on the town, Wednesday or any day. Just as I was about to bolt for anywhere, someone ordered shots of Patron. At seven dollars a shot I had to hand around just a little longer. They were celebrating for goodness sakes and who am I to argue with that. After the third or maybe the fourth it really was time to go somewhere else as it was approaching ten and closing. They came up with several suggestions and I knew exactly what I was dealing with here. All they're ideas were all night dives up toward the Air Force base and beyond. Some of the places I am welcome and some I am not, either way it was not in the cards as this is a school night, with work in the AM. I'm not really wanting to go further from home. Any stops anywhere at this point are required to be on the way back to bed. And that means alone.

I told each one straight in the eye I would see them at the next stop and then I would simply turn left when they turn right. It might be hours before they would notice my absence. That's what I decided and how it would play out. I was interested in one or two quick stops as all of my television shows at this time had already started. On Law and Order if you miss the crime in the first two minutes of the show you are lost and it is pointless, unless you have already seen them all as I had. I think I have just about given up on all that shit anyway. It's just too much commitment with so little return.

I wouldn't mind just hanging out somewhere and reading like I like to do on weekends but that is dangerous. People either think you are an elitist or pretentious and either way you are a target. As I eased on to the freeway I decided that a comfortable setting would work as the Tequila mellows me and a little quietness sounded great. Renos, that bar with the great potato salad and perfect music seemed like the logical choice so I got off downtown and cruised the block for a parking space.

It didn't take much and I ended up halfway between Renos and the pool hall. There wasn't much of a crowd with several small satellite groups of twenty something's in deep discussion...all the bar stools were taken. I picked out a small four top near the door with a view of the street so I could observe all the comings and goings, which were few. There was karaoke going on next door and for some reason it reminded me of the time I accidentally went into a country and western, gay bar in the sticks outside of Nashville. To hear a gay hillbilly with the appropriate twang sing Al Green was something all must experience at some point. It was surreal based on the fact I was on the way to hang out with a group of Pirate movie extras and renaissance fair performers from Tampa I knew who were performing that month just south of Nashville. It all seemed to make sense somehow.

Renos big screen was on and the acoustic band had just wrapped up and was packing gear into the large plastic transport containers some of them use. That was ok as the juke box had just fired up on auto with some Arlo Guthrie and would create just the right mood. You won't find rap here. I sat there for maybe fifteen minutes or so and was just enjoying the lack of pace when I made eye contact with a girl who looked vaguely familiar. She was seated with another less attractive girl and what appeared to me to be two homeless guys. There was a definite disconnection between the two couples or so it would seem. The girls were dressed well like they were the remnants of some earlier office party and as I would find out later this was the case. After several glances which I really didn't want she motioned for me to come over. To the request I complied based on the truth that she really did look familiar.

Once there it was apparent that my suspicions were valid and that the two male friends had indeed wandered in off the street and taken a seat with the front of two partially full abandoned glasses of something, making .m. Proper breeding would not allow the girls to be rude and ask them to leave. After a quiet appeal from the girls and a joke from me about what a nice evening for young couples to be out I asked the boys to hit the street. I am not above this, they moved on and I earned myself a round. Not to mention the gratitude of the table.

The main one who had motioned to me mentioned strangely that I did look very familiar to her and after going through several lists of possible connections and finding none we determined that it was just either bullshit on one or both parts or just coincidence. Either way they were grateful. They were however drunk and a little aggressive, not to mention I figured I had enough friends at this time. I decided I would have this one drink and move on. I told the pair I had to meet a guy at the pool hall who owed me some money in about ten minutes so I offered to pay and hit the door. They declined my offer based on my chivalry and I felt like once more tonight I had been fortunate and skirted off into the dark. No strings.

I went ahead and walked over past the car and went on in the pool hall. There weren't too many cars in the lot out front so I felt like things would be at acceptable levels for my needs. I had been there probably ten or fifteen minutes and was deep in a real business conversation concerning the future of the bar and my possible involvement when the pair strolled in. I didn't realize I had told them exactly where I was headed but I obviously had. They stumbled up to me like we had gone to high school together and grabbed the two stools to my left. They really weren't invited and there had been no connection so I continued my other conversation, not thinking I owed anything further. This was not to be.

The main girl, whose name escapes me started receiving phone calls with the University of Arkansas fight song ring tone at full volume not to mention her loud condescending voice drowning out my low level business drone. This was not going to fly for long. After a short time and a private conversation between the two the uglier one left with the familiar one opting to hang for round three of whatever. Next came the phone call. I was trying really hard to not listen but it was impossible. The gist on the one side of which I was privy was basically what a shit hole she was sitting in and how dangerous it looked. She went on to say that she would never suggest that any of her friends venture from out west to the downtown area for this load. That was all I could handle as I wheeled around on the stool and inquired "Just who the fuck are you and who asked you here any way". She reeled with an indignant air and said no one had ever talked to her like that to which I veined surprise. Turning back to my drink and expecting her departure I was really shocked that she just kept talking. She went on to explain that her father was the ex-mayor of a town made famous as the hometown of a very famous and prominent governor of Arkansas back in the fifties. The only interesting thing to me about this town is that it is in the middle of nothing but is home to a nice state revenue office for car tags and the like type business. The other thing is she was married to a prominent attorney from the area for several years and could basically command armies if she wanted with a phone call. After her divorce she grew tired of this power and had chosen to move to the big city for the excitement it might offer. I was unmoved by the information and was not really sure what sort of a response she was interested in acquiring. What it did do was really piss me off that she was even still in the room. It's as if my rebuke spurred her on and made her even more aggressive. This one was not used to hearing no and she did not sport the figure for that attitude as I spied the enormous ass cheeks waving at each other as she waddled to the relative quiet and safety of the ladies room.

Bed was calling as for no other reason than to get my blood pressure down so I decided as soon as she got back I would head out. I may be a bastard but I'm no prick and would never leave even a raving lunatic bitch in an unfamiliar place. The strangest thing of all was the fact that after all the disdain and rejection she saw this as some sort of invitation as I offered to get her safely to her car. I couldn't believe my ears as she offered whatever my heart desired to which I replied "go home". This finally pushed a button and soon I was loose and on the road to the house. It was starting to get a little chilly out and I knew it wouldn't take long to be ready to head. Hot shower was in order and soon I was gone. No TV tonight. I had had all the entertainment I had needed for the day.

Bedtime.

S. RAY JACKSON

SUMMERTIME AND THE LIVIN'S EASY

Morning came early again today as it seems to always do. I felt surprisingly good either fueled by anticipation of something to be determined or just because I am generally optimistic. Either way I jumped in the shower and in about twenty minutes I was warming up and defrosting the car. It was another chilly morning with a low of about 28 or so which is by no means horrible but a little lower than I prefer. The windshield was thick with a frost but was made relatively easy work of and I was on the freeway fairly quickly. As I eased onto the road I saw a crazy son-of-a-bitch wrapped up tight and riding a motor cycle. That either takes an intense love of bikes or the necessity of no options, either way I'm sure it sucks. It did remind me of my old Hells Angels buddy. Definitely the crazy part.

One summer . . ., I always seem to start periods of life like that. My existence seems to always be subdivided into three month segments. It's like getting a work visa or a pass to go forth and prosper. This has always been the way it is from the beginning and was reinforced upon joining the outdoor concert business which is defined by and lives and dies by the season. This particular summer in the early nineties was one of the most interesting although I don't think about it often. And I mean interesting not so much in a good way, sometimes dangerous but really entertaining none the less.

At the time I had been working several years for a big regional promoter out of Tulsa and I served as their local contact and show manager. We had developed a comfort level all around and I was asked to maintain a one bedroom apartment for them to use as a crew flop house. Tulsa, being close, was always a drive trip for them and all they required was a shower and a place to store gear for a day or two. Possibly a nap.

This was about every two weeks so it was really no big deal. I just had the chore of keeping things secure and making sure the liquor was fully stocked with the drug of choice being whiskey and liqueurs such as Southern Comfort and Jack Black. They were hard drinkers, as most old school rock people are, and that fit in great with me and my pals. The promoter paid for everything from receipts I would submit and for my trouble I had full access to everything including food and drink. The complex was near the river and had a great pool with volley ball and other sports every weekend. It was a great place to hang if you had time and everyone enjoyed it immensely.

Early that spring we produced a jazz festival for the city at the local amphitheater which had a sister event in another city the year before. I had served as a consultant on that event and as a result had met and become very familiar with several national sponsors and individuals who I would work with for many years. Once you're in, you're in with these folks and most of us became fast friends. One of these individuals was a charming lady who was the national event rep for the magazine "Jazziz". She was fun and vibrant but yet very sophisticated and was one of my first good acquaintances from the island of Manhattan.

The odd contrasting item about this woman of her mid-thirties was her live in boyfriend. He was the absolute total opposite from her in manner and dress. He was a Hells Angel biker so I think she had taken the bad boy attraction to the ultimate extreme.

Not a poser, but a completed, tattoo around the biceps biker, the first

H.A. I had ever had the pleasure. I knew all about the club and their customs as I had grown up in the shadow of a Motorcycle club house near my school (where we would sneak in and borrow beer while they were out at the bauxite pit rocket run races) and I had read the Hunter Thompson essay on the California club back when it was released. My first exposure to them was the movie "Hells Angels on Wheels" which my dad took me to see when I was about ten. Dad only took me to two movies in my life and why he chose that I'll never know. It was during a Tupperware party my mom was hosting for the neighborhood women and we had to remove ourselves from the property.

It was at a drive-in to boot. It only served to fuel my interest when I caught my first glimpse of the Russ Meyer (extreme busted) type women the bad boys attracted. Her boyfriend was the real deal and one of them. He was not particularly a large or menacing guy as we were about the same size. The biggest difference in us is he looked strangely like Charles Manson in hair and beard. He could have been his twin and that bothered most people who came in contact with him. It may have also been "the eyes". This didn't bother me and after the first event we were hanging out, feet propped up on his beer cooler and swapping lies.

The couple was fighting about I could only imagine what and I sensed it was only a matter of time before it was a done deal. Her attraction had to be fueled not only by the bad boy syndrome but possibly his bedroom prowess, either way I can only imagine her parents or more important her publishers reaction to his hanging around. Plus the fact he was always dressed in the corporate tank top, displaying his various yards and yards of ink.

Being from the rock side more than jazz it didn't faze me at all, but from a corporate side I can see the rub. Aside from all that we became friends and ran into each other from time to time by accident at events. About a year or so went by since I had last heard of or from him when one day my phone rang. After some quick catching up on the fact his girl had dumped him the year before I learned the fact he had rolled back down to his deceased moms' farm on the edge of Lake Okeechobee in the everglades of Florida. I could tell by his voice there was trouble.

He also had had a run in with his motorcycle club near Oakland and he said he was in hiding with a bounty on his head, his moms' being as far away as he could get in the continental US. This was surprisingly the least of his problems. I found out for the first time that he was a disabled Viet Nam veteran and still carried a small cache of metal in his left leg which resulted in a slight limp I had noticed but never really asked about before. What was worse was he had to be constantly medicated for pain through his local VA hospital as a part of his treatment. This included a litany of drugs for depression including methadone to combat a morphine and heroin addiction. Real fucked up shit.

Why he was calling he was in a jam. He needed a place to stay for a day or so and would like to visit. For some reason his VA doctor had been transferred to another state and in the process some of his medical records had been mishandled. When he hadn't received his meds as prescribed he had a psychotic break and had barged into the VA in a rage and attacked an attending physician. Once the police were called he retreated to the farm to hide out and wait. This being bad enough things turned way south. Once the VA retrieved his records it was almost too late to back up to normalcy. One detail I failed to mention was he had been a weapons expert in Nam and specialized in the creation and disarming of booby traps. One of the results of his break was a full retreat to these skills and a strong desire for retribution fueled by extreme paranoia. He felt they were coming for him and they really were. It was not just imagination. The VA had gotten with the local sheriff's department and with a little luck it was going to be a rubber room. Somehow knowing this fact he was ready. The trailer in which he lived was backed on one side by the lake and was very defendable as well as on a one lane gravel road main entry stretching at least a mile or two. The land was flat and thick with low palms protruding from the sandy loam, perfect for jungle warfare which was his preference. He had installed around the perimeter a series of trip wires which were attached to clusters of shotgun shells set to explode in grenade like fashion upon disturbance. At this point for some reason he chose to strip totally naked and sit in a partially filled kiddie swimming pool in the front yard with a fifth of Jack Daniels and an assault rifle awaiting the attack. He would not have to wait long. In a moment of clarity he had also hidden a small boat in the tall reeds at the water's edge with his backpack of clothes and provisions. After about an hour in the pool, swigging on the bottle he said he heard a blast and felt the report. One of the sheriff's swat group had tripped a wire and had been badly injured in his leg and shoulder. This changed the entire complexion of the operation and the officers fell back to a safe distance to medi-vac the wounded and re-evaluate. They could not have known the level of person they were dealing with and they would have to respect that.

During the down time in the assault he took the opportunity to hit the boat and in the confusion made his way several miles to a familiar point of land. Here he redressed and made his way north from the swamp. By the time all of the traps had been dealt with and there was a level of comfort for the officers he was long gone. And for some unknown reason I was who he thought of. There was no real traceable connection between us except for the girlfriend and I guess he felt a trip to Arkansas somehow made some sense.

It took him an hour or so to hit a main road and in no time he was making his way north at breakneck speed. Everyone likes to help a vet especially on the open road. They are always in some strange way; no matter how long it's been, heading for home. It's in the eyes. Story goes he stopped in on an old army acquaintance in Mobile, Alabama who hooked him up on some meds and leveled him out. For now he was good.

Of course I had no knowledge of all this when he called to see what I was up to and if I wanted a visitor for a short while. My first thought was "what the fuck, sure". A day or so would be fun. Catch up and drink a beer or two. My kids were little so at the house would not be cool but there was the promoter apartment for him to crash. That would work out fine and I arranged to pick him up at the bus station, which he had ridden in from Jackson, Mississippi.

He hadn't changed in the least and other than a little road wear he was exactly like I remembered. He instantly fit in with everyone he met in my group and was quite a hit at all our usual watering holes. It was a little unusual even for us to have such an exotic house guest and everyone was intrigued. The couple of days stretched into a week and sooner than later a month. He seemed to have money from somewhere being wired to him so he was covered and since there was nothing out of my pocket I didn't mind.

He was just one of the guys. Problem was he was one of the guys wanted by the authorities and I was unknowingly harboring a fugitive wanted by state and federal officials. The aborted military style assault resulting in most of the charges, but the matter with the doctor as well as the pot patch at the farm and the multitude of illegal automatic firearms and explosive ordinance found near and in the trailer helped complicate things further.

He was looking at serious time and he knew it. As soon as I found all this out I knew I could be too. I had a family and reputation and the last thing I would do is risk everything for any casual acquaintance. No matter how funny he might be. One great unexpected quality in addition to the ability to kill he possessed was his culinary skills. He made absolutely the best damned egg plant parmesan I had ever tasted. I had him come over to the house and whip it up at least twice a week for a while. It would melt in your mouth...it was so good. But that in itself is also not worth possible incarceration.

I refrained from sharing any of his back story with anyone (this act of omission would cause irreparable damage to my marriage as in this act of protection of my family I was accused of other motives by an insecure spouse) until I knew he was a safe distance out of my life. I was still unsure about the legal ramifications and what could happen to any of us even though unknowingly linked with him.

The night I told him he had to go was quite surreal. We had done some shots and I and Uncle Gaylen were out with him downtown somewhere. I think for a burger and some beers primarily, and of course the big send off. I had shared with G the details and we had agreed that distance was a necessity. Gaylen was still working for the University and of all my extended group of friends who had spent the most time with him, he stood to lose almost as much as I did.

After just the proper amount of drink I knew it was time to act. I just wasn't sure how things would go. I really didn't have a feel for how desperate he might be. Our friendship to this point had been a much laid back, pleasant trip but I was very aware of what he was capable of. I remember his hair was unusually wild and unkempt that night which heaped mounds of tension onto my already frayed nerves. Another shot and it would have to be time. He had switched to Jack, straight up and I needed him to be aware of what we were about to say to him.

He had to understand in a rational way where we were going with this. Being a school night too meant that I didn't want to be out late because work would come early. He could sleep in but that was not an option with us. With that in mind I eased slowly into the fact that he was a wanted man in fairly close proximity to Florida and it was just a matter of time before a person, as unique looking as himself would be spotted and apprehended. I knew he really liked playing with my kids Dylan and Amber (who were in the young cuddly stage at the time) and I felt an appeal on our entire collective behalf would help to even more extinguish any potential rage which might be brewing.

Did he want to see them orphaned? Father in the slammer for reasons previously unknown to him? Of course not. He really was a better guy than that and through his time with us he had grown to regard us all as his extended family. The one he didn't and never had had. We had never made demands on him at any time and only had enjoyed the pleasure of his unusual company.

And vice-versa, but this was different. It really wasn't a betrayal on his part as much as an omission. He was, like most are, a subject of many complicated layers to be revealed in their time. It was just there were some pretty important fucking layers which could not be ignored. He surprised us both with his reaction and commented that he totally understood but that he had been having probably the best time he had ever had being a part of our "family" and friends.

I could never think of it on those terms without considering a Charles Manson reference and this always made me smile to myself. Just my shitty sense of humor I suppose. He would be gone he said by the time I got off work tomorrow but he didn't know exactly where and I didn't want to know. That was the whole point, plausible deniability as usual.

In celebration of all that had happened the last two months but particularly the apparent ease of the departure we decided to hell with it all and decided to tie one on.

Old time's sake and the like. You know. Soon all of us had switched to Crown and the whisky was flowing like wine. We found out a lot more than we wanted to know about each other, especially when he glazed over and started talking about his personal horrors of war. I shared my brushes with it in regard to several of my family tragedies (Viet Nam related) and somehow I felt this information was good for him. Sometimes the only way to heal is to speak the words and ponder them as they hang there in the air.

It's not poetic and it's not always pretty but it's real. Sometimes real is much more important than you can imagine. We laughed and we bar hopped and after about the third stop I knew it was close to time. Plus, I was dead broke and having some focus problems with my left eye. On the way to Gaylens' truck at the apartment the dude was out cold. We had to get him to bed if for no other reason than to complete the evening's transaction and move on with our lives. We had to be at work in about three hours so it was no time to fuck around.

Upon arrival he was dead weight. At about 185 or 190 it was going to be a real chore to get him up the three flights of stairs and into bed. Our condition didn't help matters either as it only served to eliminate any sense of danger like most people would experience under the circumstances. We tugged at the guy to free him from the backseat and in the process pulled one of his Dingo boots off losing it under the car. I would have to come back for it. The sky was getting lighter and you could hear birds and you know what that means. It's not good. His condition, I'm sure to an outsider, would look very much like death as we would discover on the second landing.

A thirtyish local television anchor woman who had to be in the office at 4:30AM had just exited her apartment for her morning jog and had stumbled right into our awkward situation. There we stood smiling, each one on the end of a dead looking biker with one boot on. I also failed to mention that I had cut my knuckle on something in the backseat exchange and had a large red stain on my white tee shirt.

We stood in limbo for what seemed like an eternity before the ice was broken. "You boys ok?" she winced. To which we replied without a blink "bachelor party". She seemed to accept this possibly because the alternative was unthinkable and we continued in our now unimpeded path. As quickly as we could, banging his head on the door frame upon entry, we tossed him panting on the sofa.

When he landed he made a guttural sound and rolled over extolling a series of loud snores. "Later dude" we said in unison and hauled ass for a little sleep before starting the day. Next day was one of those long ones. Not so much the crown hangover and occasional puking but the expectation of what was up with the dude. Was he gone? Was he mad? Was he going to kill us and any evidence we might reveal when pressured about his whereabouts. Did he find his boot we had left in the parking lot? To all we had no answers? Only time would tell. At five o'clock I headed over to the apartment to find out what the deal was. Everything seemed extremely quiet, I guess in stark contrast to 12 hours earlier. There was a magazine and a sandal I recognized which had obviously fallen out of the truck with the body extraction. These were lying in the space previously occupied that dawn. With trepidation I made my way up the stairs and turned the tumblers on the lock.

Slowly I opened the door into a dark and empty room. He and all of his gear were gone. He had even cleaned the bathroom and hung up the towels and taken out the trash. There, on the pillow of the sofa which had just been his bed was a note made of a single sheet of paper.

I turned it over for whatever extended message it might reveal and was surprised to find it contained one word. "Thanks". That kind of summed it all up. What else was there to say? I never heard from him again but then again who would I ask? I just think about him when I see bikes or egg plant.

Present day...

I got into work on time as usual and none for wear. I usually am fairly resilient in times of crisis or adventure to which either classification could apply to the evening last. I wasn't sure what the day held but what I did know within seconds was that one of our guys' wife was sick. How this affects me is anytime she is off or not well he refuses to ride in alone. It is very interesting to observe. It must be great to love someone at that level. The type of commitment that would make one actually observe Columbus Day.

Today was going to be one of those "Diamonds on my Windshield" kinds of black and white movie, jazz club, Tom Waits kind of days. Noir if you will. If you have ever had one of these you know exactly what I'm talking about although these are usually on Saturdays.

One of the things that makes working at my office in general interesting is that its downtown. I am inherently a suburbanite but all my life I have worked in and explored urban environments. My dads' office was always in the heart of downtown and I have grown and developed as a person right along with the area and feel very much ingrained. I have known the characters and the buildings, good and bad. I've shared wine with bums behind the shell station on Broadway and dined with Presidential aides at the historic Capitol Hotel. (Legend says President Grant once when drunk rode a horse into the lobby). Such as this town is I feel a part of it all, but it was this urban training which opened the door to all types of larger and more complex environs.

My favorite artworks are the chaotic and cluttered streetscapes preferably with urban clutter. I like night time with neon and the haphazard comings and goings of the masses. It's a seedy energy. You really can't explain it but you can definitely smell it. It's a feeling you get from walking around and listening to people and looking in storefront and bar windows as you walk by. Its best no matter where you are to keep your hands in your pockets, but not in a menacing way like as if you were armed. A loose relaxed look. In tight crowds or any time in New Orleans you should carry your wallet in your front pocket. That will protect it from the sleaze bags that will slit your back pocket with a straight razor and follow you as long as it takes for it to tumble to the street and into their possession. A bold but yet a basically benign activity.

There are a million tricks and scams and that in itself is part of the allure. It's the unknown. I have many favorite cities of all sizes and in many different geographic areas. It's always based on your mood, desire and ability to stay open to new ideas. Keep in mind that locals are just as starved for an injection of new and possibly interesting characters as you are for a new face, story or location. It's this unspoken human dance we do.

Only requirement is you have to leave the house. You can certainly see it on television but you can't live it on the sofa. The king capital of fun (as mentioned several times earlier) in the south is the pre-Katrina New Orleans. I'm sure it's probably ok now but I have not visited as of this chapter and cannot attest for sure to it. One great trip there in the mid-nineties was to the Jazz and Heritage Festival held at the race track near the garden district. All the details of these visits seem to always run together but have the common thread of Bourbon Street, Jackson Square and vast quantities of something that stand out in the mind. The blur I'm sure is a result of the mass quantitiesof alcohol. This one trip involved a lot of the usual suspects as at the time we were heavily involved in several blues festivals and could usually score some type of passes or invites to activities.

In this particular case both. In the matter of accommodations (which without preplanning would be impossible) Gaylen, (Uncle Gaylen) who had attended several years and had always prodded us to join him, had leased a five bedroom home from locals. This antebellum structure would be ours for the weekend and was situated about halfway between the Garden District and Storyville. The size and expense of this arrangement would require a fairly respectable size group of fellow party goers which allowed our following to swell to nine.

This was almost unwieldy in the area of transportation once in the city as parking for one, much less multiple vehicles is impossible. To our advantage there was a cab stand and trolley stop about two blocks away so we were set at least to get to shuttles up town or to the track. For a bonus the owners of the property had properly stocked any and all appropriate liquors, beer and mixers although ice was at a premium. This made beer the drink of choice for most in order to create the appropriate pace and allow for the completion of what the extended day or night would hold.

The last thing we wanted was one of our party to pass out in a situation not suitable to the advancement of the adventure proper. Not to mention transport of the victim. This meant we all stuck together and closely monitored the intake of all. Not to say we didn't throw down but you have to have a grasp on what and when. The main day of the festival for us was a Saturday and all Saturdays start off there with a bloody Mary. Gaylen, at the time made an incredible BM from scratch (no mix) and by 9AM we were feeling great.

Showers and dressing took several hours but the beverages made this barely noticeable. The prep time was not a matter of primping but based on the fact that all were experienced enough to know they did not know when or if the next opportunity would present itself. Another reason was the lack of hot water. These older homes, although equipped with massive square footage were not fortunate to have adequate plumbing capabilities that would accommodate large groups. This would require three quick showers and then about a thirty minute wait for the replenishment of the hot water box or small holding tank. No matter because we were not on a schedule and the weather looked a little like a potential problem. Being event people we were prepared for any occasion and were soon handing out rain gear.

Most wore hiking boots and shorts anyway so we were pretty much good to go. We allowed two backpacks to be shared by all because of the festival searches and too much gear later in the evening was not desired. Clubs frown on that because it implies bums, even in a festival environment. Everything was checked and ready so off we went. Clouds were rolling in off the gulf and it looked like the sky was going to open up at any moment. For some reason, luck I guess, it held off all through the trolley and shuttle ride into the site.

Miller Beer was one of the main sponsors (and ours at home) so once we wadded through the massive crowd we ambled up to redeem a few of our handfuls of free 20oz beer coupons we had stumbled on back at our local dealership. The main act we were there to see that day was The Robert Cray Band and a sea of people waited patiently under the boiling black heavens. As the band approached the stage and picked up instruments I was feeling no pain. None of us were and in no time we had hooked up with about ten new friends in similar mode and the adventure was in high gear.

In one of the strangest choreographed events I've ever seen at the first amplified lick of the first song a bolt of lightning struck one of the stage support towers and the torrent began. It was one of the most exhilarating and awesome moments I've ever felt with just the right levels of drunkenness and adrenaline. We were enjoying life and neither the possible danger of lightning nor the rain water in our beers would deter us. The rain fell in buckets and in an unreasonable show of spirit the band played on. We (the 20K plus crowd) were collectively drenched with not a single man or woman in the audience complaining about the new element added by the multitude of wet halters and t-shirts. Fuck No!

It was stunning.

About 3:30 in the afternoon and we only had about eighty three or so drink tickets left between us. These were most certainly good times. The tunes continued to roll and some of the lighter weights in our charge were winding down by about eight pm. Gaylen and I had other ideas as he had always for years been trying to get me into one of the smaller Storyville juke joints and timing is everything. We decided to expedite things and snag a couple of cabs, cut to the chase and were standing in front of the rental house by about ten. Four of us were game to continue while the rest wanted to make a dent in the liquor cabinet and the crash pad and explore the vast collection of vinyl recordings.

I was tempted but like I said timing is everything and this would once again probably not be the first or last time I puked in a New Orleans dumpster. After a quick change to dry shorts and shirt I gathered a small ruck sack imagining the nearer than later sunrise and we headed out to the cab stand. Gaylen and I had a great old friend (Janice) who was at one time a local blues show radio DJ and was now managing one of the more notorious joints in that area. This would as a matter of course be our destination. No reason to bullshit around. Go to the source (so to speak), plus we had a connection which never hurts in unfamiliar shark infested waters. Additionally I was thinking "I've been thrown out of nicer places than this". The shot of mescal we all took on the way out the door had reinforced my buzz so courage was also not an issue. Once in the cab the driver expressed hesitation when Gaylen offered up our quest. "You sure you nice boys want to go there?" "Damn right" we all said in unison, thus relieving him of all moral responsibility and off into the black we went. The rain had stopped about the time we had gotten home and a slight fog had settled in completing the sense of foreboding.

We were in an area where we better watch our young fucking mouths and we knew it. Once we arrived the line outside for entry would further complicate the issue. Being on the guest list would open these white boys up to untold jeopardy once on the inside. This is usually the result of the pressure and badgering heaped on the boyfriends of the slighted female line dwellers. It was great to see Janice and I was even more relieved to see we were segregated to her guest area in an upstairs balcony. The first thing that struck me odd about the joint was not the décor or stage arrangement but how light it was inside. It was about two or three times lighter than most clubs I'd frequented and after about an hour I enquired why. It was like drinking in a Wal-Mart. "Weapons" was the quick response and I knew exactly what was up.

"It allows the bouncers and crowd spotters to see shit before", "It saves me about 20% on our liability insurance to have them at these levels and there was that nasty business last year." Apparently two people seated at that very table had been shot and killed in a shootout encompassing both levels that had involved about twelve gunmen all told. "Made all the papers" she beamed, surprised that we had not been aware. The incident had been responsible for a whole new set of rules and regulations concerning conduct and contraband and as they say what happens in Storyville stays in Storyville, especially the bodies.

At this point the cabbies reaction to our request was crystal. This was not exactly going to be our ideal situation and after catching up and being able to say been there done that we were ready to head out. Janice offered us a ride back to town as cabs were scarce that time of morning and we agreed. None of us were quite ready to head in, being rejuvenated by the excitement and opted to be dropped in the tourist area of the French quarter. There is a little A&P food market off St. Charles near the square and we happened by just at the French bread delivery.

When the truck opened the aromatic steam rushed out, competing with the rancid garbage shoot smell prevalent at every corner. It was just too much. We followed the man inside and within five minutes we had a loaf each and munched with added pads of butter, spread on with foil as we sat on the metal edge of the street curb. We had also scored a six pack of cheap Dixie Beer long necks made about eight blocks away and we were good for now. It really couldn't get any better and we sat there soaking it all in.

The bread was just the ticket for absorbing any excesses from the night before and the beer was cool and refreshing. Ambling up the street we passed some of the nicer,(now closed for the day last), restaurants and tourist establishments until we spotted an oyster bar trying to close its shuttered doors. They couldn't pass up four for dinner at this hour and would lock up behind us upon entry. We had about two dozen each and even bought a dozen for the day worn, exhausted shucker, who came out and joined us at the table. He had a shot of Jameson straight up, which I couldn't imagine with oysters on the half shell for breakfast and seemed pleased with the spirited company, as we were also. This place was quiet and dry and out of the fray and for that we were grateful for the break. The sun was just starting to rise now and the morning shift would be there in about an hour to open for the Sunday brunch. This fact would not stop us from a couple of more drinks and some bread before we found out the motivation for the kindness. It wasn't that they didn't like us or the company we provided, which they did, but they had closed officially at five. This meant that if paid in cash all transactions were off the books and would be split between the late guys who stayed behind.

That also meant free food (on us) drinks and cash for them, in addition to their regular pay and tips. For this opportunity they were quite grateful. "Whatever works" was our reply and since we had earlier been the guest of Janice we were able to scrape up some cash between us and then some. The sun was definitely up at this point and the horrid smell from the street was overpowering. The stillness was only broken by the occasional rat.

We finally agreed we had better get on back and after bidding our new found friends (who also floated me a free t-shirt from the bar) farewell, we hit the road. It took about two minutes on a cross street to hail a cab and within twenty we were sitting in the ancient living room of the house. We had no sooner than sat down when one of the early risers came stumbling in and thinking we had been up talking all night made comment about how dull we all were. I remember we all smiled at each other and laughed to ourselves.

After about a two hour nap, strategically situated during ladies extended shower time it was time to wash off the grime from the evening last before it became permanent. My ankles above my hiking socks reminded me of Oliver Twist. Today would begin with brunch at the French market several blocks off Canal Street. My favorite depending on the time is either Eggs Benedict with a half dozen half shell on the side or if later in the day a half mufelletta. A whole one would have way too much bread involved and would be a little harder to deal with later in the day. In these situations you have to eat when the opportunity presents itself but you should never really take on a load. You always have a lot more staying power than you would think especially when adrenaline is added. The actual necessity of a nutritious meal is vastly overrated. You have to be quick on your feet. This day it would be the eggs and oysters. We crowded around in mass at the eatery a large and ancient thick heavy table. The legs were very ornate with one corner a little loose. It was a table you could imagine coming over by ship from Paris in the late nineteenth century. The deep indents and gashes created by the crates and steamer trunks which it sternly supported with its mass and character.

The color was a deep red stain which seemed made by time and use and not by any man made oil or protective compound. It was upon this surface we would begin and plot the remainder of the day. Several of our traveling companions were new to the city so it would be required to make some of the tourist type stops.

From this position we were in a great starting point, this being just off Jackson Square and the trendy arts district adjacent to the shit hole areas. It was all there within about twelve blocks. After a quick draft beer, Abina I think, we were off. First stop was one of my favorite stores which features all items from France. I'm not particularly into French culture and especially not the style of cooking but there is something exotic and fun about this place. I guess it's because it's centered more on the empire of the 1920's and 30's which conjures up images of Morocco or the islands. Pretty sexy stuff.

Perspiration stained white linen suits and small cups of ultra strong caffeine extract concoctions. Lounge singers crying over dirty martinis. Casablanca? You know.... The music in the air also has a lot to do with it. It swirls around you in a strange mix of multi-cultural soup with the underlying flavor of that sweetest of elements, classic American jazz.

It's very strange how it transports you. You only have to be lucky or wise enough to pay attention and listen. A degree will get in by osmosis but it is best when savored. It's a sauce of life. From the French shop we decided it was time to shift things into a little higher gear if we were going to continue to hold everyone's interest. This would require some hurricanes at Pat O Brian's. Being mid-afternoon we would almost be assured of a patio seat and no more than two drinks would be more than fine for the proper attitude adjustment.

The hour, would however prohibit us from taking the customary glass for the road because we weren't sure exactly when or where or any other details. Plus the fact it is near impossible to blend and experience when you are labeled with the badge of tourist as exhibited by bundles of souvenir spoils. We also had a pantry full at home so they wouldn't be missed. As planned we had great seats near the piano in the courtyard. These were open to the bright sky so opposite to the terrible storms of the day before.

The warm front had obviously cleared the gulf and the gentle swirling breeze of the courtyard gently lifted and flirted with the subtropical growth. Another drink please! According to plan we held it to two per person and headed back out through the dungeon like entrance and to the amateur night developing on the street. It's the novices that fuck things up generally and today was no exception. Underage or first time 21's are particularly annoying to professional partygoers and it was as if the bus had just rolled into town. Young men, present company not excluded, seem to always go to unhealthy extremes when subjected to environments foreign to they're norm.

It's like when a church camp is on a field trip. It's a license to kill and the participants are not exactly sure how to cope and what to do. This is no exaggeration. When doing a rock show I would much rather work with the nastiest, most depraved heavy metal in the world than a Christian show. With the Metal I know exactly what to expect and can minimize the danger factor for myself and others. I have had many more near misses with the Christian groups. It's bizarre. The cross streets running toward Rue Bourbon were jammed with sloshing college kids and a sprinkling of high school types.

You can just tell by their volume (loudness) that they were new to town, and had possibly had some beverages on the way. The other tell-tale element of the collective nature of the mob is they ask virtually every female encountered to flash. This is not at any level appropriate due in part that it is not Mardi Gras and also before dark. The majority of females roaming this district before dark are generally honeymooners, with grooms in toe or the typical shopping tourist. Either of these classifications would emit a negative and sometimes dangerous response to the enquiry. We were above all this action and moved systematically from club to club, looking for that perfect jam to spend dusk with. After a few we found the one. It was one of those very seedy, dirty female impersonator / live sex show dives with a three drink minimum and a bathroom like in a county lock up outside of Cleveland.

This place was exactly why the rule exists. Never under any circumstances take a "dump" in a strip club. Its man rule number 2. I couldn't say who was uglier, the women or the men trying to look like women. It was a total freak show and that was most certainly the appeal. We were by no means looking for love and this was the pre-cable television era. The door man had a missing eye and the empty socket was filled by an off color glass eye with a sequin or phosphorescent pupil. I'm not sure which because I didn't want to get close enough to confirm. In just the right light it would flash at you in a lime green color almost as a signal to move forward, come in and experience some of the world's delightful weirdness.

It was hard to get past the eye but one almost had to notice the missing leg and overall attire as he held court from his high backed padded bar stool. He had one of that old man, Panama style white button up shirts with the intricate stitched front panels. This unit was unceremoniously tucked tightly into a pair of uncomfortably tight sansi-belt powder blue slacks with black belt and suspenders. Belt AND suspenders is a severe sign of insecurity not to mention a poor fashion choice. To complete the ensemble was a small brim fedora that sat cocked slight left and appeared to be constructed of sere sucker material. Tre sheik. Each finger was adorned by some sort of Masonic style faux gemstone ring with most leaning in the neighborhood of blue. His smile was pleasant enough but somehow troubled. It was a job and after all he didn't have to spend all day on his foot. The bartender was a portly woman with an enormous frog neck and what appeared to be the remains of a trachea scar perhaps from some distant past emergency procedure. The skin incision contrast of which glowed in the neon against her dark and muddy complexion. Her flowered moo-moo type tent of a dress covered a person of vast proportion who was clearly in charge as she shoved left and right every known drink, causing the skinny, gaunt waitresses to scurry like cock roaches. Her hair was pulled into a matronly bun exposing even more of the atmosphere to the girth of her head. This was clearly never a beautiful woman. She would have been beaten as a child if she had ever indeed been one.

This was one of those rooms that you just can't walk away from. As layer upon layer is exposed you get deeper and deeper in the shier weight of it all. Like Hunter Thompson said often and hard "It just never got weird enough for me". To top it all the first song played at full blast was the classic "Gimmie Shelter" by the Stones as accompaniment to a pair of Chinese twin he/she's who entered the small, dank stage juggling. You could see mold spoors rising off the stage carpet in the purple spot lights with each step. Dangerous but somehow enticing and definitely apropos. The tables, which were about three foot square had red and white checkerboard, nonflammable table cloths which were screwed down to the table tops at the corners. It really wasn't hopping yet so with no objections we pulled two together to accommodate our group.

The drinks were small, expensive and weak so we were not disappointed and after the first round we switched back to beer. It can be done but it is extremely hard to fuck up beer. I had had my fill of local brews and switched to Miller Lite. It's not that the local brands aren't good but it's a lack of quality controls. Dixie Beer is hard to beat but I've never had two bottles in succession ever taste exactly the same with some being downright rank. This is not only true of small southern beers as the worst green tasting pitcher of Samuel Adams I ever had was at an outdoor joint on the square in Boston believe it or not. The beer was cold and wet on my tongue and just almost succeeded in cutting the thick cigar smoke which was creating a film on my face and neck. The first act was very weak as topless juggling just doesn't have the appeal to me as it perhaps once did. I sat there for some reason hoping for midgets. Some excitement was called for as the atmosphere had gone as far as it could and midgets looked to me like they would fit this place like OJ's glove. Midgets are great ice breakers and one of my favorite sayings involves them. When meeting a person or group of persons you are unsure of or you may remotely want to impress this always works. I was once with an after work group of nurses and surgeons I had never met before when after the sufficient number of drinks I blurt out as if to begin a story "so I'm beating this midget. . .". the trick is to trail off after the initial statement like your musing quietly of how great or pleased you were with yourself at the adventure of it. The gaggle of professionals just stared and I knew exactly where I stood. They had no sense of humor and there was no need to make an extended effort. They were obviously not my kind and never would be.

It's just fun to toss that rock on the frozen pond. Cut to the chase as it were. After several lackluster performances by stone faced strippers staring at something just above our heads (unusual as most are trained to increase tips by making eye contact and creating a personal connection with the customer) we were not to be disappointed. A totally nude male black "little person" whose member seemed to be literally touching the ground rambled on to the stage deck and glared at the audience. Everything seemed to halt, with the exception of the help for what seemed like an eternity. I'm not sure yet exactly what his act was but it was awesome. It was hard not to look as hard as we tried to divert our gaze. His head, which was shaved and shaped strangely like a peanut, was almost as big a distraction as the obvious.

The obvious, as I would determine later was an object lesson in optical illusion as his manhood was only slightly larger than normal and was accentuated by his shortness of leg. I think it was the shock factor that made his act successful. We sat in anticipation of what possible music on earth would be appropriate to this strange exhibition and were in no way disappointed as "My Guy" by Diana Ross blasted out of the system and hard into the rear wall.

The place erupted like Krakatau as the crowd howled and threw coin toward the gyrating Nubian. Now that's entertainment! As fate would have it and as things often work we somehow invited the little man to join us for a drink. Our only stipulation was that he don pants and not get ugly with us because we had questions and he had answers. It's not that we were perverts but how many opportunities come up like that. The only initial faux pas was our collective laughter when he asked Jabba the hut behind the bar for the phone book to sit on. After apologies it was on with the evening. It seems that he was originally from Houma, Louisiana and had six full size brothers and sisters with him in the center as the seventh, meaning three normal sized, him followed by three additional normal sized siblings. He seemed to harbor no resentment about the hand dealt him and quite the opposite he seemed to welcome it. He explained that after some adjustment (particularly in his school days) he was able to become the only member of his extended family to be gainfully employed and had even earned a bachelor of science degree from Tulane with his specialty being Agriculture management and more specifically catfish farming.

His current cash paying occupation was serving the purpose of staking his ground floor investment in several catfish ponds north of the lake close to I-10. Never judge a book. He also seemed pleased to interject where else can you make that kind of money for just dropping your pants, this being traditionally a paying not income proposition.

He "hung" with us for about an hour as we talked specifically about the "ins and outs" of fish farming. My main contribution being that one of my favorite rock stars (Ian Anderson of Jethro Tull fame) had turned much of his music profits over the years into pretty much controlling the majority of England's fish farming industry (or as I had been told). Beyond that I pretty much just sat there impressed by how on top of his game this guy was. He was a man with vision. He had a plan and he was on it.

I'm sure there's a lesson in that but it escapes me at this juncture. Soon he was back up on rotation and had to change into I guess . . . nothing. It was pretty much time for us to move on anyway and we requested our tabs. The infinitely less than arousing performances had left us a little flat. The one legged, one eyed door man should have been the red flag about the entertainment value. Very uninspired. Other than the midget conversation it was more or less just a light show. Well fuck it, we headed back to the street.

We exchanged numbers first with a few of the staff but all parties knew they would never be called once sober and the spur of the moment urgency revealed under the bright light of day. The street was shimmering with neon and loud. Walking the blocks was much like going to a state fair. Every door passed had a totally different sound and feel all blaring at you in an effort to entice. We had just experienced plenty of weird shit and sex was just not gonna do it for us. We switched to music. Blues was out because its soooo depressing and I can only listen to it for so long. Jazz was obvious but Dixieland sounds too touristy if you've been here before. The way around this issue is for it to be the real deal. This means like Preservation Hall or Al Hirt (who was alive at the time). They took it to a level like Armstrong. It was not the homogenized bullshit you would find in places like Club Mason, who would rip you with a heavy cover charge and drink minimum while the shitty band went on a thirty minute break. After a while of door peeking for just the right deal we settled in on one of the open air courtyards. This had been an older structure with a large patio which had been partially destroyed by fire. The end result was a large bar area open to the sky surrounded by restroom and service areas. This allowed the showcasing of a moderate size covered stage. I would say that the capacity was probably about a thousand or so and it was sporting every bit of that. With the stage size and the ten dollar per head cover charge it was no doubt they could handle some decent reputable acts.

I think the band that night was "Sweet" or one of the other pre-huge hair techno bands of the late seventies and early eighties. They all kinda run together after a time. The crowd was a very odd mix (as you would expect) and included older, wide eyed tourists in Bermuda shorts and black socks, the remnants of an apparently near toga party and last but not least the typical voyeur much like our party. We were relatively regular Joes slightly south of preppy and leaning hard toward earthy, before there was such a classification. Again a reference to our day packs and hiking boots. Standard event equipment. The one novelty of this joint was the test tube shot. These were colored vodka concoctions served up from whatever exposed body part of your choosing from your bikini clad stripper/ waitress. They would slip the full size loaded test tube into cleavage or whatever and then dispense the liquid into the waiting mouth of the recipient. I just couldn't get this right as for some reason my instinct was to grab the tube with my teeth and pull. The result was I kept spilling about a third of the sticky fluid on the breasts or stomach of the server. This was a big laugh for our group causing several to be purchased on my behalf just for the show it provided. I think on the fourth I had mastered the maneuver without incident, thus the novelty of it ended.

The wind somehow was reaching us about midnight usually meaning rain off the gulf. Just some air movement was refreshing and blew new life into the group, allowing us another hour or so here. After a jaunt back over toward the river through the square, there we sat on the curb with our backs against the black wrought iron fence. Where to now? We sat there for probably thirty minutes or so before a plan developed.

It was the night breeze that made our decision to head to the moon walk which stretched along the water's edge. Not a place to be that late without a loud group such as ours. Before we went we ducked back in the A&P and picked up some forties for the road. Once there the moon was on the decline and we took it all in. We talked about our dreams, desires and we laughed. The soft breeze blew and tossed our hair.

Sitting there at that time we could have no idea at the injury that would happen here in Katrina. That thought is even now beyond my capacity. It was perfect and so were we. I think that may be the reason I resist returning to this day. Some things need to stay ingrained in their original condition.

Just like snap shots in a shoe box on the closet shelf. There is no doubt the images will fade with time and at some point disappear all together. This is how it should be. It is a cycle of things that you and only you can call your own.

Like that trip and others the romance is much more appealing than the reality of the aftermath. When a group of people stop for that moment and participate in a joint experience it becomes an important element in the collective makeup. In the DNA if you will. When you attempt to chart and follow the continued saga of the individuals it can easily spiral out of control and context.

Such is the case with this particular group. This is the type of realizations in hind sight that makes that trip in its entirety more special. It perhaps is also what makes us human and unremarkable. Every voice in its own distinctive pitch. Upon our arrival back to earth and subsequent dispersal into individual paths not all things ended well. Myself and my issues notwithstanding the party becomes a good case study in the preciousness of moments. One of our group, which was a dear friend and actually lived with my little family for several years give or take fell into an almost immediate disrepair in the form of alcoholism. At the loss of her father to a sudden illness she slipped into a depression compounded with a stay at home job allowing her the luxury of limited outside contact. No one has seen or heard from her in many years and she is missed. There was the newlywed couple on the trip who were great fun people and worked a lot with our shows. The guy was a bartender and semipro blackjack dealer and his bride was a petite blond stripper who worked nights with him. After some early marital issues she was found in the front yard of their rental house with a single gunshot wound to the face. The official story was there had been a fight between the two during which she had burst out into the yard and committed suicide. As people residing just below the societal importance bar in their community there was no further investigation and the matter was closed. The guy within a month closed up shop there by quitting his job and skipping out on his home lease.

It is rumored he traveled to Mississippi where he works as a dealer in one of the river casinos and I believe that he has never remarried. The pretty boy of the clan was the son of a very successful businessman in town and had had the good fortune of much travel and extended stays in locations like the Keys and Hawaii where he was employed as a lifeguard.

Being an outdoor type he was always accompanied by his extremely handsome and well behaved retriever dog. Soon after our trip his father died of a heart attack leaving him broken and without direction. His inattention to matters of the family business soon forced him into a position requiring a sale to the second in command. This move hurt him deeply and all but erased any connection he had with his so called permanent home here. Last I heard he was roaming the Teton Mountains with his dog or the latest incarnation and doing odd carpentry jobs when available or required.

Gaylen is just Gaylen and he went on to greater things as one would expect. Aside from the hiccup of his department at the University being disbanded upon the death of his benevolent boss and old friend he has always maintained a forward motion, later marrying a truly wonderful and fun woman. A real gem. Upon his news of dismissal at work we threw a huge "getting fired" party where my sons rock band at the time played in the carport during a rain storm and at some point I projectile vomited on the side of his house behind the hedge. Hell yes! Seems like I also walked in on some girl on the toilet but I can't be sure. Our main goal together was to always get to the Burning Man Festival which happens on my birthday each year. We have yet to make the trip.

Another one of my part time guys dropped unexpectedly out of sight for about six or seven years only to reemerge as if nothing had happened or changed. Typical of the road and its students. He is currently married to one of the most obnoxious and annoying women it's ever been my displeasure to lay my damn eyes on but that's totally his bad. I believe her to be a succubus.

My ex-business partner and her husband seemed to grow apart not too long after in our goals and interests and we were soon a thousand miles apart in geography and ambitions. And that's how it goes. These types of stories taken in context only serve to prove that when individuals find a true moment of contentment you have to hold it close absolutely as long as possible. Not just big assed dramatic things but little things. They don't always come back around and never in the same form.

The other Saturday I stopped into the pool hall for a beer and some chips, maybe a joke or two, when one more example of the weirdness attraction to me came into the door. There was a small pool tournament going on and I had just flipped channels on the above bar TV to the movie "Gangs of New York" when someone tapped me on the shoulder. I turned expecting as I should someone I knew to only be greeted with the overwhelming stench of day or two old whiskey smells. The smell as you would expect was accompanied by a pair of wild, bloodshot eyes bulging out of a weathered nut sack of a face. I studied it closely and tried to process the tale which was tumbling out of his mouth and falling to the floor. The initial request was without a doubt unusual even for me as he inquired if I had a hunting rifle he could borrow. I just sat there and listened trying to wrap my head around the request. As he expanded his tale I motioned for another beer which seemed an appropriate measure.

Apparently he had for some reason left his car running in the parking lot (keep in mind it is 3 o'clock in the afternoon and he is pretty much wasted) where someone had while attempting to steal the car opted instead to steal the gun on the seat. Eyewitnesses had determined that a local pair of pimp and ho that had been frequenting across the street for about two weeks were the likely suspects. In the exchange they had left their own Buick Skylark in an adjacent lot so later I sauntered over and recorded the license plate number for future reference. I wanted badly to ask him the urgency for the rifle but thought better to leave sleeping dogs lie.

The bartender, who is a very nice elderly pot smoking old hippie lady was obviously disturbed by the situation and gave me the high sign to please intervene. I was so enthralled with the whole deal that I had almost finished my drink before I quipped back explaining we had no rifles as this wasn't the old west and that maybe it would be best for tournament play if he hit the bricks. He seemed pleased I guess that there was not a more aggressive response and wheeled and headed for the door. He had almost reached the front door when he quickly turned direction and headed into the large bank of pool tables and players and began the incoherent story. I could see it wasn't resonating with the crowd based on the nearest two participants were pinching their noses to combat the wafting scent of stale Wild Turkey or maybe Dickel, perspiration and god knows what else. I'll bet he had velour interior. One thing that did cross my mind as I looked into the yellowed and glazed eyes of the wayward stranger that had opted into our universe was the fact that in a lot of respects it really sucks to get old.

Don't get me wrong. There is no fucking way that I would ever want to go back and repeat or undo anything except with one possible exception. I would never have put my physical body through the abuse that I did. I believed this happened for a couple of reasons off the top of my head. One being my love for working outdoors and the other being bad advise from a multitude of poorly trained and inadequate sports coaches over the years. In my sideline line of business, which as you know is concerts and event production we always have vast crews of day laborers for a multitude of tasks. I have always, as I was recently reminded, felt that it was important to lead by example and was always comfortable holding my own with work crews. This would mean 16 to 24 hour days of extreme physical and mental stress over many years which I readily handled.

My epiphany on the subject came about a year and a half ago when at the gym lifting weights (a passion for almost 35 years) I tore a bicep loose from my shoulder attachment. At the orthopedist during my MRI I was shocked to learn that yes I had a severe tear where my muscle had fallen 3 inches from normal but also I had no attachments of any kind in either shoulder. This was, as I was pointed out, not a normal outcome of gravitational pull and I obviously had contributed. What I do attribute it to is many things, spilled milk and all that. Sports coaches in the sixties and seventies were pretty much individuals who may or may not have a propensity for athletics but were more likely the one who drew the short straw or was not intellectually acceptable as a regular teacher. This was very evident when you were forced to attend (usually social studies or speech) classes taught as a mandatory requirement by coaches. It was amazing looking back on the shallowness of their depth of learning. Recently as I have run into some of my old coaches who have retired and doing the math I have determined most were in their early twenties. Not who I would have entrusted the health and well being of innocent children. Example: In Arkansas heat in the summer can be brutal and August and September are not uncommon to be in the triple digits. Two a day practices for football traditionally start in August which means the late morning and for sure afternoon temperature will most likely top 100. Based on an article that our head coach had read (probably up his own ass) he had been convinced that to save on his ice and water budget that it was to be encouraged for us to consume handfuls of salt tablets at breaks. The theory for this was that when you sweat you relieve your body of vast amounts of salts and this was a way to readily replace them. We in no way felt good about this and after running and working in the heat to be given a hand full of twenty or thirty solid salt tabs, the end result being severe dehydration and heart burn, we were all but done in. We were very lucky that no one had heat stroke. That was the mentality. We, as good little non-complaining soldiers went along with anything as gospel. My love of manual labor is legendary. (In my own mind) I can to this day stay on my feet and function for unending hours. It has been a long standing joke that when we have a new guy at a show they tell him he has to follow or shadow me in case I need something done or as added security in case I am carrying cash. They usually last three to four hours no matter how young and either quit or ask to be reassigned. I usually have no help like that anymore as it is (I'm sad to report) that no one under 30 is pretty much worth a shit. This being a contrasting whole reversal from the "don't trust anyone over 30 principle". If you question this try going into MacDonald's and ordering anything you may or may not want. It's quite sad. And KFC?... don't get me started.

As Forrest Gump would say "That's all I have to say about that".

And then as an extreme leap there's the search for truth. This as you know is a very old and complicated question and one that is engraved deeply into every man, woman and child. The thought can be somewhat suppressed by busying oneself but it is always lingering just below the surface. It usually first manifests itself as a quickening of the pulse. This may be all that may happen but depending on the subject and what other areas are affected it may spread to other symptoms such as sweaty lip and brow or overall panic.

My best example of the basic and unexplainable need for truth is television shows concerning UFO's. A moderately sensible man (such as myself I think) will sit through a two hour docu-drama style program on the subject and stay riveted to the seat, unable to move. Why? Is it some unknown revelation of truth at the conclusion? If there had been some recent discovery wouldn't I have heard about it on the networks or at the least CNN? Why would the only purveyor of the potentially earth shattering information be the History Channel? Common sense would dictate upon reflection that there is no new information and the two hours would be spent rehashing eyewitness accounts with accompanying grainy terribly fabricated footage . . . or whatever. We can't help but do this. But it is wise to recognize the need. Truth comes in many forms. We don't mind the vilest of creatures as long as we know and understand what we are looking at. More important is that the subject is exactly what it presents itself to be. This is our order of the world. Our comfort zone. On the other hand we can often manufacture our perceived truth about others and our surroundings and dwell in that. It's tolerable and depending on the depth of the plant, unflappable. This is mostly true of older people.

The day is really dragging now and I've let my mind wander. I know I'm relatively stranded in town right now. I am considering the Warhol exhibit that's at the local Arts Center the next couple of months but I may wait until my daughter comes in from Chicago. She's reading most everything she can right now about Edie Sedgewick and "The Factory" so it may be a little more interesting with her in tow. Or I could go twice?

A road trip is really what I need. When I look at the calendar I always realize it hasn't been long since I got back from somewhere. I guess that is why I never feel like I have any roots anywhere. I'm just always heading somewhere for a recharge. It's been so long for me to not have a home, in the settle down sense that it seems unnatural and awkward to have the opportunity.

I was thinking the other day about the Carolinas. North to be exact. This area which is my ancestral home was also the site of some really good times and I never really get back enough. One year I was hired by one of my bigger corporate clients to aid and participate in the corporate village for the National Special Olympics. This was a great honor and I really enjoyed the advance trips and everyone I met along the way. The event combined several elements such as staging, corporate hospitality, Nascar and the Olympic games themselves.

This required contract labor that could and would swell up to about fifteen bodies. I handpicked the best and most comical that would be up to the challenge, fun loving and adventurous spirit a must. Needless to say every day was hard during the day's activities and even harder during the nights. The event itself was in Raleigh at the campus of NC State so there was an abundance of college town bars, taverns, pizza places and the like. It took us no time to get acclimated and become regulars of sorts. We being more or less southern like the locals eased the transition. An abundance of cash beer per diem pretty much put us collectively over the top. One of the high points of the trip had the distinction of being over of all things... doors. In the corporate Olympic village the main tent belonging to our client was an air conditioned monstrosity which for some reason had been delivered without its main double airtight doors. This being a weekend meant the situation could not be rectified until well after the closing ceremonies. This would not be acceptable so after numerous beers a plan was formulated. Earlier in the day we had been invited to a swank reception at a 68 degree Fahrenheit football stadium sized tent structure hosted by the Kennedy's and Arnold Schwarzenegger. It had it all and was populated by several Hollywood types. I ran into a shorter than expected Jon Bon Jovi at the cheese table. This being said, I and the group being from the event side of life took note and admired the facilities, including a plethora of air tight double doors. We also admired how they were held in place only with wire and zip ties and how the frames and doors were self contained.

The more we drank the more we admired. It was a short time later over a pitcher or two that the plan was hatched. We had a truck and six guys handy so we could handle the girth and mass of the six-plus foot double doors. Our female clients with the credit cards were gleeful about our covert moxie and we ran with it. They were practically beside themselves at the prospect. It would all boil down to how sober and responsible we could act while bull shitting the guards who would most certainly be posted. The plan was simple. Under cover of darkness we would swoop in, acting in an official capacity and requisition (borrow) a pair of the doors from the Kennedy reception tent. They had more than they needed was our justification and they certainly had the resources for replacement. We had been told a clerical error had been the culprit in creating the gaping hole at our tent entrance and nothing more. Whatever the reason, the challenge of creating something good from the error was too tempting. I think the beer was also a factor. If successful we were promised beverages for the rest of the trip on the client. We were motivated. We were smart. No doubt in our minds this crazy band of gypsies was on the top of our game.

Our wait for darkness was essential on a myriad of levels. One, it gained us the extra measure of courage afforded by libations and another, item one would contribute to the plausibility of the story we would weave for the security we would surely encounter. After a reasonable amount of distance and with ten o'clock approaching it was go time. As a protective measure we felt it would be best if the pair of clients hang back out of the actual operation in case things went south. We had gotten the general lay of things the day before when at the reception and felt a measure of confidence. Our collective hearts thumped as the enormous tent came into view. Young Billy who had just turned 21 the day before and wanted to see 22 shifted nervously in his seat, head shaved like a space monkey.

We had our snips and wire cutters and were poised to the task. Besides, it wasn't like we were actually stealing. We were just settling accounts. We were doing good at some level I was convinced. As we circled the tent it was easy to settle on the far side set of doors, these which were relegated to wait staff and deliveries. This would certainly be the least offensive to lose and would cause a lot less outrage than if we had chosen one of the main entrance pairs. Clouded mind reasoning.

We backed the truck up into position and readied for attack. We had briefly discussed it and had decided it would make much more sense if I was to seek out security instead of the possibility of discovery during our impromptu visit in the night. This task only took a minute or maybe two. I think the heavy security coverage was based on the vast amounts of silver service and products poised in the structure for the next day's activities.

The pair of guards was atypical. One, an older black man with a paunch and slight limp and a gun belt laced with at least three speed loaders for his snub nose 38 police special revolver. It was obvious to me the gun had never been drawn much less fired and the thought of this man engaged in a gun battle requiring 21plus shots was ludicrous.

   The other was a much younger, slightly built white kid whose pimply face and oversized uniform were reminiscent of Barney Fife. Both were smiles as I approached as if the suddenness of our visit was a welcome element in the otherwise quiet and boring night. I launched into our story about the fact our large air-conditioned tent in the Olympic village had flagrantly been denied its allocated doors, the result being a very substandard situation which allowed all the mid-summer Carolina elements into our otherwise immaculate environment. This injustice could not stand. My passion peaked as I approached the portion of the tale including the fact we were to appropriate this set of doors and immediately install them into our tent. All this action was to take place before midnight so the tent AC system would have time to kick in and catch up cooling the area down. I was even amazed at the story intricacies that I threw up into the night air and watched swirl and dance under the stars.

   The eyes of the older guard grew wide as he felt exactly what my mission was. "Do you need a hand?" the pair tossed out to which I grunted approval. As we lumbered back toward my group the kid tried to contribute to the conversation with his appreciation to the older partner for getting him the job. In a spill of his guts he quickly volunteered that as a new 18 year old father he needed the extra night work to supplement the heavy expenses of a child that his day job at the small engine repair shop would not cover. The older man, who greatly slowed our procession, said it was ok because he liked having the company of the boy. This helped keep him awake he contributed adding that if he was caught asleep one more time he would be dismissed. He also had a long time day job and a daughter attending nearby NC State which caused an intense drain on the family finances. In an odd twist of fate his income was just high enough by a few hundred dollars annually to make him and his offspring ineligible for aid or grants above the 3500.00 level which is pointless in taking anyway these days. Funny how things work.

   Even in the pitch dark I could feel the weight under his muddy dark eyes. Each step I took made me more sober. In the distance I could see the alarm creeping across the faces of my compatriots. The last thing they expected was for me to invite the very group we were trying to avoid into our midst.

With such ease and grace? Everything was in place and ready for the trigger to be pulled . . . with four extra hands.

With a "thump" the shoe dropped and in a moment of clarity we did the right thing. My mind raced from the temporary fleeting glee of my clients to the embarrassment, disgrace and job loss for the pair of agreeable trusting souls. I looked into both pairs of eyes to take one last measure and make double sure about my decision. In surprise to all I explained to my team that we didn't have the proper written authorization for the exchange and these gentlemen would not be able to permit it.

I thanked the guards, shook hands and told them to have a good rest of the night. They replied with appreciative smiles not knowing or understanding what had just happened. As we piled back into the getaway vehicle I explained the alternate plan I had just shit. In the AM early we would take a trip with the same group to the Lowe's store on the interstate and purchase a set, do the install and be done by mid-morning. They (the clients) would have to understand.

When we got back to the bar I informed our clients that we had been stopped just at the brink and that a plan 'B' had been formulated. "That will work" was the quick reply and in the process two lives were spared. I felt good about that. Beer tasted a little bit better and the laughs were a little louder the rest of the night. It was all ok.

We completed the early task at a cost of less than $300.00 and got the install done. The rest of the event was relatively stable until the music portion just outside of the Olympic village. With the entertainment tailored to the participants and children's theme the adjoining amphitheater area featured the trio "Peter Paul and Mary". This seemed a perfect match and in my mind very low maintenance. The catering tent was nearby and consisted of a 20x 20 foot tent with four side walls and an open flap on each end. I was lounging and taking a deserved break near the rear service opening when I heard a scream and saw a medium sized roasted turkey attempting post mortem flight as it was hurled through the opening and onto the ground. Closely following was what I would assume to be dressing. From the comments of the attending staff I would assume that Mary had had some problem with the offerings and this was her distinct show of disapproval. The stream of profanities was electric and people slowly but surely moved from the line of fire. Amazing to say the least. I stood there unable to move as if under the spell of what I could only imagine a cobra or possibly a bear or sloth like creature. At least the athletes and other children were out of earshot. About five full minutes of this action was it for me so I moved on to calmer environs.

At the end of the day it was tear down and whisky with a side of rib eye at the O' Charlie's Restaurant in the hotel parking lot. All-nighter possibly so we would look and feel our best for the long trip back across the "Smokies". Good times? It took us about twelve minutes to shower and change and we were pulling on the door in no time. The collective smell of cologne was mind boggling. It was a mixture of Arimis and Polo or something, sort of sweet but not an Old Spice kind of thing. Either way I thought I would surely puke. Any doubt I had about not puking evaporated when we walked in and gazed upon the seating hostess, a real beauty. We had been joined by a few others who were equally fun loving and we decided quickly to play a little game that we often resort to in similar out of town situations.

It was very obvious from the stares that we were new and unfamiliar to the locals. We were not from around here. We had a little bit of a rock look about us as some of our party were complete with the long hair and tattoos and the more modern end of the spectrum with the short spiked locks dyed almost as white as mine was naturally. The game consists of the choosing of alter egos which we work into a collective story. The locals enjoy, we usually get some free drinks out of the deal and we get to see how far we can take it. Our whole plan was reinforced when our waitress shyly approached giggling and awkwardly stammered that they knew we were somebody famous but they didn't quite know who. I just smiled and said you may be right, planting the initial seeds, adding that we would like some privacy and drinks now and perhaps we would clue them in later. My job in this process is to decide and assign the names and back stories to the various affected parties.

The sudo-identities we selected were as follows:

Subject one: Jim. Jim was a lead guitar player in a local band I was helping book at the time. Jim had slightly reddish long hair halfway down the back. He was a little overweight and very quiet. He had no tattoos. He was a very accomplished guitarist with an acoustic guitar in his hotel room across the way. He would be Elijah Blue, son of Greg Allman and Cher. This was based on his shyness and slight resemblance to Greg A.

Subject two: Jerry. Jerry was a very muscular and tattooed up employee of the staging company who had homes in Dallas and Little Rock. He was dating off and on a model with the Ford Agency I think who was fed up with his road life but very fond of the money he would wire home. Jerry was very good with numbers and could very well have been a structural engineer. (Possibly in another life). His drink of choice was the vodka tonic which he could almost keep up with our draft beer drink for drink. He was a god in a bar room. Hair was very washed out blond short spiked like a punk. He, by virtue of his look was going to be the lead guitarist of the rock band Stone Temple Pilots. We had to be a little obscure yet believable.

Subject three/ four: A husband and wife team who were in town working at the Nascar track a hundred miles south at Rockingham on the South Carolina border. They were all decked out in the traditional Nascar shit and almost looked like pit crew members. Beyond that they contributed little. I had only met them the day before through some mutual friends and they had a permanent home in Little Rock. They would play the role of famed Nascar driver Mark Martin of Arkansas's team captains who would just be dining with the rock people by virtue of the Arkansas connection.

Subject five/ six: Two women who worked with us over the years. They owned and operated an event design company and specialized in large scale decorative element rentals. They would play the role of staff support to my company.

Subject seven: Young Billy. Billy had worked for us about two years with this being his first road trip. Billy was a good kid. He came from a religious background and his family in south Arkansas owned the longest continuous operating business in the state. The other significant thing was he had just turned twenty one two days before and had taken to beer like a pig to shit. Billy had shaved his hair to fur for the trip and naturally had the look of a roadie. This would be his designation.

Subject eight: Me. I have an air sometimes, good or bad, of taking charge from the get- go so would play the part of manager of something or other.

No one ever asked what.

   Sometime it's the information you don't supply that takes a life of its own and creates the path for the evening. Not being obvious and from the corner of my eye I could see the entire wait staff whispering and trying to get a look without seeming too obvious. We knew to act inconspicuous and like we were just trying to have a private dinner heavy with a hint of party. This was not difficult as these facts were the only totally true elements of the exercise. Things started to gel as we started our second round of drinks and were informed that they were on the house. I truly expected that would be the case at some point but nowhere near that early in the evening. This was working out. After a few rounds we decided on steak and the evening was officially launched.

   I think it was about halfway through the meal when two of the waitresses got up the nerve to make another pass. They held each other as they approached the most intimidating yet somehow approachable member of the dining party, me. I looked over my glasses at them as they once again offered the inquiry concerning the potential fame seated in the round. I politely told them I'd introduce everyone after dinner and maybe sign some autographs if they wanted.

   You would have thought I gave them a car. I followed them with a diverted, uninterested gaze as I saw them enter the kitchen and at least eight folks entering the speculative conversation. We were buzzing pretty good by the time dessert came around to which I passed. It was as if vultures watched our every move and waited for the opportunity to be invited back for the full story. After several more drinks we all had the courage to go into our parts and play to the hilt. We never really said more than a few words to set the stage and let the imaginations of the youngsters run wild. Guess they don't get out much. After a bit more time lapsed I motioned with my index finger and it was game on.

   It took a few minutes to make the introductions. The funniest thing about this was that the characters were so obscure and had nothing particularly in common as a group, yet as they were made several comments by our hosts inferred that that's who they thought they were. That's the bizarre power of suggestion. We were totally immersed at this point and with the place emptying out I decided to step it up for the possibility of staying later or after hours now that the young night manager was in the loop. I asked the excited group if they wanted Jim (Elijah) to play them some songs on acoustic. I added that he was really fond of the darker draft beers and I'm sure he would be happy to for a pint or two. He agreed and headed back to his room to retrieve his Gibson. I also inquired that if anyone had the STP CD in their car and a sharpie that we could probably get it signed. The beauty in that is there is never hardly ever a photo on dust jackets of support musicians. It's also a funny thing about autographs. They are often rough dramatic scribbles that are illegible. That is what is expected and what they will get. Amazingly about four individual covers were produced and about the time Jim made it back with his axe they were signed and handed over to the proud owners. As the last paying customers left, as I expected, the door was locked and an impromptu performance area was created. Jim can sing a little and in karaoke style I gave him a hand as we stumbled through some Allman Brothers classics such as "Whippin Post" and "Sweet Mellissa". The songs and the draft flowed free from the newly liberated taps. The entertainment didn't disappoint and everyone seemed thrilled. The dining floor was cleaned in record time and ready for the breakfast crowd.

Shit like this and that with the crazed bum in the pool hall always follows you if you will occasionally sit still and wait for it to happen. You never know from what direction the excitement will come but it most certainly will come.

The day today is a lot like most and as usual I switch into automatic pilot and attempt to get it done and in the bag. I'm not exactly sure what I want to do later and where I may or not eat but the rumbles down there reminded me it was in the cards. I don't think I'll have any beer tonight. I'm just not in the mood. Perhaps a movie. I think it was about three o'clock when Mexican George called. . .

The Era of Mexican George

Every once and a while you will run into a character who clicks into your system as if he has always been there. A fixture. Not like a lamp (nothing that illuminating) but maybe comfortable like a sofa. George is that guy. We met almost by accident. There is an area on the Riverfront which we had just developed into a new concert venue and that's how it all came together. He lives on the property of his employer just behind the sea wall on the river and is an expert welder, painter, ladies man, philosopher, hard drinker and student of life and the road. That's why he fell right in without even missing a step.

The new area we were using would eventually have underground power and water but for now that was not an option. This necessitated the need for us to find some alternate water source which happened to originate from a fire hydrant in his yard. The first time we met he was very helpful and offered his services for whatever we needed to which we gladly accepted. By the end of the day he was driving a forklift for us and helping spread gravel and was a fully fledged member of our site team.

He is 60 plus years old and from what I understood was born in very south Texas but he seems more like the original item. (Whatever that means). He has worked in pretty much every field of specialized labor and seems very well versed in all. There doesn't seem to be anything he can't do. He has a great sense of humor and can pretty much drink at the pace that I often employ. Although after about the eight or nine hour point I have noticed he gets a blank, shallow look just behind the surface of his eyes. This is the signal that I need to drop him somewhere, usually the house. He has a fondness for beer. Particularly liking whatever brand I may be drinking at the time. He also doesn't mind work at the spur of the moment and actually understands the value of it. That's rare but he is from that generation.

We have had some great conversations sitting on the docks at the river near the police boat launch. He lives as I said, just behind the sea wall in a large house with 16 guys who he lovingly but with an edge refers to as the "yo-yo's". Most are almost certainly illegal as they don't speak English and seem nervous at my presence and any other Anglos for that matter. I am picking up more and more Spanish and that's not a bad thing.

I mentioned earlier that he was a ladies' man. The bar is pretty low sometimes for him and that's ok but I have seen very attractive Latin ladies drive 5 hours for the privilege of his company. He must do something right. The other night he had some crazy bitch over that he had rescued in an alley from three drunken kids who were kicking the shit out of her. Details were a little sketchy about what provoked them but regardless she had at least one tooth in front missing and multiple other injuries. She was really out of it. Without much prodding she offered up the fact that she was part Hispanic and was visiting her son in jail from Southern California here in Arkansas. Beyond that the story spiraled into idiocy and included murder charges, juvenile detention and the fact the boy was a star quarterback at a local college. All this was between shots of an unlabeled and I'm sure illegal tequila. She was so out of control that after a short while I had to confront her about the fact that none of her info made any sense in a technical context. This was of no matter to her or the others who had begun to fill the room, enthralled by the exploits. They had hunger in their glassy eyes. That was my queue to excuse myself for less seedy pursuits.

It's always like that. There is either a lateness of the hour or mosquitoes or some other form of treachery that I am not in the least interested in pursuing. One important thing our relationship has brought me is a new sense of the racism in our country today.

I know that probably sounds very odd, given my geographical location in the traditional south with its ghosts of old and new tradition. This and the fact that I am a product of an all black Junior and Senior High School experience so I am very well versed in all types of hatred and violence that cross all lines. What I had never really considered or even noticed was the underlying current of hatred and distrust against Mexican Americans. It's not upfront, outward things. It's hidden. It's in people's looks. How they cut their eyes. How they answer questions. Where I first noticed was one afternoon after he had helped me work on something at the park I decided a nice cold beer up at the Irish pub Creegans would be a great reward. As we sat at the bar no one approached us for several minutes and in a very uncharacteristic move for me we sat quiet and just cooled off in the air that billowed hard from the ductwork. I thought, as we sat at the bar, that possibly the bartender was just busy until I saw them alternating to the back for a smoke break. This annoyed me a little but the last straw was when a tourist couple came in and sat adjacent to us. The bartender almost broke his neck to get around us and serve the pair. This pissed me off as it occurred to me what was up. I was embarrassed as I tried to measure what was on Georges mind by studying his features. He stared straight ahead, unmoved. Or was he so used to this type of treatment that he was not aware of it.

Regardless, he was my guest and this was not going down on my watch. "What the fuck is up, dude?" "How bout you pour us a couple of draft Lite beers before we get shitty". "And some chips would be great . . . thanks bro". George seemed pleased and smiled to himself, trying hard to not show too much emotion and void the small victory he had just been handed at the bartender's expense.

After that incident I made it a point to always take him to my favorite haunts and very loudly proclaim that he was my friend and with me. I also introduced him to all the bartenders and made damn sure that everyone knew he was not to be fucked with at any level. All this was done quietly of course by winks, nods and inflections. Once accomplished, he was soon a fixture and cherished local character around my world and I was always tickled when I would walk into a joint and it would be announced to me that Mexican George had just left, usually with some chick.

The other day I got a huge surprise when I called his cell to see if he wanted to pick up a couple of bucks doing a security job at the submarine for me only to have his phone answered by a stranger. On the other end of the line was a very frantic acting black woman. She proceeded to weave a tale for me that caught me totally off guard and seemed a little more than out of character. Apparently he and the woman had been riding in her car in Brinkley, Arkansas, which is near Memphis. Why he was there is unclear but what were clear were the alcohol and the traffic stop. The result was several outstanding warrants in Jefferson County Arkansas for DUI and failure to appear. She went on to explain that he had given her his phone for safe keeping, which I didn't buy and subsequently corrected, and was taken straight to jail where he was given a mandatory 60 days and a fine. This was the entire summer. He missed all of the shows that I really needed him on. I'm sure he's a lot sadder about that than me. The jail time would only add to his allure and I'm sure he had no trouble picking right up where he left off. As my dad would always say "Did you learn anything?"

Another example of what "Mexy G" has helped me notice. The other day a kid drowned. This 18year old Hispanic kid was blowing leaves from the seat of a riding lawn mower at the Clinton Presidential Library. The hills there are very steep and slope toward the Arkansas River. Near the Rock Island Bridge or "Bridge to the 21st Century" it is speculated that at a tipping point he and the mower flipped into the drink.

On television within the hour pictures showed the Sheriff's department hoisting the mower out and onto the shore but no body. Three days of searching by divers and patrols turn up nothing. Distraught, the family gets involved when the department suspends its search. The news report photos showed about twenty family members, some with waders standing along the bank. With ropes tied around the waists of the others as safety lines from the current they proceed to swim and search along the bank. In about an hour they locate and retrieve the beloved son, cousin and brother and the coroner is called. The body is in about ten feet of water and is twenty feet from the original accident site. My eyebrows are raised at this point. George and I sat at the pool hall one Friday night and talked about this. It had been about a week since and I had looked at it from many angles. I told him my conclusion was I was angry. He looked at me with his usual cloudy, unsmiling and sullen eyes and shrugged. I knew exactly what he meant by the expression. I also understood exactly why he didn't have words. He didn't want to go there. As the point was pushed by me he just looked a little sad and still said nothing as he stared into his half full beer.

When your super heroes can't fly...

All people have them. Heroes. Usually it's early on when they are developed. Not as early as in the childish infatuations that mark developmental milestones and are prone to change like leaves in the wind. These are influential people and ideas that somehow shape who you are and what you may at least attempt to mold yourself into. It's in the way you walk. The way you dress. Hairstyle. At least it is in phases. However, even with the changes of opinion you always retain small bits that end up making up how you are and what you have become.

When older you become more and more reflective. It's very interesting how you feel and cope with the passing or short comings of people you once held in esteem. In my case one was the Marshall Tucker Band. When I was an early teen the group and their strange mix of southern rock and jazz fusion hit the scene in my area like an atomic explosion. All my friends had the same sentiments and a type of kinship was born that stands to this day.

They touched me in a way that seemed to say that where we were from was more than ok. It's called southern affirmation. It was almost desirable to be from the south. And then there were the songs and lyrics. Every bad or failed relationship was somehow healed by the pain and hurt oozing out of "Can't you see". It's as if we were somehow spared from the worst of it by relying on the experience of these voices in the dark corners of our rooms. They were always strong and reliable and men to count on. Not at all like an absentee father.

We even had a small cottage industry making handmade t shirts with images from album covers. Later in life I had the good fortune of working with the band on several occasions unfortunately after the death of the original lead singer. His place had been taken by the very capable Doug Grey who was also the final remaining founding member. In one of my Northwest Arkansas engagements I really bonded with them and spent some time after the show. There we sat in production, passing around a gallon of Jack Daniels and swapping war stories.

I was in heaven but they, including my guys, would never known it. They were genuine and true as I had always imagined. The first chink in the armor was on the same show. Our sound man was one of the best in the business at turning knobs and with reluctance and a binding contract we turned the board over to the bands sound guy. The great clear sound we had for all the opening acts was destroyed within minutes as I noticed that Doug and his inner ear monitor were either not functional or he was deaf. Turns out the latter.

Like Pete Townsend, years of over amplified music had taken its toll. He was unaware of the fact he was having his man totally distort the sound to accommodate his hearing loss in an effort to hear the music. This caused him to strain on vocals and the overall band to look at each other through each selection as if searching for direction. It was a little disturbing but unnoticeable to the overly intoxicated crowd of zit covered pancake tit flashing yokels.

I also joined in the passing thought that must have circulated that it was just a bad night. We all have them on occasion and this was no different. A couple of years later was a different story. There is a large established event in Little Rock called Riverfest which is held each Memorial Day weekend and one that it has never been my displeasure to work. This particular year I noticed that the band was headlining, albeit on the final night and on the south forty stage which would be par for the committee. My group and I couldn't wait and planned a whole day around beer and Bar B Que in anticipation of the evening. We were early and had the proper head on our collective shoulders appropriate to the occasion and took our places in the parking lot under the bridge. The stage that would accommodate the band was on the small size but probably suitable for an enterprise whose last hit was over 25 years prior.

Before they went on I eased over to the backstage fence to say hi and got the proverbial brush off. It could have been my attitude or condition, either of which was understandable. I let it pass. As they took the stage and I took to my feet I noticed something wrong. It was obvious to me as I saw Doug in the wings punching his ear while the rest of the band was on the second approach of the first song. A lump was coming in my throat. I was embarrassed for him and me. The buildup of the day had allowed me to shower enthusiasm on my guests and I could feel their eyes on us both. When Doug finally hit the stage I could see his pain from across the asphalt surface. They had started with one of the classic hits. As he parted his lips only a squeak tumbled out and fell on the deck of the stage. He, for whatever reason was unable to sing due to a catastrophic failure. It was as if his voice had been strained to the point of injury and there was nowhere to hide. He was front and center in the glare of the spot light. What I could see clearly was a glisten on his cheek as he turned in terror toward one of the younger yet equally talented band members. Without hesitation the youngster jumped into the vocals without missing a beat strangely like this was not new, Doug faded back into the shadows.

For some reason, which I will blame on hormones, I began to cry. I'm not big on showing emotions in public but this was totally unavoidable. I had done all I could to discount what I had known to be true. Here it was in living color. To see your heroes crash and burn. It was one of those moments when you have a rush of emotion that is a combination of your own mortality and feeling for someone your senior who is now for pasture.

It was a little more than I wanted at the moment and I hugged my friends and they knew. I took a slug of flask whisky and said a prayer. That's all I can do.

The Circus Witch...

I have over the years had an interesting relationship with circuses and carnival folk. I'm not saying I ever aspired to run off and join the circus. I would never be that arrogant. But I did somehow associate myself with the lot and often to this day enjoy their company.

It must have all started when at about 13 years of age a fortune teller at the Arkansas state fair while palm reading looked me straight in the eye and informed me I would someday be killed by a jealous husband. Hoax or not that can scar a kid. I took it to heart even though I was somewhat unclear to what was actually implied.

This encounter though sparked a curiosity which had to be quenched. A fire, however brief, had been lit. Subsequently I began to seek out other fortune tellers and mystics in the area for further clarification as to what I could do to save my precious life. It was a little odd to me that most of the mediums were in their forties and mainly slightly overweight, cake makeup, heavy around the eyes. Seemingly in an attempt to keep the orbs from sinking ever further into the skull from which they gaze. They never wanted cash which I had little. Love was often on their minds.

As a young man I didn't mind this arrangement. I guess this may have led to the fact a fair measure of my girlfriends prior to my 18th birthday were generally in their mid forties. I loved them every one. It was hick town trailer park bliss. What it was short of was answers. It took no time to become aware of the fact it was all bull shit spun from bad liars. One visit was all I needed to see clearly but I never let on. I never complained.

But…the real carnival people knew how to live. They were pretty much a collection of misfits, as one would guess, but could party with the best. We would befriend some of the group, usually at the fair, and go back after closing to hang out. They generally were never allowed by management to leave the site to go into town and would be more than willing to pay us to provide the hard liquor they were unable to obtain through traditional means.

The midway would be closed and it would be surreal to be drunk on your ass in a deserted midway. Drinking whisky and riding rides with the thin, tanned skinned women of the road. They knew how to live. They only took what they needed for the day and may or may not leave some for tomorrow. Usually not. They required less sleep than anyone I've met before or since and loved with a passion in the straw that would cause a bovine to blush. They were goddesses after dark.

But in the light they changed. They had previously shadow hidden paunches and dry aged wrinkles that traced roadmaps on the face to almost match the miles logged. Dark circles of sleepless nights, alcohol soaked livers and Y's that gleamed in the overheads like prizes the night before. Much like Christmas presents the next day. Piles of debris. They were a metaphor for what they had chosen to be.

Nothing is ever as it seems. In the light of day everything always loses its magic. Things change. Soberness and clarity make truth out of mud. We didn't at this time give a shit about clarity. Clarity didn't keep us from crawling under the tent flap. Thank god for the autumn and the dead leaves that would love us till dawn.

Gone fishin. . .

    I don't fish any more. This is a little unusual in a state called "The Natural State" partly by virtue of the fact it is home to a multitude of rivers and lakes that hold many fishing world records. I'm not saying I didn't ever. The Arkansas River has always pretty much been in my backyard and I can't remember when it wasn't there in the background.

    This river is a very dangerous place with its sudden drop offs and sink holes peppered with hidden swirling currents. Many foolhardy drunks or depressives have ended it all there by choice or not. My mom always knew if I had been in for a dip based on my underwear being a consistent shade of pale brown.

    When my Dads work had moved from mid-downtown to a block from the river a whole world of leisure time woke up and a tradition of lunch time bank fishing for catfish was born. Just across the street and down Rock Street was the actual "Little Rock" for which the city was named. The monument sits at the base of an old railroad bridge called the Junction Bridge built around the turn of the century. The way the bridge piling is situated a very deep hole formed by virtue of a natural whirlpool along the bank. Over the years this had become home to some of the larger and older fish who would sit in the shade and wait for floating edible debris.

This would be my home for lunch breaks. I had begun the habit of packing a sandwich to expedite things and had a cane pole like they use in black and white movies as also the old men over by the airport. This instrument was dutifully kept on the back loading dock.

You always in the back ground hear news stories that generally have no direct impact on you until somehow through a strange series of events one is developed, in this case a double murder suicide. One of the other major road bridges just up river is the elegantly designed Broadway Bridge. For some reason this bridge is the frequent site of many suicide jumpers who choose the 100ft plus fall into the center most preferable for selfish purposes. This generally places you 1500 ft from either shore if you survive the fall and the plunge into water that is up to 80ft deep. Not promising for you. Then the fact the sheriffs rescue boat will take fifteen minutes at the minimum to launch and get to where you might have been earlier.

You're just pretty much fucked which I guess was your whole plan. In this case it was a little more tragic than the routine suicide of a homeless person or jilted drunk. This was tragic and sinister. Happens that drugs were a factor as is more and more customary. Seems that a young black couple with very small children had become desperately hooked on drugs. They had decided in a terrible fight over drugs or money or both that they were going to split and go separate paths and to dead ends no doubt. The two details which had not been resolved had been the 3 month and 16 month old children who had been a result of the somewhat better days of times past.

One can only guess in a cloud of poor judgment the father had decided that his spouse was ill prepared as was he to take them to raise. I guess they had no family support to take them in and the state was not an option for whatever reason. The decision was unthinkable. He chose to park his shitty Toyota Camry at the foot of the bridge, take the children and hike to the bridge center. Here witnesses stated that one by one he dropped the desperately clutching children over the side in broad daylight and subsequently followed in suit. Three lives were lost in the muddy water that

Tuesday afternoon.

Like I had said these events, however disgusting, were of no real consequence to me in my life. The last day I fished was like any other. The sky was clear and blue. The transistor radio I had with me was playing one of my favorite songs. My sandwich was peanut butter and jelly and I washed it down with a Dr. Pepper in a 12oz bottle I had purchased for twenty five cents from my dad's vending machine.

Traffic was light and I gathered up my tackle and headed on over. The horrible events from the Tuesday last were well out of mind and all I even remembered was that no bodies were ever recovered. This may sound weird but not unusual. Often time's jumpers will get held to the bottom by current or become entangled in debris such as logs. When this happens they often are not found for weeks and often wash up downstream in the town of Scott. They are at this point usually unrecognizable shells after being toyed with by the predatory turtles and bottom feeding catfish.

This was not the case today. I had been there maybe fifteen minutes and just got settled into the shade when I noticed something odd. Catfish are a bottom feeder and generally you sink your bait to the bottom to lure them. With this in mind you generally do not use a float or "bobber" to signal a strike. This day I was using a line only. The last thing I remember was watching the people across the river on the other bank having lunch time clandestine rendezvous.

I bit into my sandwich and then I saw the doll floating in a circular motion in the whirlpool about twenty feet or so from the bank. It was in a pink jumper and looked exactly like some of my sisters dolls she used to have as a kid, plump and somewhat off color, A non racial look of off grayish tan. Then there was the other. As soon as my eye trained on the one another doll bobbed up just behind the other and chased it as if in play. At first it was just odd to me, the coincidence that two objects so similar would be in the same whirlpool in my catfish hole. My first impulse was to snag one and drag over to at least end the disruption.

I pulled up my line and noticed my bait gone so the opportunity arose. I pulled my line up high and after the third try my small treble hook grabbed the meat or as I thought plastic of the calf of the smaller form.

As I pulled toward me I noticed the eye color. My sister had always had many dolls and I was very familiar with the flip up plastic eyes of the standard toys. This was not like that. The eyes were milky white and filmed over. Where the ears were had been chewed off and only openings were visible on the sides of the head. The skin was light grey at the outer edges and I noticed the fingers were also gone.

I pulled the one onto the bank and with the smell hitting me I puked the third of the sandwich and my drink onto the "Little Rock" and tried to collect my thoughts. After a minute I realized I had to suck it up and get the other secured. This was a little more difficult as it was a little farther out but after about ten tries the pair laid face up on the bank in the mud like snow angels or silhouettes. I knew the police had to get involved at this point and I hauled ass across to the shop and made the call. It took about five minutes for the first to arrive but soon there was a crowd. There were three police cars and two ambulances. Several of the local business people started to congregate and were not allowed to cross the hastily erected police crime scene tape. No one knew exactly what the deal was but soon I had pieced it together. These were the young ones that had been dropped into the dark place by the one they trusted…to play with the monsters? I answered questions and just the gist of them confirmed my suspicions about what exactly I had come across. I had never seen an unprepared dead body before and there was something about the scale of a dead child that I was in no way ready for. I sat there on the bank for awhile. At my feet was the remainder of the sandwich and the empty soda bottle.

I remember the bodies being bagged in bags that were five or six times too big and how they shifted around while being carried to transport. I remember seeing them drive away under flashing lights. I remember the police officer shaking my hand. They never found the father and the mother I heard moved I think to Houston. After I noticed the crowd going back to work I felt like it was time to head back and I grabbed up my pole and looped my line and hook as I always would around and secured. I went back to the office and laid my pole back on the rear of the loading dock just under the edge so as not to allow rot. I was about ten minutes late back and my dad gave me a hard look that really bothered me as if I had done something wrong by unwittingly participating. He wanted no details. I was late.

I didn't fish again and years later I saw that my pole was where I had laid it that day. I never visit the "Little Rock" either. Anytime the wind blows just right and I'm near that site I sometimes think I hear a cry or I may see a flash of pink in the water. When this happens I always get back to work whatever I'm doing and remember what my dad said. "You're late".

Uncle Buddy...

Buddy was not my uncle. He was my dad's boss and the owner of a local printing company. He went by many nicknames, some acknowledged and some not. There was "little Caesar", "Bubbles", "Uncle Buddy" and "Satan" among many others. We used to say he was too evil to ever die but the other day he proved us wrong.

There was no family outside of an older bedridden sister who is virtually blind and deaf at this point. He was 91. Buddy started out his life downtown on the east side of present day Interstate 30 in the final year of World War 1. I believe his childhood was probably spent on the porch and away from the ire of the local thugs and more athletic and rambunctious locals. That was just an impression I got because I never knew him to have any real friends and he never spoke of any of this. Old habits die hard so to speak.

What I did know I found out by accident once in the storage room behind some boxes. There in the shadows I found an object in an old and important looking case. Once pulled out and opened it revealed its cargo of a brass plated trumpet. Upon further investigation I learned that in the big band era he had been an accomplished trumpeter in several regional bands. This fact was very odd to me considering I knew for a fact that he had never tasted alcohol of any kind. Working in a club would in my mind be an unbearable temptation for a young man but I guess he had his reasons for abstinence.

During the war to follow he received a deferment due to flat feet or some such shit and I'll assume out of guilt chose to serve as the reproduction person at the Little Rock Army Corps of Engineers office. Little Rock at the time had a large regional presence primarily to serve in the development of the river navigation route with its later multiple locks and dams and several manmade lakes.

This was where he learned his trade. The Farrell brothers had actually started a blueprinting company a few years earlier and decided to bring him in as a partner toward the end of the war in 1946. He owned no particular great skills in his field but was more of a conduit to the lucrative government printing contracts currently in the wind. His partners were not of great stock either and were prone to terrible bouts of depression and alcoholism. One of which would end his life with a single 38 caliber bullet to the temple in 1961 and the other a failed liver almost ten years later to the day.

Both Farrell's regularly cleaned out the cash register on Fridays for poker and gin cash. My dad stood by as manager and watched. With them out of the picture Buddy was allowed to hold court and operate virtually unchecked aside from the yearly stockholders meeting with the widows. A pair which included a maniacal lunatic alcoholic named Alice and a dense headed misshapen doll with fish eyes calling herself Ruby.

At an early age I began to recognize ineptness toward the most benign tasks in him. He always seemed to do things the long and most difficult way and seemed to draw great displeasure at being corrected by others, especially children like me, of which he had none. His evil twin was his wife. She was a very sick and bitter woman who slept every night under an oxygen tent. She had a cane and I seem to remember a metal head of some type that was always tightly enveloped by her boney pale hand with the throbbing blue veins.

She hated us and saw us as a necessary evil. We did what she could not and we enabled the coin that would flow to her and her husband. At our older location in the basement at 3rd and Spring Street we all shared one chair for lunches at her request. Each guy got ten minutes to eat after which the wooden arm chair would be turned over to the next. When we moved our location toward the river in the late 70's there was a room on the mezzanine that was originally for storage. The company had no particular need for it so we were allowed to create a lunch rooms for ourselves. We attacked the project with optimism and zeal and after about a week of effort we were ready. We had used old plywood and 2x4"s to create a counter on two sides of the room. A collection was taken and a used ping pong table was purchased and placed in the room center. It was comfortable and more important it was ours.

Everyone felt for once that things were going to change for the better and an up-beat feeling was contagious. Then she showed up one afternoon. The room had been used by our group for about two weeks and even my dad was amazed at what this bunch of kids had accomplished. She was walking around on the 2nd floor and mezzanine when I heard the yell crash over the huge metal fire door that hung in the stairwell.

It was my dad being summoned and it was not pleasant. Once he had made the stairs all I could hear was a muffled somewhat heated conversation and the occasional tap of the aluminum walker on the hard concrete floor. The vibration from the tap seemed harder and more violent with each tense passing moment. Shortly my pop came down, went straight to the cash register and grabbed a twenty and motioned over Carroll. He was our senior delivery driver and after a muted conversation was handed over the bill and promptly left the building. We kept to our work until the wicked witch had departed and tried to make eye contact with anyone who might shed light. After a bit Carroll reentered the business carrying a small brown bag from Besser Hardware on Main Street. Everyone was still totally in the dark and could not imagine what could be happening. The next day would yield answers when a couple of us arrived early and went up to play a little table tennis and were met, to our surprise with our room padlocked.

Evidently after everyone had left my dad had returned and installed the hasp and lock. He had been instructed that we could not effectively serve the company with those kinds of distractions. The other bitch of it was our table and furnishings we had constructed were locked inside. It was back to the lunch chair. She was most assuredly the dominant force in their relationship which lasted fifty years. They had as I mentioned no children and allowed only the comfort and companionship of a pair of Pekinese dogs who had continual eye infections. After the over ten year old dogs passed into the light they were summarily stuffed and eventually put in a room housing other trophies purchased such as mounted bass and deer heads.

Because of the affection for the pups and lack of family upon the wife's death a large sum was donated to the local humane society. It is rumored he would do the same. Buddy was legendary as a miser. He would argue over the slightest amount of money where others were concerned but would drive an RV to work every day at four miles to the gallon of gas.

We received raises on our minimum wage every time Congress mandated it. I took the janitor position and mopped twice weekly as a supplement and seemed to each week garner more and more resentment when I received my extra $15.00 in cash. It was almost not worth it to be brow beaten. I decided to take a job that would immediately double my salary for almost the same duties at a time I had been married almost three years and was expecting my first child. You would have thought I had burnt the building down. I had always been despised for trying to do better and ambitioned was frowned upon. This would cause even more of a rift and although I would carry the company as its best customer through several recessions including black Friday in 1987 I would never have a seat at the table.

I was dead to them. This fact was of no consequence to me and I had hoped that at the very least he had gotten something for our captive game table. I had already developed a deep dislike for them and everything they represented. In some weird way I think they by their actions had caused me to work hard toward a positive direction. I can't bother myself then or now with overly negative people. Life is too short. What sealed it all for me was my Dad's retirement party.

Something happened of which I'm not sure one day. My dad got mad. This was not uncommon but this time was different. That very afternoon he walked into Buddy's posh but garish office and relayed his intention to retire. On the anniversary of his start in 1951 he would clock out with 50 years under his belt. This is an impressive feat on the surface but even more when we discovered in his personnel records that he had accomplished this with only two sick days and no tardiness.

He was the one who opened the doors and the one who locked up at night. Buddy had a terrible dilemma and decided in principle to close the business within months of the party. The party, which was held at noon at the office, was well attended by many old and familiar faces. Some not seen in over twenty years and some important broken fences (Andy) were mended that day.

Buddy chose not to attend. He decided to go to Hot Springs and bass fish that day. In addition the check to contribute to the party expenses had by an error not been authorized. My dad never knew but my mom picked out and paid for cake and she and I took on the gold plated watch engraved with a big "50" and in script "good job". The bar-b-que and potato salad was the result of a collection. Never had Bill been so proud and down deep I was glad the bigger asshole than myself had taken a powder. His final gesture for an entire life spent spoke volumes about the character of the man.

As is common with a trickledown theory all I could associate with the dedication to service was how many games of catch I had been denied because of work. Selfish I know, but I'm just being honest. I thought of how my youth had been squandered by this man and his demands and how I in turn would perpetuate this cycle with my own offspring.

These things crossed my mind. They did not stay there long and we celebrated the day. The cake was cut into big squares of white thick icing with vanilla ice cream on the side on red paper plates. As promised soon after the party the business closed its doors. The drive and fire that had sustained it was not there any longer. The car would not function without an engine and for once the truth poured out and nobody really cared.

I can't say it was a sad day. The man who would not die finally succumbed the other day. I heard the news several days later and in a twist he died on New Year's Eve. It was almost symbolic of the end of things on the final afternoon of the final day. He had been in the hospital for pneumonia and had actually been doing better. During his late afternoon bed check he was discovered by a nurse face down slumped into his serving tray. I believed it was to be spaghetti day. For some reason he was buried almost a week later and at his request had a closed casket. The day of the funeral was a terrible day weather wise with sleet and freezing rain complicating the all outdoor service. We were going to attend but bailed at the last minute due to the inclement mess. My dad went anyway and sat in the car for the sparsely attended ten minute service. Ice sickles formed on the casket he said and dripped long into the waiting hole.

Adios Bubbles!

In an even stranger twist the other day I was hanging in the old man section at the pool hall bar when my phone rang. This is not unusual in itself but it was my dad calling and that was out of the norm on a Friday night. On the line there was an exuberant voice of a man with big news. Seems a letter came in the mail informing him that he was the beneficiary of an inheritance from Buddy's estate. I think I shit right there on the stool.

Ghosts of Vietnam

I'm not exactly sure where I fall on the whole ghost or "spirits' if you will concept. I think it's one of those things where if you see one you believe and it's maybe best just not to discuss it either way. If you draw too much attention you may become a target, a lot like I feel in Park Slope Brooklyn or China Town San Francisco. It's an over the shoulder uneasiness.

Why I'm saying this is I think on one occasion I had an experience. The story starts with Viet Nam and the war. I was fortunate to fall into that narrow slot of too young and too old that sometimes benefits certain generations of young men and women in this country. In the case of the Viet Nam conflict it ended close to my sixteenth birthday and I was sweating the proverbial bullets. I had witnessed at least half a dozen of my school mate's older brothers coming home in boxes or worse just shy of age nineteen. This created a strain in the air for everyone my age as we considered a prolonging of the conflict and the callousness of the people who ran the country at the time. Anyone who tells you those kids were not cannon fodder is full of shit no matter how patriotic you may feel. It was not like World War 2. My dad served in the Pacific theater fighting against Japan and was the only member of my immediate family to be regular army. The rest of my family were all Navy. One much older cousin in particular went to diving school and graduated into a munitions salvage operation in the Vietnamese inland rivers. This was considered extremely hazardous duty as one would expect. The job consisted of exploring the murky waters for sunken US boats, locating and destroying left behind ammunition. This was in an attempt to keep the enemy from doing the same operation but for salvage purposes.

The water, in a constant state of churn was described to me as soup like. There was no apparent life except the occasional large and alien like turtles and the ever present crabs of various sizes who fed on the constant supply of the less fortunate. You could not see your hand in front of your face. Most of the divers in the group would only last about three months at a time before transferring by necessity or request by superiors. Either way it was not a long term occupation by any stretch. Stress like that kills.

My older cousin Butch seemed very well suited for the duty and for some reason volunteered for two tours. He really had nothing at home except a house full of younger asshole siblings, a disabled dad and an obese mother who could only carry her girth short distances. I assume the job was a more appealing prospect. As it was described one particular mission was in a very dangerous hot spot. The area had been left simply under surveillance for about a month in an effort to allow some sort of stability to engulf the area of the sunken wreckage.

Once a comfort level was achieved a detail was scheduled with Butch in the lead and it was time to go. The water was particularly churned from upstream shelling and visibility even with high power flood lights was literally about six inches. In these types of conditions the only option is to feel your way around the wreck and locate the objective. After a short while of groping around the torn metal of the deck he reached an open hatch that could be reached from below. Apparently the boat had settled on its side in the mud with its payload of dead weight pressing it deep into the muck.

It was not good procedure to enter the vessel until it had been cleared to do so and the thickness of the water had prevented this portion of the operation. He did however reach into the opening as he had come this far and felt like at least a futile effort was better than no effort at all. As he reached into the abyss his hand brushed against something uncommon and unexpected. First reaction was to grasp and pull the object from the hatch and to the surface. The object seemed buoyant to a degree and was perhaps a bag of something, possibly important, and was retrieved. The trip to the surface was a matter of minutes as more debris in the form of broken logs floated by causing an obstruction. He held tight to his prize.

As the surface was growing nearer he started to realize the consistency of this hand full was changing in his grasp. It was starting to feel more of an organic nature than that of a knapsack or other object. He and the object both broke water at the same instant and as he cleared his fogged mask he started to realize yells in his direction from the waiting crew on the deck of the boat. A few moments passed and as he looked into his glove he realized he had retrieved the upper torso of a black soldier who had been submerged with the parasites of the river for possibly the month.

As he studied the empty eye sockets he blacked out and passed below the surface from shock. His buddies fished him and his gear to the deck. The visitor was sent adrift after retrieving his dog tags for identification purposes. There was no way to transport the remains in their condition and the living was the current priority and keeping them that way. For butch it would be a regular hospital in Saigon for some months and then a transfer to a more suitable psychiatric facility.

Things got better and soon it was determined that he could travel and be a functioning member of society. With this decided he was soon on a troop transport and a relatively short time later touching down on his home turf in Kansas City. It was a joyous home coming and us being eight hours away by car we piled in and headed north for the series of supportive gatherings that would surely be planned. We arrived the next morning to a totally unexpected scene at the family home. We were to soon find out that there had been a terrible accident on his first night back. Having not driven in a very long time but insisting to he had traveled with one of his two teenage sisters over to pick up a friend who would be his future sister-in-law.

Along the way after the stop he lost control on the Interstate. Witnesses said the car left the road at a high rate of speed and rolled over several times. Seat belts were non-existent at the time and his sister was partially thrown out the window and rolled over by the vehicle. Every bone in her body was broken and death was instant and merciful. Butch survived with minimal injuries with the other passenger suffering a broken nose and lacerations. It was suspected he had been drinking beer, probably the first in a year. All were in shock.

No one could believe that this could be the outcome of his ordeal in the jungle and his long journey back to life. Dad called his boss in Little Rock and with hushed tones explained the situation in the small back room near the washer and dryer. The next day was quiet. The leaf was put in the kitchen table adding the extra eighteen or so inches that would be needed to accommodate the bowls of mashed potatoes, corn on the cob and tins of fried chicken of various earthen hues that would seem to fall from the sky.

No one made eye contact. About mid morning, possibly 10 AM people began to stir toward the front entrance. It was like the unknown and silent language of bees as possible intrusion threatens the hive. A car had pulled up, hugging the curb. With the help of his slightly younger very unattractive brother he was pulled from the backseat of the Century Skylark. Butch had an enormous cast that would cover in totem from ankle to hip. It was bright white and fresh as were the aluminum crutches fresh from some hospital supply storage room. What seemed an eternity was his triumphant walk up the driveway and into the house. As before, no eye contact was made and nothing was heard except Invasion of the Body Snatchers on the black and white console living room TV and the shortness of breath at the weight of the cast.

As the threshold was crossed and he embraced his poor excuse for a mother tears erupted and emotion filled the room thick and stifling. The parade proper had caught all the attention and no one even noticed that Candy, the other surviving passenger was following the rear with terribly large and leaking bandages hiding tears in her forehead and chin. She was not the subject but merely collateral damage. At this point I excused myself as I felt an outsider to this private pain.

Eventually he was given more of his pain medication and was tucked into his old bed in his old room. It was strange for a badly broken man to return to the bed of his youth. A bed too short for his frame. A bed for dodging school and the occasional wet dream. A comfort zone surrounded by old track ribbons and wrestling trophies, some without men on their perches, long broken off during play. There he slept and dreamed his dreams that hoped the last 48 hours to have not had passed. Dreams that he had just not made his last kill in a battle that began two years and three months before. The funeral was worse. Two days of mourning had passed. The unending supply of food had been partially consumed.

I always wondered why food is thrown into a situation where a meal is the last thing on your mind. At the insistence of the family there would be an open casket at the funeral home service. The casket was a pale rose metallic color and had brass or faux brass hardware. It was very nice. The brothers were pall brothers along with some friends. All were still in high school.

The condition and lack of structure in the body had required the introduction of an expansive gas into the cavity allowing it to be stuffed with paper into a near appropriate shape. The effort was not the desired one and she came off very rounded and without form. There was also a purple discoloration above the eyes, which were naturally exceptionally large in the expansive sockets. Sort of a Cro-Magnon look. There would be no graveside service as everyone was ready to turn the page on this scene plus the 650 dollar savings for the tent and chair rental as well as the motorcycle escort that stayed in my uncle's pocket.

Butch sat on the front row with his cornstarch and flour hardened appendage protruding into the isle. Great things were said. As many as could be said about a sad and ugly tenth grader who had been snatched out of first period, none of it her fault. A true victim in every sense of the word. I couldn't say what was transpiring as I was studying the intricate stenciling that ran along the ceiling line of the chapel room in the strip shopping center mortuary. I believe it was paper that had been applied by some method, probably glue. The maroon wall paint made the room look smaller. After the service everyone retreated once more to the house. We opted out of our tenth chicken dinner in half that many days and prepared for the eight hour journey back up and down the mountains and home. We would stop in Harrisonville, Missouri and have burgers and fries that would become our entire on the road consumption.

Dad had to for sure be back at work tomorrow and me in school. We pulled into the driveway in 7 hours and 59 minutes. I didn't think much about any of this for many years and after skipping the next years Thanksgiving in Liberty Missouri things began to seem normal. Normal as you can be under the circumstances. Butch, I did believe received some VA counseling and within a short time would re-enter society and his rightful place in line. The walking wounded which were everywhere at that time. Then it gets weird.

When I was in the eleventh grade I was dating a girl a year younger than myself who lived out in the country near my school. We had had a mutual attraction of a purely physical nature. A girl of a high school boy's dreams as it were. Our relationship demanded many late night trips through the farmland down narrow and dimly lit roads. The main road back toward the highway and my house passed a strange extremely tight switchback, no doubt a property dispute settlement which had been the site of several traffic fatalities over a forty or fifty year period. A proverbial dead man's curve.

It was very dark here with a single light on a single pole at the height of the turn. Most of the victims had been wasted drag racers of the red neck variety, drunk with Jim Beam or Jack and the need for added quickness in the night. Not from the area, unfamiliar with its perils. I was very aware of this area and slowed for the turn almost slow enough to read the names on the Styrofoam makeshift grave markers leaned in memoriam against the aging and scared pole.

I was also familiar with how the lone night watcher light would play against the mirrors of my Pontiac and light up the back seat. I was totally unprepared for this night. At about 9:30PM, as ten was curfew on school nights I approached and began to round the curve. There was a strange low slung fog on the fields encroaching the road heavy enough that it could not be easily sliced. About the time I turned the wheel I began to feel the hair on my neck standing on end as if by electrical inducement. The light began to shift and travel up the black bucket seats and there it was in my rear view mirror. I looked up and in the flash of pale light I saw my cousin staring silent at me from the backseat into the mirror. Her eyes were unmistakably large and round as I remembered and looking at me with a dull stare, not exactly angry or menacing but obviously startling as you would expect.

My first reaction was to attempt to brake but in the confusion hit the nearby gas petal propelling me just past the pole, through the ditch and fence and into the field. At 20mph this was not necessarily a perilous maneuver. I rested there for a moment in the safety and cover of the corn.

In an instant I had popped open the glove box and retrieved my flashlight, the beam I directed immediately into the rear compartment. Empty. The feeling I had on the back of my neck before was also lifted and I sat there with my thoughts for another moment.

The only sound being my heartbeat and shortness of breath. After I collected myself which involved puking into a bush I backed up and eased the car back onto the road. Luckily I had sustained no damage short of my own mental. I made record time back to the house and upon entry ran directly down the hall and to my parent's bedroom closet which was home to the massive volumes of family photo albums and clippings. After my third attempt the proper selection was located and the article found. There was a tattered news clip scotch taped in place describing the accident which had drawn my cousin into the light. Upon inspection I realized the accident had occurred at around 9:30 on the same date as that day five years before. I closed the book, sat there a moment and went to bed. I never spoke of this.

The big move. . .

I quit counting many years ago how many times I've driven coast to coast. I know every single wretched stop that is worth a shit. Where to get a burger. How far you have to go in one day. Where to get gas. Where to piss. Where to sleep. This particular trip was totally different. This one was special. One way it was different was it was a winter trip with a trailer in tow and particularly treacherous in westward mountain situations.

Around Christmas Amber had graduated college in Chicago and with all her worldly possessions in Little Rock in storage it was time to gather all and head west and the next chapter in her life. Three weeks before we had headed out to find an apartment after singling out a hit list in the Long Beach California area, I was somewhat familiar with the town and felt pretty comfortable with all aspects of it. The recon trip went pretty much without a hitch save for the fact it rained much of all the three days we were there. Unusual for Southern California. They were in a terrible drought and several people informed us that before the rains came they were just weeks away from water rationing. The mountains were also receiving some much needed snow pack and had gotten almost forty inches in the past few days. The primary realty company we had been working with from the get go was turning into total flakes. We wasted several attempts to see a property including the agent's car wreck on the way to join us and other strange missed cues. Once we finally saw the upstairs apartment about 12 blocks from the beach we added it as number one on our list to the point of making a tentative deal.

The next few were a succession of overpriced semi-clean flop houses that I'm sure even my son of relatively low-bar threshold wouldn't even have considered. Bohemian kids like that sort of thing but the eyes from blackened screen doors I felt on my neck told me to move on. We were overdressed even casual and my jacket made me look like a cop we joked. Either way it was an arduous task to wade through. Most took about 35 seconds to get the vibe and most all were no good. Towards the end of our list we saw one that at first was a strong maybe based if for no other reason than its clean condition.

The building was relatively modern and 3 and a half blocks from the beach just down from the harbor. Across the way from that point is the Queen Mary, its attractions and the ferry to Catalina Island. The apartment was not cheap but more than made up for it with new appliances, carpet and more than adequate square footage for her meager belongings. It was on the second floor next door to the owner, a very nice 60ish local school administrator with Mississippi roots. Seems he went west in the 60's as part of the "movement" and somehow evolved over time to become "the man". Funny how things work out sometimes.

Another plus in my mind is it sat next door to the area Fire House. I work a lot with firemen and grew up next to a firehouse so there was a sense of the familiar and a comfort in the proximity. She was not moved by all of this. The breeze from the ocean also created perfect flow through ventilation which in my mind meant more than manageable utility bills. This was plan B.

Each late afternoon we retired to my favorite Long Beach hangout which is "The Yard-house" on the marina. From the outdoor table vantage point you can observe the small boat traffic as well as the sunset near the lighthouse on the port of Los Angeles. Beer is tall and cold and as in most establishments I frequent they seem to know me and my guests. I'm sure just my imagination. For some reason I always feel like I'm in a place for the first time and am always surprised that I am recognized. Over drinks and a light dinner we finalized our decisions and felt confident enough to return the rental car and board the plane back to the heartland.

Once back we made preparations to do the deal with the flaky realtor on the first piece of property and over-nighted the application fee and all the signed and notarized forms. We were locked and loaded. That's when things turned south. A day or two later after several assurances we were informed of the glitch. It seems the owner in the crux of an unnamed financial calamity had opted suddenly to potentially live in the upstairs available apartment. This action spurred on obviously by our willingness to dive into an ailing housing market.

I knew that the property had been listed for several months and this would in the real world work in our favor. I knew the country and particularly California were in the throes of a terrible recession but I never saw this coming. They never offered to return my deposit. At the news, gears were shifted and to my delight plan "B" was still available and moved to the front burner. This felt very much right to me and after several email exchanges and two phone calls we were in what I felt was a comfortable position.

At that point it was real. I kept my head down and charged forward. Our plan had evolved and with a signing date on the ninth of the month we would have an extra week of preparation. About a month before we had gone shopping for some furniture. Her taste leaned toward bright art deco or 50's quiche and the second hand store around the corner from the pool hall was just the ticket.

Two trips later, each followed by a celebration at the Irish pub across the street, we had secured a 1920's era dinette set and a perfect condition couch I would peg as from the mid 60's. This was her own personal stuff and after her breakup and split of shared property extremely symbolic. She picked it out. She owned it. I would haul it.

The owner of the store, as an occasional friend in passing, had agreed to store it for us prior to our trip so only one move was required. I thanked him for that and offered to buy him a beer sometime at Reno's next door. The plan required a U-haul trailer of the 12ft variety, which I preferred in the mountains because of the additional breaking capabilities and the aid of a one adventurous Mexican George.

Several months before over beers I had thrown out there the possibility of a cross country excursion and he was more than game. He was even excited. He owed me 150 dollars from a long forgotten emergency so no pay would be required to him, only lodging and food. I knew from experience there would be no beer until the mission had been accomplished and only on the return. We would be taking my yellow truck as I knew of its towing prowess and all seemed in order on a fundamental level.

As the day approached everything was in place. The weather, as I knew, was a concern in the higher elevations and our route could not avoid it. The Weather Channel became the first and last thing I checked daily in the days prior. The route I had selected was the most direct on Interstate 40 which traveled a basic straight line from Arkansas to just outside Los Angeles. This was pretty much most of the year a non-eventful path but not in February.

Even in the spring I was all too familiar with the freak snow storms on the mountain at Flagstaff not to mention the higher elevations of New Mexico at about 7000 feet. We would surely get some weather. I don't mind snow at all but I don't care for snow blind conditions where you can't see lines on the road or shoulders in mountain areas with no guard rails. I've done that many times and know that all you can do is go forward until things improve. Pulling over is not a credible option.

Even if you could feel your way to a shoulder chances of being pushed over by a speeding snow plow are better than average. To compound this problem was pulling a loaded trailer being shadowed by an inexperienced driver who I did not want to have to have surgically removed from my ass. This would no doubt be interesting. I tried to prepare Amber for the potential and explained the rules of thumb. In that type of situation follow the tracks in front of you. If the tracks go off the hill, don't follow them anymore. She saw no humor in this. The morning before I was excited to be heading west as I eased toward my office downtown. I think the fluid nature of our plan with its huge blank areas for spontaneity was the key to my attitude. Once downtown while sitting at a red light, just by chance I glanced at my dashboard and notice something odd. I knew the temperature outside was around 40 and there was no way after the ten minute drive I should be near overheating. This was not right and not an option when dragging a trailer up and down the lower end of the Rockies. Around the corner was my local repair and fix it so I wheeled in, explained my schedule and its lack of room for this type of activity.

Sensitive to my plight it was rushed in. I got a ride to work and awaited the news which came like a lightning bolt up my ass. My radiator was cracked. I saw this as a good sign that it was discovered at home and not on the road. After the radiator and replacing the two busted rear shocks from years past I would finally be ready about 3pm. Still on schedule and just 700 dollars lighter I was still feeling ok about myself.

The trip to the U-Haul counter was a little easier than expected; again I think a product of the ailing economy. A quick 20 minutes later and I was ready to head back downtown and get the held furniture. The two pieces would be the first items in the trailer anyway so this should work perfectly. I had to park temporarily in the mayors spot at the stores front due to a Christian festival at the arena but Friday night was not a problem for this intrusion into city government. (until he pulled up as we had sofa in hand and he frowned at me.)

In a jiff we were loaded and I was working my way around the block and back toward the river. As I passed I noticed there was only one car in front of the pool hall. I think it was David Duke's (The infamous artist and advertising man). Darkness was coming quick now and I headed over to get the rest of her gear from storage. This portion of the plan required us to finish loading so I could pick up Mexy G at 7 in the AM and pick up the Interstate by his place. All was well till I saw the flicker.

My dashboard lights flashed and in an instant I was absent of them as well as tail lights on truck and trailer. This again a potential major scheduling setback. I had just left U-haul less than an hour before, called information and automatically placed a call. There was an immediate and slightly bored answer to which I explained my plight. Before I could finish I was abruptly forwarded to National roadside assistance, which I did not need. Seeing this potential conversation was clearly a waste I jerked the unit into a "U" turn and headed back to the outlet. Luckily I caught them still at the counter. They were not sure what to do with me and after two different guys for naught I settled onto the curb with an aging tired mechanic and my owner's manual. He clearly was not going to solve this as he was in the "changing flats" section of the book to which I could not make the mental connection. After I used my spare 15 amp fuse and restored power he deduced the short could be the crushed wire housing at the hitch. He replaced this and sent me on my way. Just about an hour off so not in terrible shape. Just down the road the same problem arose and a second fuse was gone. Being proactive I stopped for fuses and went on to load.

I felt the staff was just guessing and decided road side assistance was in order and made the call. It would be several hours allowing time to load. Over the phone with the tech I traced the problem to a naked wire in the rear lights that was shorting against the body and made arrangements to meet him at the shop to fix. With fuses in hand I took the back roads to avoid a rear end accident and met the young faced savior just about ten PM. I quickly showed him the problem, changed the fuse and was soon eating late dinner before bedding down.

I didn't alarm George as to any potential problems as he had already been privy to the radiator and we were set as far as I was concerned. 7AM came early. I was running just a little late for some reason but I wasn't going to sweat it. Like clockwork I met Amber at the office, we swung by and got G and we were off.

I tested the load at different speeds for proper weight distribution and decided a reshuffle was needed about ten miles out of town. I eased off at the exit. After a bit we were back on track and heading northwest toward Conway, Arkansas.

To prepare for this excursion Amber had apparently went to a friend's house for a little going away get together and crawled into a bottle of Jim Beam until about 5am. Glad I wasn't riding with her. Dylan gained his infamy for this trick just a month before in Chicago where he was going to hang a minute with a female acquaintance and was subsequently found the next day at noon, drunk and missing the scheduled departure by five hours. Not pretty at the time but allowing him to be the butt of many jokes later.

I was a little concerned by this development but press on we must. If it became a problem I was prepared to put George in her car and let her sleep a bit in mine. Gas prices were way down from my cross country the year before but the added weight of the trailer and its cargo made frequent stops a necessity. One of these was at the Travel America just across the Oklahoma border. I always frequent the TA's or Flying J Truck stops whenever I'm out. Like the success of McDonalds you always know what you'll get. Its consistency, not necessarily quality but it is what it is.

This particular stop Amby gained a prize in the form of a hologram photo of a pair of white puppies complete with faux brass frame. She seemed quite pleased and who am I to argue. Back on the road because of the force feed of billboard advertising I decided we would have the treat of a late lunch in Amarillo at the "Big Texan" steak house. It was going to be four or five PM which was not a problem as one large meal would tide us over until 10PM or so when we would approach the mountains of New Mexico.

It seemed like no time at all because of the dullness of the area and we were soon seated at the old style checkerboard table cloth tables of the famous eatery, famous perhaps in its own mind but however noteworthy as the home of the old 96er. This is an aged humongous 96oz steak which is advertised if you can eat in an hour is on the house. If you fail however there is about a fifty dollar price tag. To even enhance the experience the whole culinary event is held on an elevated stage above the main dining floor at a table covered by black and white spotted cow hide. "Festive". By the time we arrived it must have been between shifts as all the surrounding tables remained un-bussed and stayed in that condition the entire length of our stay. Another odd observation I had never noticed before there was how gay the entire staff looked in their cowboy garb. I don't know if it was the juvenile ill fitting hats or the abundance of gingham but it was all slightly disturbing. It's hard to make eye contact with a "pardner" dressed like an eight year old. Once we exchanged jokes we placed our order and were not disappointed. Who was disappointed was our Mexican traveling companion. As most things are advertised in Texas as large it was all he could do to not drool over the 64oz draft beer specials of which we were not partaking. His track record in these matters being what it was had caused me to put a lid on any and all alcohol consumption until after our mission was complete.

Besides, as a result of his recent incarceration (60 DAYS in solitary at Jefferson County Detention Facility) he was without driver's license and already a risk behind the wheel less the complication of beer breath. He would have to wait just like me. We had miles to go before we rested. At dinner we did the math and determined we might need to call ahead and reserve something not knowing the state of accommodations for a late arrival. George slipped behind the wheel in her car.

After a little investigation and a to-go glass of tea this was done. Darkness was falling even though we were traveling with time and soon we were near the lights of Tucumcari. A strange and familiar little town situated perfectly at the beginning or conclusion of a long desert stretch depending on the direction traveled. I've stayed there many more times than I can count and am always struck by how genuinely nice the people are. It may be an act but I don't think so. It's strange to see such hard exteriors, no doubt attributed to the desolate surroundings, turn and melt away at the slightest inquiry.

Maybe it's just boredom…everyone, all the time, just passing through. This night we were not stopping and cruised by without hesitation knowing we were closer now to the first day's end. Amber was trying to cat nap without much success and after about 30 to 45 minutes back behind her own wheel. This made me feel a little better too considering the before mentioned lack of proper credentials. Funnier shit has happened.   Before long and after a couple of refuels we were hitting town. Albuquerque is a jewel of a city. I really like the attention they pay to their heritage with public art along the freeway and bridges. I haven't spent a great deal of time there but it has always been my jumping off point to either Santa Fe to the north or Socorro to the south. None the less it seems very nice. That night we could pick and choose lodging as travelers were light and we opted out of our reservation. This was for a more convenient stay just off our path near food and gas. We would only be staying to sleep and it was important to be up and out early as the temperature was obviously dropping and we could only guess what lies ahead. This would be our gut check day. I knew it was uphill from here and tried to convey to Amber once more the rules. I knew Flagstaff all too well and could tell by the west wind and cloud banks ahead it could be rough. I seem to always be dragging a load in this type of shit. Just a few hours in and we got our first taste.

It was pretty amazing to see in the vast expanse distant snow storms with bright sunshine overhead. At about 5000 feet we started to get a little flurry much sooner than I had expected. I really thought we would be at least across the border into Arizona before we saw anything measurable. This would not be the case but in our favor the temps were just high enough to not allow total road coverage.

This would work and we plowed forward at about 70mph. Flagstaff dead ahead. On the approach at around 6000ft things began to turn sour as we noticed our windshield began to fog. The snow was much heavier and wet and before long my wipers were beginning to freeze into jagged chunks.

I didn't like this development as I had not alerted Amby to this possibility and only hoped she had the presence of mind to deal. My other least favorite development was starting and soon the entire road and shoulders were snow covered and packed. This is extremely dangerous at night due to snow blindness but even more this day due to the lack of bearings, heavy tow load and a kid in the trail car shoved up my ass. She was obviously having difficulty seeing as she was so close behind my trailer I couldn't see her in my side view mirrors, another potential development that had escaped me.

But when and if I ever do this again, I will have an added cautionary tale. We were finally on the approach to what I believed to be the worst at about 7500ft. It was about this time we started to see the wreckage. First was a horse trailer almost perfectly balanced on a metal guard rail? Next was a succession of various small and mid-sized cars off the road in the woods ranging from twenty to fifty feet away from us. We pressed on.

I was in the mood for a piss, some gas and a large lemon Arizona tea and I knew Amb surely was also. As we passed the town I knew that we had reached the crest and the conditions should improve at any time. We got off at the exit after the Grand Canyon off ramp and slid with the others up to the pumps. The Shell station was part convenience store and carried a wide array of provisions for the camper. There was a deserted Shoneys next door. Nothing more…nothing less. Two chicks in fish net hose and miniskirts, obviously off course, gingerly maneuvered over the ice in platform shoes toward the respite. Mexy G without hesitation rolled the window down and began to cat call. Something about a ride to Arkansas, which made no sense since we were heading west? Must have been the altitude. They seemed unimpressed. The cold wind he let in during the exchange caused me to shudder and I yelled at him to shut the fuck up. When Amb got out of the restroom I got the low down on the conditions she was experiencing and found that as I had guessed I was right. She said she almost pulled over several times but had no cell service to alert me. I'm glad she didn't. Her final comment on the subject was now she understood when I said my ass was tight the time similar in Colorado when she and Dylan were young kids. I had to laugh.

In making small talk with the stores counter girl I enquired about the foot of snow that had fallen that afternoon to which she replied "It ain't got bad yet". Apparently there were much worse conditions on the way but we were relieved to learn the elevation would drop 2000 feet in the next 17 miles. That should put us just out of the snow range where we would see no more straight through to Los Angeles. The lady was exactly right as I'm sure it was a common question in the winter months and in about twenty minutes we began to thaw.

The ice flew up in chunks off the brush guards of the yellow truck and smashed against the windshield with its intermittent wipers. This didn't bother me in the least as long as we were all safe. I was requiring gas at a ratio of almost three to one to Amber in the Sentra and I know it had to be annoying to her. Whenever we would get cell service George would get a call, held over from some distant area, and he would repeat the same story I had heard at least ten times in Spanish of the fact he was on the way to California. They all thought he was lying. To counter this disbelief he had already used about four rolls of film in an effort to document his travels. Once in California it was as if the world had flipped. All bad weather was behind us to the east and ahead was the mountains and the sunset. I took cell phone pictures of the postcard setting and sent to friends. We were making good time again as the mountain passes on this leg of Interstate 40 are much less extreme than the southern Interstate route more direct toward San Diego. This was good considering my load. Before we reached Barstow and the end of I-40 we decided to get gas which should get us to Long Beach. I used my credit card and when Amber was prompted to enter her zip code on her card she drew blank and twice entered wrong.

I told her to cancel her transaction and use my card. This was a mistake. Apparently those anti-theft safety precautions really do work as one of my companies had been tracking my westward movements. This was not an issue until I tried to use my card on both sides of the same pump at the same time. None of us were thinking clear at this point. We were just so glad to be out of the Snow Belt before dark. My credit card had been officially tagged. Past Barstow traffic picked up quickly. This was Sunday night and a heavy stream of cars were retreating to LA from Vegas after a weekend of who knows what. They were tired and in a hurry and a yellow short bus with a U-Haul and a Sentra extremely close behind was not what they needed in their collective paths. I totally understood and did my dead level best to stay in the truck lane. I could pretty much do this with the occasional pass and I just hoped Amber was still behind me. She was blending in too well with the sea of small imports that seemed to surround and somehow propel us forward. It seemed surreal or maybe I was just a little tired. I was also stupidly texting (a practice I no longer advocate) to stay alert, which Amb later said she knew I was doing as I listed in and out of the edge of both lanes. It wouldn't be long now as we hit the connecting freeways like clockwork to go north of downtown and find a due south route to the 405 and Long Beach.

The Grammy Awards were being held that night and I chuckled as I overheard George telling friends we were late and hurrying to go. Soon the 405 was in sight and before long we had passed the North/ South 710 or Long Beach Expressway which goes direct to the Queen Mary complex. Our exit at Lakewood would be just up the road and once there traffic seemed to die. We had made great time and eased past the U-Haul yard and into the hotel parking lot at about ten PM. The trailer partially hung out into the street as I went in to get our reserved rooms. Behind the counter was a very young and unhappy Pakistani kid who was obviously the unlucky son of the owner, obvious short straw drawn to work on Sunday night. All seemed in order for rooms until I asked him where I might best park the truck and trailer. "May you unhook it please?" to which I just stared at him. "Not an option" was my quick reply as I went on as kindly as I could to explain it was fully loaded and weighed in the neighborhood of 4000lbs. he seemed to respect that and quietly the asinine nature of his question evaporated. I went on to suggest I could hug the curb in the far end of the near empty lot to which he replied with an enthusiastic yes.

With the truck secure we shifted shit around in the tightly packed trail vehicle and headed out to eat. It was late but we had already decided on the 24 hour Del Taco up the street on Pacific Coast Highway. One of Amb's favorite restaurants and one I'd never tried. That was the final straw concerning my transactions by credit card. As I often do on trips I like to preserve cash as much as possible and charged the fourteen dollar total. This consisted of about eight hard tacos and various burritos and drinks. This late night Mexican restaurant transaction in Long Beach coupled with my near double gas pump entry sent my credit card company into code red lock down. I would find out later that the card had been suspended and only after personal assurances that I indeed had the odd assortment of purchases was it reactivated. My history supported some odd and varied behavior but nothing much as rabid and viral as this. I am glad they are looking after my interests and hold no malice. After we pounded down the grub we retired to the rooms to watch some "Law and Order". No beer. Nine AM would come early and we were not yet acknowledging the fact we had traveled over 1800 miles in two days. Fuck No! It was top of the world mad when considering the trailer in tow.

The next day came with rain. We had been alerted by the future landlord that the days of rain should break and create a window just about moving time but we would have to make it quick. The window was about an hour earlier than we had planned but we were up and jazzed on adrenaline so we were good to go. I called Mac (the landlord) to see if earlier was ok to which it was and within about 12 minutes we were in the spot he had held for us at the front of the building.

The papers were signed and within 30 minutes I was returning the empty trailer back to U-Haul. As we sat in the vehicle inspection lane the rain regrouped and commenced to drench us. We had been just in time. As we sat patiently in the truck every radio station was talking at length about the Grammy's the night before and the teenage singing star that beat up his teenage star girlfriend. He had left a rented Lamborghini in the hood with the girl inside and walked to civilization. I asked Mexy G if he had seen that and he told me to shut up.

I think the lack of beer was getting to him. I was about ready myself. Once we got back to the apartment I felt so relieved we had beat the rain and even better that I was no longer a tow truck. The yellow vehicle handled so much better and suddenly gas mileage was relatively spectacular. It was late morning and we all realized about the same time we had neglected to eat. Piling into the truck we headed to downtown LBC to eat at the little Americana Café hamburger joint we had found in the rain two weeks before.

They have great soups and a strange eclectic crowd of locals who seem to float in and out as if from a mist. The windows have stained glass images of rock icons like Elvis but it's as if the money ran out or the owner died before the motif was finished. The window frames and bases seem to have more of a ginger bread feel totally foreign to the window subject matter. None the less I like it for some strange reason. I can't tell you why. After the late lunch we headed north on the 405 to visit the local IKEA superstore. I had learned years before with Dylan's move to Greenpoint Brooklyn how convenient and perfect the IKEA concept was. Bookshelves, beds, small furniture and accessories could be bought new for a song and packed tight in boxes flat.

Tools were always included in each item. It's the Swedish way. Amber was in the market for some closet storage bins and lamps as well as a coffee table. We scored on the bins and lamps. Additionally with my and Georges insistence we secured a small white chair. The empty apartment seemed bizarre to only have the kitchen chairs and sofa as primary seating.

Guests would have to sit around the corner or on top of you. I was assuming of course there would eventually be guests. The huge amounts of rain the days prior had for some reason caused the escalators to be shut off so we found ourselves tramping up and down the stairs to the various levels of sleek ultra modern furnished sets. A couple of hours later and we were around the corner entering the super Target store. At this stop it was to be light bulbs, toilet paper and beer as primary objectives. That's where I found out about my credit card company and its anti-theft system.

The near transaction at the gas pump and Del Taco I had mentioned before had caused my account to be suspended. I had received several strange calls from an unrecognizable number and no message so I didn't realize they were trying to verify my transactions. Once I took the call and undid the freeze all was well but the decline at Target had me a bit unnerved. I had once before had my calling card number stolen over my shoulder in Vegas and saw it rack up over ten thousand dollars in overseas long distance within 24 hours. I knew what could happen and how quickly. Luckily this was not the case this time. Next stop the apartment to unload and construct the few meager items we had acquired.

We were in a little bit of a hurry. The feeling we had accomplished a lot and the fact we were in between storms caused us to see the opportunity to go to my favorite bar at the harbor. The self imposed beer exile the entire trip to keep our focus had weighed on us. Our alertness made us more than ready to tap one.

In no time I sat at an outdoor table with my traveling companions and we ordered a round. The sky was stunning as it broke and re-gathered, seemingly with the lighthouse as some sort of divining rod or focal point. The boats at the marina were still and silent being a Monday afternoon and I guess technically winter. It almost seemed fitting as we were allowed to observe in silence what would soon to be the home of my baby girl.

I felt good about it and after many candid action shots and several more rounds we were ready for food. I know they didn't remember us but that was about the tenth time I had been there on the patio for up to six hours at a stretch in party mode. I just couldn't get enough of how the whole vibe would change about every thirty minutes. Always for the good. I was making Amber, although all the furniture was in place and complete, stay in the hotel one last night. The utilities had not been transferred and perhaps it was my fatherly hesitation at leaving her.

We had had a great trip across country and she had always been one of my favorite traveling companions. We always have a wonderful time and I am very proud of what she had become. Most important beyond being her dad is I genuinely like her and her company. There is always love for a child but it is rare to cherish the time you have together as I do. I knew this was all she had wanted and all I could do was be supportive. This was where she had chosen to start this chapter of her life.

In a lot of ways I admired her courage. It takes some real sand to move 2000 miles cold into an area where you know no one and have no support structure. You have to make it all on your own terms, all while remaining upbeat and confident. I'm glad there is such available and ready communication today like texting so that you really are never farther away than you choose to be. The next morning I decided the three of us would go about mid-morning to I-Hop for a big breakfast. I somehow felt the thing to do was to stuff her as much as I could somehow thinking it just might be her last good meal for some time.

We had left her car at the apartment to preserve the space the night before so I kind of crawled snail pace in a stalling action to drop her off. We are not a touchy feely family and never have been so I know it seemed odd to her that I felt compelled to embrace in a hug. We had been so focused on the mission of the trip that the reality of the outcome had somehow eluded me. But here it was. I was leaving her in LA to her own devises. I didn't push it because no one wanted tears and soon George and I were pulling away. Chapter three of her life had just begun and I loved her deeply at that moment. Good bye kid.

Next stop for Mexican George and I was Vegas. We had an early enough start and should get there by about four in the afternoon. This was much earlier than I can ever remember pulling into town and the prospect was interesting. To follow in the footsteps of Hunter Thompson I always when possible do the high speed burn through bat country. This was the I-15 route through Barstow and Baker (home of the world's tallest thermometer) and the couple of casino oasis along the California and Nevada border. Drive as fast as you can. They wouldn't follow.

We had beer on the brain and George was giddy as a school girl about just the possibility of being on the strip. I had called my friend Brian Saliba days before with the prospect and would let him know when we hit town. I always liked to hang with him, catch up and get the real no bullshit perspective of the current left coast business.

First stop is always the Motel 6 on old Industrial Boulevard by the In and Out burger. A couple of years ago they changed the road name to Dean Martin Road but it's still the same early morning hookers and bright sun on the empty pool. This is a perfect stop at 29.00 per night, just off Tropicana and the strip and right on I-15 across from the Excalibur. I found this location years before and never considered any need for change. All you do is get a couple of hours sleep anyway.

Second stop is always the Harley Café on the strip where I get the southern fried chicken platter, complete with mashed potatoes and corn on the cob. That as our second meal of the day would certainly tide us over until possibly 2am and some In and Out burgers. The other big plus for the Harley was the joint had its own private parking deck out back with full all access for patrons. We could leave the truck there, eat, drink and hit the shops next door, working our way on foot wherever on the strip.

We would retrieve the vehicle later when the situation demanded. Everything was like clockwork and after picking up a jacket at the Lucky store I was ready to roll. I had poorly underdressed with the trip joke being

I hadn't brought any real shoes. I had socks and my huarache sandals I wore everywhere but this was inadequate for the snow we had encountered not to mention the fast approaching desert night cold. Keep moving being our mantra. The meal was in no way a disappointment as I expected and after a couple of large iced teas to hydrate us it was time to seek out what lies beyond the double glass doors. Construction was in its final phase across the street on the enormous shopping (slash) condo complex, City Center, although I remember thinking this very thing the last two to three years. I think the design contributes to it's almost but unfinished look with its fluid and ultra modern lines. This would truly be a marvel once open.

My main thought all along is why on earth anyone would shell out the bucks for a condo at such a location. I guess maybe higher up executives at the strip casinos but it doesn't seem like much of a family life. Constant 24 hour a day traffic and the ever present purveyors of snap cards we will address at a later date. Not at all wholesome but who am I to throw stones. Another walk through the adjacent mall was in order so Mexy G could take some pictures for unbelieving pals. The Miracle Mile shops for some reason have a Moroccan theme and a sky painted ceiling which changes through the 24 hour day cycle on the hour.

It is a direct rip off of Caesars Forum shops but is a crowd pleaser none the less. It also has the thunder and rain shower in the designated area near the seafood buffet every thirty minutes. From that type of atmosphere we would attempt something completely different. I had contacted my friend Brian there and needed a suitable rendezvous spot so we settled on the Cantina Diablo. The one great feature is a life size Elvira titted type female statue in devil attire adorning the roof just above the front entrance. This always reminds me of the movie "From Dusk till Dawn". Down side is they don't carry my brand of draft beer and are heavy on the tequila. It's also very crowded and seats come at a premium. Miraculously we ended up with two bar seats perfectly situated near the swill (Budweiser) dispensing taps and two plasma television monitors set on alternate sporting events.

Not a bad deal for two semi-professional bar hounds who just stumbled in off the strip. As I mentioned our joy was short lived as the only choice of draft beer was Bud and Bud Light and those are not the beers you want to start with. Not to cast aspersions toward the millions of Bud fans but the after taste is something that can taint the palette for the remainder of the outing. Especially on account we hadn't partaken of anything thus far on the trip. It was a matter of focus. We were parched and even after bitching it went down relatively easy. Any port in a storm.

It wasn't long and Brian called with a parking issue. The strip was packed and he understandably didn't want to pay for deck parking to just hook up. With this in mind and the Bud problem he suggested and we opted for further down the strip at Mandalay Bay. This was fine with me because I had wanted to check the action at House of Blues, where I had several other old friends in security, plus I knew they had the proper beer for my liking. Brian showed and we grabbed a corner table near the gaming floor. We hadn't talked shop long when George asked directions to the restroom. They were delivered and off he went, not to be seen again for almost two hours. Seems on the way back he was attracted to the pretty lights of the quarter slots and stopped to make some pulls. That was fine but a little unnerving at first. I was his ride the next 1200 plus miles back. We were joined by a few others who revolved through and by 8ish we had pretty much caught up. From our vantage point the sport was sightseeing all the trophies that were gracing the adjoining restaurants with gaggles of split skirts in tow for the early dinner or snacks.

Our next stop I would learn would be the House of Blues VIP club on the roof overlooking the entire strip area, with its back to the Interstate. Of course George was still MIA at this time and a thorough search would ensue. After some deductive thought our prey was identified and apprehended and within minutes on the elevator shooting skyward. The level of buzz from the suds was just enough to eliminate most forms of self doubt. This fact would allow for full enjoyment and just the proper level of confidence required for such situations. I had never gained such access to this club and in tourist fashion bee-lined for the balcony with its vistas for photo opportunities.

After every conceivable combination and photo angle we ambled in to perch on a deep, rich leather pit group. In this environment you must at all times remain poised almost to the point of indignant. This is the only proper air to carry and will be responded to in suitable fashion. George was in awe. I could tell by his awkward posture and movements he was terrified. He was certainly the only person in his family or acquaintance to have ever had the fortune of this treat. I tried to draw him into the conversation but it was a tough sell. As we ordered appetizers and more drinks I saw his first smile crack as we discovered all was on the house. It couldn't get much better.

We discussed and considered staying an extra day as we were technically ahead of schedule by at least a day and were fully capable of doing the full load at once back if need be. It was a haul of about 26 hours but I had done it on several occasions. It had been a long enough time since Dylan and I had done it that the memory of how insane it was had escaped me. After a time we felt we had absorbed all this exquisite room had to offer and ached for the dirt and gritty reality of the ground floor.

Brian headed home to get ready for the next day at his day job with the County and we were off. When street trolling the trick is to hit the convenience stores along the way for tall road beers and totally avoid the casinos and bars. Bars may charge six to seven dollars per beer which covers the cost of an entire six pack if you are chugging and not concerned with beer temperature. This was not how we roll so a strategy of cheap stops in between stretches requiring single cold beers was employed. The exception in this plan is O'shay's, a shitty dive of street level casino like you would expect to find on Freemont Street in old Vegas. This was designed for the common man. These could not be found just anywhere. Hell no.

The beer was cheap just like the women. This eyesore is famous for its 24 hour dollar draft beer happy hour complete with leprechaun outfitted midget and haughty décor. I believe from 1977 or a year earlier I was there so I know. The big O was in the geographic center of our trek between the car park and the furthest reaches we would venture to. Not much past Treasure Island. You can only drink so much technically, or so we thought. About this time I learned George had parlayed five dollars into forty back at Mandalay so we were staked for the dollar dance. In the distance just past the constant bells and beeps of the penny slots you could almost discern the low beat of Da Do Run Run. Just around from the bar is a small lounge complete with stage which houses some of the finest "has been", low level entertainment on the strip. All bands of whatever caliber have a certain level of acceptance after just the right amount of alcohol and this was no exception. It was a five or possibly six piece if you include the window dressing, with somewhat matching suits in various degrees of distress. I do recall ruffles like a pirate costume and tan tuxedo style pants with some type of satin stripe about ¾ of an inch wide sewn down the leg.

This for some reason unnerved me and caused a reaction that inched me toward hitting at least the closest person I could find square in the face. I put this aside for the moment. I hadn't felt this urge so strongly in this town except possibly the Utah redneck tobacco floor spitting incident at the female nude bull riding competition in the Frontier, Super Bowl weekend several years prior. It was ugly and I knew only more beer could drown and suppress this rampant anger. The eye in the sky cameras were also a deterrent I think. This early in the evening the last thing we needed was to be banned from this shit hole not to mention the shame and ridicule from these low life sons of bitches.

I swallowed these feelings and pushed them hard down the diaphragm and deep into the gullet. Keep moving still being my mantra. Never let them see you sweat or cry as the case may be. After a cruise through the main gaming floor and a stop to take in the usual mariachi band near the men's room we decided to venture further up the strip. This would be towards the higher class areas housing the likes of the Venetian and Caesars.

These places are great fun to walk through if for nothing but the architecture but not practical at any level for drink or purchase. The places always remind me of a sign I saw at the entrance of the Atlantis Casino in Nassau which reads "NO locals allowed!" It's an air. When the cheapest pair of sunglasses in the Forum Shops is $250.00 then it's time for a full retreat. That's the equivalent of 250 one dollar beers at the previously mentioned crap trap and roughly two times our consumption for the entire trip.

There was severe disparity in this disturbing fact but the numbers do not lie. Your friends do but numbers no. That meant a quick stop at the ABC store for a 40 ounce. That should suffice for the walk through and the free shows in the central hallway intersections. George was really into seeing the talking statues in the Forum and Baucus in particular. I explained his relation to wine. I personally was indifferent but not a spoil sport so we hung around and nursed the beers. Our perch was near a revolving lighted advertisement and for a brief moment I entertained the thought of seeing Cher. That is until I saw the 300.00 per ticket price attached to all that was left. That is the equivalent of 300 one dollar beers or in our case because of the two tickets required it would be like 600 one dollar beers!

Just the thought of that borders on the insane particularly in light of the fact I know Cher's body double personally and can see for free most anytime. The fifteen minutes went by with relative ease and George sat with wide eyed wonderment like a kid at Christmas. I felt my destructive urge returning but pushed it back into its pink fleshy container. The show was brief and we were soon on the move. As we navigated through the maze of sculpted storefronts something unusual caught my eye. Toward the main exit onto Las Vegas Boulevard there is a high end sports memorabilia store. Near the entrance at a small folding table sat a very tired and worn looking Pete Rose signing autographs and posing for snapshots with trophy wives and mistresses.

It struck me odd that none of the men were on the business side of the camera and chose, I suppose the allure of a sports celebrity with their respective special lady friends. We sat there a good few moments and considered approaching for the novelty of a cell phone picture and observed this cruel situation. He seemed pained but readily accepted the tens and twenties palmed him none the less. His hair, which I remembered was the thick dark Dutch boy cut of his youth, had been replaced by a thinning bald look reminiscent of a cancer patient. Several times our eyes met and he must have sensed my indecision in this matter concerning him. I don't know if he thought me a potential stalker or what and in my drunken condition I could not accurately access my state as I had no idea what he was seeing. I didn't know who was a bigger asshole… me or him. Fuck it. Back out into the crisp night air.

It had been about an hour or so since we had gotten any snap cards so we dove back into the game. This action required a slight detour back down the strip, reentering into the shitty part. The finer establishments shun away such purveyors. If I haven't explained in detail, snap cards are a great prize because they are both abhorred and admired with no one admitting either path. This is similar to the fact that no one actually masturbates. It works like this: Mexican illegal's seeking employment come to the city which is saturated with cheap labor. This is almost identical to the plight of the Oakies coming to California in "The Grapes of Wrath"(A Steinbeck novel of note). They are hired by the escort services to stand in groups on prominent corners where pedestrians are forced to cross and are often stopped by traffic signals. These groups of men and women attempt to pass off playing card size full color printed advertisements featuring nude women in various poses and a phone number. This magic number was usually accompanied by a bargain price sometimes as cheap as $29.00 per visit. If the card is accepted and a call made, the person handing out the card will be compensated a commission making them by proxy a type of pimp. This pimp, as it were, has developed and employed a card delivery system which involves a clicking or snapping of the card between the middle and index finger thus the "snap card" phrase.

(snap cards)

Most respectable tourists and gamers with the exception of frat boys would never be seen on a public street accepting these handouts. It is an admission of need and a primal inadequacy to produce sexual results by more traditional means. There is also a level of uncertainty based on the illegal feeling of it all. Most if not all potential clients are from other areas of the country where this practice is an illegal form of solicitation. Not in the great state of Nevada, also known as the "Silver State". The fact that it is a foreign practice to most compounds the feeling of shame and guilt accompanying the acceptance of said cards. "This is what we embrace in this wild and lawless place in which we thrive". I think Abraham Lincoln also said that .

Several years ago we started a game which mainly involved my grown children and friends such as George who would appreciate the sport. The object is to accept as many cards as possible while loudly exclaiming an enthusiastic "snap cards" to the Spanish speaking purveyors. At the end of the night the stack is measured in inches with I believe the record being ten to twelve solid inches of the collectable soft-core pornographic items. Once the game is complete it is not unusual to have secured upwards of a thousand of the high gloss slips. You may be asking, "What do you then do with that many cards?" considering between all the players who win or lose you may have acquired three to five thousand units.

The answer is you mail them to your son, if he is not a current player. He never is expecting the useless items and the shear bulk of such a thing gives it incredible shock power. Can you imagine opening a nice unmarked and unsolicited UPS package to find thousands of racy advertisements spilling onto your living room floor? Just the thought of the surprise is enough for a low level chuckle. The other interesting and entertaining angle is the looks you get from airport personnel if flying or people in general if driving at the shear depravity of such a collection. Regardless, we were back on track in an intense competition and I sported a backpack which was ¾ full at this point. The snap carders were very pleased to see our outreached right hands tucked just slightly out of pocket indicating a stealth move. This was the proper delivery acceptance motion adding to our glee. The game resumed.

Being once again bone dry it was also time for a stop. Coming back down the strip and the lateness of the hour we decided a snack might also be appropriate. In the same general direction we opted to cut through the Miracle Mile shops past the magic shop where Dylan had once secured the man size rabbit suit and jet back across the street to the Harley place. I always like the late night macaroni and cheese. It is a little known fact that macaroni and cheese is the signature dish of Las Vegas. Often times a city will try and attach themselves to a particular type of food as a promotional ploy. Amarillo has steak. Kansas City has bar-b-que. Little Rock had that silly attempt at Velveeta and Rotel cheese dip and Vegas has macaroni and cheese. If you go to pretty much any chain or casino type eatery you can be assured of finding some type of exotic rendition.

Just notice next time you have the opportunity. Mine is at Harley. It's an elongated deep dish with large elbow pasta smothered and baked with three white cheeses, very tasty and filling. It's the carbohydrates you are after in this situation. As usual this time of night the restaurant is winding down and we are relegated to the bar. The one saving grace is the friendly familiar face of the slightly chunky tattooed up Betty Page look alike seating hostess I've had my picture with on several occasions. I think she likes me. Within a short while I am digging in with my seat situated so I can just see the crosswalk at the corner and its constant activity. This is always entertaining. This was the same stool where I witnessed a drunk driver hit a drunk pedestrian about three o'clock one afternoon and the ensuing riot.

Police came and about ten officers were required to untangle traffic and the lock of drunken aggression. The strip at its finest. This was the center of the party universe and we were there to suckle the teat. The break was a good one and after a couple of drafts and the restroom opportunity we were once again off. Next stop was the karaoke over at the outdoor margarita and egg joint. This was without a doubt the most depraved group of hardcore and amateur singers I had ever witnessed in my short life. The lack of talent coupled with the shear sand and blind willingness to subject oneself to such criticism was staggering. Even stranger was the concept of coupling eggs and margaritas. In my world it kind of makes sense as I'm sometimes known to order eggs over easy not found on the menu at my favorite bars with beer. This however in relation to this particular location is somewhat odd. The bar is almost not officially a location as it's found at the edge of a walkway through a sea of kiosks in pedestrian mall form.

The walls are defined by rope and stanchion, contributing to its open air atmosphere, the only defined structure being the thatched roof over the bar and the bar itself. The roof doubles as bottle display and glass hanger although no real glass is served this close to the street. There are several styles of plastic containers from the standard souvenir 10 ounce clear to the lime green yard of beer which measures the full 36 inches. These come with extremely dangerous thick straws close to 24 inches long which under the right conditions could cause one to lose an eye. My friends and I have come close to this so I am an authority on the subject. I've seen it happen. This is just one of the dangers inherent in the "last stop" mentality. It's always the last drink that gets you. It was about 2am at this point and most all the singers were either choosing "Take it easy" by the Eagles or a Whitney Houston selection. There was a clear division in relation to the level of inebriation and shear gall. The Eagles is a group anyone can fake sing through much like "The Band" just by being normal and relaxed. Minimal effort is required. This is the patron who is at ease and having fun. Not trying to impress or influence. Whitney is the other end of the spectrum. This is a pretentious lot. It's the female or she-male as the case may be who perceives themselves several levels above the average patron of this shit hole. It's the high note never achieved except in the mind of the participant. This is also a good possible reason for the plastic glasses. A regular glass could shatter from pitch or someone could be cut manually as the case might warrant. It can always go either way.

This tug of war in ideology goes by for some time before stools open up at the bar and we can stop standing around like a couple of fucking hoboes. We wouldn't stay long. That's always my mantra… don't stay long. After a bit we are clued into the fact there are only five singers signed up in a rotation with each round more slurred and clouded than the last. As brother Alex in "Clockwork Orange" would say "pure horror show". Around three am we would get a shiny green pair of ten ounce margaritas and head out for tacos at Del Taco or wherever we could find open off Old Industrial road or near our hotel on I-15. This was not a huge challenge. The biggest challenge was to keep George from whore mongering the tired hookers that slide from the gas station on the corner past the before mentioned "In and Out" burger on Tropicana and the hotel. It's very depressing this time of night, although not as bad as 8am when they are viewed in the bright light of day spending spare change on video games in the corner and playing scratch off. Everybody is a winner! I always smile and say hi, not to be so much like the other jerks.

It took some work but I got him in and to bed. We had an early day tomorrow and I wasn't sure how far three hours sleep would get us east. The fact we were getting used to the four to five hours and averaging five to seven hundred miles a day was in our favor I think. This was the few days prior to Vegas however and we had been dry to this point. Regardless of how we felt, George had to be at work on Monday so it was not up for debate. 7am came and I hit the shower first so I could catch some more of the Twilight Zone marathon on TV while he got ready. I require 0% primping and can be totally packed and ready in usually ten minutes. George is another story. Sometimes I think he has a vagina.

I-15 was busy as usual and after a quick stop at the corner for a fuel top off, a pint of strawberry Nestle Quick and some light fraternization with the wide eyed, battered and tweaking teen girls we were off. Once more students of the open road. George had never seen the Hoover Dam so that became our chosen however necessary route. That would as usual hook us up at Kingman, Arizona with I-40 and the straight shot home. As we approached Lake Meade it became apparent there was heavy duty construction in an effort to widen the US Highway to four lanes and bypass the switchback road which actually crosses the dam.

This would be accomplished with a new bridge which would traverse the narrow canyon on the spillway side. The bridge was being carefully constructed from both banks simultaneously, not yet meeting in the middle but hanging in mid-air approximately one hundred yards from making center contact. This was a little spooky to see. No one was working today and the scene had a deserted eerie look. We stopped and took pictures from the overlook below, one with George like a proud papa, the unfinished structure in the background. From here we snaked back and forth till we stopped and had an early lunch and much needed restroom break. This would be just prior to Kingman and the high speed burn that was to follow. From there it would be about 1800 miles, give or take and we would have to hit it. It was my goal to drop G off at home in as close to 24 hours as I could get, grab a shower and a few hours shut eye and head to Mardi gras in New Orleans. I know that sounds stupid but when you're on a roll and your system gets in the proper mode it's totally cool to continue.

Anytime I drive straight from California or any other trip over 1000 miles it usually takes me a couple of days before I can get into a normal sleep pattern. It's pretty strange how one can become a machine, without the help of mind altering drugs, of which I don't approve. Alcohol is different to me because the effects can be controlled to a degree and are short lived. It was with this in mind that we decided on a pint of Jack Black label to ward off the cold in the higher elevations we knew were dead ahead. I had been monitoring the temperatures on the weather channel periodically and knew that the front we had met on the way west had dropped everything into a deep freeze in the lower Rockies and all the snow would most defiantly still be on the ground. I'm sure the roads would be graded and the clear skies made for a totally different situation. I timed it so we would have good daylight to get through Flagstaff and the worst of it. That should pretty much coast us right on to Albuquerque. I constantly kicked my own ass for not having thicker socks to go with my lack of solid shoes. Dumb luck that. Especially when we hit the rest stop at the approach which had walkways cut into the three and a half to four feet snows. Ice sickles hung at least two feet long and even with a small pipe saving space heater my urine still made a plume of steam as it splashed into the urinal drain plug. This made the stop quick but photos were still taken demonstrating the depth of the snow in relation to the human body. Very impressive but I longed for the low desert and an end to the unpredictability of this bullshit.

It would be a few hours but the crisp, clear air seemed stable at the moment and no squalls seemed on the proverbial horizon. We both took a hit off the bottle and turned the heat on full tilt. Ahead we pushed only stopping for fuel, bottled Lipton iced tea and piss breaks. We were feeling pretty good and the thought never occurred to me to allow George a turn behind the wheel. That's not how I roll.

The high country, with its reasonable evergreen growth flew by at breakneck speed. The lower country was near and the long straight stretches that were customary. We were about a third of the way back to the heartland. Not great but not shabby. The snow, even though graded, had caused us to lose some valuable time. I hit the bottle again as a precaution. We put on some of our trip CD's and flowed into the piece of a road with no turns or twists. In my calm a road less traveled. But not really, just long straight-aways toward the approaching darkness of the east. That's always the downside of the eastward route. You are hurtling toward the past and its loss of hours and light. New Mexico was ahead and the last of the high country. About dark thirty we were topping the hill overlooking Albuquerque. I really wanted to take Bugs Bunny's advice and turn left. This would head up to Santa Fe and Jim Talisano's place but I knew I wouldn't want to leave. George would miss work and I would miss work and I would be late for Mardi gras. Not to be this trip. Seems like last time I dropped in on him it was Halloween night just prior to him splitting his time between here and Manhattan and his new teaching post. I think I stayed a week.

That was when it was rumored Gene Hackman, who lives there, was arrested for beating up two teenagers who rear ended him at a traffic light. They had cast aspersions his way it was assumed. He can be seen around town in painters pants. Maybe he really does shop at Lowe's.

Pressing on, don't look right or left. Hit all the Travel America's. Look at the other warriors stumbling past the cheap Indian blankets, made in China hats and pecan rolls in search of the restroom. Legs a little dysfunctional and wooden from atrophy due to the tight cockpit area. Stretching legs. License plates from Kansas, Minnesota, Tennessee and Utah. A kid, maybe 12 with no shoes, a Mohawk haircut died pinkish purple. He has real tattoos on his neck and face. He is trying to give away a large yellow dog on a makeshift rope leash to the entire passerby's. His parents or possible kidnappers sit near the air pumps watching intently from a weather beaten blue Ford escort with Utah plates and dolphin window stickers. Perhaps in need of gas money? Regardless, no takers. All have shifty eyes and noticeably look right and then left probably fifty times. A small gathering of American Indians pile out of the back of a truck camper and bee line for the MacDonald's counter with its listless check out girl, dreaming of the five o'clock shift change. All the natives are at least 30 pounds overweight with the bulk of it surrounding faces marked with weather and despair. All counter lines head either parallel or due south I believe as a result of gravity. You can learn all you ever want to know of this country from a Travel America gas and convenience store parking lot. Like the fact virtually all old people have small dogs and under no circumstances should you partake of the white gravy sitting stagnant in the buffet vat. Trust me, just don't fucking go there.

   These stops are strategically placed several hundred miles apart for the use of the long hauler much like Stucky's was in the old days. An idea about 30 years ahead of its time. Although much more skewed toward children and the casual tourist. How many pounds of praline candy and Indian blankets can one party manage? Good concept on the surface. We are fast approaching midnight and Tucumcari at this time. The pint is long empty and after some deliberation we determine that our current rate and the hour would make a bargain stop for a shower and a little shuteye go a long way. This would also work out as a fuel stop at first light and the hard push to the finish. Or should I say Georges finish as I would still have about 7 hours from Little Rock to New Orleans.

   This time of night is prime for a cheap hotel room. Most all rooms that will be taken will be occupied by ten pm and it is known that most night men are allowed to negotiate with the late arrival road weary traveler, especially with the economy in its current state and the total absence of travelers…slim to no pleasure seekers, not to mention winter time. After surveying the main drag and identifying a near empty Regal 8 just off I-40, across from an all night BP station we coasted silently in and hit the buzzer. After three minutes or so and several pushes I saw a stir in the shadows just behind the counter. A balding and overweight younger guy, maybe mid-thirties, pressed the release and I gained entry. The most predominate feature of him I noticed was an extremely bushy yet sculpted mustache which crowned the upper lip and cascaded down either side of the mouth to a length of about an inch.

My first thought was that of a seventies porno star but with the rest of the package added a child molester or pedophile might be more accurate, an unsavory character. I wasn't there to make friends and within moments proceeded to explain our story and the briefness of our intended stay. Under most other circumstances two adult males and a hotel stay of less than six hours might be misconstrued but in the context of this location and time was considered beyond reproach. It wasn't difficult in light of the fact he wanted a return to his hidden cot and slumber. We were soon stretched out in a double for a total of twenty in cash. This would be an off the books transaction with the condition we would be off well before 7am and the day shift change. Not a problem as I set the automated wake up call for 6am. We would be long gone or at the least at the BP blending into first light with the stirring of the other walking dead. At first adrenaline still pumped and I watched about thirty minutes of some show about whale migration on the Geographic Channel. This led me to a quick series of strange dreams concerning whale boys and some sort of dispute with Japanese vessels.

I don't know but I was deep into it to the point that I never even heard George snore. Sooner than later the phone broke the still dark air and within moments I was trying to negotiate the postage stamp sized complimentary soap into an underarm lather. With some skill I made this happen but resorted to my stash of various collected shampoos and creams for hair treatment needs. Within about five minutes I was in clean underwear and pants and shoving George out of bed for his turn. Reluctantly he complied. I parked my ass against the headboard and switched back on the 19 inch color television customary to this type of room.

To my surprise the programming loop had been accomplished and the whale show I had viewed earlier was in conclusion. Amazing! After about fifteen minutes it was done and I shoved my small leather toiletry kit back into my yellow bag and slipped into my coat. This time of day the desert is always bone chilling and this day in February was no exception. Light would not be for about 45 minutes so we felt like the rest had not been a squander of time. We were also surprisingly refreshed and ready for the big push.

At the BP about a half tank topped it off and George got a large coffee. Black. No sugar. I had a bottled green tea and some berry and nut trail mix which I shared with my traveling companion. Traffic was light as we had beaten the crowd, such as it was. Hurtling past the semi trucks parked on road side ramps with steamed windows and sleeping drivers with small dogs. I often thought of taking my dog on a trip and almost did this one until I considered how the responsibility would hamstring spontaneous potential plans. Anyway, I heard a wise man say once, "Never take a dog to Vegas". He was correct. We were cruising now and it felt good as we crossed into the Texas panhandle, toward Amarillo and the approaching dawn.

This direction we were meeting the present. Mid-morning the Big Texan restaurant was passed we ate at on the way and I began to consider real food at a future stop. Once in Oklahoma we could smell the end of this leg. Following the billboard advertising for about a hundred miles touting the Golden Coral buffet outside of Oklahoma City and its senior after 2pm special of $4.99 all you can eat. Senior being defined as 65 and older. I, being 50 and G being late 50's with darker hair than me, would cause this to be a stretch. We would have to see. As luck would have it the almost full parking lot was approached at the appropriate time. A single, late afternoon heavy meal stop made the most sense.

The girl at the register, a disheveled girl of maybe 20 years and definite local roots glanced our way and asked blindly if we wanted the senior special. Without hesitation I responded yes, paid the fee and grabbed the plates. About the time we sat down and got our tea the realization of what had just occurred flooded in. Did we really look 65 plus or was the exchange the product of a bored and disinterested employee. This would never be known because to ask would throw a bright light on our deception. It would be a matter of the practical nature must outweigh vanity, the cost savings being substantial. Another mound of mashed potatoes would drive away these thoughts. Soon it was back on the road with fresh large iced teas in Styrofoam cups laced with "sweet and low" from the little pick packets. Refreshed again, full of belly and gas tank. So close to Arkansas and the last 5.5 hours it could be tasted. Just outside of town (Oklahoma City) we passed the truck stop where Dylan and I had lost the timing belt of the yellow truck in a previous trip and strangely I felt like I had accomplished something. This was a good boost and any thoughts of fatigue soon evaporated. This was also caused by thoughts of the third leg of the trip which would involve my first New Orleans visit post Katrina. I kicked up another five to ten miles per hour in response. There's nothing to see here anyway.

Crossing the Arkansas River and then entering Fort Smith made us speed up even more. This was familiar home turf now and somehow not as vulnerable to mishaps as one would expect in more desolate and inhospitable surroundings. A quick rest stop at one of former Governor Huckabee's border palaces made all even better. No more stops would be required before hitting Little Rock and a little rest before the 9am morning departure for points due south. Time was working out fine. Knowing the traditional speed traps always leads to expedited travel and this was no exception. We were almost home or what we considered current home, a respite for our stuff. I wanted some homemade chili spaghetti and called ahead with the request. I knew my carbohydrate level was down and a recharge was in order. It was comfort food, chicken soup for the soul or some such shit. Within about three hours I had dumped George and his junk on his front porch and was sitting in my favorite chair, petting my favorite dog and eating spaghetti.

The Armor chili variety with American cheese slices and wheat toast. All being washed down with a tall glass of 2% milk. It was all good. I had started some laundry and after a few loads would have everything clean used on the trip prior and ready to repack for round two. My traveling companion and I were pretty excited about Mardi gras and knew at the least the sub-tropical temperatures of the "Big Easy" would be welcome after what had just been endured. Everyone in the know thought I was insane for extending a literal cross country trip to include another couple days of drinking and the required 1400 miles round trip south. I didn't think about it much. After a good warm shower I cat napped until first light. With it I was up and within an hour or so ready to roll. As I said this was my first post hurricane Katrina trip and I was both anxious and apprehensive about what the scene would be like. Regardless this was the first ever legitimate Mardi gras trip after many aborted attempts over 30 plus years. The road down was just as I recalled and had been taken hundreds of times. No map required. Most all landmarks including the giant slogan "Duane Allman Lives" etched several feet tall in the limestone cliffs at Vicksburg remained unchanged.

Only new storefronts on the travel centers in Tallulah, Louisiana were the most noticeable. Same bumpy roads. Same depressed areas flying by. Not least of which is Poverty Point and Lake Providence, voted once as the poorest city in the United States. Easy to miss that turn on Hwy 65 which when missed puts the traveler indeed in real peril. Things remained the same although it seemed like more businesses were closed than usual. Must be the economy and its accompanied decrease in traffic. No Obama bailout here. When we got through the short jaunts in various states and landed on the Interstate due south from Jackson, Mississippi it started to rain, soft at first, then developing into sheets of a tropical nature as to make travel treacherous if not impossible. We pressed on. The worst thing you can do in zero visibility is give up and pull to the side to wait. The other vehicles will in most cases not expect or see you and a 'target" situation is created. I have found what works best for me is to get situated in the fast lane so as to easier spot the left shoulder stripe. It becomes a visible landmark and allows you to regulate your speed accordingly. This avoids the slower blinded vehicles as well as stopped ones on the right shoulder. You just have to punch through until it improves. Even twenty miles an hour is progress as storms here this time of year are slow movers and any reasonable speed is usually adequate to get you beyond.

This was a bad ass storm with the occasional tornado siren heard in the distance. According to the weather service we would be in and out of it all the way. Our best bet would be to haul at every opportunity of cloud break and try and make up for lost time. This strategy worked well and soon we were on the approach of the causeway bridge, the long, low level bridge over the swamp and marshland adjacent to Lake Pontchartrain. The rain was in short intermittent bursts at this point which made the close quarters of the vehicles extremely hazardous. Traffic was picking up as the metropolitan area was approached. We had made up our lost time and were pretty much on schedule when dead ahead red tail lights could be seen. This stretch is the section which had generally collapsed in the hurricane and was tight and without exits until the other shore and the city proper was reached. It was a dead stop in both lanes making it almost impossible to clear the wreck most certainly ahead. The nearest emergency response was coming from the rear and all traffic pulled to the narrow shoulders right and left respectively. A middle lane was created for the fire truck, tow truck and ambulance to gingerly make their way. Must be a bad one no doubt created by the combination of blinding rain, high speed and Mardi gras ambitions. As the stop agonized past thirty minutes I began to wish I had filled up prior to the causeway. It would probably be ok but it was hard to tell. I knew I didn't want to be too far into the inner city with a near empty tank as this was just not advisable.

Luckily we started to pick up a little speed with about five miles per hour gained about every two miles. Within about twenty to thirty minutes we were off the causeway and approaching the Canal Street exit. For many years I had stayed at the Canal Street Days Inn in the shadow of I-10 for several reasons. Not least of which were the cheap price, walking distance to the French Quarter and closeness to the Interstate and its quick escape. This hotel had always been medium level even for a Days Inn but I was totally unprepared for what I saw. The basic structure seemed intact with its concrete block basis but it had obviously gone without some storm repair. Only one elevator was working and quickly I realized the majority of rooms had been surrendered to the street trade for sex and occasionally drugs. Never saw so many gold teeth, women and men alike. Indoor smoking laws were non-existent or not enforceable as even the front desk person was smoking during check in.

From the outside you could spot some drapes flapping listlessly in the breeze. Torn and discolored from multiple rain and sun. Days Inn had apparently abandoned the property and it had been reopened with local ownership. The structures color scheme was haphazardly attempted at purple and jazzed themed. You could see exactly where the money had run out. With this buildup I was still unprepared for what the room had in store. Upon entering, first off I noticed no pillows or trash cans. This being an easy enough fix. Then there was the 19 inch color television with the severed power and cable connections. What the fuck? I knew we would spend little or no time in the room but there was the principle of the thing.

Being reminded what I had paid I made a call to the front about the pillows and made note of the electronics. The gruff desk woman seemed genuinely surprised about the vandalism but assured me that as probably the only white people in the hotel we would get prompt attention. After getting unsaddled we were ready to hit Canal and head down to where the parades were starting to form. This walk was the most depressing I had had in many years. High rise office buildings with broken windows and blinds, boarded up at once active ground floor entrances. All left to the ravages of nature and the occasional squatting homeless. Courtyards used as human toilets and gangs of youths in uniform colors and sunken eyes, with no visible whites surrounding pupils even in the corners. Being open season almost everyone sported a 40 ounce beverage of some sort. We picked up our pace feeling watched.

Subconsciously I wished I had armed myself but like my sandals in the snow I had been too relaxed and unthinking. We would be ok and would certainly shell out ten bucks for the late night cab ride back. A walk after midnight past the permanently darkened doorways of the shell buildings would be certain suicide. Cash and maybe more lost to the night. Get the cab you cheap bastard. Even drunkenness doesn't create the lost sense of security. Get the cab. As we approached the river and the hoards of revelers the feeling of urgency evaporated into the fog and swirled with the melodies emanating from every door. The notorious NOPD was in force and still couldn't stop the purse snatching I witnessed two steps away. The group of ten year olds scattering in two directions and just out of sight like wisps of smoke. Very third world. Locusts. No one seemed to mind and kept on gathering for the parade or the beginning of the bar to bar migration.

Turning left down Bourbon Street the neon lights of the bars and sex clubs created a Disney like atmosphere of temptation and pleasure. The barkers were in rare form with a state or county fair passion and fervor. Working on commission. "Come on in and get fucked up twelve ways to Sunday!" "How much you got boy?" We kept moving surveying the offers before settling on a country music bar more or less. The three for one happy hour may have been a factor of which we were snugly in the middle of. The fact that this was a later night offering and there was more than adequate seating also figured in. After about a half dozen watered down margaritas and some stale chips as a warm up we were officially started. I, as is customary, introduced myself to the bartenders and after a couple of hours was on a first name basis. I have always found this to be a good practice at the beginning of a multiple day drinking binge. This creates a repot with just the right folks which allows for a multitude of later date potential.

Soon the open doorway was calling with the throngs that traipsed past east and west. Once on the dirty pavement the wave of humanity scoops you up and moves you along. Keep your wallet in the front pocket. The old razor blade trick never goes out of favor with the patient thief. Especially with all eyes up watching the balcony eye candies with large plastic breasts and dark glowing nipples the size of silver dollars. God bless America. It wasn't too long and just a few mobile beers and I decided I wanted oysters. It occurred to me I hadn't eaten since the pair of sausage egg biscuits from MacDonald's in Tallulah, La. That meant about six to eight hours and the drinks I had consumed on arrival required reinforcement. The best combo we could find was a traditional oyster and steak house that had a few street side tables available. Perfect for people watching and a restroom break before hitting the street for serious and of course the chowing down. I started with a pair of long necks in anticipation of a long bar wait and two dozen raw oysters. These were gone in a flash and before long I had sunk into a well marbled rib eye, medium. It quickly became obvious they were turning tables so nothing would be long including a potential linger. They were pushing dinner on the tourists and the last thing desired was a pair of beer drinkers tying up a prime table street side. Not enough profit margins.

I was satisfied and full and had no problem with this harsh economic reality. Soon, after several dirty looks from wait staff it was off to the street and more gawking. One contrast I noticed to the abandoned destruction of upper Canal was how clean the French quarter looked. Having been there many times over the years I had always accepted the filth and depravity as part of the local flavor. This was what New Orleans was and had always been. A stopping off point to other places but this time it was very different. I'm not sure if it was the light crowds, which were noticeable, or it was as if the flood had swept through and erased hundreds of years into the river. Either way I wasn't sure if I liked it. The different feel, the different smell. Somehow it reminded me of the homogenized look of Church Street in Orlando, or maybe Printers Alley in Nashville. Almost Disney. It wasn't quite right.

We bounced into a couple of art galleries who remained open braving the crowds and made our way down some side streets. Along the way we witnessed some beat cops tuning some drunks who under ridiculous odds remained defiant. That's how it always is. This one guy sat square on his ass under a single bulb street lamp on St Charles. He sat stoically in about two inches of rain water left from the earlier storm, which threatened to reemerge. A small group had gathered, to which we joined, listening intently to the dysfunctional conversation between cops and drunk. These exchanges, no matter who's in the right always sound like shakedowns. Just something in the rhythm of speech, the tone of the negotiation. The action had quickly become mundane on the main drags so any personal exchanges such as this are viewed with intense interest. This particular issue involved a wasted young mid-westerner who, being separated from his frat friends had been traversing up and down Bourbon violently pulling down girls' tops and slapping ass. This had become a problem with several victims' boyfriends chasing and catching the kid down on St Charles.

The guys had done a pretty good job of subduing the misguided youth when the ever present boys in blue arrived and took over. It wasn't long into the explanation of why this wasn't appropriate even at Mardi Gras before they realized to say more would be futile. His eyes were a blank and searched the crowd over their shoulders no doubt looking for more meat to violate. He was toast at this point. In a flash it was determined he would eventually hurt someone or himself and he was handcuffed and hoisted to his feet. I remember how tall he seemed next to the overweight middle aged officers. This entire diversion took about ten minutes and it was once again time for a mobile brew. The street was getting crowded now and for the first time ever I began to notice the semiprofessional party photographers, this type of development obviously an offshoot of the internet. The girl's gone wild syndrome? The ambush tactics I was not too fond of. As is customary women on the street flash the party goers who occupy the balconies. If the girl is acceptable the very prized and collectable beads are tossed down. One important element is the eye contact. A girl is having an unspoken conversation and a transaction is taking place. Here is the problem. In the shadows under the balconies the photographers lurk for stills and video. This takes place while the girls' eyes are distracted upward and is a little like fish in a barrel. They may not care at the moment but most women in attendance have jobs and families and are very luke warm about being featured in all their glory on internet porn sites. I had never noticed this before. The spontaneity of a beautiful flasher with your memory as witness is totally ruined by the gaggle of ass holes clicking away. That's progress I guess but I didn't like it, especially with pro looking rigs on mobile single leg tripods.

About an hour more of milling and it was restroom break time, of which none were readily available. The shakedown for this necessity requires that you enter a club or restaurant and buy the minimum. Once this is done you can do all the business you require. No questions asked. Just a watered down six dollar drink in most cases. We really were not hungry so we opted for one of the several advertised live sex shows. The interesting thing about these aside from the shitty drinks is you are crammed into a series of flat bench seats surrounding the performance stage which is never occupied due to frequent break times.

What you do get is a tired mid-forties stripper who does fire tricks and a tongue piercing with a large nail. The only upside to this freak show is the bathroom and the swag you come across on the continuous padded seats. I have never failed to walk away with at least an umbrella and at most some folding money. It's all good. We throw down ten in cash for the drinks as you never . . . ever use plastic in these places. The neon is calling. Same old, same old. The seeds that had been planted at the country karaoke bar should have sprouted by now so back toward Canal was the immediate goal. Stumbling in the familiar surroundings of the bar previous I was hit with the reality of a growing and massive crowd in the room.

The only option being to perch near the bathroom corridor linking the club to the restaurant and hope for the best. It was easy to spot the potential seats but no one budged their asses for what seemed an eternity. The upside was the bartender from earlier I had become acquainted with recognized me and continued the happy hour specials for us. That being three for one. Even a watered three-fer is better than nothing.

We waited patiently and after a bit things paid off. Out of the corner of my eye during a karaoke version of Johnny Cash's Cocaine Blues I saw a chair fly violently back into the dark. With my full attention now I could make out a couple in their fifties. He had the professional variety of beer gut reserved for many NASCAR enthusiasts and she was coming in a close second. She also had probably three inches on him in height and incredible posture. It was in a total, indignant uprightness that that she took the punch square on the front teeth. The head snapped back slightly and I swear her eyes glowed to match the stream she was spitting on the floor accompanied by two teeth.

In an instant the fat man was rolling between tables clutching his gushing nose. It was that quick. It was a fucking blood fest. He was crying as she towered over him begging him to get the" fuck up" just one more damn time. In another instant the twin bald bouncers had the pair pinned arms back and restrained. Crisis averted. While all this was going on I had gradually moved toward the now vacant table and without hesitation slid in, sat down and topped off with a portion of the now abandoned pitcher of beer. They wouldn't be having anymore. It tasted a little bitter and I decided it might be Amberboch. No matter. Table and two chairs gained in fair play. The bar tender smiled in our direction. We didn't create the problem, we just made lemonade. From this vantage point we could see the hand off to the street NOPD patrol and the ceremonial administering of the handcuffs. I was a little concerned because in cuffs neither party could try and address the blood issue, which by this time was covering the front shirts of the pair.

Whatever the fight was over it was fast and to the point. It was grand to behold. What was not grand was the singing. This place, being advertised as a Bourbon Street cowboy bar attracted as you would expect a vast assortment of true and dime-store shit kickers. All in all a pleasant enough crowd even when loaded. This did not translate to song selection and quality of performance. The chairs were a huge plus and even made things tolerable to a point. As these things often do, a theme was developed. One person will sing a type of song and it will have some sort of appeal or maybe strike a chord of competition. In this instance I think blind drunken appeal. The vein was "done me wrong" songs. These songs, if you are not familiar are not very upbeat with the exception of the comic ones. These

were not the comic ones. They were creating a depressing downward spiral which from our outside of the fold position would have been amusing if they hadn't been so inebriated.

About an hour was it. The twang had begun to strike me at the base of my skull. We paid our tab which had been reduced by half at least. This development was much unexpected. The reasons could be two-fold. One: The bartender could have been very impressed at how we capitalized on the misfortune of the couple. Two: It was a common house shakedown request. This is accomplished in chaotic situations such as this where the house will not ring up complete sales. The purpose being the additional monies required to make the transaction whole are transferred to the tip side and will go directly to the bartender in full or to be shared. It is a quasi legitimate way of stealing with a legitimate paper backup if suspected by management. The key is draft products which are not as easily inventoried. Considering most kegs have a 3% waste factor in foam and spillage this is all in the realm of possibility. I decided the later as the reason and doubled the amount as tip. My instincts were on target and I got the wink and nod. Street action again.

Bourbon Street was really crowded now. You were almost buoyant in the flow of humanity. The one thing I noticed for the first time was the abundance of stop action street performers creating the periodic island in the otherwise natural flow. These guys were ingenious in their simplicity.

What they had done is created super hero or sports figures done in full size metallic looks. They were totally homemade and had a junk yard style similar to road warriors but somehow familiar. Some were space cowboys. Some were more robot like. All were covered in metallic spray paint which glistened in shades from silver to copper as they balanced on five gallon buckets for the added height. People flocked to tip for a photo with the still life figures that would move only to create an accommodating position, even more so for the ladies. You could also tell the guys were a loose confederation who recognized the importance of boundaries in commerce. Only one performer per block created a menagerie of life size characters. It was interesting the first three blocks. After which, it became a little silly as you realized just how thrown together the whole operation was.

I was much more interested in the bevy of exposed plastic breasts which had multiplied exponentially, that and the small dogs on leashes. I never understood why on earth a person would bring a dog into this mêlée. They were obviously locals and even though I didn't approve they had my undivided attention. They all seemed to be having just as much fun as the revelers and owners. Especially the Chihuahuas. I had my picture taken with a pair. A blond named Mitzi and a fawn called Skooter. I mean what the hell. The trek up the street was getting a little old so we decided one more food stop and bathroom break before heading in.

It was decided there would be a lot less traffic toward the river on Decatur near French Market and infinitely easier to catch a cab so it was that direction we headed. Always pick up the pace in these less populated areas. You never know what's in those dark holes waiting to pop out. Luck was with us this night as we ambled off the side streets and back into the hustle and light. Fried seafood sounded good as an element to soak up some of the alcohol. This was required before sound sleep. What was chosen was a fried oyster po-boy to get the added fortification of the toasted bread and light coleslaw common to that sandwich.

One more beer with the meal was good and I'd be done. We wolfed down the delicacy. Time to move. Within five minutes we were in the back of a beat up gypsy cab rolling slowly down Canal toward I-10. Once again experience won out as we passed the roving groups of treacherous thugs off the beaten path. We slid down in the seat. They wouldn't notice just in the shadows. Not that they would attack. We had us some protection as they say. I could just make out through the scratched and stained Plexiglas barrier the wooded butt of some unnamed revolver peaking from under the day's sports section. It was all cool. The best ten bucks I had spent that night. At the hotel the driver skillfully made the u-turn in the boulevard and we were standing at our door.

I washed the black street dirt off my feet as it made a road map like pattern where the skin had been exposed. I hit the sack and didn't wake up until the very next day. The sun was shining and the blur of the massive amounts of breasts and alcohol didn't even register. It was as if it had all been an illusion. I think the last twelve days were catching up to me as I had logged in the vicinity of 5000 miles to this point and was probably delusional. In years past I would go full speed about two to three years and would crash usually in the fall to sleep a couple of days straight. This sounds extremely unhealthy but seemed to work for me. This was not one of my crash points but I could absolutely use a haircut and my own bed. The weather had cooperated in light of the fact I had run out of clean socks days prior.

Socks and sandals is considered a little "fresh" by most anyway and reminds me of how I felt watching my dad mow the lawn in shorts, black socks and house shoes. Creepy, but as you age, more and more becomes perfectly acceptable. You're not really trying to impress. You're just trying not to get your ass kicked in unfamiliar surroundings or circumstances. As planned we threw our loosely packed shit into the car to depart. First a quick check to see if anything had been stolen by the valet. Not that we would ever get a return or confession but it felt like a responsible action. It was again our lucky day and all seemed secure. We had been traveling light and had not left too much in the vehicle for the opportunity.

Regardless it was a fleeting proud moment. Also as planned I made the quick u turn on Canal as employed by the cab driver prior and was heading up the freeway ramp in a flash. Feeling really good at this point. The light traffic in contrast to the cluster on the way down was much appreciated. I always enjoyed the view toward Lake "Ponch" going north because of the sea of grave monuments on the surface of the massive municipal cemetery. It always reminded me of the scene in "Easy Rider" when Fonda and

Hopper were tripping acid with the two hippie chicks. This day it also reminded me of the bodies that floated up and into the 9th ward during the hurricane. It also brought to mind the parish sheriffs who armed themselves at the other foot of the bridge and wouldn't allow the crime and hopeless panics leave its basin. Old wild west shit. It was all gone now but if you squinted in the bright sun you could almost make it out.

It was one of those things that will remain with us throughout our lifetime. That was a fact. Pushing the pedal down we began to cruse onto the causeway bridge. This thirty or forty mile stretch was basically over water with little or no shoulder so never any highway patrol. There was no cover for them plus the likelihood of being killed for your effort by hung over traffic was high, particularly on a Sunday morning. We had exited town prior to breakfast and after some debate my traveling companion Pat and myself decided to push on to Jackson, miss the church crowd and grab a single day's meal at a buffet. This was sound logic and the thought of soft serve ice cream as dessert was appealing. This dairy craving is my body's way of asking for vitamins and minerals of which I have none left at this point. I must heed the call. Even with spot on timing we hit heavier than usual food lines. I hadn't accounted for the late staying Pentecostal groups. That was ok as I had made good time to this point and could relax and take in the locals in their Sunday best.

It seemed like on this trip I had seen virtually every type of person imaginable and this all seemed very natural. After about forty five minutes and two bowls of vanilla, one with chocolate topping and one strawberry, I was getting gas and pushing west. This was the last good haul ass section of the return as you skirt the corner of North Louisiana, just before hitting Hwy 65 and back into Arkansas farm country. Slow going. Speed traps. Very depressing but its home. One ray is its afternoon and February. Both these points make the need to stop several times and scrape exploded insects off the windshield to see unnecessary. Due north again and within hours pulling up to the house. Sunday afternoon with shadows growing long. Better shower, grab a sandwich and get some shuteye. I have to be at work in the morning and that comes soon.

Kid stuff...

It is a known fact that young people are inherently stupid. They can't help it. Its part a lack of fear and understanding and a level of naivety that has to be driven out usually by years of disappointment and reality. My friends and I were no exception to this rule. One major example was the use of a vast network of storm drain pipes running under the freeway as a playground. Looking back with older more claustrophobic eyes I can't even imagine crawling several hundred yards in pipes so tight you would have to literally back yourself out. The only option was to go forward until you enter one of the multiple box rooms which funnel and direct flow into various areas. From that vantage point you and your compatriots could go in any direction including a complete turn to exit the way you entered.

We never lost a man and we never left a man behind. This by all accounts now was a very stupid game. Sudden rains in the spring or summer have been known to trap and drown more unfortunate mother's sons. We knew it could happen and had heard the warnings. Water builds pressure against the poor kids body which acts like a solid plug. The force propels you against the rough unfinished concrete tube, scraping and removing skin. The thin layer of slime found in the very bottom, usually about four inches wide is of no help or protection. The limited light at either end of the tunnel is extinguished. You are pushed in directions beyond your control. If you are unfortunate enough to be pushed into a reducer pipe which is usually several inches smaller you will most surely die. Only the backup produced by the wedged object of your body will alert anyone of the obstruction. This was a stupid game but one we often played.

In a still undeveloped area of town on the way to my middle and high school there are many abandoned ore mines. The area was widely strip mined during World War 2 and until the seventies for bauxite ore which is a key element in aluminum production. The end result of this process is incredibly deep "bauxite pits" with captured beautiful turquoise water dropping off at the bank sometimes as much as 300 feet deep. The water was cold year round as a result of the depth and was a depository for many "hidden things". My best example of this is Mrs. Goodspeed. On my school bus "56"route there was a semi attractive girl in my class named Carol. She was the second oldest of six kids of stair step age and had a brother two years older. He would later in life be shot in the throat in a robbery gone wrong just off Baseline Road.

This day in her seventh grade year was like all others. She got up. She helped bathe and dress the younger kids for school. She cooked some breakfast while her mother slept in, no doubt tired from a late night at Atlantic Billiards on 65th street. All was normal. Everyone caught the bus or walked the short distance to Wakefield Elementary. The day's schoolwork was typical and soon all piled back on the bus and headed west. Next day at the third stop there was no Carol. Carol with the bright blue eyes. That day came and went and I noticed there was none of the family group that always filed out like clockwork.

The third day they all came out and acted semi-normal except for Carol. I noticed tenseness and made a point to sit with her on the return trip and make some inquiries. Perhaps I could be of some help. After several awkward minutes of grilling she offered up the fact her mother had not been home after school Monday and still hadn't returned. Food was in short supply in the house but she knew where her mom's cash stash was hidden so that could be rectified. What bothered her was her mom's purse was in its customary perch on the kitchen counter. Cash and drivers license as they should be. Car and keys however were not. This was a very strange situation as what I knew of the woman would not allow for this. Whore? Perhaps... Lush? Most certainly, but always responsible and somehow providing for the brood the lord had blessed her with. Days turned into weeks with no word. It was amazing the façade the family presented.

Carol was more than a little distraught. She not only feared the worst but had been thrust at a tender age into the role of mother and potentially provider. The older brother would certainly be of no help and never had been. Father abandonment issues I suspect. More time passed with no word. Every day, like clockwork they would show up dressed and fed and go off to appointed rounds at school or other appropriate errands. To the outside world things were as they should be. As a matter of fact too good as this would be their undoing.

All of the smaller kids were regularly referred to by teachers in evaluations as "spirited". Not exactly trouble but not squeaky clean either. Carol, in an attempt to keep the family intact had become the disciplinarian her mother never was. This was the first red flag. This was probably the first time in history "excellent behavior" led to personal downfall. Noticing drastic change some of the teachers sent notes of congratulations home for signature of acknowledgement. Several were not replied to. This did not go unnoticed with finally an attempt at forgery. Signatures were compared with office records and within days a school administrator was at the door. Something seemed amiss. After several surprise visits and the customary "moms not home right now" answers through cracked doors. It was a matter of time.

Six months had passed and the family had carried on. Carol and her older brother had assumed the bitch had had enough and moved on. At home the jig was up. Social services intervened and the kids went to separate foster families. They suspected the same abandonment scenario. Carol petitioned for emancipation and was granted a waiver to live with a distant aunt who had offered to take only her, perhaps because she was older and more self sufficient than the others. I never saw any of them again.

I caught an article in the police beat section of the paper about ten years later. The water filled bauxite pits are searched by sheriff's divers every few years for stolen items such as cars and trucks and objects of vandalism and theft. Many weapons are found, most with no serial numbers. This day was not a routine search but a search for a suspected drowning victim. Lots of teenagers partied regularly at these secluded spots and after a few beers or a line or two it was not uncommon to have impromptu diving competitions. With a drop of two feet to two hundred in a single dark step even the most sober of swimmers could find trouble. This day a boy from McClelland High School had been seen across the way walking along the shoreline rocks, one moment later not to be seen. The revelers had driven to Lawhon's Grocery on Arch Street Pike and called the authorities from the pay phone. Beer was hidden from view and a search began. In about two hours the river patrol specializing in "recovery" arrived on the scene. The water was incredibly azure and clear at great depths and near the spot of the disappearance the lifeless 16 year old floated as if in space in about 85 feet of water. He was tagged with a float and it appeared the job complete. Before the diver turned back toward the light he noticed something more just below the boy at about another 100 feet. There was a fairly undamaged white Cadillac resting comfortable as if parked. This in itself not so significant but in the windshield he could make out movement. This would be impossible for any type of air pocket to somehow remain a viable option for survival. The water at this depth was also bone chilling cold year round. It was his duty to investigate and within ten minutes or so he approached the car and grasped onto the familiar hood ornament. The movement now was more visible and distinct yet strangely serine. That's when he realized it was a woman looking direct at him with a puzzled smile; her long blond hair floated gently and crowned a perfectly made face. She was strapped in and sat perfectly in the front passenger seat with impeccable posture. It was the missing Mrs.Goodspeed. The water temperature and enclosed car had perfectly protected and preserved her just as she had been ten years before. The youngest kid by this time was a senior in High school. The older brother was dead. Things had moved on. The pit had hidden and held her there and may have continued to except for the young boy who led them here. No one ever found out what had happened and it didn't much matter. She had probably crossed someone or a deal of some kind obviously went bad. Either way there's no backing up. No do overs. I saw Carol many years later at a reunion. She looked much older, almost like her mom when I saw her last. I wanted to ask if anything had come of any of it but I kept quiet. We laughed and had a beer.

Just down from that particular pit was a strip mine dump ground, long since abandoned, which had found new life as an off road motorcycle race track and club house.

This was not for traditional motocross but choppers and hybrids owned by the notorious (I cannot feel comfortable naming as they are still quite notorious.) motorcycle gang out of Central Texas. They were the real deal and partied most days till all hours out of a make shift shed of a bar. This was all private for members with booze served free paid for out of dues and illegal gain. It was known as the "Rocket Run". There was a loose form of mutual respect between us and the gang. This was rooted in a fear of certain death on our part and the desire to not involve County law enforcement on their end. Quid pro quo.

The chapter membership fluctuated between thirty and fifty strong plus "old ladies" depending on who may or may not be traveling through from Dallas and to or from Kansas City. They were into all manner of things including drugs, prostitution and weapons which you could hear on the practice range if you happened nearby. We didn't need the kind of trouble they could deliver. I was sure they had contributed their fare share of stolen vehicles and lives into the nearby bauxite pits across the road.

It was the perfect setup for such a group with its footprint just outside the city limits and during the administration of a weak and ineffective county sheriff. They were what would be commonly referred to as "bad ass". They had a rough look almost as worn as the herd of ugly leatherette faced women often seen in their company. Over time we had developed a party spot of our own just adjacent so we could hang out, drink beer and see two of the turns on the race course, one with a slight jump. This was comical to watch with the longer chopped bikes with it not uncommon to see a crack up or at worst forks breaking off the bike.

A couple of times requiring the very timid approach of the local ambulance service, all very entertaining from our perch. One other development as a result of our frequent viewing was a basic understanding of their schedules. The comings and goings on a Saturday afternoon and night. They were very predictable and deliberate in their movements. I'm not really sure why? Perhaps a subconscious compensation for the otherwise unkempt existence. Either way a door was opened in our collective minds and within a couple of months a plan was hatched. Being aware of the amount of beer brought into the compound we were able to determine the amount that would not be missed on a regular gig night. That amount was determined to be two cases of cans. Two cases of free beer was a great amount to us and would go very far. The other strong enticement was the brand they drank was regular Coors which was illegal in Arkansas at the time and had to be bootlegged in. This was also an incredible opportunity for the beers we didn't consume could potentially be passed on for five dollars per can on the streets minimum. What that meant was a great buzz for free and a stake of cash for pizza or Churches chicken later in the evening. All of this information figured into the plan and made the myriad of risks, which were great, almost worth it.

Down side we would be caught and simply disappear from the earth. Our parents would never have a body to bury and would either have a sudo-memorial service or just a newspaper obituary, both probably several years after the fact. Not a promising prospect. These things would be for normal people to consider of which we were not. The plan was as follows: according to their schedule just after dusk, everyone was required at the track. This was primarily to aid in hooking up the multitude of car batteries to the makeshift event lighting along the course. This would create about a twenty minute window where the club shack would be totally unattended. The shack was a wooden plank structure about sixty feet wide, with a tin roof and no windows. It had blow through screen doors front and back in perfect alignment with each other.

Four of our guys would traverse along the perimeter ditch on Arch Street Pike at a point where it was about three feet deep. Two of the guys would remain in the ditch while the other pair would emerge about 100 feet from the building. There were multiple scrub bushes creating large shadows for some cover. Speed was imperative but movement that seemed ordinary was even more important. Two would make way to the back screen door, slowly open and pull two cold cases from the stack. One carried by each while making way to the ditch and hand off to the other waiting pair. Through trial and error we had determined it was too tough and risky for two guys to make the entire trip. A case of beer when in a crouching position can be incredibly heavy, particularly at sixteen. We only attempted this five or six times but we knew arrogance at our success would surely cause a slip and the resulting disaster. Just the fact we had the sand to attempt it seemed a victory over adversity of sorts. Or it could be construed as stupidity from wherever you stand on the issue. Regardless, after that summer we never did that again. Anyway at that time pretty much anyone could buy beer on 65th Street. The novelty was gone. Plus it was about this time there were large scale bootleg operations into Louisiana with widespread Coors and we had graduated to Miller Beer in "pony" bottles anyway. Even more faddish bullshit. It was like when my dad as a high school graduation gift gave me a used suit case. "What do I do with this?" I asked to which he replied "you'll figure it out".

Saturday Last

Saturday started off like most. I was a little disheveled and my new longer beard I was sporting had a slight bend to the left. Slight yet distinctive. I wasn't sure yet the look I was going for but "the most interesting man in the world" from the Dos Equis television ads was quite appealing. The night before was the start of two low stress and maintenance gigs for me and Mexican George. The kick off involved loading up some sound gear as support for a DJ at a high school reunion for my day job boss. Kinda interesting considering this was also my alma mater; just this class is several years after me. This was the "grad night" and was an outdoor affair held in the Rivermarket Pavilions. Music was to begin at 6pm. I was in the quickie mart down from George's house and ten minutes from the gig when the phone rang.

The DJ had shown up a little early and was alarmed by the total lack of equipment. We had not worked together before and knowing the general flakiness of these sorts of things he didn't want to get off on the wrong foot. I assured him all was well as we loaded an eighteen pack in the cooler and dumped on the ice. As prescribed we were there quickly and set up in about five minutes. All seemed in working order so we started dipping into the ice chest searching for answers. I knew they have to be down in there somewhere.

I knew quite a few of the guests and actually had a good time catching up. I was three years older than the average attendee but if I say so myself I had fared better than most. After a couple of hours we had nothing but ice left in the container and decided to excuse ourselves across the street to the "Flying Fish" for oysters and more beer. I wasn't sure how the oysters would be as we were almost thirty days into the massive oil spill in the Gulf of Mexico. I was very surprised and commented on the fact they were the freshest and healthiest I had seen in years. I sent Amber a text about this fact and she commented they were probably "oilsters". That was cute and it was suggested she should copy write that. After two dozen half shell, two po-boys and a bucket of long necks we were ready to cruise back over to the gig.

As is customary with these things the party goers wanted to hang on and we obliged about an additional hour. After loading and dropping George, who had to work at 6am moving some steel, I stopped at Zack's on the way home for two or three for the road. That got me in bed at around midnight. Much later than I wanted to start off a two day deal. Saturday at 11am I had to be at the submarine museum on the Arkansas River to guard and help direct traffic a few hours. Dehydration was an issue because of the night before but I was able to scrounge up several old bottles of water in the back of my work truck to tide me over. In my zest to clean out my yellow truck (suv) and make room for the audio equipment I had somehow mislaid my folding chair, an essential piece of equipment for such endeavors (guarding submarines).

I wasn't sure where it was at all so I made a quick call to Sheila who managed the nearby RV Park and barrowed one within minutes. After exchanging some pleasantries and being told I was full of shit I moved on and took my position. It was relatively uneventful considering I was in the apex of a High School graduation, a large company picnic, a river boat cruise and the regular museum Saturday traffic. It was all handled and before 3 PM I was ready to move on to the next task. The same audio equipment as the night before had to be set up in the Doubletree Hotel Ballroom before 6 PM so I took the opportunity to walk the dog and made a weak attempt at fixing a cable television issue. The latter to which I was unsuccessful.

After my brief stop I reached George, who had washed his face and slathered on some cologne. Plan was we would set up the equipment and head to "Pep Boys" for a rear tail light bulb for the yellow truck. I had known I had a tail light out and had been slightly spooked by all the police traffic stops I had seen the night before. Once there we popped off the lens in the parking lot and were rolling again in about ten minutes. Pep Boys just happened to be in the parking lot of the shopping center that housed my favorite cheap Mexican food joint "Los Palmas" and it was happy hour. Two bowls of bean dip with cheese sauce and much cerveza and it was time to hook up with Pat at Zack's bar for round two.

All seemed well till I opened the truck door and found my door locks unresponsive as well as the ignition. She was stone dead. Apparently when we were testing the lights I had forgotten to shut them off for a couple of hours. I called Pat to report the fact "We really screwed up…man", when a very nice man and wife in a huge truck next to us felt pity and gave us a jump.

In no time we were back on the freeway heading south. We didn't have to be back at the hotel till between 10:30 and 11pm so there was no hurry. Zack's seemed an appropriate stop as it was now early evening and the DJ would be in by now. The new DJ was a real man of a woman complete with wall to wall tattoos and short butch haircut. Multiple piercing, plaid pants and a gas station attendant work shirt rounded out the ensemble.

She had really taken a liking to me for some reason and had been texting me periodically for some time. Perhaps because I seemed to show no fear with her look and sexual orientation. She also liked what I brought to the table as far as obscure musical background and my many years of exposure to the like. For several months I had fed her on Fridays a list of about twenty songs and artists per outing. This she kept posted in the sound booth. She seemed to be able to always tell our moods from across the room and programmed accordingly. She liked when she did someone else's request and I would barge into the booth and demand that whatever (usually rap) shit was blaring to cease immediately. We had bonded I suppose. As was expected she was at her station and feeling no pain. We surveyed the room and sundered up to the bar. We were in the usual range of seats on the far south end where a claim had been staked as far from the original bar regulars as possible. No animosity intended but we just didn't mix with those types. We were Nuevo-regulars and seemed in much more control than any of them dared to be. It was in part the fact we never looked at them or the video poker games they constantly played. No real cash exchanged, just points in a cyber world of faceless players in dark rooms across the country with code names like "High Pockets" and "Lefty". What total bullshit. I never really played much poker in my life but if I did I would have the decency to sit at a real table, feel the felt and toss the chips. Never got into the game. Never really got gambling at all. I would much rather throw down at an expensive restaurant, drop a wad and feel like I had accomplished something. But that's just me. I'm no authority.

As expected the DJ could somehow sense our joyous presence and burst into some Marshal Tucker, specifically "This ole Cowboy". A classic and one of my favorites. Perfect to start an evening off correctly. The best jobs are the hurry up and wait types which allow the indulgence of an adult beverage. We were at the crest of one such job. After a bit we got hungry and decided to peruse the menu. I'm not sure why exactly as it hadn't changed in at least five years but one could always hope. I considered dip but remembered how shitty it was considering we had had two bowls earlier of the best dip in the western hemisphere. After the debate I had had many times we all chose cheeseburgers. I'm not sure why but George often lingers slightly behind my choices in eating situations and nine times out of ten orders the identical thing. I'm not sure if it's a respect thing or he genuinely cannot make up his own mind. I guess I'll never know. One thing we both agree on is we like our French fries "Las Vegas" style as with white gravy on the side. I've had this at Caesar's Palace on many occasions. After about ten minutes we were sitting in front of three heaping platters of bliss and proceeded to dismantle the culinary creations from the sides inward. We were drinking now. This can maybe be attributed to the refueling and the addition of a series of palate delicacies we hadn't known that day to this point.

It was quick work and I checked my watch periodically to make sure we were in reasonable time. Things were all good. Additionally we had not received any audio distress calls so all seemed in working order. More beers were ordered and slid down easy. A tapestry of great songs were being woven as a comment and perhaps a sing along on our part accompanied almost every selection. Within no time we were about thirty minutes late. Quickly paying our tab and moving on to the truck we were soon on the freeway and headed back toward downtown with its luxury hotels. Ten to fifteen minutes later we entered the Riverside drive- through at the Doubletree Hotel, where we legitimately parked in loading and headed in.

The dress banquet had ended probably thirty minutes earlier and a very inebriated DJ sat at the controls of our gear. He was playing something I didn't recognize and chilling out with a couple of longnecks. What I consider the greatest invention of the computer age sat before him. He is one of the fortunate folks in his profession to have an internet pass to literally millions of songs waiting for him to summon to his personal download storage. This miracle can happen in seconds which is truly amazing. With this in mind I pulled up a few banquet chairs about five feet from the large Peavey SB2 speakers, ordered four more beers from the banquet bartender who was cleaning up. I plopped down for the show.

George looked a little worried as he is not from the culture and a generation that appreciates such pursuits. Never the less he took a seat as did the DJ. Next a chair pulled up beside me and was soon occupied by one of the reunion hostesses wearing a wonderfully cut outfit reminiscent of a medieval serving wench. She was quite welcome to join the to this point all masculine party. She had overheard our conversation concerning the fact I never get to hear my gear at high volume on songs I actually liked.

This obviously intrigued her. When she heard my selections were all Pink Floyd she was sold and bought us all rounds. I suspect the bartender sold more beer after the party than during. I made sure the cleanup staff was cool with us and they smiled large, broad approving smiles over the blaring music. We were obviously entertaining to them. The song list was extensive and about three songs into Dark Side of the Moon we were given the high sign. George was also on the verge of projectile vomiting as I had seen that pleading look before. He knew full well I was certifiably insane and with the slightest encouragement would take the party into the next day. He had witnessed this on occasion and had learned to say no and get off the runaway train when he had enough. This was one of those times. I informed our new found guests it was time to tear down. After a quick search for a luggage cart we had stashed behind a curtain wall we were loaded and on the elevator down. We stopped on two floors but could not receive additional passengers as we commanded the entire available space. Once in the lobby something happened we couldn't explain or put our fingers on. We discussed it the next day in an attempt at the truth but could only come up with the fact it was bad. Best of our knowledge as we pushed outside with the loaded cart we had to move through a designated smoking area inhabited by a young man and two ladies, we would assume tourists. At that point things began to get strange.

I remember vaguely the guy holding the door open for us at which point he evidently did or said something I took great offence to. I remember shouting obscenities and I recall yelling at them to go get some authorities and tell on us for being rude. I remember them almost sprinting to the lobby elevator to make an escape. I felt terrible the next day if they were tourists but it must have been a huge line crossed. You know the main rule of tourism. "Never piss in another man's yard". I think Leonard Nimoy said that. Or was it Terrance Trent Darby? Good times.

Matt and Marty

An odd couple if there ever was one. These two guys went to my High School and both were products of the all white neighborhood known as "Wakefield". Marty was in my class and Matt was two years older. Marty lived two streets down from the top of the hill past the fire station. Matt lived further over near the ball park, maybe a half mile. Marty had a very slight build, about five foot three or so and maybe one hundred pounds soaking wet. A very weak maybe. He had red hair brushed high and puffy as was the style at the time. He had braces on his teeth, upper and lower. He always had really cool tennis shoes, usually Puma brand, usually some unusual color like fluorescent orange. Marty liked to drink beer but because of his size three was usually his limit.

Matt was his polar opposite. Matt was a washed out jock. He was probably a little over six feet tall and had a relatively muscular build for his age. He had a permanent snarl on his face as a result of a bicycle accident several years before. He was known to sucker punch people when provoked. He was unusually tan and had jet black hair piled tall. A high and tight before there was such a thing I'm thinking. He had been kicked off the football team as a junior for stealing wallets from lockers during practice. He was a dangerous guy, more because of his unpredictability than his menace. It was unclear the motivation of their friendship. I suspect Matt was taking advantage of a person needing to fit in a higher profile and notorious crowd. It was quid pro quo and both benefited.

RAY MAN

One summer as a gift resulting from a home newly broken Marty received a relatively new 75 model T-Top Pontiac Trans Am. This black beauty was very similar to the Smokey and the Bandit car of Burt Reynolds movie fame complete with the gold firebird emblems on the hood and upper quarter panels. From that moment on they were inseparable. Marty often let Matt, who had a suspended drivers license for reckless driving and two DWI warnings cruise around town with Marty slouched down low, sinking into the black leather.

We never understood the fact Matt acted like he owned the car. It was in the way he parked one arm on the top of the wheel and the other out the window, kind of a pimp style which fit his reputation. Marty almost seemed embarrassed but never complained. He was very much the bitch in the relationship. We even sometimes saw Matt driving alone while Marty was at work at the local burger joint on 65th street. There was also the fact they always changed seats around the block just out of his mothers scrutinizing view. A covert action in response to warnings about Matt. The parties about this time in space were getting pretty intense at Harper's field, a farm area down a dirt road just off the freeway to Dallas, perfect for parking and drinking under cover of darkness.

They were part of one of the first groups who brought Tequila on the scene, ratcheting up things a bit. Marty seemed almost smug as he let Matt skid sideways in the low grass upon arrival and again at departure. They obviously fed off of each other's enthusiasm. It almost seemed gay except for the reputation that Matt exhibited at every turn of ultimate machismo.

Matt had been warned by the lenient local police about his drinking and driving but this new to us hard liquor was more than he could realistically control. It was a Friday and hot and sticky in mid-summer. We had seen them earlier in the evening in line at the liquor store drive through getting the customary fifth. After that they were MIA. About midnight the news was spreading through the neighborhood like a foul wind.

There had been an accident in which there had been a death. Later we heard the details and realized we had only thought we knew what a clown Matt was. Apparently the pair for some reason was heading up Allsopp Park Road around 9 PM at a high rate of speed moving west. Allsopp Park Road in this area is extremely dark and narrow with no guard rails and a drop of about forty to fifty feet into a creek bed below. Alcohol was a factor. The T-Tops were off the car and open and the car careened off the edge and slowly flipped, landing on its top. As a result Marty fell out of the open top and was crushed by the weight of the car. He died instantly. What bothered police was that the extremely drunk Matt was unharmed. Also alarming was the fact he claimed he was in the passenger seat with the broken Marty nearer the driver's side. The seat was pushed all the way back and locked. Not in a position appropriate for a driver of his stature.

Questions were raised. Within about a week Matt was taken down for questioning, mainly at the request of Marty's family. As a result of the extent of his injuries Marty had a closed casket on Thursday. Everyone knew who was behind the wheel that night. Years later I even heard him brag at a party about what he had gotten away with. I never saw him again after that. I didn't easily lose the image of him changing seats with the lifeless little boy, not allowed to grow up. Matt left the state as he spiraled down further into drugs and bad behavior.

Thank god for small favors.

Hard Day's Night

The other day I had to go to LA for a meeting with some concert execs and one of my clients who I believe owns some exotic properties. I had about ten days free with only two committed for work. I had considered getting a rental car and busting east to Vegas to hang out with my buddy Brian and his friends. Maybe grab some lunch. Either way whatever would be fine. My trip was paid for by the client so it was all gravy at this point. The meetings were typical with the exception I got to select the dinner spot one night which naturally was the Yard House in Long Beach. Typical LA weather. 75 during the day and upper 50's on the shore after dark. The striped lighthouse was functioning. Queen Mary lit up year round like it was Christmas. Second night we were at the Rainbow Room and the Whiskey on Sunset. My client is huge into hair bands and just creams being in these filthy fucking places. Vomit smell and all. I think it was on the Rainbow's outdoor patio when the idea was first thrown out. Alcohol was a factor and at the time it seemed like a simple and almost sensible thought. "Why don't we do some fishing?" All these drunk bastards thought this sounded like a great idea.

Sometime in the wind and sun would do us all some good. Nothing better than a cold beer on the open seas. I had assumed we were talking Catalina or maybe Santa Monica or Huntington. "Where you got in mind?" was the next question. "I'm thinking Nassau". Nassau? I was familiar with THE Nassau but us being on the left coast I figured it had to be some area maybe I was unfamiliar with.

The conversation began to accelerate as a plan fleshed out and took form. I sat silent for a bit, drank my tepid draft beer, ate my chips and patiently waited to see where this was going. When airfare became the topic and a private jet belonging to one of the rockers was thrown in the mix I knew what they meant. It would actually be far to the right side in the Bahamas. I had the time and they were paying so what the hell. Sounded good.

Deep sea fishing is impossible for me after my biceps tear but I can certainly bait hooks and drink suds. It all sounded like crazy drunk talk but I knew us all and we were just crazy enough. We cut things short and went to the hotel to get on-line and seek out lodging. After about thirty minutes we settled on the Wyndam Resort in Nassau, settled just up the coast from downtown and just across from the shipping channels carrying cruise ships to and from the port of call.

Weather was not exactly great. There was a tropical depression near Florida that funneled extreme winds on the wayward side, exactly where our rooms were on the twelfth floor. Luckily I had my passport with me so after an extremely long direct flight populated by dreams filled with horror we were touching down at the third world airport. I never understood why none of these places invested a damn dime on airport design or amenities.

Did they not realize? Did they not understand that first impressions really are important? When the first thing you see is a shit hole that tends to set the tone. Not however in our case. We could really give a damn at this point as we grabbed our bags and headed to customs. The line was relatively short and we were greeted by a smartly dressed uniformed agent with a broad ethnic smile, very Bohemian.

Our stuff was loosely searched as who would smuggle anything "into" Nassau. The return to USA proper is always the bitch if there is going to be one. After being stamped I made a quick bathroom stop followed by cramming all into one of the many mini-van taxi cabs at the ready.

This particular one had a recently broken side hatch door which we were instructed to please hold shut for the remainder of our journey, part of the adventure no doubt. I was starting to lose my buzz. The cab was on empty and the very happy and polite driver pulled over to fill up. Gas was over six dollars per gallon. I took the opportunity to go into the convenience store and bait shop and grabbed a liter of Meyer's dark Jamaican rum. Great with Coke.

The one great piece of advice from the driver involved the local bus system. Our hotel was several miles down the two lane road from downtown and would require a ten dollar cab ride each way. The number ten bus which circled the Nassau area and landed in the heart of downtown stopped just out front at a cost of 25 cents one way. Mix with the locals. The route also took you past the big daily local party known as "the fish fry". This consisted of many shacks of multi colors and shapes which served the temporary food purveyors handling the fresh sea catch of the day. Every night, seven days a week.

There were three bars on the outskirts of this area but for locals only. Tourists were not welcome. Cash only…no plastic. The local favorite is fried conch. Grouper fingers the size of your hand goes for two dollars. Tourists can buy beer in 40 ounce cans across the highway and take in as long as left still in the bag. Palm the cop a single at the crosswalk. I love these fucking places. Third world but not really. Dusk is more or less curfew for tourists in all areas except the heavily patrolled dock areas which are home to the daily cruise ships. Reminded me a lot of San Juan. If you are outside of this protection I must imagine the wide broad smiles turn very dark. They want some of our money during the day and all of it at night.

In the distance across the cove is the "Atlantis" resort, another example of corporate excess that points directly at the local wide divide between rich and poor. It was almost embarrassing. Especially later when we walked through to throw some bones at the casino and noticed the "no locals" signs posted conspicuously at all entrances. It didn't feel quite right.

We had made some calls about charters and after some haggling had one secured for early the next morning. We would be departing from the large seawall at the harbor. Heading that way anyway we checked things out inconspicuously. The boat looked fairly clean for these parts and was captained by a tan, older looking American and his two Bohemian mates, about a 33 footer with good paint. We were satisfied and didn't want to be caught staring and draw attention.

It was getting a little warm for October but this is Nassau. A margarita to start sounded appropriate and we dove headlong into the first tourist dive we found which oddly enough was a Mexican themed fish joint featuring karaoke at eight o'clock Friday and Saturday. The drinks were cold and not watered down as was also reflected in the price. Conch fritters as usual to start. After a few it was time to dig a little deeper into downtown before we would have to head over to the bus stop and the totally environmentally controlled tourist refuge at the resort.

We were kinda disappointed that there weren't more dive joints, perhaps like you would find in New Orleans. That's where the people are where you can take the true measure of a place. Most bars and restaurants were theme type places and either high end or fast food. There was not much middle ground. The first thing that jumped out was the Hard Rock. This didn't sound terrible for some nachos and beer so we were soon on the second floor veranda overlooking the side street. Cool view. Lots of commerce. Lots of movement. Very busy on the brick pavers peeking out periodically from under the broken asphalt. Who's stupid idea was that public works project? Soon an hour had passed and someone suggested the steak at our resort. Sounded great plus there was the second biggest casino in town just off the main hotel lobby.

This would not be an all-nighter because of our early date on the water. Last thing you want is a touch of hangover on some potentially rough waters. Can make for a very long day. After the bus ride, dinner and drinks, I found myself balancing on the back legs of a chair with my feet on my twelfth floor room balcony rail.

I was pouring Meyers Dark rum from my second bottle into some Coke I had secured in the lobby liquor store and lit up one of the six Cuban cigars also purchased near the casino. The cruise ships were lined up and departing in orderly fashion just out from the shoals in the shipping channel. The shallow area below was a beautiful turquoise color by day in contrast to the deeper ocean beyond. This was what made Nassau so appealing to the pirates of old I learned. The rocks that surrounded and signaled the harbor protected bigger ships from running aground but allowed the shallow drafting pirate vessels safe passage all the way to shore. The larger ships of war had no weaponry capable of the span so they sat helpless at the barrier, unable to pursue. I read this all on a brochure. It had full color renderings.

   This was perfect for me. Watching the massive cruise ships, Disney, Carnival, etc, etc. pass by and watch the lights dim as they turn starboard and out to sea, straight to Florida or elsewhere. More important was I was alone. I love the camaraderie but I can only take those assholes in small doses. You know how it is. But it was basically their dime so a degree of attention was required. Next morning arrived early but more so.

   My balcony faced east so the sun coming in on my face woke me a couple of hours before the alarm. I had forgotten to close the sliding glass door. The sound of the waves crashing made me wish I wasn't going and could just catch up on some rest. I never sleep real well on planes. Never the less this fishing trip was the whole point. It wouldn't be too bad considering my infirmity as I mentioned wouldn't allow me to actually fish.

   I would guard the beer cooler and catch some sun. The waves were a little choppy but easily able to navigate. The water seemed clear once we were free of the docks and the oil and debris trapped there. Birds followed us out as well and a pair of dolphins picked us up a little ways out in deep water. Might as well go along... everybody else is as Josey Wales once said. All looking for a free ride. I peeked in the cooler and found it fully stocked with our favorite beer brand and about a case of Red Stripe. I popped one to test its tepidity and was pleased to find it as cold as it looked. This was going to be a very good day.

   Hooks were baited and wet and we were on our way. Just in view of the shore, maybe two miles out. The sky here was bright and clear. You could see a million miles if that was your objective. Only downside I could spot was no cell phone reception. Not that that was a problem. It was all ship to shore radio at this point. The captain was skilled and knew his spots. It wasn't an hour and we had our first strike. The drag was slight on the line but the reel still needed to be wetted on the initial run. This fish was not to be and the line snagged on the hull as the catch circled underneath the boat and snapped it. That's ok. The beer was still cold. The rest of the trip was just trolling around with little action. Nothing big. About mid to late afternoon we had about enough sun and expressed the desire to go hole up in the relative cool of one of the bars downtown off the pier. It wasn't long and we were stumbling along in the mass of humanity, a huge contrast to where we had earlier been. There was every type of person you can imagine. Some well dressed in English cut linen suits with straw hats. The other end of the spectrum were the street beggars, some white and some black, all with the seat worn out of cut off pants, rope belts around gaunt waists on most. No doubt from sitting daily on the rough pavement, all these guys looking beaten and worn. The sun and rum had made the whites of their eyes a dull brown. They looked down most of the time. The other type of street character was the sneak thief. Like in the French Quarter of N.O. in these tight quartered overcrowded streets it's always good to keep wallets in front pockets, especially when drinking or drunk.

These guys look similar to the street sitters except about half or less the age. Perhaps this is the natural evolution of a sneak thief turning into a street sitter. They usually travel in groups or packs if you will. They will fall behind you walking on the sidewalk and wait patiently for the opportunity to strike. Again, like the Quarter it's not unusual for a light cut at the bottom of the back pocket to be made with a single edge razor blade. After which you will be tailed for however long it takes for the wallet to work its way out and fall to the ground to be retrieved by the group. Ill gotten gain.

Like my dad always said "be aware of your surroundings". Very true as you should always be aware of people around you, most of all those who linger a little long. Throw your shoulders back and be confident in any location has always worked for me. Avoid back alleys at all cost after dark. We wouldn't be having this problem. Not getting dark until 8:30 or so and the last number ten bus running at 8pm made it imperative we move along. Within about ten minutes we had departed off the street into a deep hole of a bar marked by a weather worn plank with a rough cartoonish looking skull on it in addition to some indiscernible writing. Our kind of place. These kinds of places even if not officially should be treated as cash bars. Credit card info is traded by insiders and many thousands of dollars has been lost by tourists before they were able to get home and back into real world routine. This bar was a little more local than the norm and seemed geared to dock workers and the like. Very blue collar. I fit in more than the rest of my party and I suddenly had the urge again to dump them as I had at the resort the night before. I didn't because I had about fifty bucks in cash and hadn't eaten yet. Chances were they would pick up the check.

Cash money goes a long way on an out of country drinking binge. The bartenders were two very overweight black chicks with British accents and bright colored off the shoulder outfits to fit the personality. I think we might have been a breath of fresh air to them after surveying the room, a typical joint with a rough nautical theme, one pool table in the rear by the single male/ female restroom with the hasp lock. Juke box with half the lights out and a slight rattle in the bass speaker. Songs were a quarter. Heavy on Buffet and Reggae, with a spattering of Merle Haggard and Willie…no doubt requested selections. Roughly half the stools were padded and they were taken by regulars hunched over various whiskies and rum pours like vultures. We ordered beer and were quickly advised to stick with a bottle and not draft. It seemed most of the glasses had been broken the week before in a massive historic fight and would not be replaced any time soon. The other reason is you never know what they put in that draft beer or so we were told by several. Always heeding friendly advice, unless it doesn't pass the smell test, long neck bottles were ordered.

They weren't the coldest but were acceptable after our long parched afternoon of downing several power punched Red Stripe. Pretty soon conversations were struck up and it was as if we had been here all our lives. Things happen that way sometimes. Not always, but sometimes. Drinks were exchanged in a variety of shots much to my dismay when we discovered the great food one of the bartenders had garnered from the "fish Fry" area and brought to reheat and resell as her own. I hate to do shots with fried food. It just doesn't seem to ever work properly and often leads to disaster. Something about the mixture I'm sure. I had a couple of more conch with some white bread and a side of some pickled mixture of vegetables and fruit. We chowed down at five dollars per plate and were quite full and satisfied well before dark. Drinks and bull shit continued to flow in a positive direction but I could tell how quickly this place could turn. Several of the older rummy types had filtered on out to who knows where and were replaced by guys just off work, way behind in drinking and a lot less charming and hospitable. We would be leaving soon. I kept thinking about all the broken beer mugs and exactly what that must have been like. Clear projectiles at rocket speed slicing through the low light. We paid our tab which was very reasonable (filed the name of this place away) and after getting our bearings, stumbled on down toward the number ten bus stop.

This had been great fun but I was kinda interested in getting back to my room and the remainder of my bottle of Meyers, get a shower and watch the cruise ships depart again. It's funny what appeals to you sometimes and at this stage of my career I have nothing to prove particularly to these bastards. Plus the next day was Halloween and surely there would be some wild island carnival action. Wrong!

The Hard Rock was having a costume contest which was out of the question. Can you imagine us dressed in make shift outfits and riding the city bus downtown for an after dark judging with a fifty dollar prize?, spending five times that in over priced sissy drinks and shitty food. Losing the competition to some tourist bitch with thong swim bottoms on, getting mugged and robbed on the street waiting for a cab which never comes. Good times. There just didn't seem to be anything practical going on.

Having this conversation in the lobby a very helpful hotel employee with a wide ethnic smile informed us the hotel casino was the place to be with drink specials, a live band and costume contest. Sounded good and very promising with no travel required. That alone would potentially save the cost of several drinks. Frankly watching for sundown was getting a little tiresome.

The plan was made to stay on property so I hit the pool, just after a quick stop at the lobby package store and two 40 ounce Miller Lite beers. I had the chick at the counter, who was becoming accustomed to me by this time put it in a plastic bag with a little ice. Very accommodating.

The wind of the last couple of days as a result of a nearby hurricane had started to subside and it was finally possible to grab a few rays in a sublime position. The boat had only exposed my back and shoulders leaving the other areas in stark contrast. I tried hard to kill the first 40 as quickly as possible cause I knew with the quickly melting ice that second can could conceivably be piss warm by the time I got to it. It took about five deep swallows across my teeth. The third was better than the second and the fifth was just fine. I was back in the saddle. The Rasta guys were starting to roll around offering the pool or beach go-er everything from heroin to ankle bracelets. All for a very good price "mon". After brushing off the third I guess they collectively got the hint and I was left to my I-pod for a bit.

My hosts were really bugging the shit out of me at this point in the trip and I was very much ready to get home the next day and pet my dog, among other things. I was really enjoying the low music when I had just one more interruption. It was one of the guys in flower print shorts and Tommy Bahama shirt partially hiding a massive beer belly coming to join me. That's just great man. I stepped up action on the second can in an attempt to run. I was going to be with the gang the entire evening at the Halloween party and really needed this quiet time. It was not to be.

He was obviously going to hang so I shoved all my electronic devices back into my black leather backpack and prepared for what may. He wanted to get my opinion on some marital issues or something, I don't know for sure… I wasn't listening anymore. I was concentrating behind my sunglasses on the pair of co-eds just over his right shoulder. Other than being diverted occasionally by his hideous shirt I was pretty much locked on them. I would guess about 21 or 22. One had a pale yellow thong with string top. The other similar in lime green.

I took a long slug of the now luke warm beer and nodded at him with enthusiasm. The things I have to do sometimes. After what seemed an eternity I suggested we grab a cold beer at the beachside bar. Anyway the chicks had moved on and I saw two empty stools. I also knew firsthand he still had an open tab there. The water was a really nice color today and I soaked it in as the continued conversation blew past my ears and into the ozone. About five o'clock and maybe ten beers later I suggested we get ready, meet the others, eat and then hit the party or whatever it was. This seemed like a plan and after a shower I retreated to the porch with a quickie rum cocktail to watch the ships. This had become my ritual. It was what I wanted to do without influence or prejudice. It was great but I knew if I ever wanted to work with these guys and more important get home, I would have to attend the party. Perhaps it might actually be fun. We had reservations at the upscale Caribbean fusion restaurant on the top floor of the resort at seven and were admiring each other's outfits in the lobby at 6:45. I bucked the entire vibe with a linen sport coat I had picked up at the Vegas Forum shops the month before. Very sporty but maybe a little dated, black shirt underneath, very Miami Vice. Probably dumb looking but I was comfortable and didn't really give a shit. My personal plan was to get a steak if on the menu with some rum on the side and hit some slots before the live band started. This all fell into place and with limited conversation. Before too long I was parked in front of my favorite "Double Diamond" haywire machine and plugging in for quarter plays. I had upped my play limit to fifty in observance of the holiday and was pretty much keeping up with things. Staying ahead about $35 and deciding to cash out about 10PM when the band was to start. We were able to snag four stools actually at the bar which doubled as a stage. It was a peculiar arrangement with a platform built on top of the back bar with hidden stairs behind into a storage room or something.

The drum riser was an additional eighteen inches tall. The result from our vantage point was a strange, neck straining view straight up the noses of the front men. Truly bizarre. To top this off the band was local Rasta type dudes in costume. The lead singer dressed as Dracula although the painted on widows peak was more reminiscent of Eddie Munster. The very short, ill fitting cape may have contributed to this. In the spirit of fun I immediately requested "Thriller" by Michael Jackson.

Unfortunately the band only knew the intro which by the fifth or sixth attempt became a terrible tease. The singer really wasn't bad but the costume greatly distracted from his potential talent. Kind of a shame. I became embarrassed for him. After scanning the room I also realized there were no single people of any sort with every table supported by tight couples. Several obvious honeymoon parties…you know the drill. It began to look like I would be entertained once again by the conversation of my hosts. What the fuck was I thinking? After about an hour I saw an opportunity veiled as a restroom stop and hit the gaming floor on the return. I had the gain cash and thought just hanging back would be cool. They would understand a weakness like this even though it was totally for my benefit. They would not question. The band had played a repertoire of about ten songs, gives or takes, and was now repeating. Most we recognized not that we were too drunk to notice.

The band members even craned their necks searching for me as the band launched once again into the "Thriller" intro. I had been screwing with them hard and it had become a running gag. Kind of like a catch phrase. I was thinking what would Chuck Bukowski do in this situation but I knew he would be much more brutal than I was capable. It was regardless an interesting passing thought. Within a few minutes I ferreted out the machine I was on earlier and was glad to find it unoccupied, although a sweating drink and smoking ashtray proved it hadn't been long.

Regardless, I parked my ass and inserted my voucher ticket. I was balls in and ready to sit a spell. Unusual for me but even my distaste for gambling was outweighed by the possibility of more "buddy" conversation. Never, ever get stuck on an island with egomaniacs. The coin was falling and pretty soon I was up about $135. Feeling pretty good I ordered three Miller Lite longnecks from the cocktail hostess who I would tip a twenty.

She looked more Spanish than black and had a very pleasant smile. An orthodontist at some point? She would be back. My luck continued. One of the guys walked by on the way to the head and gave me a knowing wink. I was in the zone. Thirty minutes later I was up 225 and stupidly thought I had a system. What I really had was probably a system error where I would gain five for every two given back. It didn't matter and I decided if I reached $300 I would cash out. No voucher for future play but three crisp Benjamin's, tell the others I lost the fifty so they wouldn't try and borrow and be none the wiser. I felt good about this concept and shortly reached my goal.

Probably grinning like a possum I headed back to the awkward seat at the bar. Just as I walked up a smiling band of idiots on the stage stopped dead in mid song and cranked up the "Thriller" intro. I got a few dirty looks from the snuggling couples. The drunks thought it was hilarious but the marginal did not. Around midnight the "suave" came in and circled the room like literal vultures. They were old and tan and they were three. Crests adorned navy blazers with white button down shirts floating out of pressed trousers. None wore socks. They lived here and they were here at this time to take your date. Don't dare leave a young lady unattended. You could feel the newly added tension. In the low light they slinked. They were lean and tight and had various degrees of facial hair, very well trimmed and maintained.

Overweight men pulled wives and girlfriends closer in sheer terror. The leagues here were finally defined. This was not Disney Land. These were not elves friendly or otherwise. Suddenly tables of patrons began to systematically disappear to the gaming floor and within the hour we were sitting at a corner table with the men. They were French and Spanish and as suspected living on the island near Atlantis Resort since the mid seventies.

This explained the style of dress. They were decent company after what all I'd been through. Having resigned themselves to the fact all potential female company had exited we would have to do. The tallest guy whose name I didn't catch had opened a tab and the rum drinks were once again flowing. They seemed as glad to see real people as we were to see these Boogie night relics with a platinum card. It was all good. Again quid pro quo. I had the $300 deep in my pocket with my room key, a fantastic buzz, 3 new fairly interesting people to chat with and a large bowl of spicy trail mix snacks. The band played the "Thriller" intro and I nodded approval.

The singer grinned ear to ear. All seemed right with the world at that moment. That's when it started. I can drink with the best (except NASCAR enthusiasts) but even I have limits and the room began to spin. The others were feeling no pain either. I was somehow aware the three were watching us intently with snakelike eyes, much like vermin awaiting the demise of a victim.

I stumbled into my chair trying not to puke on the table. The room was really doing flips now and I began to realize this was not a typical alcohol result. I remember falling toward the floor and not feeling any pain at all upon the landing. There was just the image of two of my friends slumped in chairs and the third on the floor about eight feet away. He had obviously tried to flee before losing all motor functions. The band struck up "Thriller".

Darkness falls.

Next morning I heard the waves crashing. The always soothing sound seemed to find and burst in areas inside my brain I had been totally here to fore unaware of. It took about an hour to be fully aware of the room. The television was on and gently playing an Andy Griffith rerun. I think the one where Howard Spraig's fiancée wanted him to shave. I was fully clothed under the covers and had apparently wet the bed at some point within the last several hours. It was still relatively damp. A large puddle of last night's steak with grilled vegetables was just over the edge to the right and melted into the semi-shag carpet. The sight and smell of this caused a quick and sudden gag reflex. On the night stand were my wallet, room key and passport, neatly stacked with a note on hotel stationary stating "had a wonderful time and Happy Halloween? Trick or Treat! "And signed "Warmest Regards…your island Friends.

   Credit cards and Travelers Checks were all intact…cash gone. I searched my pockets to also not find the $300. I had always read about this kind of shit but you never think it will happen to you. Especially in groups. I called the guys and each reported the pretty much same outcome. We were cleaned out of US and Bohemian cash but in good sporting fashion left with a smidge of dignity.

   Even our watches were spared. These guys were obvious professionals but certainly not pricks. On another occasion and circumstance even someone I might like. I had to think the Hotel at some level was in on it but after some reflection I discarded the notion. Although it was much too smooth and set up it was humanitarian to not just dump us in the street. I had to appreciate the civility of it all. A real class act.

   If I ever go back I may seek them out. Who knows? Revenge may be in my heart at the time but not likely. I slowly gained more and more strength and in a couple of hours I was showered, changed and sitting in front of a large glass of sweating juice, orange in color. This beverage could only be handled in small petite sips, very gentile. Eventually the glass was empty and I decided to attempt some raisin toast. A very slow and deliberate proposition but somewhat successful. About that time the others joined me. They looked like some of those wax figures at the Disney Hall of Presidents. Very unhealthy. No one spoke. Everyone stared straight ahead or into coffee or water. The only thing spoken came from the head prick with the plane. "We will never again speak of this". I can only assume they had lost much greater sums than the $400 and some change that had been absconded from me, $300 of which was the slot machine gain and could be considered only a cosmic loan of sorts. In a weird way I almost felt lucky. Strength came much faster now. Pretty soon I was packing. When I picked up my passport to stow in my backpack a folded bill fell out and onto the floor.

   It was a hundred, possibly from the casino, neatly folded and with a smiley face drawn on the face with red felt tip. Have a nice day? Maybe they spotted I was not such a jerk as the others? So cryptic... What could this mean? I decided it was probably a joke on the others after the thieves obviously saw I was the financial lightweight of the operation. A little payback showing they understood?

I felt much better about everything at this point. I gathered up my shit including the two cheap Hawaiian style shirts I had snagged from the market near the fish fry, two for five dollars. I hit the elevator. As the elevator door closed the overhead music speaker cranked up as on queue. "Thriller" by Michael Jackson. This was very weird and I almost felt I was being watched...had to be.

"Fuck Michael Jackson" was my only thought.

The Volunteer

We had worked very hard. Harder than we had ever thought possible. The running. The pushups. The conditioning. A little light on the fundamentals, but that was ok. It was only 7th grade football and this was a great day. The first game of the season. Cloverdale. To a sandlot veteran this was the big time. A proud moment for friends and family alike. In the pre-game warm-ups, our butterflies were so thick you could see them.

I spotted my parents in the stands but I looked down and away as a grownup student athlete would. How proud I was as I performed my callisthenic's. I had worked after school and during weekends for 2 months to earn enough money for those shoes. We, being of an intense work ethic, could never be bothered with something as trivial as athletic shoes, making their mere presence somewhat of a miracle to me. It was like my father's blessing incarnate in leather and rubber.

As game time approached, I noticed a flurry of activity within the coaching staff. Coach Jack, a man of affirmative action, motioned suddenly for the team to line up for what we thought was going to be a pep talk or a the least an inspiring prayer. As we soon learned, one of our star players, an economically disadvantaged black kid from Sweet Home, had worn his tattered Converse All-stars. These were the worst looking pair of shoes I'd ever seen, obviously hand me downs from at least two brothers. The slick soles had become dislodged causing one to flap loosely as if begging for its well deserved retirement.

   The coach carefully studied his nervous, shuffling recruits with his star halfback in tow. His intentions were becoming obvious. As he neared me, I felt a large lump forming in my throat, choking me. Please walk past…walk past. Don't humiliate me in front of my pop. As the coach reached the spot where I was standing a smile of relief crossed his otherwise ignorant face. "What size shoe ya got there boy?" he bellowed out. I hoped pop hadn't heard him. "Seven, sir" I said hoping my answer would be undesirable. "Perfect" he smirked while adding "you want to help us win don't you?" "Now trade shoes with Tim". I'm sure the color of my face mirrored the color of my maroon jersey as I slipped on the ragged rejects I had been given. I hope my dad couldn't see me but down deep I knew this to be unrealistic.

   I saw no action during the game and of course, Tim refused to return the shoes, with full approval of management. Coach didn't interfere and based on my limited experience at that time with such matters I relented. After the game, as I approached my waiting family and knowing the wrath that was about to descend on me I noticed something quite odd. He had a smile on his face, we walked in silence for a while. As we neared the car, he touched my shoulder and said "I'm proud of what you did today…now let's go buy you some shoes".

The sun was shining now.

RAY MAN

Letters from Tee

Tee died the other day. He was one of those people you might call a "character". He would float effortlessly from lucid genius to bat shit crazy, often without warning or influence. You never quite knew what you would be getting. He was a lifelong New Yorker and kept a rent controlled apartment on the Upper East Side.

As one would expect this apartment would be crammed in hoarder style with hundreds of finished and unfinished plays and manuscripts. He had had me read rewrites of "The Ashcan and the Cobra" many times. When my son, Dylan, first went to Stella Adler Conservatory in the City he and Tee struck up a relationship where he quickly evolved into the role of mentor. The amount of knowledge he possessed concerning playwriting could not be measured.

He was only looking for an empty vessel to fill with even a portion of that knowledge. This was his passion. He had been working most of his professional life on the development of a comprehensive textbook on playwriting which to my knowledge nothing like had ever existed before. The project had somewhere along the way become open ended and had swelled to over seven hundred typed pages, much like his life, more to say than typed pages to contain it.

I first met him several years after Dylan did at a play premier. Dylan had written and directed a three act play in a competition at an off Broadway Theater. I flew to New York to be supportive and check out all the progress I had heard about. At the premier Tee was just as proud as I was if not more. I met him and immediately we made a bond. He would say later he was struck by my stark white hair. He said I seemed noble and distinguished. I didn't get that but I think it was his projection of images on anything that entered his world.

All was dramatic, extreme highs and lows. This was his craft. His calling not entirely realized. Success of others that he had touched thrilled him to the core. Tee was a chain smoker although I got the impression he did not touch spirits. He always threatened to have a beer with me when I would be in town but we never made the date. He wanted to discuss my stories. He liked the fact I had lived. I thought that was the process? To do and then document. He didn't like some of my language but understood this was my "voice". He would call me sometimes at odd hours and leave me long rambling messages. Some I would answer, some I would not. In typical style the work was more important than the person and he allowed a case of pneumonia to get too advanced. By the time his sister got him to the hospital there was nothing to be done and he was dead by next day.

Dylan had decided to leave the City for a few months to take some University courses and this death seemed to confirm the decision. It was the end of a "chapter" as I tried to rationalize the event. About a week after receiving word I searched around my desk at work and somehow went straight to a batch of correspondence from him. He truly enjoyed the written letter and shied away from many things electronic in nature.

As I began to read each letter I could feel a passion I hadn't noticed before. All he wanted was to touch people and pass on the gifts he had been given. He had seen the light, in a non-biblical sense. I read each letter very carefully. Each neatly typed with a manual typewriter and signed full name with blue ball point. It took about an hour and I was amazed I had immediately found them, particularly all together. I enjoyed them as much as the days they were received and in my typical "closure" style I started to toss the lot into recycling.

At second thought I put them all back where I found them. I may want to read them again sometime.

Snowed in with Russ…

Occasionally during Arkansas winters we are visited with severe snow and ice storms. These usually form with a low pressure system over the Dallas/Fort Worth area funneling gulf moisture up and over an arctic air mass usually rocketing from Kansas City. Depending on the levels of moisture these storms can range from a light dusting of snow, gone by early morning or several inches of debilitating thick ice. The later and more severe are known to snap trees and power lines as well as collapse unstable structures.

This particular year was something in between. There was a snow base of three inches followed by a good layer of ice in the form of sleet. The surface was completed by another several inches of heavy wet snow. For most everyone this was a horrific combination and required a total shut down of most business and commerce. That is not the case with me. Driving in Rocky Mountain white out conditions on steep grades over the years as well as upstate New York and New England have acclimated me to pretty much anything which comes along. I like to think I have total confidence in the capabilities of myself and my Xterra SUV and often take on the responsibility by giving rides and aid in these types of situations. This time was no exception. The sparseness of the ice caused no disruption of power which is always a check in the plus column. We had plenty of firewood and I stopped by Kroger on the way home during the initial storm for comfort foods such as beans and corn bread as well as a fully cooked ham shank. A second stop secured mass quantities of beer and harder alcohol. I decided on flavored rum and as a kick one of my all time favorites in the form of a fifth of Southern Comfort with 7up as a mixer.

I rarely drink hard liquor anymore for a multitude of reasons not least of which in my small and tight knit crew someone generally has to be the "daddy" and be in charge. This day was an exception. Once errands were complete I decided to see if I still had "it". With "it" I mean the capacity to drink 100 proof alcohol in a controlled environment where little could go wrong at around the same rate as I do beer. It had been about twenty or more years since I had attempted anything of this type. This opportunity just felt right. I think I was just in the right mood.

In addition to having power I had received a collection of Russ Meyer DVD's for Christmas which I hadn't viewed in even longer. To those unfamiliar Russ Meyer is the cinematic genius behind such titles as "Faster Faster Pussycat" and the "Vixen" series. The "Vixens" were particularly dear to me as one of my initial pubescent Drive In movie experiences. Each film had recurrent themes of very busty main female characters, angry cops and the famous escaped Nazi Martin Bormann. Meyer...a truly inspired visionary.

From where his inspiration came is still a mystery I'm sure to all. I am a huge fan and always will be. This played into my plan and I called Mexican George to see if he preferred to be snowed in with us or at home with his yo-yo friends and an intermittently working dish network. He chose us no doubt knowing we would be well stocked with food and beverage. His other option was a crap shoot at best. This would cause me one more stop downtown and the ice was just starting to fall steady again and thinly coat my windshield.

In these situations it's always the other guy who will screw you up, usually a young receptionist who didn't get out in time and is panicky...jerky in her movements. These drivers will take you out. Cause you to take chances you wouldn't otherwise. It took about thirty minutes of caution through town and George was soon buckled in the passenger seat. Before heading back I banged and scraped the thick collected ice off the wipers and we were right as rain for the return. I called ahead and asked that the fire be stoked and some water started boiling for beans. Soon we were safe at the house with even the truck backed in just in case another trip became necessary. Four wheel drive in the locked position. It was all too dreamy. The heat on the inside fogged the windows and made for a toasty entry. This was even better than I anticipated.

After some idle talk I informed my snowbound friends of my plan. I wanted to watch Meyer films and drink the hard spirits in an experiment of sorts to see if I still had the proverbial "stomach" for it. Not even I was sure, but I was willing to try. The first glass was tall and a little biting. The trick is to more or less keep a continual drink going by refilling elements anytime the glass became no more than one third empty. This allows the level of alcohol to be slowly increased without notice until it becomes almost a pure glass with a splash of mixer. The second glass was better as my dormant taste buds remembered the intoxicating flavors from my distant past.

It got easier. About an hour into the experiment and the first film it was time for a large bowl of beans. This may sound like a foolish mixture but seemed very appropriate at the time. The drinks we're going down really smooth and fast now. From my perch in my chair with my best dog I was feeling little or no effect. Strange to me in light of the fact half a fifth of 100 proof alcohols was gone. I had urinated only twice. We were into the second movie by now and the drinks tasted better than ever. I was really enjoying this.

I could see the soft snow falling outside the window and the fire cracked. I threw on another good sized log. Sparks flew up into the chimney and out into the night air, dying when striking the cold. About two thirds into the bottle I recieved the first shivers of a buzz. It was a mellow feeling and seemed to intensify the fire warmth on my face. In short order I realized the heat was from flush and not the fireplace. I poured another tall one and leveled off the glass with fresh, clear ice.

This seemed to push away the blood that had started to accumulate in my ears and cheeks. Pat and George surveyed the bottle and estimated probably two reasonable sized mixed drinks left. I still felt good and in control with a slight mellow, comfortable buzz. The movie was Super

Vixens and was everything I remembered from the Drive In. It always cracked me up with the recurring themes such as Martin Bormann owning a desert gas station and always making an appearance somehow being made important to the storyline. We were at the part where the motorcycle cop Harry Sledge was killing Angel in the bath tub. What a scene "man" as they would say. That was about the time I felt the first all too distant yet familiar flip. The room seemed smaller suddenly and the front of my chair seemed to rise slightly. It was a feeling I had long since forgotten after I took on my role as adult in charge. My function being to make sure everything and everybody came out ok in the morning.

This was not an exactly pleasant development. Deciding to not be cheated out of finishing the fifth off I stepped outside a moment to check the snow depth on the windshield. It had been cleaned off when I went to the store earlier but at this juncture about three new inches of fresh powder had accumulated. Coming down hard I looked straight up and let the soggy flakes hit my face and tongue. Wood smoke smell filled the night. This was exactly what was needed to revive me and allow the last of the bottle to be consumed.

Immediately hitting the kitchen before the sensation of strength left me I mixed the next to last drink. The remainder could probably fit in the glass as it was only about a quarter of an inch deep but I was determined to stick with the method and formula which had worked for me thus far. The drink was a little harder than all the pervious and my tongue felt a little thick. My speech was in disconnect with my otherwise racing mind. The others laughed as I tried to explain. I started to salivate. The pup wanted back in my lap but had suddenly become a source of intense heat.

I put her back on the floor. By now I wasn't feeling great as all the sensations worked in a medley. I salivated more now in the roof of my mouth. Halfway done now with the last big drink. I could do this. The flipping was now accompanied by spinning. Eyes open or closed. With eyes closed I felt falling backwards in the large leather chair only to be pushed violently forward in two third intervals, never having actually moved at all. Fascinating... The movie was all but a blur of bright colored tits and ass with the sound track of sixties acid music of the period. Strawberry Alarm Clock I believe, one of Meyer's favorites.

Mexican George was talking some shit as a result of his beer drunk which I couldn't quite make out. More Spanish than English. There was a fleeting thought about alcohol poisoning but only for an instant. It had only been about three hours and a lot of alcohol had been consumed. The fire continued to pop and was uncomfortably hot. The last gulp went down with reservation and I sat there a moment reflecting my next move and evaluating my physical well being. Emotions flooded over and through me, a combination of stomach and mental distress with a good dose of upheaval.

Most distressing indeed.

The dog made one more attempt to crawl up and was once again rejected. I would have given anything at this point to have had beer all evening. Then it came. In one swift and deliberate move I had reached the bathroom just off the living room and began an immediate campaign of projectile vomiting like no human being had ever experienced. Everything consumed all afternoon had pickled with the caramel colored liquid and created a paste most foul. The only thing in my experience of compare would be lake hawk excrement.

Thinking in my fog I had safely reached the toilet it was not known till later about the disaster on the walls and floor undoubtedly upon my dubious approach. The small black and white dog was defiantly interested in the new developments and had to be kept at bay with the use of a Swiffer jet broom. At this point death could not come soon enough. After collecting myself slightly with my friends help I eased off into the yard once more and laid face down in about ten inches of soft snow.

This remedy was remarkable but not practical or suggested. In this condition frostbite and hypothermia are certainly possibilities as well as potential drowning. The wet snow loosened the material stuck to my beard and left a strange film on the lower portion of the face imprint I had created in the yard. My friends admired it with a flashlight as they attempted to hoist me back in deadweight into the warmth of the apartment. About twenty minutes went by as I dried by the fire and bathed my forehead with a wet washrag. Ice water sounded good at this point to just have something wet and non-threatening. When getting this together I noticed the bottle on the counter with just the slightest amount of liquid floating at the bottom.

I'm a lot of things and quitter is not one. It was stupid and made no sense but in slow motion the bottle was to my lips. Straight up. I could do this. So close to greatness I had to try and finish this. The sticky liquid stung my injured and raspy throat but somehow brought a slight bit of comfort. Thus the name? Chasing with water seemed to make it stay down as I limped back to the safety of the chair. The dog followed trying to make eye contact. The bathroom cleanup would have to wait a bit.

A crooked smile crept across my face as I realized I had done it. I still had it after all these years. As they say in the Special Olympics "I'm a winner!"

Thursday PM

Last night I heard something that made me stop for a moment, sit down and think for about a full five seconds. No small task my friends. It may sound funny but with the way information is disseminated in today's "techno" world it's a little unusual to hear something even in the potential realm of profound. The more interesting angle is that the source of my interest was a blue jean commercial, Levi to be specific. I'm not sure the original author, maybe Wordsworth, but it read as follows: "Maybe things are broken on purpose so that man will have work to do". I thought a lot about that. It has several layers that can be pulled apart. In one line it implies a higher power, mans relationship with that power and the reason for mans existence. That's a pretty heavy fucking statement.

Today wasn't a terrible day. The recession recovery still hasn't taken full hold but Obama insists it's any day now. I have been moderately busy. The lake is twelve foot down from normal depth based on the idiotic decision to lower it five feet in one day for some non-essential dam repairs at the beginning of a summer drought. Sailing is treacherous at best. Fishing is ok as the mass of fish are compressed by the low levels into several deeper pools. Fish in a barrel? There are several new bars just open but they are very proud of their drinks and I'm a little short of cash. Kindness of strangers? Things are cyclical and I know this…things will change. Always do. Spring will be here soon and hopefully improved cash flow. One of the most promising new bars is a little high brow faux-English pub on the ground floor of one of the new multimillion dollar condo developments on the Riverfront. The actual bar is only about twelve stools so I can see competition there for the older seasoned non-posers. (Professional local color). There is a fireplace with nice stone accents in the middle of the bar and big screen televisions throughout, outdoor covered seating for warm rainy days in my mind. Darts as one would expect but maybe only decorative, I'm not sure.

I think maybe me and one of my friends may go for a late lunch Saturday and have a couple with maybe a Sheppard's pie. Watch a game maybe. It's supposed to rain.

A dangerous fellow

It's rare that we have a bona fide mystery in Little Rock Arkansas but recent events caught and held my attention as they unfolded in print and television media. In one of the gentrified areas near the hood and the Governor's mansion off Broadway downtown there are many beautiful older homes in various stages of restoration. This is a part of the original residential tracts of town and were once the mansions of bankers, politicians... movers and shakers. Many have high stone and ornate wrought iron ivy covered fences.

Courtyards and gardens. You get the gist. It's I think today referred to as mixed use. Crime in the area has never allowed it to really develop to full potential in the last thirty years. Gangs over the years systematically creep into the area from the real hood to plunder and vandalize. Tags are painted on most blocks. The local Mini Mart gas station closes just after dark because they got tired of the robberies and parking lot shootings. Their insurance may have mandated this... I wouldn't know.

In the midst of these homes is a federally subsidized high rise housing project. This building covers several blocks and towers above the neighborhood to a height of about twelve stories. There is a single controlled secure entrance. It is affectionately known as the Parris Towers but there is no connection with France or Europe at all even with the addition of the extra "R".

The mystery started several years after a man purchased and spent hundreds of thousands of dollars on the refurbishment of a neglected brick mansion back into a single family dwelling in the shadow of the "towers". The man seemed of adequate means and other than the poor judgment of residential location seemed quite normal. Just a guy who wanted to enjoy life and the fruits of his labor. The back yard was fenced and secure and was a great domain for his beloved black chow dog and his latest restorative project in the form of a late model Ferrari car, red in color.

The fence was high and ivy covered and the yard in no way visible from the street. That was at first what puzzled the man. It started as chips in the cars window glass. At first he considered a hail storm he had missed or maybe rocks from kids hurled blindly over the wall. It made no sense at all.

Daily he would find more damage to the glass and then deep dings in the body of the immobile object. Impossible. After about a month of observing he was no closer to an answer. One Saturday while rinsing some dishes from lunch he decided to let the dog out to chase the brown squirrels as he often did. Just after he closed the sliding door he heard the dog cry in pain and after searching discovered the animal cowering in the corner of the yard under a hydrangea bush.

He stroked to calm the dog and after several passes noticed a sticky substance on his fur and his hand. The blood was slowly oozing from what appeared to be a small wound in the neck just below the custom made white collar he had purchased in Eureka Springs, now stained crimson.

In a panic he loaded the terrified animal into his SUV and headed to the emergency vet. After a bit he was surprised as the vet extracted a tiny silver pellet from the chows' skin. "Someone has shot your dog…and at high velocity". "You should call the police".

As soon as he left the vet he called the non-emergency number, left a message with details and all essential information and waited for a reply. A week went by. Every morning he would take his camera out to the car and document the last day's damage, download the pictures and mark it with a date / time stamp. He was creating a historical record of what was happening in a very controlled manner. The chow couldn't understand why the yard was now forbidden. The squirrels were not to be seen either. One afternoon after several "quiet" days the man was filling his bird bath with his white garden hose when a whizzing sound came close to his ear and hit the sliding door just to his left. The window shattered.

This time he called the emergency number at the police station. Within minutes one of the police prowlers cruising the area was at the front door and two officers were knocking. Once in they were escorted out back and photographed the damage while taking a statement. The man downloaded to a flash drive for them the mound of photo documentation on what had been happening as well as a copy of the veterinarian's findings and the spent pellet. He was very thorough.

The police were as baffled as he was and promised to send a real investigator with bullet trajectory experience over the next day to render an opinion. A file was started. This attempt on the man with such force took the events to a new level only reinforced by the car and animal damage. The next day, as promised, a lone detective was at the door. He spoke little, wrote notes, nodded and listened to the man's excited ramblings.

His heart pounded as he spoke. With little effort about twenty spent pellets were recovered from the damp ground and bagged before it was sufficient evidence. Next the detective pulled a small laser pointer from his jacket pocket and stooped to the approximate location of the hole.

In moments it was determined the only possible point of origin was the Parris Towers.

This discovery presented its own set of challenges. As a public enterprise the management structure created multiple twists and turns including misinformation and smoke screens that went on for weeks. No help whatsoever. Management jobs and reputations were more important than the neighbor's safety. It was unfathomable that there would be a sniper in their midst. Not seeing results and still enduring daily bombardments the man set up a private video surveillance with a telephoto lens trained on the building facing him.

What was produced was a faint, blurry photo of a man and gun emitting from the seventh floor laundry window which had been illegally pried open. With all this evidence to establish the harassment the man bypassed building management and the police and went straight to the press, shortly appearing in print articles and television. All he wanted was to be able to enjoy his property. No one had any answers. Months dragged on. Residents of the tower were questioned. Residents were threatened. A reward was offered. The car had more new dings. Paint chipped and littered the yard like bright foreign specks, then somehow a break.

One of the residents had been evicted off the seventh floor for non-payment and loud odd behavior. As this housing is usually the last stop before the street he had left all his belongings behind with the exception of multiple articles of clothing. Upon cleaning out his possessions management discovered hundreds of rounds of pellets along with several short and long range weapons. This was the guy.

Seems he was a sixty six year old Viet Nam veteran who had been on some sort or another of disability since 1968. As one would expect he was considered a loner and subsequently left alone.

Upon the discovery the police were summoned. They soon had sealed the room and began collecting evidence. The man was in the wind. A bulletin was issued with arrest warrants and weeks went by. On the third week the North Little Rock Police alerted Little Rock that they had their guy, or at least his whereabouts. Seems the guy was at a serious dirt floor type beer joint called "The Forge" and after a solid day of drinking had slipped off his stool. As he fell his head clipped the rail on the base of the bar and peeled back a large portion of scalp from above the right ear, in the process fracturing the skull.

The resulting hemorrhage and swelling had put the man in a coma. Upon the accident the bar had sent him to the local hospital by ambulance. Once his condition was determined in emergency trauma and he was stabilized, he was transported to the local University Medical Center as indigent. He came out of the coma suffering from severe brain damage. Police knew of his location and waited for an outcome. At some point the Medical Center decided he shouldn't be there and transferred him yet again to the VA hospital, which subsequently lost him in the system.

The police couldn't locate him and best as anyone could determine he had been transferred to a long term care facility as a non-functioning resident. No one was quite sure though. The police closed the case. The pellet rain had ceased. The dog has its yard back I do believe.

Lost weekend

Every once in a great while seventy two hours becomes something worth remembering, but not often as usually one "major" event defines a time period. This was really weird even by my standards. I had taken Friday off in early September. In a no spending frenzy because of the recession I had opted a day here and there sailing and fishing on the area lake which doubles as the cities primary water supply. This was one of those long weekends.

The sun was warm but not too and the beer was cold as usual. Pat and I headed out after lunch with the plan of hitting the dock on the return about 8pm or so. Pat was in fishing mode and I was designated pilot. Nothing makes me happier than to anchor in a channel or near an island, put a chair on the top deck, read and drink beer.

Occasionally my help may be needed but not often. This was one of those quiet perfect days. The warm winds had shifted from the due south as they will meeting and rising with an approaching cold front not due until late afternoon the next day. My company picnic was also on Saturday the next day around noon so the plan was to drink and fish today, do the gathering in North Little Rock, pick up Mexican George and all head back for a few hours before the front moved in. It was a perfect day but would cool off quick once the sun went down. We were anchored beside a fish haunt called Rattlesnake Island about three and a half miles due north of the marina, into the wind. Nothing was biting. I decided I thought we could slowly sail out of the cove into the main lake with a directional wind shift in our favor. It was about thirty minutes before dark. If anything would bite this day it would be now. The heavy rod and reel was bated with shrimp and dragged slowly behind, while under sail there being no danger of wrapping the line around the prop, killing the engine.

The wind stayed true and we gently moved south. We were talking about some such shit and watching the shifting sky of a powerful sunset when the fish hit. I had just popped a beer and was in initial deep gulp when I noticed the rod bend almost double. No small feat with the heavy duty catfish rod outfitted with fifty pound test line.

We were working toward the middle following along a channel about thirty feet deep where major fish lurk and we had had some success with bass and some catfish.

The sun was setting fast now. I cautioned against reeling in too fast, the drag was set and we waited to see what was next. About five minutes after the hook set, in the blackness we heard a huge splash about fifty feet behind us. You could make out a flash of white in the wake. We looked at each other and exclaimed "Oh Shit!" in unison. We had caught larger fish before in the five to seven pound range but this acted totally different.

It pulled about twenty more feet of line out before it started swimming toward us at a clip allowing all the lost line to be recollected. We were a little concerned. I had seen the movie Jaws in high school and even though we were at a high profile above the water's surface in the boat we were still at least three miles out and the marina bait shop was closed for sure. I didn't think we would be swamped but it briefly crossed my mind. Pat held the rod and shouted something as the fish approached. Holding the tiller with one foot I reached around and grabbed the high power spot light used for night approach and searched the surface for a glimpse. The first time we saw it we were both in shock. The fish came up slowly and broke water on our starboard side maybe three or four feet from the rail. With the light shinning down you could easily make out a solid white mass in the three and a half to four foot range in length. A giant cat. Jaws once again came to mind. Neither of us could believe what we were seeing. Remarkably the pace of the boat was just a comfortable swimming speed for the monster, which I would find out later from a Game and Fish agent would be in the eighty pound range. Every fifteen minutes or so the fish would fight back slightly but soon would settle into swimming at the surface just to our side. It was majestic and terrifying to watch. It was about a mile and a half out I came to the realization that we might actually land it. Being pulled along had obviously tired it out and the buoyancy of the water versus the line weight worked out perfectly to keep it in tow. What was the plan? I couldn't say. I didn't have a fucking clue. I had seen the monster fresh water fish on some of the cable TV shows and had a clear picture of what the sheer weight of this fish could do to one or two normal drunk humans in the dark. I began to be really concerned at this point. I got on the cell and began calling everyone I knew who had any sort of big fish experience. Most were out and I got voicemail. I left dramatic messages about our plight but had no calls back. I did get my dad but philosophical wisdom was not what I needed this moment. I needed to know how to pull this fish up without losing fingers in its mouth or wrestling with it and losing even more use of my right arm and its torn bicep. We tried to take pictures in the mean time but the reflection on the surface caused all attempts to come out jet black.

We were now about a mile out. Slowly we sailed along. The fish had been on the line about forty five minutes to this point. Next conversation was what we do if we land it. Being firm believers in catch and release plus the fact we were almost wasted getting the fish on the dock for a picture seemed almost reasonable. The other option was holding the fish in the truck where it could do incredible harm to us (Steve Irwin?) or surely cause an accident. How would you explain to the arresting officer? Yes we have been drinking. Yes we have a live albino catfish the size of a twelve year old boy in the seat with us. Yes sir, I am bleeding from being stabbed with the fish's barbs. Yes I am bleeding profusely because I am on blood thinners. No sir, the transmission will not shift because the fish broke the shifter by knocking it in reverse while traveling at fifty miles an hour. Yes sir, did I happen to mention I have been drinking? You can see bringing it back was not an option particularly when considering the fact a fish such as this can live an hour or more out of water. We would surely be killed. Our minds raced. We had had way too much time to consider all this information. At this point we were heading into the marina no wake zone and I really needed to drop sail, put Pat on the bow with the flood light and motor the rest of the way in.

The fish was not fighting anymore and acted somewhat like a dog on a leash. This worked out fine as I couldn't pilot and hold the rod. Pat worked up to the front while reeling closer and pulled the fish and line up to the bow avoiding the spinning prop. This was going to work at least at this point. The tricky part was the narrow slip. The boat and fish could certainly not fit at the same time which would require P to slide to the rear and let out line in perfect unison with our approach. We talked over what had to be done and without any hesitation made the maneuver and eased into the slip. Luckily the dock lights were on so we had a good view of the line just at our stern.

That being the only portion of the plan devised I quickly tied up the boats bow and jumped over to the edge of the dock to survey things. Pat gave me the rod and it was determined we would reel it to the edge and see if we could perhaps roll it onto the wood at least for the photo before we would be killed, pulled under the surface in an alligator like death roll I suposed. Pat held the light. I held my breath. Reeling was easier than I imagined as the tired monster came closer as if ready to give up. Pat trained the light on the surface. Then without warning the head came up, being half again as wide as my head and processing bluish humanlike eyes.

I have seen eyes similar on some of the buffalo fish in the Arkansas River but not this close and certainly not alive. What makes them distinctive is they have whites with dark colored pupils. When the eyes roll or move side to side they look almost human. Almost like some intelligence was in there working. Not like the flat, dead eyes of most ocean fish. It was unnerving.

It was much larger than I had dreamed and the thought of falling into the dark water with it wouldn't even process in my clouded mind. Instinctively I pulled forward and as if helping with the effort it eased up and onto the dock, about a foot of the body showing just below the head.

We stared eye to eye and I saw a sudden look of fear although I'm not sure if it was the fish eyes or my reflection in them. It was one of the strangest things I'd ever seen. I was starting to position myself to reach around when gravity intervened. Out of water the entire dead weight of the beast had stretched the line to its limit and beyond, suddenly snapping and throwing the rod behind me. The fish sat there a moment, looked at me once more and slid over toward and underneath the orange boat in the next slip, the exact location where I lost my good sunglasses a month or so prior. In the gentle glow of the flashlight it slowly swam off into the night about three miles from its normal environment. We both sat there exhausted. After securing the rod I popped a fresh beer and sat quietly for a moment or two. Pat did as well after mixing an extra stout rum drink. No one will believe us we both agreed. Around this time the advice riddled return calls began to come in, one right after the other.

The drive back to the lights of town was the longest ever. Next morning was clear, bright and breezy. It had rained a little after the fish had gotten away but maybe for only thirty minutes to an hour. No drought buster by any stretch. The cold front was supposed to come in from the north that evening so it was not even a factor in any plans for the next day's activities.

The company picnic on Saturday was to start around noon so the plan was at that time to attend, chow down on some Whole Hog Café award winning bar-b-que, stop by the Visitors Center and see me pops, pick up Mexican George while in North Little Rock and head back out to the boat. The plan from there involved retracing our steps, dragging shrimp in the channel and finishing by anchoring in the shadow of Rattlesnake Island AGAIN, three and a half miles out, as I said a great bass spot.

These steps went like clockwork and soon without fail we were drifting in the channel, Pat, Mexican George and myself. The sun was warm but about mid-afternoon while at anchor I began to notice some subtle changes. The wind in the treetops of the island had begun to swirl and I noticed a gray cloud bank flat to the North from my perch on the bow. I was halfway through a decent book (Goodbye Columbus) and had several beers fueling my lack of concern. Then the wind shifted hard from the north...

The boat swung around the anchor line heading into the wind as that was the direction the tiller was secured. This movement dug the anchor deep into the side wall of the eighteen foot deep channel at the east base of the island. We wouldn't be going anywhere unless by design. I put on a button up shirt. Not thinking too much and having more beer I became aware of the difficulty in holding my book pages secure. The wind was really whipping now and the temperature had dropped at least ten degrees with the sun covered by the cloud bank of the approaching front. I checked my watch and was surprised the front was about five to six hours earlier than predicted. The wind now was about twenty miles per hour gusting to thirty five. There was no fishing to be done and Pat and George went below to close up the windows against the approaching cold. I tried to secure the lines and debated whether we should shove off and sail back.

The wind direction was perfect to take us directly into the marina but I was concerned about the building gusts and the lack of control the tail wind might create on the open water. Wind was now gusting to forty plus. The wind and anchor tension now made it virtually impossible to weigh anchor. The current created swept around the island and in a weird twist stabilized our movement somewhat. We would be stuck until the wind died enough to release the pressure on the anchor rope.

Not anytime soon. We looked around at food rations and discussed sleeping arrangements if it might become necessary. I was most concerned about my dog, having not really prepared for this. It was a couple of hours until dark but the thick cloud cover negated this fact. That's when I noticed the silhouettes against the grey sky and the call of the hawks. Apparently several hawks had taken to roost in the taller trees above us on the island and had been disturbed by the high winds and our now obvious presence. They looked strangely like vultures when viewed without my glasses as they circled and cried out to us. We had bigger fish to fry and I discounted them as just another ominous trend of a yet to be determined outcome.

I went on down below, closed the hatch secure in the fact we should stay put, not crash into the rocks and proceed to discuss our options. We certainly were well supplied and had almost a full gallon of vanilla flavored rum, a half gallon of cheap vodka, maybe a case of beer, etc. etc. Provisions were not an issue. The wind howled another hour or so and we sat, drank and shot the shit in the comfort and calm of the cabin. Strangely above the radio I could still hear the cries of the large dark birds.

It was now officially dark even though it had looked like it for hours. More discussion ensued, probably influenced by strong drink, and it was determined we would wait for the first opportunity and head across. The rain had not yet come and the prospects of the unpredictably on the open water would require us to secure the main sail, cover and motor across. That would be fine with me but the anchor was dug in deep and would not be freed easily. The wind subsided slightly and I thought it time to evaluate exactly how stuck we might be. Easing to the bow, George held the light and I attempted to pull us against the current and position directly over the line, where I could "milk" it causing the anchor to collapse and free.

The current and wind were still too much at that time and George and myself were unsuccessful. The hawks still screamed at us and circled the mast at high altitudes. They obviously didn't understand we were trying to leave. After a bit we decided to retreat below, have another beverage and wait for the next opportunity.

After some more discussion I suggested a risky move, again I'm sure fueled by strong libations. According to the charts I felt fairly confident I understood the lay of the underwater trench at that position. The proposition was to start the motor and circle to the other side of the anchor location in reverse, against the wind created current and gently pull the anchor free. Stopping the engine at just the right time, pull the anchor aboard, re-start the engine in time to get out of the current and miss the large rocks in our wind path. Aside from the obvious we would run the risk of hanging the anchor on the wall or unseen bottom debris if I was wrong about the terrain, at the least losing an anchor and deck cleat or at worst breaking apart the bow and sinking the boat in about twenty feet of black water. Upside of this potential development would be the short swim to the island. I asked the long time dock master once why they called the island Rattlesnake Island to which he answered "why the hell do you think they would call it Rattlesnake Island?" These were not great alternatives but within a minute I had the boat in reverse and circling the line dipping into the drink. Mexican George was on the bow to help guide me as to location as best he could.

I got in position and gently pulled back. In a great stroke of luck the wind subsided at that moment increasing the chances of success. I killed the engine, threw the tiller to Pat to keep us in alignment and quickly proceeded to the bow. When I got there I saw the gleam of Georges knife as he was about to cut the line and free us the shitty way. "What the fuck? Don't do that!" I eased him out of the way and tugged at the line. Like butter the anchor popped free. I pulled it up and secured for George to stow and headed back to phase two and the avoidance of the rocks portion. Like clockwork the motor came to life and stymied our drift. It was about that time I heard the screeching caw. George stood motionless like he had been shot and Pat started yelling from down below. I had no idea what had transpired as the rocks were my top priority.

Apparently we had been dive bombed by a low flying hawk that had proceeded in dropping an unbelievable amount of the foulest smelling liquid paste all over the back of George's coat, on the top deck and down the stairs into the cabin. It was a perfect shot and only I was spared.

Pat got paper towels and attempted to rake the literal shit off George's back but it wasn't easily happening due to the deep pile of the fabrics weave. The smell caused a gag reflex and soon he was also swimming in rum puke and the hawkish substance with the consistency of runny cement. He puked over the side a second time.

I glided into the channel, clear of all the rocks and proceeded into the main lake area. The only option was the coat would go overboard. George, in his short sleeves slowly climbed down below and attempted to stay warm. Pat used Windex with ammonia "D" to clean the stairs and the splash area which covered the counter and instrument panel. I popped another beer, pulled my coat around my neck and headed due south toward the flood lights of the marina.

As suspected motoring was the proper move as the boat tossed three directions often with the motor lifting periodically out of water at our severe angle. We would make it. After about an hour on the main lake the wind died enough to make the remainder very manageable. The retching below had subsided and I was unsure what horrors I would witness in the daylight the next day when I came back to clean and secure for the week. I had time for one more beer before the dock and partook. The front had passed and I pulled gently into the slip. It was 3 AM. For some reason I thought of the Gilligan's Island theme song. I read somewhere later that if a hawk shits on you or especially your boat it is an unbelievable source of good luck. I'm not so sure but I will be going with that. We never saw George's coat again.

"The Dharma Bum"

The cat dude

In the realm of bizarre occasionally something comes down the pike that astounds on multiple levels. Much like the train wreck you are drawn to, the details and drama you can't turn away from. The cat guy was one of those train wrecks.

There is a neighborhood in Little Rock known as Stifft Station. I believe it derives this name from its standing once as a trolley stop and turnaround about the turn of the century twice removed but I'm not for certain.

This destination is on the edge of the more and still affluent "Heights" area, although it is noticeably a tad more tired and worn. This is a result of the hippie culture and mentality. A strong majority of property owners are second generation counter-culture stoners who by luck inherited their family homes and benefited greatly by the property value booms of the eighties and nineties. As a result there is a higher than normal concentration of multi-colored wind socks and bamboo porch blinds. You would have to be there but you get the picture. There are two main bars on the primary street. One is a seedy pizza place populated with a good cross section of career alcoholics; food is fair but not recommended. The other is a long established oyster bar with odd ideas about what constitutes red beans and rice. After the gulf oil spill I recently attempted to buy a dozen oysters on the half shell. They had jacked the price up to $1.25 each and I swear it took three of the postage stamp size little bastards to cover the face of a standard square saltine cracker. They do take credit cards now.

The other major attraction is the deaf and blind school which is housed in an ancient structure which once was the Confederates Soldiers Home. The deaf school used to field great basketball and football teams. The blind school…not so much.

This area is the backdrop.

The first noticeable element in the advancement of this tale was the posters. Because of the nature of advertising in the area (particularly band advertising) it is not uncommon to see all types of flyers plastered to basically every telephone pole at almost every block. At first glance no big deal. The band gigs came and went and over time the abundance of "lost cat" posters was overwhelming, some with photos done well with Photoshop. Some with large type and detailed descriptions, all disturbing. There was a trend here that couldn't be ignored.

Fluffy was missing, as well as Tabby. This section was definitely a cat town. I'm guessing the fact that cats require less attention which is something most of the residents had in spades. These types of things are generally not a priority to law enforcement so the posters on the poles grew thick and fat in a natural sort of progression. This went on for who knows as no one was paying attention until a bright Tuesday afternoon.

It seems a gay Argentine national new to the area with beautiful long black flowing hair was walking down the alley behind his apartment in an attempt to find his black and white mixed cat. About two blocks away he spotted the cat squatted cautiously as it was being approached by a thin young man in an ill fitting red jogging suit. He looked Hispanic. He had a short fresh haircut (almost prison style). The Argentine was alarmed as the man bent down to coax the cat closer with something in hand, possibly a treat. Startled from his task, whatever that may be, he became combative when questioned. Behind the man in a pile was a soiled small "igloo" cooler and a pine stick or walking staff about an inch in diameter and in the range of six foot long which he proceeded to swing at the head of the hapless cat owner. Screams were heard up and down several blocks. The first two attempts missed but the third connected just above the eye and the blood began to flow. The attacker disappeared near a garage and was gone. The injured man and several neighbors called 911. The police came and took notes. The ambulance came. The injured man was treated and released. The cat was safe. The attack alarmed most of the "peace and love" crowd who met and determined that they would be watchful. The injured man was fine as his injury was superficial which is common with pine stick beatings being it is a relatively soft wood. The next day with his cat secured indoors he took to the alley and search for clues to what had happened to him.

To his amazement the same man, in similar attire was back in the alley coaxing another cat. Knowing what he was capable of he opted to call the police first and once in route he would approach. First he would watch. The man seemed oblivious to him. The cooler and stick were at his rear as before and he crouched hand outstretched in "cat whisperer" fashion. In his hand seemed a cat treat of some sort.

The gay man must have made some sort of noise alerting of his presence and startling the attacker from the previous day. The police had not yet arrived. The South American would not be beaten again as he realized his size advantage without the element of surprise used against him day previous. He cornered the guy. This was gonna go out a whole new door. In an aggressive move he had kicked the stick away and dialed his cell 911 again to check progress.

The man reminded him of a rat with pointed facial features and his overbite. Both were angry. The cat sat still in a trance at what was happening. Sergio stayed on the line with the operator and reported every move as if choreographed. After what seemed like three days, police arrived. Assault in that neighborhood, being rare had attracted the right attention and in proper police procedure both ends of the alley were capped off with cars. A third circled down the most immediate street. There would be no escape today. It was a hot day and none of the officers dressed in black were in any mood for any "fucking fruitcake bullshit" as they would put it. The rat face kid hit the loose gravel and broken asphalt and was almost immediately cuffed, seemed like on his way down. In the search of his pockets all that was found was a Kroger grocery store card, three dirty single one dollar bills and a pocketful of tuna flavored treats, the ones shaped like little fish. All were bagged and labeled as evidence for some future proceeding. The gay man had to be led away to the rear based on the unhelpfulness of his sudden hysteria. He had however identified the man as his attacker and was helpful in this regard. As the search continued it became a more than a little disturbing in its implications.

A pin knife was discovered in his slumping left sock and tucked into his right tennis shoe was a Salvation Army business card. This guy was homeless. Next the cooler was searched. As the officer slowly opened the heavy cooler he was surprised to meet bright frightened green eyes. A full size cat cowered in the bottom of the cooler, frozen with terror, unable to move. It may have also been affected by the lack of oxygen but this was unclear. About this time other officers arrived, no doubt enticed by the unusual radio chatter and the otherwise slowness of the day in the world of crime fighting. How could you stay away once the cooler contents were discovered? The contraband pile in its entirety was neatly bagged in clear plastic and labeled.

The entire proceeding was photographed for posterity. The gay man had calmed and was no longer hyperventilating. No EMS would be required. The "perp" was seated on his ass, leaning with his back against a shed in the alley, only allowing enough room between for his cuffed hands. He asked for water but the request landed on deaf ears. The officers talked among themselves and it was determined that for liability purposes an animal control person should be called to the scene to deal with the cooler. No one was quite sure what exactly the poor animal had been through and how it would react once it got its bearings. This took about fifteen minutes for the officer to arrive, carrying crate in hand for transport. All were amazed at how docile the animal was during the transfer and it was questioned if it had really been necessary to involve another city department. All agreed better safe than sorry. Once empty, the cooler was also bagged and tagged and added to the evidence pile. The rat faced boy (young man) seemed unconcerned by the whole situation and stared skyward, singing some sort of tune in a low hushed tone. The gay man was breathing heavy again it seems after he caught sight of the pin knife in the clear plastic bag.

Somehow the pine stick was in his mind nowhere near as potentially lethal when in reality that was not the case. A person from a sandwich shop around the corner, being it was lunch time more or less came offering free sandwiches to the officers. Only two were taken.

After interviews were finished with witnesses and potential theorists the suspect was readied for transport. The circus was building.

News outlets, from monitoring police channels and having received anonymous tips from residents were in route to central booking to garner camera positions. Most interesting, high profile suspects are led at least sixty feet from car to building allowing decent camera exposure and not being sure where this fit in the spectrum of crime this was also the plan.

Cameras were ready and in focus. Reporters seemed reluctant to approach and in unusual form did not, opting for the long shot. Everyone had speculated about what was up in their own minds, nothing was verbalized. When the cars arrived and parked in the municipal lot everyone was in position and ready, expecting some sort of monster.

What they got was much different as the odd looking fellow, who was as unconcerned as a man on a Sunday stroll, chatted politely with the arresting officers. Only in the last twenty feet did a lone reporter have the nerve to advance and on camera ask rat boy what he was doing with the cats. In startled amazement the boy in a voice most sincere answered "I don't know nothing about no cats?" The police smiled. The guy's voice was nowhere near what was expected as it was more of a backwoods ignorant twang than Hispanic as one would expect by his ethnic looks.

His overbite hidden to this point became prominent when he spoke. He looked like a multitude of cartoon characters I had seen over the years. I really hadn't known what to expect. With the door closing that was it. Speculation was he was trapping and eating the cats although no evidence would support this aside from the obvious. This being his overall healthy physical condition in light of no visible means of support or housing, the abundance or "rash" of lost animals in the area and probably most damning being caught in the act during an abduction and the subsequent cooler animal.

Based on the news coverage the rightful owner of the "cooler cat" came forward a few days later and claimed "Mittens". The suspect soon dropped out of coverage for a more recent house fire and some Obama stimulus legislation and was not heard from or about again.

I'm not sure either if the cat disappearances subsided based on his incarceration but I would suspect so. I would also suspect that after further investigation it would be determined he was as crazy as a shit house rat and sent to what used to be called the "nervous hospital". Perhaps this was the plan all along. Winter was on the approach. I guess we'll never know. Either way I think the cats are safe again in Stifft Station. That is till I saw one last week smashed on the pavement of Markham Street near the Deaf School. Maybe rat face was framed?

The Vietnamese Hick

So Mexican George and I walk into this bar. Not just any bar but our old stomping grounds, the pool hall and our last stop... not first or even third. I'm not sure the circumstance as these things usually are organic. They take on a life of their own. We were on a tear drinking as much beer as possible and not necessarily in great moods. Not exactly angry but more like stewing about something. It seems like we had had some words earlier at Zack"s Bar with a very loud and intoxicated soldier but I wasn't entirely sure.

We were in the mode where things were running together. I do remember someone made a remark about my eyeglasses and possibly my sporty newsboy cap. When you live in a town like I do and have been anywhere else and possibly been exposed to any fashion at all you become a hard target for every hickory nut son of a bitch on any random adjacent bar stool. It can be very annoying. Generally not but when in just the right mood you tend to become a little volatile. You are like an explosive that only requires a catalyst or spark to send you into orbit. If others would only leave others alone. This however is not the game. As I said we had had several quick stops at various haunts but was either not fully impressed with the crowd, the music or something.

We had moved on. The pool hall was a definite afterthought actually on the way home. That's why they call it a "way homer" in that old joke. Neither one of us had been in the door in probably eight or nine months and wasn't entirely sure what to expect.

At one time about two years prior before the owners divorce giving ownership to the wife (and fathers checkbook) we had been intensely loyal regulars. Many a new years eve was spent on those stools. One of the things or the beginning of the end for us was the banning of music over the PA system. Management had opted for a pay for play internet based jukebox under the assumed theory that it would become a cash cow. Obviously a good sales job by the rental company. What it did do was insure dead air, a terrible element to have contributed to a bars atmosphere. I've sat at the bar watching television on high (above the bar) and I've seen couples come in, look at us and hearing nothing, turn and leave.

It must have seemed like walking into a closet occupied by the disenfranchised, not exactly festive. Regardless of the extremely cold beer in frozen mugs we saw the handwriting on the wall and sought greener pastures, only occasionally looking back. The few instances we had dropped by hadn't been terrible and we had been treated generally well.

I believed the current bartender to be an old friend from the place out by the airport who generally would often buy us several beers in an effort to lure us back. This night free beer was not to be. Opening the door was like opening a vacuum. It was like opening an old refrigerator with a burned out interior bulb. The first thing to hit you was the still flat intense quiet. Apparently the juke box mandate was still law. The second thing was the stale air, in typical pool hall style.

A tournament, which had been started that morning was winding down and only involved three tables back in the corner near the men's room door. The same men's room door two years before a crazy drunk bastard I had smashed with a pool cue had accused me of kicking a hole into. (I was later exonerated by the video surveillance tape). The only sound was the clinking of balls. All eyes and I mean all eyes, turned to greet us. This was of no consequence in our drunken state and we sauntered over to the end of the bar once housing, the I believe, illegal gaming machines and grabbed stools. I was very familiar with this perch as it allowed a full view of the entire room and especially the two exits.

The one and most important face to greet us was the bartender. It was the same guy as before. He seemed glad to see us as well either because he wanted new blood or thought he might actually move some product. Pool tournament players are notorious for having bottomless cups of coffee or nursing sodas for hours on end. There is no money in this aside from entry fees which also cover the prize money. We had cash.

He was glad to see us. After taking our order, delivery and some brief catching up I began to smell a stench of tension. Near our seats two championship tables are positioned, one occupied, one not. I noticed more eyes on us.

It seemed a money game had just ended, a fish was skewered and blood was in the water. The hustler (I use that term very loosely) yelled at me about twenty feet away and made the challenge, interrupting our pleasantries. Stopping I eyed the guy, just to see what was up to require such an intrusion. Before me stood an oafish figure, early to mid-thirties shaped similar to an inverted twenty watt light bulb but not as bright. He had a slogan t-shirt and some hunting logo ball cap which may have been camouflage in design. I'm not sure. I was more drawn to his teeth. He had a slight overbite which he clicked almost like a set of ill fitting dentures on a much older man. "What?" I asked as I really wasn't listening to his initial comments. "You want to play for two hundred?" As I processed this I noticed his sidekick who no doubt would hold the cash.

He was in the neighborhood of three hundred pounds and was literally as wide as he was tall. He had a ferret style face with characteristic pointy teeth grinning for what seemed a mile. I think his shirt and pants matched, possibly a jogging suit. He looked a lot like the animated main character in the Disney film "Despicable Me" but larger and of more girth. A couple of redneck bozo's.

We all three turned and stared as the question hung in the air. "No" I replied "we're just here for a beer". I turned back to my conversation. George sat between me and the guys at the table. "Didn't think so you old prick with your funny hat and your queer glasses". "Pardon me?" I replied. "You heard me faggot". George began to recoil and tense, squirming in his seat. He knew what was coming. With lightning speed and without thought of any kind I whipped off my hat and whirled it in Frisbee fashion into the face of the speaker. This flipped up the bill of his ball cap. "You can have it you bastard" followed the lid in their general direction. "I don't want it" was the cleaver comeback as he flipped it back. More mouthing ensued.

The bartender picked up the phone and in "Sling Blade" style was ready to call an ambulance or a hearse. Whichever was required? About that time, Debbie, the owner became aware of the commotion at the other end of the bar. Storming up she suddenly recognized me and came over all smiles and hugs.

This surprised the pair. She wanted the story of what had just happened and became very angry that they had so publicly attempted to force illegal gambling on to, unknown to them, common strangers just off the street. This could cost her liquor license.

In a closing shot the huge one told us we were lucky in a threatening manner. "What you gonna do? Roll over us?" I threw back. Quiet once again took hold with the occasional snicker making its way to us. They were angry but they were the regulars now in place of us. They were compelled to behave and would have shot us or something if this had happened outside, as crazed gamblers are known to do. We were not afraid which is our mode when wasted and laughed with the bartender who replied "See what shit I have to put up with?" One more beer each and we would go.

All the players, including the antagonist had retreated to the back corner by the tournament. We sat and visited alone with the bartender. About this time a lone figure walked up with confidence and sat mid-bar to our right. He was the striking figure of a Vietnamese man, early twenties and wiry as they often are. He wore a vest and headband in gang fashion and had tattoos of dragons and shit on each arm and shoulder. George was blitzed and oblivious to him. I was expecting trouble as he ordered one of the tired hotdogs from the roller machine.

He eyeballed me. I knew he had witnessed the entire exchange and was certainly not on my side. Making eye contact I decided to take the offensive and seek his intentions. "You with him?" seemed a quick cut to the chase. "I know him" was tossed back in the purest Arkansas hillbilly accent I have ever heard outside of exaggerated movie dialog. I stared in amazement as the entire potential exchange diffused. George and I looked at each other trying not to laugh. The guy ate the hotdog.

Where in the fuck did this guy come from? We would never know as he rejoined his friends and said no more. "Let's get the hell out of here" George contributed and after shaking hands with our buddy we were soon in the ride, slowly cruising Main Street toward the river.

Home again home again ziggety zog.

The River

1962

The river came one day. The brown torrent rushed and raged as it breached the dike and poured itself into our lives. We gathered all we could and quickly piled into our getaway vehicle.

I pulled my grandmothers quilt tightly around my body as if an armor to shield me from the impending flood. Making mental notes of our escape, I checked the back seat for the few personal effects we had gathered in haste. My one eyed bear, my favorite shirt, two pairs of socks, a coffee pot (percolator type) and our family bible.

Not much to start over with but it would have to do.

My dad pumped the accelerator the customary three times before gingerly turning the key. Surely it will start. It has to start. The water was already halfway up our wheels as the V8 slowly began to turn over.

Easing our way out near the tree where our drive once was became increasingly difficult. The rising waters laid claim to the processions we once called our own. Toys I had left in the yard floated away, perhaps to some more deserving boy. My dad began to swear and I knew it was my cue to retreat under my quilt.

After awhile I felt the tension ease and could no longer resist the urge to peek. We were just coming off the old road to Jacksonville.

The sun shone brightly and soon there stood my grandmother with open arms. "Y'all get in here and we'll clean ya up…hungry I bet?"

New Years Eve

Arkansas is a truly strange and magical place indeed. There's a saying here that if you don't like the weather hang around a minute cause it's going to change. This was the situation we found ourselves in on December 31. As the jet stream arched to the north of us south winds rushed into the state as far north as the Ozark Mountains and near St. Louis. This meant overnight a balmy change from the highs of forty or so to a little over seventy degrees. Aside from potential illness based on the temperature swing there was but one thing to do. Sail.

I had never sailed this late in the season and that alone was incentive. The plan was made. New Years day fell this year on a Saturday so I was off work on the Friday prior. To not totally flip out of routine I decided to get up early mid-morning and head to the gym. Finishing the year with a good workout seemed like a splendid idea so this became my stage one. The fact I was alone was an icing as it gave me a sense of improvement over the younger guys who had obviously "blown it off". They were weak of soul or possibly just early thrill seekers. They were not dedicated. I felt really well and finished strong.

Next stage was picking up my sailing partner and "PIC" and head to the liquor store. I had had an English muffin with raisons earlier and would not require food until stage four of the plan. The liquor stage would be broken into two parts. Pat was a huge rum drinker (vanilla flavor) so a trip to the discount liquor barn was first up in route to the lake. To complete this portion Wal-Mart was next at the corner of Chenal Boulevard and the state highway heading due west and to the water. It began to sprinkle a little with some passing potential storms in the parking lot but bright sun could be seen to the west. Still only 12:30pm so time was working with us.

At Wal-Mart we had secured some snacks and I got my beer and ice. I've been having a little infatuation with the Miller "vortex" bottle and I secured eighteen. This should do. In about fifteen minutes we were pulling up to the marina. To our dismay half the gate on the right approach side was shut and the sign read "marina closed". "They can't close the damn lake" was shouted in unison as we proceeded in the open side reserved for exits.

The bait shop was indeed closed for some reason but from it we required nothing. Two trips unloaded the car and all day sail provisions were dutifully stored on board. The south wind blew about ten miles per hour and dark clouds came and went. My dad called several times as he monitors weather as a hobby and profession warning of high winds and rain. Maybe. We had heard about the tornado earlier in the day in the Northwest part of the state which had killed three. It was a risky proposition but we wouldn't go far. Before going anywhere I attempted to install two sail slides I had gotten modified to fit the mast. They didn't fit.

In the mean time we fished. I was two thirds through reading the Wizard of Oz trilogy and was at the part where Uncle Henry and Aunt Em were transported to Oz to live out their days. They were about to lose the farm. An almost appropriate storyline based on current events. The fish were not biting and the wind began to shift from the Northwest. This changes everything when on the south shore in the fall or winter. Any wind from that general direction has to blow across the entire lake. The fact we had had an uncommonly warm day was totally erased. The cold water from the last few weeks' exposure served to drop the temperature by at least fifteen degrees in about fifteen to thirty minutes. The only saving grace was how trashed we had so quickly become. Still, the fish were not biting and darkness came at around 5:20 or so. With all that factored in I determined it was time to pack up, secure the boat and head to the next stop. I had pretty much mentally mapped out the series of events I would like to see happen the day before so I had a very clear vision. Next stop on the way back to town was dinner and drinks at Buffalo Wild Wings, a local sports bar on Highway Ten. Beer was cold on draft but not overly. Margaritas were ok but different somehow. When you've had real homemade you can spot and not appreciate a tainted or haphazard pre-mix. Regardless, we had a good head on our shoulders and wouldn't be deterred in the least. The waitress was somewhat entertaining as she was extremely unhappy.

She had a scowl which would not turn no matter how hard she tried and very small ears (freakishly) which would not support her "Happy New Years" mandatory employee plastic crown. Perhaps this was the reason for her resentfulness. We watched her navigate her station of tables and for good measure I knocked over a half full beer. Or maybe Pat did, I'm not sure? After a bit our food arrived. We had ordered a large cheeseburger which we split and a sampler of ribs and wings with Bar B Que sauce. It was similar to our version of a smorgasbord.

The spill insured we would rarely see our waitress again which suited me. Sometimes you just want to punch someone in the face. She was one of those. Again we didn't allow this to seep into an evening well underway. Some time had passed and much was consumed. Sitting and observing the room I developed a strange urge to hear about the Mercury space capsule mission, pretty much impossible in a chain store sports bar. Must have been a subliminal message from somewhere distant. I was correct in my assumption as I realized I was staring at a video trivia monitor perched high to my right. We were really fucked now. On to the next stop.

Stage five for the evening would be our regular bar Zacks. George would not be joining us this evening as he was spending a holiday month on the Mexican border in Laredo at his ancient moms. (He's bringing back a load of Sauza tequila and homemade hot tamales on the bus). Our regular section of stools seemed open and soon we were in our normal position at the bar, fresh drinks without ordering. DJ Debbie, my butch dyke buddy was once more in the booth with a new totally white hair dye job. I texted her asking if the carpet matched the drapes to which she replied "Go to hell!" Home sweet home. Videos were being shown on the large projection screen and she almost immediately popped off three or four from the permanent laminated request list I had given her last summer. At some point that crazy bitch Lady Gaga came on. While watching I was struck by the fact that young people think they are the only ones who have hot sex. Older people are the most sensual and amorous people I know for several but one main reason. No dramatic games. Funny how life is. Sooner than later that video was done thank god.

More drinks came. I started to play some trivia and a musical question came up whose answer was "squeeze box" by the Who. This had reminded me of my kid Amber. She had been home at Thanksgiving but had opted to spend Christmas at her home in LA. After being off a few days with a nice bonus she had gone shopping, or probably just piddling. Downtown she ran across a homeless trumpeter on a corner with a hungry looking rat terrier with a petit Santa hat. It had rained almost ten days straight prior and panhandling was at a premium. She gave him a hundred dollars and he began to cry. I think so did she? While this was happening I was having a beer at US Pizza and reading OZ. She was texting me play by play periodically. About an hour after the street incident she sent me a photo. It was an antique squeeze box she had bought for $67.00. "Do you play?" I asked. There was no answer.

The bar was starting to fill now but as regulars our place was secure. Just down the bar two black couples had relocated and we tried to engage them in conversation. There seemed no interest. Perhaps we were slurring. We had switched to rum with a beer chaser and suddenly felt nautical again. Had we gone full circle? The couples requested some rap music, which was obliged and the air changed. Even the black bartenders said they didn't prefer it because it was bad for business. I thought I understood but didn't ask for an elaboration. Something to do with tips. It was about that time I started again to feel buzzed. The seal had been broken hours before and like a man with an enlarged prostate I had a going problem. I soon found myself standing at a urinal between two guys at least a foot taller than me. One white, one black. I'm not sure why that seemed significant. For some reason I once again thought "what would Bukowski do?" I ruled that out and relieved myself. Never shit where you eat.

It was 11:35pm. I told Pat I felt like it was beginning to get serious now. "What?" was the reply as the head seemed forced against air to swing around and answer. It was prolific and almost grand in its simplicity. I began to laugh. "What's next?" Having completed the six planned stages of New Years Eve there seemed a void which needed filling the last twenty minutes. We had squeezed all we could from this location but I needed a strong finish. Pat was toast and wanted sleep. That was when I found my finish. Dylan was working at the pizza place downtown by my office and I knew they would be closed or closing and just hanging out a minute.

After dropping Pat I gathered my next best traveling companion, my little terrier "Max", who was ecstatic at being allowed to participate. I got her harness on and in about ten minutes we were at the restaurant. She loved the attention and everyone seemed in great moods. Money had been made and work was done. I had one beer. I swear the dog was all smiles or maybe it was me on the inside. It had been an unusual day but it seemed to give a positive cap to an otherwise pretty shitty year. I hugged my son. He hugged my dog. We all shook hands. It was 12:03am. Happy New Year. I thought about sleeping in as my phone began to vibrate with celebratory texts. George really missed it. I think I'll go make some eggs.

"Let's go pup…"

"Own"

My gym has a cardio area. It's divided into two rooms, one large and one small. The large is an open air with a twenty foot ceiling and glass on three sides overlooking the downtown Riverfront entertainment district. This one is crammed full of treadmills and automated skiing machines with twelve inch color video monitors.

The small room is separated from the large with a glass wall and a fifty inch flat panel TV with a ceiling mount. This room is significantly smaller and has only two rows of machines. The back row against the office is a pair of stair masters which sit extremely high. The front row is comprised of low slung recumbent bikes strategically placed so that all may share the one large TV monitor.

The rule of thumb is whoever controls the remote controls the programming. The remote is usually obtained by being the sole occupant or occasionally by abdication. If asked nicely the holder may choose to change programs or may not even know they are in control of such power. Such is often the case with women who don't care or understand the system. Some time the remote also gets misplaced. It usually shows up in the drawer at the checkout area in what would seem an attempt to keep a show on in which an employee is interested. Strictly against health club policy. This particular day was a Friday and I was early. I had decided to break my current routine of iced tea and Chinese food on Fridays and had opted to do some bar hoping. It was 2:10pm. The gym was pretty much empty save for some hotel guests who seemed to themselves and their I-pods. My routine was usual for a Friday and my shoulder and arm injury were feeling quite good for a change.

I breezed through upper body and moved on to some core work. This being done it was time to settle in for a thirty minute recumbent bike ride. All very usual. Once in the room I scanned the usual spots and searched for the remote. Not to be found. Being so early I did not know or really feel like approaching the front desk guy so I let it go.

My ass hit the seat and I dialed in the usual settings of difficulty and distance. I began to ride.

I had decided I would just hang with what was on from either the previous guest or the desk guy and that would be fine. I assumed it was probably CNBC. I was two minutes into my ride. The commercial on was trying to sell seniors reverse mortgages followed by a lively "huv-a-round" ad which should have been my first clue. Red flags began to rise. Oprah was up next in all her glory and sat two thirds of the way in a semicircular grouping of assorted guests. They were on a stage before a studio audience. My blood began to run cold and I felt (or thought I felt) the blood thinners I had taken at first light. Impossible I know but I had the mental sensation none the less. I had successfully gone my entire life without viewing a single episode of Oprah to this point. Additionally I avoid Oprah book club endorsed books with equal enthusiasm. I saw half of "The Color Purple", the parts with Whoopie. I'm not an Oprah supporter although I am amused how Stedman kept her on a string (and may still) and how a person of such self importance has such weight fluctuation. She seems like a different person every six months.

She begins to talk and the audience leans forward as if for some golden nugget of truth. I notice she has no dialect. Years of training have obviously created homogenous speech patterns which hold no discernible national origin. I began to squirm. I am five minutes into my ride. As she talks I see her lips moving but I have no frame of reference to associate with the conversation. I am not really processing the discussion and I'm beginning to sweat. Sweating is to be expected as I am technically forty five minutes into my overall workout but this is a cold sweat.

Like a dentist visit, somewhat calm but uncertain. She talks on only interrupted by obvious manually prompted applause. She smiled broadly and I detect dimples in the large round face. Popping fresh? I look over my shoulder for the desk guy but he is in the back washing towels. I am eight minutes into my ride. I decide I can tough this out but am acutely aware of being alone. It's good in a way because I'm not sure my reputation wouldn't be tarnished if thought to be an Oprah viewer. On the other hand I had no one available to sympathize with my situation. The same commercials I had seen earlier came on; no doubt a heavy rotation to compensate for senior shortness of memory. I was at this point hoping they would continue. They did not.

The scene was a continuation of before. After some quick thought I decided to hit it head on. Best defense is a good offense type shit…you know. In this effort I looked around for some help one more time and then attempted to focus and concentrate on what was being said, casting aside all preconceived notions of "hen parties" and the like. Once locked in I was shaken to my core. I am fifteen minutes into my ride. To my horror the discussion was revolving around the fact the Oprah show was ending its 25 year run. This is not a totally unpleasant thought considering it is the only show in the world that garners loyalty by buying its audience cars and vacations. The grisly aspect is yes it is dying but by its death a metamorphosis. A phoenix rising from the ashes. (or so one would think) The hour long show was just not enough time to glow on the audience and discuss issues like teen pregnancy and displaced African Americans. The show would be replaced by an entire network of twenty four hour a day programming, all in the image and with the message of her majesty the queen. With a sweep of her mighty large arm and about a billion dollars she would launch on an otherwise unsuspecting world the kingdom to be known as "OWN" (Oprah W. Network) Am I the only one that reads into this plans of world domination? A land of perpetual "Touched by an Angel" episodes and self help books on video tape.

Do as I say don't do as I do. Pay no attention to the man (or woman) behind the curtain. She is handing out hearts by the bucket load to all who will kneel. The wizard in the flesh. My head began to swim. I am twenty minutes into my ride.

On the screen the seniors are once again riding outside the complex at three miles per hour on red and blue beauties respectively. I'm not even annoyed by this as my brain tries to process what I had previously seen and how a human being can possibly have the gall to do such a thing. When the show resumes they are discussing the top ten finalists in a show host search.

The plan was an open solicitation throughout the country inviting talented (or not) individuals to record and send in audition tapes demonstrating why they should be awarded their own hour long shows. Describing how cool it is to be in "show business" a vaguely familiar looking gay guy from one of the cable shows and a woman who rang no bells blushed and moaned about luck and hard work. I tuned out. Where were the seniors when needed? Apparently thousands had responded and ten were chosen to compete further. Or so I thought. Each ones tape was shown with its respected owner allowed to adlib or elaborate. A little into it I was surprised to learn (not really) that Oprah alone herself would make the selection with slight help from the before mentioned pair of who knows what.

Hardly fair as I am more accustomed to at least an obstacle course or possibly an arm wrestling match to make the decision. The queen herself would choose. My real clue was about the third selection and her choice comments complimenting big O's outfit and hair. The tone was set. What ensued was the most insane orgy of ass kissing I have ever witnessed before or since with each picks face and nose covered with more "brownness" than the one previous. It was madness. There was no rhyme to it. O sat up straight and pleased, never fending off the remarks with even an ounce of humility. She was like an ever growing sponge. I was also reminded of the Steve McQueen version of "The Blob" (not the shitty remake with Kevin Dillon) where the monster grew with every human it devoured and absorbed.

I began to feel seriously ill.

I'm totally not used to this type of human behavior. I almost wished for the ASPCA commercial about abused animals to help neutralize the switch that had been turned on in my brain. I began to squirm again but I couldn't look away. Her hair, big and long was complimented again. I was twenty six minutes into my ride. We were doing reverse mortgages again with the presumed portly killer of Natalie Wood at the helm. Two minutes and thirty seconds elapsed. I knew with a minute and a half to go I could get through this however I did survey the room for waste receptacles in case I projectile vomited. Immediately the ass kissing resumed. I looked away but was drawn with some interest to the overweight female comedian from Phoenix. I'm not sure why.

Like manna from heaven the bell sounded alerting me of ride completion. This was a routine I regularly do but I was completely drained, both physically and emotionally. This would take me some time. I believe this is how she will do her world domination thing as she sucks your life force out. A succubus perhaps? Now she has a host of minions to keep the onslaught going 24-7. Mind numb I stumble away before learning the winner and soon stood motionless under a Luke warm gang shower head. The nausea had subsided but it was replaced by a pain in my left side. I feared stroke. Thirty minutes in the glow of her show had almost destroyed me. I had won this day but first thing tomorrow I would check with my cable provider to see if available so I could cancel. I have to warn the others. I may need a reverse mortgage.

Fear

I'm not a particularly heroic figure. I, by and large do the right thing but I think that should be expected and is appropriate in a civilized society. This should not be categorized as heroic. That being said I will say I have an inner confidence and am not prone to experience the emotion of intense fear, especially when under the influence of spirits. This fact has led to many scrapes over the years often ending in potential establishment banning and occasionally worse. All these facts are what I point to as I was shook to my core the other night. I felt vulnerable and I felt fear plain and simple.

The evening started like most. I found myself on the fifth from the left end stool at Zack's Bar, Mexican George to my left and Pat to my right. There were several ballgames on television but I opted for electronic video trivia. I logged in as a guest player under the name "Hi-Beam". No particular reason, it just came to me. It was eight o'clock. The usual routine of draft beer for George and I. Pat had vodka and cranberry juice. The third or fourth drink was followed by a catfish sandwich (not terrible) for me and cheeseburgers for the others. They have a new brand of frozen crinkle fries. Very typical bar food. My third game clicked for me and I won by about twelve hundred points. Feeling pretty good now, drinks continued to flow. Our usual bartenders were not there. Casey and her boyfriend we learned had moved on to work at Willie D's piano bar downtown which had been purchased by Casey's mom the month before. Erica was working the horse shoe portion of the bar inhabited by the jerk ass long time regulars we choose not to associate with.

Our end was being handled by a couple of very nice black guys I had seen before around on the day shift. They seemed to know me by name but I couldn't return the courtesy. Around ten PM Pat was tired and headed to the house. A short time later George walked up the street to the store for some lottery tickets. I thought he had said earlier he had no cash but I may have been mistaken. All very typical and no big deal. I finished the current game and went to the head to" break the seal".

As I hit the door I was greeted by an empty restroom and settled up to the middle wall mounted urinal of three to do my business. In about mid stream I saw a couple of guys slide through the door from the corner of my eye. Didn't think much of it being home turf. The main guy saddled up to my left. I felt his gaze for some reason and to be polite I glanced over to nod. In a stranger development we made eye contact. This was more than a little strange but I chalked it up to just two drunks or maybe alcohol poisoning.

The guy wore a puffy camouflage jacket with a matching ball cap pushed back slightly exposing a bald head. He may have been thirty and of the white redneck variety. His face was clean shaven and swollen red like he had been in a cold wind. He started to talk as I finished. I was immediately uncomfortable. He asked my name like he might know me but I well knew he did not. Then I glanced over and noticed his buddy. Over his shoulder there stood another guy much thinner than the first, dressed similar, same style coat and hat. He had a backwoods style goatee beard and large bulging eyes. He never seemed to blink.

I remember thinking he looked wired on something as he stared straight at me, maybe meth. He looked crazy and I really wanted out of there. I zipped up, hit the door and made my way back to my bar stool. I had all but sat down when I noticed the talker sliding into George's empty seat. "I'd like to buy a shot for my buddy Ray here" he announced to the bartender. I declined and he ordered one for himself and the staring guy who was almost in the same position over his shoulder as he was in the restroom. He continued to stare and I felt anxious. This was very unusual for me in the state I was in after a dozen or so beers. He kicked back the tequila and I understood his flushed appearance. He ordered another. The guy behind had none and continued to size me up. I tried to log back in and play more trivia but in mid key stroke the talker inquired on how it worked and what you win. I was starting to get a little pissed but that strange feeling of fear suppressed it. I'm not sure why but for the first time since I was maybe twelve I actually felt vulnerable. He was actually "sizing" me up. The other guy stared backup. "Where did you park?" "Out front?" the talker asked. This question really alarmed me.

I had no idea where George was so there was no backup for me. I squirmed to my right looking up and down the bar for a friendly face. There was none. He kept with the odd questions. He had another shot slamming the glass on the bar. I got the feeling he was working himself up to something. Where the hell was George? I once again looked nervously over my shoulder. The other guy stared at me. He offered once again to buy me a shot and once again I refused. He wanted me to drink. I stuck with my customary beer so I could maintain. He had another. I really didn't like him in George's chair.

I tried to ignore them and play my game but they wouldn't have it. I felt old. I'm sure I looked it. The questions and overall situation had really sobered me up. They were going to rob me or worse.

I thought about the young "stockbroker" guy a few months back who was kidnapped coming out of a bar in the Rivermarket area. He had closed down one of the bars on a weeknight and was approached in the shadows at his parked car by two young men. He was forced to drive to an ATM at gunpoint where he withdrew the maximum amount of cash available. From there the trio entered the freeway heading south from downtown toward Dallas and the airport.

Leaving the freeway they took a dark fishing road to a retention pond underneath the Interstate. At the end of the road the man was pistol whipped, crying "why?" since he had complied with all demands and totally cooperated. This whimpering enraged the pair. In a fit they broke out the front teeth of the cold and cowering man, after which forcing him to perform oral sex on them to completion. His mouth bled down his starched white dress shirt and mixed with the semen. Tiring of the game they asked him why he should live. "I have two kids…what have I done to deserve this?" Copying Clint Eastwood they answered "Deserves got nothing to do with" and two shots were fired. One for each kid they explained.

The first shot broke the collar bone leaving him unable to support his own weight forcing his face into the warm damp earth. The second shot entered the base of the skull and exited just north of the badly broken mouth. The ground became sticky.

The right eardrum was ruptured due to the pointblank gunshot. He was found the next day by fishermen. He survived. His car was found in almost the same spot it had occupied earlier. Surveillance cameras showed the car being re-parked about 5am, an hour before dawn but the pair could not be identified. They are at large. To protect tourism I'm sure, the City's official stance is the event never happened. DNA evidence was inconclusive as no matches were in the system. All of this went through my mind. He had another shot and asked me again about my car and its location. I was really sobering up fast. To change the subject I asked if his friend ever drank or was he just decorative? The talker thought this funny and slapped me hard on my bad shoulder. I felt old again. Where the hell was George? Feeling on the ropes I decided to interject. "I'm sorry to say but you're in my buddy's seat there and he'll be back any minute". "You ain't got nobody here dude... I haven't seen nobody" was his answer and it was confirmed to me it was a shakedown. I thought again about that poor bastard under the bridge and how he had to eat through a straw. The guy ordered another shot. His buddy stared. I was terrified. I focused on the game screen above the back bar but I could feel him piercing a hole in the side of my head with his bloodshot eyes. About that time one of the new black bartenders sensed there was trouble and came down to inquire what was up. At the inquiry the otherwise joking smiling talker turned his smile totally and told him to back the fuck off, he was talking to his new friend (me). He grabbed me around the neck in a friendly but rough style.

I pulled away and warned him to back off. The door guy had been paying some attention and eased over behind the staring guy and waited for what was next. "Give me another" the talker demanded. "You're done, so pay up ass hole" the bartender answered. For the first time the tweeker behind him blinked. It was as if his trance had been broken or maybe he felt the looming bouncer over his shoulder. Either way he was back to earth and surveying something other than me. I finally breathed but was not out of the woods. Being ejected for harassing me would not endear me to them and it was a long walk to my car past about ten potential hiding places. I was still in danger.

He threw down a waded twenty on the bar and headed to the door. No tip. They walked in a line with the staring guy in the middle and the bouncer coming up the rear. As the parade exited my long lost comrade entered. George, with his wide Mexican smile made way to his previously occupied seat clutching three power ball tickets. "I got them!" he bragged. Seeing an obvious look of concern on my face he inquired what was up. I explained all that had happened to which he just laughed and told me I was full of shit. "Wish I was, Amigo" was all I could say with levity. At closing I told the bouncer of my concerns and a couple of the guys agreed to shadow me and George out to the car. I had a little bit of a buzz again but still felt I had dodged a bullet. I was a bit shaken but took great pains to not show it. They were not outside that I could see. We hit the car seats quickly and fired up the engine. The bouncers waved and we hit the freeway heading north. The evening had made a real impression on me. Always feeling confident was no longer automatic. I would once again take my Dad's advice from forty years earlier and often since. Be aware of your surroundings. Damn, I feel old.

Trade Unionism

I ran across one of my prized possessions again the other day. I say again as it surfaces about every ten years from whatever "safe" place I determine that particular year to not forget. Never works. This is not so unusual for a person of my ilk but what is interesting is the irony I feel with each emergence. The object is a small blue hard bound book about six inches by ten inches in overall size and about a half to three quarters of an inch thick. The first and last pages are blank and made of tissue paper in the method popular fifty years or so ago. This type of binding denoted an air of importance to whatever subject matter may be contained within. The outside front cover was emboldened in stamped gold leaf about 18 point size standard Century Schoolbook type, all capital letters. It said "Trade Unionism".

At first glance one would wonder exactly what could possibly be the significance of a "blow by blow" accounting of the initial development, principles and rise to National importance of such an institution. Truth is, it was a gift. I was about three months from my eighth year (I know because I wrote my exact age along with my name in the front jacket as a child will signifying ownership) and was a relatively studious and lonely kid. My father was all consumed by his job and had little time for sports or games involving cavorting with me (boo hoo). Aside from this fact I faithfully watched at the front glass storm door for his arrival perched high in the black bentwood rocker we had by way of extreme guilt persuaded my religious zealot grandmother into giving me one year in Kansas City, the one who never seemed to know my name at holiday time.

He arrived at 5:15 PM each day. Dinner was at 5:30. This was the routine. The routine did not vary. Today was no exception. It was June and bright outside for several more hours. There was a slight overcast and had rained a bit some time earlier as it will this time of year…heating showers. Only the grass still held any of the water. The streets did not. As he parked the Datsun B-210 with the weird "honeycomb" pattern hubcaps in the yard I pushed the chair back from the glass, dismounted and headed to the back door for the official greeting. I'm not sure today what exactly I was trying to accomplish with this action as the result was usually the same.

The big brush off as he parked his shit, grabbed the waiting glass of tea and watched the news for approximately fourteen minutes. These weeks it was usually a Viet Nam related story, today was different. Once in the door he paused and I noticed tucked under his arm was a small blue book. I wasn't sure what this new addition meant but waited with relish. He noticed my interest and I have to assume this played into his plan. "Whatcha got?" I enquired. "I brought you this book" was the reply. This meant one of several things, none of which made much sense. First of all my dad had come from work. I had been to work with him before and knew he only allowed fifteen minutes to eat his eight homemade peanut butter and saltine crackers wrapped in foil, usually standing. This would not under normal circumstances allow for a foray to a bookstore. Second, at this time there were no bookstores in the downtown area. Third, I was not sure the importance or significance of the gesture. It must be very important. Fourth, being totally unfamiliar with subjects of this nature I was a little lost in how to react. I fiend extreme interest which was not far from my true feelings.

He handed me the edition. After I grabbed and held it at a length to survey the title I was still unsure. T-R-A-D-E U-N-I-O-N-I-S-M. I sounded it out in my head, probably moving my lips. This sounded really important, regal in a way, historic in another. I started to open the book when his hand closed it again. At this he looked me dead in the eye and spoke these truths "Read every bit of this and learn it…It will help you." I was a little scared at this point. No one, even at school had mandated such an undertaking. It was a fucking mystery. It had small type. It had no pictures. It contained large pronouncements of which I was unfamiliar. I took it to my room and cried but not too long. After a bit I knew it was supper on the table so I wiped my face and joined the group. I had hundreds of questions but no opportunity arose. It was as if it never happened. Conversation leaned toward LBJ and the war escalation. (The TV on in the background) I picked at my potatoes.

The book and its looming importance were paramount in my mind. After eating I excused myself, dragged the chair down the hall and started my directed task. I scanned through the edition once more in a quest for pictures and came up empty. As I struggled to read it became abundantly apparent to me that not only was this an "adult" book but very "dry" material. I pushed on. The first day I averaged about a page an hour. At this pace it was near impossible to garner any nuggets of truth when the mere mastery of the words was the problem. I pressed on. It was important. He had directed me to do this and that is what would be done. Chapter One…Chapter Two. I was getting a little better over time but I was still not seeing great significance with the material. It was boring and stale but press on I did. After a few months I'm sure my dad had all but forgotten about the gift and the directive.

I pressed on. Don't get me wrong it wasn't my only entertainment and I broke the monotony with the occasional comic or "Brains Benton" mystery. (I owned six of these editions.) However, the little blue book was my bible though I knew not why. I pressed on. In about a year I was halfway through and still didn't understand the significance. I began to again question the origins of the book but was too afraid to bring it up. It had to be important. I pressed on. The deeper I delved into the fundamental principles I began to wonder what the dynamics of worker / management relations had to do with an almost nine year old boy. I began to feel a little duped, but I kept at it. Surely there would be a revelation soon. My father, who loved and cared for me had taken the time in his busy day to select this volume and bring it to me. I would not let him down. I kept at it but felt a little worse and worse about it. I was investing valuable play time and it wasn't paying off. There was no good end to this. It took two years to finish and when I did all I could do was sit and stare. I was no doubt the stupidest little bastard ever who held a wealth of invaluable information on the topic.

I finally had had enough and questioned the books origin. I was to learn he had picked it up in a trash pile of old office books headed for the dumpster. They had belonged to the alcoholic one of my dad's bosses who had eaten a 38 slug from a snub nose despondent over losing at checkers to his also drunken wife. When quizzed about what was so important about it he drew a blank. He didn't know what I was talking about. The book that I thought was a wonderful and important gift; a gift my father took the time to get me was just trash. I was crushed. I didn't get the joke.

I slid back to my room and put on some "Monkees" 45's on the record player but was only half listening. I'm not sure what I actually learned but what I became aware of was how careful you have to be with people who may idolize you, especially the young and impressionable. I'm sure there were other lessons here but I had already invested enough time. I kept that book and today have it on my desk. I think it is a reminder to question things that may not be what they appear. And sometimes things only appear to be important . . . or it's the idea of something and not the substance that makes it significant. Either way I'm the jackass of 1967.

The Cushion

I sail a dead man's boat. I'm not saying that to be shitty, I'm just saying. The boat now known as "Dharma Bum" is a Hunter sailboat approximately 25 and a half feet long. It was built in 1984 and has all the higher end interior appointments popular at that time. It has bookshelves, a kitchen table, and galley and head, all highlighted with fine stained wood which may be teak but more likely mahogany. The engine is a 9.9 horse power outboard which saves on gas and insurance. When I came across the boat it was housed at a lake about a hundred miles to the north and was in immaculate condition.

It was like it had been in storage or something even though it was obviously kept on the water. Taking a boat of this size out of the water is a major undertaking and requires special equipment.

The sail covers and Biminis top showed some signs of wear and age but everything else was tip top. The owner was the receptionist at a local architectural firm and through a series of connections I had arranged to drive up and see the craft. The woman's son in law knew much about boats and led the tour. The lady, who was extremely nice, refused to board and instead stayed on the dock mostly looking down and shuffling her feet. I thought that odd but was more overcome with the excitement of the find than idle curiosity. I was informed that the sale price would be a couple of thousand below market on the condition that it would be used often and enjoyed. After a little investigation I discovered that indeed the boat had not been taken out in three years. I was very interested. The son in law took me aside and asked me to call him at the office and discuss.

He would be brokering the deal on the woman's behalf. He obviously had a story he was uncomfortable exchanging at the moment. I called around 10 am. In hushed tones I was told the story of the previous owner. The craft had been the pride and joy of a local attorney and his family. There was the husband and the wife, two kids (a son and daughter) and a small terrier mix dog. Weekends were a ritual. The lawyer was an avid outdoorsman but not a hunter. He leaned more toward mountain biking and running and competed in many iron man competitions. He was I think 45. One event, at the end of the marathon portion of the triathlon he became unusually dizzy and could not continue. Alarmed at the possibilities he scheduled an appointment at the Family Practice Clinic where his fellow iron man competitor doctor practiced.

Tests were done. More tests were done and he was sent to the Medical Center for a consult. After a week or so it was confirmed that he had advanced cancer of the endocrine system. He would be dead within three months. There was no real explanation. The family was devastated. The boat sat and waited for its friend and master to return. He did not. Knowing this back story made me more determined to do right by the vessel and it was purchased, although I gave market value, feeling the widow could use the money. I appreciated the intent but it was not necessary. I had it moved to the local lake and the Biminis top became torn during the transport, being rotten as I had suspected. Early on I began to find things, mainly tools and packets of parts mainly. Old items used once and stored for another time. Stowed below I found a great stash of several hundred dollars worth of cushions and regulation life jackets. Everything you could possibly need was there. It became a little odd when I would have a passing thought about needing something and within moments it would surface and be at hand. This went on for some time.

Once when digging for something I ran across a custom made life jacket for the family dog. That kinda bothered me a bit. The thought that the fun ended so abruptly. However I felt whatever presence here was friendly to us. Whatever residual feelings obviously approved. After a few years I had it pulled out and the keel and hull below the water line color scheme changed. It was fading little by little from what it once was but I still sensed approval. More years passed. Eventually I quit discovering secrets with the only things left starting more and more to resemble just junk. More years passed. After a point I never thought much more about the man (the captain) and his family outings. Then the other day we were out on an unseasonably warm winter day. We had sailed across at a leisurely pace to anchor and do some fishing, pretty much normal and ordinary. Usually I like to "bunch up" a couple of seat cushions, one as a seat and one as a seat back to give me some comfortable height to navigate easier. This time was no exception. When at the spot I anchored and moved to secure the tiller. The cushion lodged at my back flipped into the water and with the wind began to drift quickly away. The lake was extremely low and in no time the cushion had drifted into waters much too treacherous for an attempted retrieval.

I just sat and watched. It slowly moved away from me and seemed at peace somehow, although I have no idea what I mean by that statement. It was just a feeling. Like happy and sad at once. The faded green material was shinning in contrast to the liquid dancing surface surrounding it. It had belonged to the man and I had let it go. I hadn't thought about him in years but at that helpless moment he came flooding back. I watched it float away and wondered on what bank it would land? If a fisherman might retrieve it or will it stay there for more years and rot? I watched it float away and it made me kinda sad.

I opened a beer and drank deep.

Facebook

I know that "Facebook" is a remarkable social networking tool which has literally transformed in several short years the way people communicate. (Or so I have read) I also know that among other vices it must be used in moderation much like heroin or wild turkey. Hell, I even saw the "Social Network" movie back during the holidays. I get it, however I am what would be considered a casual user. I update my status about every three months, usually on a lark on a Friday night. I am mildly amused when I "reconnect" with someone from the distant or not so distant past, however my rule of thumb is to never, ever meet in person.

This particular day I broke my rule.

An old female friend from the late eighties to early nineties had requested to "friend" me and I had accepted. We had been part of a drinking group who spent every Friday happy hour at "Slick Willies" with about thirty others playing shuffle board and ping pong. Beyond that there was nothing. Her home page photo was exactly like I remembered her about sixteen or seventeen years earlier. She had aged well. About two or three days after being "friended" she sent me a message to which I responded, all very innocent and casual. There was absolutely no interest on my part whatsoever. Several days' later more small talk. The next message was decidedly darker and I became a little concerned. Not for myself but here was a person reaching out for something I would have to assume was short term cash. After about a month against my "rule" and better judgment I agreed to a lunch.

I figured the restriction of my one hour lunch period would allow for a timely escape if what I figured was accurate. I also selected a very public location approximately ten minutes from the office which would cut an additional twenty minutes from the overall meeting time. I felt comfortable with a tight forty minute time frame. This I could live with. Even with the built in preemptive precautions I still postponed twice and felt terribly guilty at the rejected tone of the reply texts. Something serious was up was my gut reaction. The third time I decided "what the hell?" and let the plans go through. That morning I got pretty busy so time passed well. That was good as she was unable for some reason to meet at my regular lunch time of 11am and opted for a leisurely 1pm. I'm ok with that on occasion so I didn't complain except to myself. At 1pm I texted her I was on the way and headed out. About halfway there she replied she had secured a table and would wait. The parking lot was beginning to empty as the noon crowd was getting gone and I took my choice of spots, very rare. I speculated which was her car. It was a tough call and I didn't dwell. After crossing the street and pushing the door open I felt a little reservation but it passed as I did through the threshold.

I scanned the room with my terrific new invisaline bifocals. She was easy to spot with a slightly updated hair cut in mid dining room... there was no doubt it was her. Nothing seemed out of sorts except perhaps her posture, which was bent slightly forward. She was overdressed. I knew from previous brief conversations she was currently unemployed and I had a feeling she had spent the better part of the day putting her outfit together. I was being sold something.

She wore a deep green pant suit with jacket hanging over the back of her chair. The color immediately reminded me of the green velvet dress made of draperies Scarlet O'Hara had manufactured for her jailhouse meeting with Rhett in Gone with the Wind. Eerie. The shirt had ruffles that seemed a little out of place and reminded me of the puffy shirt on Seinfeld. I'm really not trying to be a prick but these were my honest impressions. Her hair looked good and suited her. She must have felt my gaze and commented it had just been cut, I assume for the occasion so I'm glad I followed through.

I gave her a hug and noticed several smells which seemed unnatural to each other. We sat. She already had ordered a soda so I ordered and swiftly received an un-sweet iced tea which I loaded with "Sweet and Low". (The pink packets) I asked how she had been and she began to answer with a series of several one liners, like the speech had been prepared. The first being "She felt old enough to be a waitress at the last supper." It went on from there. I wasn't sure how to take it so I tried in vain to access the menu and make a selection. The clock was ticking. After the third joke I interrupted and inquired how she had been and what all had happened since seen last. After ignoring me and telling two more she launched headlong into her tale.

The waiter came back and we ordered. I requested a prime rib sandwich. I'm not sure what she ordered but it came with salad. I was too busy studying her. At first I thought she was nervous but then decided she must be tweaking on a drug of some kind. Her eyes seemed squinted and her face make up incomplete but I couldn't quite put my finger on exactly how. As I listened I started to feel her story was inconsistent with what little information was available on her Facebook profile. The glaring item was a slip about her "trailer" which contradicted the "Heights" residence which is much more than I can afford. I was suspicious. It didn't take long for money to be mentioned but not as a request but more as a victims comment. She shook physically with simple tasks and was obviously not well. My uncomfortable feeling was gaining root. Her salad arrived. While eating I noticed a disconnect between the bowl and the face leaving about a third on the table. I felt the waiter watching us. I was now thinking drugs. It was a lot like watching a wasted Mexican George attempt cheese dip. Soon my food arrived and I had not spoken ten words since "How are you?" She drifted from topic to topic, all very depressing and I waited with two napkins for her hand gestures to take down her soda. One of the facts gleaned was she had been married three times since I had seen her.

The first to a doctor who had made millions in private practice, I believe a podiatrist. She had not been required to work and had kept house in an exclusive "Heights" neighborhood, somehow this sounded familiar. After a few years he had become more and more unreliable in his personal and professional life to which the answer at some point became exposed as cocaine addiction. With this soon came philandering and eventually physical abuse. In the "last straw" episode he came home late after an intense day of drug and alcohol abuse, at which time he proceeded to urinate on her mink coat and pass out on the sofa.

She, also in an altered state I'm sure, beat the unconscious man into a coma with a large strap of some kind. The paramedics were not sure how his ribs had been broken and tufts of fur were extracted from his throat. He was lucky. Divorce proceedings followed as soon as he was able and he would later be incarcerated penniless for Medicaid fraud.

I had finished half my sandwich. I finally noticed she had ordered fried oysters. The second husband had only lasted four days with the service being annulled. Not much there. She shook and dipped her oysters in cocktail sauce. I was really uncomfortable now and felt everyone, in addition to the waiter was watching me. She talked on. The third husband was responsible for several surgeries and her permanent disability status with monthly payments described as "not enough to live on". In the middle of this story I learned about the multi-million dollar inheritance her 87 year old father had refused her and her brother from their grandmother. Soon she was back on track and I was beginning to really feel sorry. The third husband had neglected to tell her he was bi-polar and schizophrenic, a startling fact discovered after he discontinued his medications. His "last straw" was the occasion he held her hostage at knife point for three days straight and killed her dog. During this ordeal he explained in detail his plan to have her dead a day or so before he would break her skinny legs, allowing her body to be hidden inside the well in the side yard. On the third day (somewhat biblical) he passed out from sheer exhaustion and she saw her opportunity for escape.

Most people would call 911 but she opted for the revenge card first. Rummaging through the closet she retrieved her prize aluminum baseball bat and after enhancing his slumber she proceeded to break all extremities.

This being done she called John-law who in turn called medical personnel. Before this portion of the lucheon she apologized as I was trying to finish my sandwich. I studied her. She shook, ate and talked. It was about this time as I sat quietly nodding she looked up slightly and crashed her face on the table…asleep. The entire room including the cooks looked at me. I drank some tea. I tried to ignore them as if this was normal. Her head sat there in salad for maybe ten seconds after which she raised up and jumped back in mid-sentence as if nothing happened. Remarkable. It was like something I'd once seen in bat country.

Her strange mix of perfume and old lady smell was not allowing me to continue my food and I soon gave up. I had about five minutes before needing to leave, waived for the check and interrupted just long enough to bring this fact to light. She seemed unmoved and continued. "I really have to go back to work…I'm sorry", I injected into the air. She continued. I paid the check and got to my feet.

At this she asked "If I had been disappointed with meeting her" to which I took the high road and replied "No way!" On the way out she slid into her coat and asked that if I knew anyone with some part time work could I please let her know. I wasn't sure at what but she said she could do most anything if it required no walking, sitting or standing. I thought about this. She was still talking as I got into my car and headed out. I had never been so ready to leave a place in my life although I did feel absolutely terrible for her. I'm glad I went but it was kinda like a barium enema. It had to be done but it wasn't pleasant. I think tonight I'll go home and delete my crappy facebook page.

Renos

It was a long week, the kind of week that keeps on giving way past the appropriate time. Every other Friday I get off at 1pm but this was not one of those days. Five couldn't come soon enough. I had psyched myself up to go to the gym but as the clock neared the hour I lost my steam. About three I texted Mexican George and the Dylan to see what was up. George wouldn't get to his house until about 5:30 and would have to get cleaned up. That gave me about an hour for him. Dylan had to be at work tending bar at a show at six but was game for a couple. I chose US Pizza on Kavanaugh because I could be there in five minutes and the ultra cold beer mugs with floating ice. It was a decent day and outdoor seating was in order. I hadn't really sat down with Dylan in a couple of weeks as we have non- convergent universes so even the short time was pleasant for me.

We made small talk and watched people walking dogs go by. We sat up high near the stone wall overlooking the entire street. It seems he was going to a country club dinner the next afternoon and was a little apprehensive. He was going to go by Target and buy a no iron white button down shirt just prior. It should be a good deal I assured him. The shirt and the dinner, just be yourself. Do not get toasty first. Six o'clock came and he moved on.

I called to make sure George was ready. He was and climbing into my ride within about ten minutes. After a quick debate on destination we headed to Renos on Main Street in downtown Argenta. We are semi-regulars there and the food is good, particularly the homemade soups, which is appealing to older gentlemen such as ourselves. The bar was not terribly crowded except the long side.

This meant we would be seated in the two stools on the high end. This end is elevated as it sits partially on the now deserted stage. It was a little uncomfortable because of the harsh angle your body contorted to rest elbows on the bar and the whole "public display" aspect. We dealt with it and ordered "dos" beers. After a couple more and some catching up we each had a large bowl of soup. I had chicken and rice, he had the gumbo, both with extra saltine crackers. We inhaled the food.

The bar was populated by regulars sprinkled with a few fresh faces but not many. From our perch we were unable to see the televisions above the bar so our only choice was to people watch. The corner nearest was an older drunk chick who was working hard to make some sort of eye contact. She drank hard and alternated between rum shots and bottled Budweiser beer. It seemed to be some sort of system. Every third drink she would receive a cell phone call from what I would gather to be a disgruntled daughter from what I could overhear. They would fight fiercely after which she would smile and show me the bottom of her glass. It was later I would notice she was wearing slippers. Beside her was a pair of bikers, Male and female (one of each). The man was big, with a shaved head and goatee beard in typical fashion. He had a pleasant and uncharacteristic smile; the girl seemed a little younger and was decked out in a leather vest, skullcap and chaps. She was in a "club". I noticed the wind burned nose and asked where she had ridden from. Seems she had come down from the Joplin Missouri area to join the man and look for work. She was interviewing Monday at a coating plant. She was obviously in love with the big dude. I wasn't sure what had prompted her decision and didn't pursue the question. It's often best to leave such matters lie. Next to them was a hipster poet with a short beard on his second date explaining a strange Nietzsche-Frost connection? He had a great hat but not for someone of his age. They shared potato skins with sour cream and she stared deeply into his eyes as if he spoke truth.

It was about this time I noticed the red head. She sat across the room with her back against the wall and stared a hole through us. She was smoking and nursing a pint and reminded me a bit of Maude on "The Big Lebowski" with her sculpted red hair cut framing an unremarkable face. She continued to stare. Not understanding exactly, I wiped my face to remove the possible object of her attention. She sat alone. I was considering this when my field of vision was disturbed by the bum and the two white trench coat ladies. This was very unusual and I lost all thought of "Maude".

It seems two young twenty something's walking the street to the wine bar were approached by the homeless, shoeless man. In a naïve effort they brought him into the bar to order him a burger. Being barefoot was the first issue. As he stood there awkwardly listening to the girls explaining their intentions he opted to steal a smoke from a pack on the bar, grab a deep drink from the drunken ladies beer and make a quick break for the door. The drunken lady screamed and hurled the remainder and the glass at the man, just clipping his elbow and shattering the mug ahead of him on the floor. The two girls in matching vinyl jackets stood wide eyed at how wrong things had become. Embarrassed they hit the door and turned north on Main.

More odd people filtered in. Next was an ugly blonde in a purple Beatlemania type coat and her portly male escort. They continued straight through and sat by the aquariums. Again I felt the gaze of "Maude" but I still was unsure the exact game we were playing. She was obviously meeting someone as we were outpacing her three to one. The cook who doubles at the pool hall spotted us and came out to say hi. He had on a killer camouflage pirate baseball cap which we tried in vain to buy off him for six bucks. All the cash we had. I glanced back at Maude. During the interlude with the potential cap deal a group looking like American Idol contestants had moved in next to her. They all had bleached teeth I could see from twenty five feet away. About that time Maude's face lit up. An older man in a double starched white shirt and dyed jet black hair slid the chair up next to her and engaged.

By the body language I determined they were on a first date of possibly the internet variety. I noticed his shirt had a Nehru collar, uncommon for these parts. I haven't seen that outside of a magazine in many moons. She seemed to lose all interest in us with her new prey which was fine by me. That's when I noticed they were being watched. This younger hustler looking guy with ball cap turned backwards "gangsta" style was working around the room for better and better vantage points. He was casing them. He had noticeable "shakes" even from where I was. I've noticed a lot of young people seem to have this affliction. He moved in and joined them and my suspicions were founded. She introduced them and I began to fear for the old guy. I've seen enough CSI to spot a set up, robbery, killing. I watched until bored and moved on. Things were getting a little blurry and people came and went as they will do. It was about ten and George reminded me he had to be at work the next day at six. This was code for lets head out which was fine with me. The crowd was turning young now that live music was beginning and our stools would be required. We paid the friendly, female Mexican bartender, bid Tony farewell and were soon at George's door.

I think I might go sailing tomorrow.

Do NOT serve Paul

The scrawled hand written note read "Do <u>not</u> serve Paul booze, Thanks, Louis". It was written on notebook paper of the three hole variety, I'm thinking school grade, and had been gingerly placed on the bar back mirror with two pieces of 3M, ¾ inch clear plastic tape, a piece on each upper corner. Mexican George and I were seated directly in front of the sign at the bar. It was very hard to miss as it blocked my reflective view of the TV on the rear wall at Reno's. Louis is the young owner whose father bought him the building and subsequently the bar.

I knew of Paul and had seen him around on occasion. My mental images of him would not allow me to visualize the need for such a public admonishment. He always seemed quiet and shy, always seated in the corner at a table or end of the bar. A wallflower. He usually sips wine, possibly Merlot, and watches other people and their fun. I would guess his age upwards of seventy and possibly seventy five. He is well kept and in good physical condition. He has excellent posture however he does walk slow as one would expect. His longish gray beard has no wayward hairs; I'm sure requiring regular scissors and comb attention. He was also I'm sure considered attractive in earlier years. His clothes always appear clean.

I would see him at all manner of places in the Argenta bar district, always quiet, always in his place. What on earth had happened? What had pushed the owner Louis over the edge with the kind old man? George and I discussed this for some time. After a few beverages I decided to dive in and ask the friendly Mexican bartender chick what had happened to warrant this action. At the question she smiled that toothy crooked smile of hers, looked both ways for privacy and began to explain. We leaned forward on our stools to insure the hushed conversation private. The following is what I believe we were told although I have slept and partaken of beverages since then (This story may or may not be at all accurate as we were not witness but is somewhat entertaining none the less). The story began on the Friday prior. Paul had been in just after lunch about 2pm and instead of his customary wine ordered a Jack Daniels straight up with a beer chaser, unusual but no deal breaker all being adults. After the fourth in two hours questions were asked. "Everything OK Paul?" was whispered at him to which he only replied with a look... just a cold stare. He was obviously bothered. About 5pm Louis came in to prep for the evening along with the happy hour regulars. No one much noticed or bothered. He sat at the bar and tossed them back. About 6pm after near a hundred dollars worth of shots things turned. The shift change happened and when the new arrival noticed the unusual number of hard drinks attributed to the 135lb frame of the old man he became concerned. As is customary he went to the boss for advice.

He went to Louis. Louis went to Paul and probably a little abruptly cut him off. "That's enough Paul, time to go". The last thing Louis wanted was poor old Paul passed out on the floor just as the crowd began to shift young. It just doesn't look good, especially if due to his employee's inattention or lack of care in such matters. Paul didn't react well to the sudden rejection, a reflex not uncommon to "Jack" drinkers. Before the boss knew what happened Paul's glass in hand flew dangerously close to his head and smashed into the mirror, miraculously making only a small hole maybe three inches in diameter as it hit directly on a wall stud. She lifted the paper sign to reveal the point of impact, somehow fitting. This enraged Louis as he had already had a couple and came close to coming over the bar at him. Paul was not deterred or intimidated by the man forty years his junior, another trait of the Jack indulger. He reached with both small aged spotted hands over the bar, grabbing the owner's shirt by the collar and held on. With all his might he crashed his prey's face to the rough bar surface and the blood began to flow. The regulars were quickly up and had separated the men. "What the fuck, Paul?" was shouted in unison and surprise by all in attendance. Things calmed and breaths were caught. In the still Paul flipped off a shoe and with cat-like speed hurled it at Louis, striking him broadside of the head. This hurt him. Cops were called and soon arrived, the station just around the corner. No one knew quite what to do. Police didn't want to run him in but Louis insisted. The compromise was they would escort him out and banish him for life. In his present state possibly not a long banishment. This seemed to work and was carried out as soon as his shoe was retrieved and laced.

Paul crossed the street and disappeared. Everyone was in shock just shook their collective heads. What they didn't realize is he ducked into another bar and a similar scene ensued. Cops were called, more property damage and less forgiving. Paul was on an old man rampage. He seemed fueled by many years of pent up rage, alcohol and adrenaline and it was unclear what to do. Within an hour he had earned two more "for Life" rejections.

The slight humor of the Louis attack was now replaced with serious concern. He would have to be sent home. At the fourth bar, a gay bar in which he was shouting about the "fag" sized drinks he was finally subdued and handcuffed. No one knew or could imagine what had provoked all this. All were baffled. It was not risked for him to ride the trolley home, lest he fall off and be run over, not to mention the metal bracelets. Police took him home.

Nothing else was said. After a week the swelling on Louis face had subsided. The sign on the mirror remained. I believe this was the end of the bartenders account but we still had many questions to which no answers existed. After a few beers we moved on to other topics. We ordered the potato soup of the day. Several weeks went by and one Tuesday I was having lunch at the Starving Artists Café in Argenta. As I was walking in, a collected Paul was exiting. He had on smartly pressed jeans and a white button down. His tennis shoes looked clean and white. Perched high on his head and contrasting with his white hair and beard sat a pair of blue mirror lens reflective Revo sunglasses, the kind astronauts wear. He looked like an eighty year old rock star or maybe a movie producer. I and others have no fucking idea what all this was about or why it happened if it actually did. (Again this is rumor and speculation). Bad day I guess. I guess some bridges needed burning. After seeing he was in good form I felt a little bit better and made my way on in. Luckily I was given a window seat where I had the white bean soup with extra crackers. They have really exotic crackers. I wonder where they get them.

The Wind

The wind was howling on the lake. Lake Maumelle is a little unusual as with steep mountain ridges bordering on the north and south a strong convection current is created especially in warm weather. It's not uncommon to be triple digits in actual ground temperature with a twenty plus mile an hour wind. These winds may even gust to forty, being cooled by the several miles of open water between the ridges. This was one of those days but much more widespread.

It was Memorial weekend and I was in between responsibilities downtown at the big annual city festival so I opted for a few hours of sailing. The wind was stout at times and made the outing a little more like work than I had hoped, but it was ok. An hour or so in I had the notion about what would happen if someone, maybe drinking, was to go overboard, exactly what that would mean. It's the law that life vests be worn on power boats but not so much on sailing craft. There are many life jackets on board, most go untouched. There is also a life ring which is mostly ornamental. We would be prepared in theory. Truth is it would not be instantaneous to retrieve someone less fortunate in that situation, particularly in a wind like this.

The craft would most certainly move a great distance from the subject before dropping the main sail and starting the motor. This maneuver would be done into the wind which would prolong the amount of time to the rescue, assuming whoever is treading water. Factoring in the amount of alcohol the pilot and the unfortunate one may or may not have consumed and it is easy to see the dilemma. God forbid if the pilot lost footing. I considered all these facts about 3PM that afternoon, after which I popped a beer and headed east. I say all this because a strange event occurred at basically the same instant I had these thoughts. At another lake, in another part of the state the same intense wind was blowing. My friend JR (the event electrician) had a buddy on that lake taking his excited six year old on a fishing outing. All had gone well with the exception that the wind had caused great issues with fishing itself. The use of a bobber was not practical but in great need and the gusts would not permit it.

   It is a known fact that young boys new to the art of fishing often require the visual stimulation an active bobber affords. They lack the patience and finesse that bottom fishing requires. This is an older man's game and has no color. The stiff breeze wreaked havoc on the line below and caused an action scaring the fish more than attracting. It was not going well and there had been no bites. No fish had been landed. This fact however did not dampen the spirits of the anglers on their outing. The sun shone bright on the glass surface, no clouds visible any direction

   After several unsuccessful spots the Dad turned the small flat bottom boat into the wind to cross the lake for another secret spot to share with his boy. The trip across was a couple of miles and under normal conditions would be no problem but at this depth the water had begun to whitecap. The boats draft was not particularly high but the dad was confident all was well. Once across in a cove they would have some shelter from the stiff wind now causing all eyes to water.

   They pressed on throttling up a little to speed the process. The gust came from nowhere as they will. The boy at the front of the boat felt the lift and quick removal of his baseball cap, watching in vain as it flew high and landed in the waves. He burst into tears. This was no ordinary hat as he had just started to participate in League baseball and this was his first official team cap. He would sometimes sleep in it as boys will do. The dad knew this and felt for his son, not knowing what to do. The quick and first reaction was to release the throttle, essentially killing the engine. Once drifting he could evaluate the situation. The hat skidded across the surface, propelled by the wind and wave action. It would soon be gone if he did not act. The boy welled up and watched with interest. In an instant the dad had decided the best plan was to drift alongside, ease into the water if necessary and retrieve the object. He slowed the motor and closed the gap but the wave action made it impossible to lean over and grab. The boy sobbed. The dad quickly determined he would have to go in, swim the five feet or so and get the hat. Not his first choice but there was not any time to debate. Being a strong swimmer he was confident. He felt a life jacket would cause him to have less control in the wind and would not be required.

He would go straight to the object and straight back, piece of cake. Without hesitation he went headfirst into the depth trying to gain distance with forward momentum. He didn't want to be in any longer than necessary. In two strokes he had reached the prize in question and had the hat firmly in his grasp. The next gust came like a warning. The man had made his turn to come back to safety and treaded water a quick moment, catching what breath he had lost. In an instant the wind had shifted to the west. The man felt panic as he observed the craft move a few feet further away. The boy looked over the edge and cried harder. The motor was off for his safety and the boat was dead stick. The man had the hat firm and lurched toward the boat. His lungs were now burning as the whitecaps filled his nose and mouth. He swam harder. The boy stared, not knowing what to do. Another gust came and slapped at the broad side of the flat bottom and the gap widened farther. The man swam faster than he could imagine but the gap grew. The wind had a firm grasp on the vessel and shuffled it east as if on point. The man swam and held the hat, kicking off his tennis shoes to hopefully gain some advantage. The wind blew and the gap widened. The man's arms were heavy and on fire. The water soaked hat seemed made of cement. The boys face was no longer recognizable as the boat headed further east. The dad thought there's no way this could be happening. The wind blew harder. Tears came to both and the dad's concern shifted from himself to his pride and joy alone in the craft on the open lake. The blue sky was replaced by a whitecap wave to dark green and he knew this was the deal. He held firmly to the cap and relaxed. It grew dark around him.

The wind continued to drive the boat further. After about a mile it began to subside and die and the boy ran fore and aft, screaming and frantically looking for his hero. He was not there. Nearing the cove several anglers heard the commotion and spotted the small boy alone on the craft, making a beeline to investigate. The boy could hardly speak as he choked out about the wind and the hat. He could only point in the general direction that he had last seen his father. The men were joined by others in the search. Night came soon and the now empty boat was towed to the marina. The boy wrapped in a blanket sat in the lead boat. He looked at the stars. He had never seen so many stars.

Two more days came and went and the man was never found.

I think about that when the wind kicks up now and then. I popped another beer and headed west.

An Outing

    This will sound stupid but at this moment I'm tired of sailing. After some discussion it was determined that a totally left field option be exercised. This option became one of the Mississippi casinos just across the Mississippi River on the east bank. Several years ago casino gambling was legalized in that state making it a Mecca to surrounding states in that regard. I'm no gambler but I'm an excellent driver so I was totally in. Twenty bucks, even in Vegas is my limit (unless I win big) and slots my game of choice. It takes the human interaction element out. Double Diamond Haywire to be more specific. I like the pretty colors of the lights which are predominantly purple.

    The day was hot and the thought of sitting in an air conditioned room also had some appeal. The drive was pleasant enough and took about an hour and forty five minutes. I took my time. One restroom break on Interstate 40 before the fifty miles or so on the back roads with no opportunities.

    The large tea I got earlier with the free steak at Buffalo Grill had passed through and I opted for no more till the destination was reached. Lula, Mississippi just east of Helena Arkansas was selected instead of Tunica near Memphis to save some time. Isle of Capri is the first and sits basically at the foot of the bridge. Coming over the bridge I notice the parking lot was only about a third full, unusual for a Saturday afternoon but I wasn't complaining. I'm just not into huge crowds unless I'm working with them at a show I'm managing. A parking spot was secured quickly near the front drop off and we were soon inside seeking our games of choice. Every few years I come to these places and am immediately reminded why I don't come often. It's not necessarily the gaming but the clientele.

It's depressing to people watch unlike Vegas. Vegas has some of the most beautiful women in the world in their natural environment while this is the polar opposite.

I have yet to see any attractive people here and most tend toward the oafish or freakish. I don't want to sound elitist but it is painfully obvious. The farmers (40% of gamers) looking as if they just got off the tractor seem to have no cares or cash. Toothless grins are everywhere. Obvious welfare recipients of some kind surround the penny machines like moths to a flame. The room is relatively warm and crowded so we decide to head over to the other gaming room, only to be met with a large banner and two bored looking guards alerting that the second gaming floor is closed for renovations. This explained why the parking lot was so empty and the one room so full. Walking back we scanned the one open room looking for particular machines and finding only row after row of penny slots. The prospect of playing hours for a stake of twenty five cents was in no way appealing. We split up and settled into convergent rows at one of the few quarter machines. Pat found the one of choice and I settled for a Red White and Blue which had no sound. I didn't realize when I plopped down that I had sandwiched in between an elderly couple in which the wife had been playing two machines, mine being one of which.

I guess I looked unapproachable so she let it slide as I started dropping coin. The lack of sound seemed very startlingly odd. My standard twenty was inserted and off to the races I went. I had some initial short gains. The old husband to my left seemed a very kindly sort with deep wind worn features, his perfect farm mate to my right (the wife). They feverishly played and complained their machines would not accept his hundreds. This required them to go to the changer and break to smaller denominations leaving the machines vulnerable to seizure for a moment each time. I agreed to watch the chairs.

About thirty minutes in the man's phone began to ring. His loud machine caused him to miss several calls and when he did answer he couldn't distinguish the caller. At one point he handed me the phone to hand across to his wife to possibly hear better. Seems it was their son Gary. "It's Gary" she shouted across me. I had $17.50 showing. "What?" he replied at the same level and pitch as her? After three or four exchanges like this I told the man it was Gary. "You know Gary?" He seemed surprised. "No…No, Gary is on the phone…that's what she said." I shouted at the kindly prune of a face. "Oh great!" He grabbed the phone and after a brief exchange offered to me that his son Gary had noticed his truck in the yard and no one home. He was just checking on them. It seems the truck was low on gas so they took the car I went on to learn. Gary was fine with that.

I was losing big now. It was if the machine sensed the distraction and was trying to spare me somehow. I'd love a beer at this point but didn't really want to get started this far from home. Sobriety checkpoints terrify me. After a little less than an hour I went bust. I wandered about a bit and tried to look interested. Funny how you act when under surveillance.

Pat was up $200 on $20 so we weren't leaving soon. Plus with a potential on top finish I might be in line for some ice cream on the way back to Little Rock. I could wait. I found a support column just out of the way to lean on with a decent view of the Haywire machine and the floor. From this vantage point I could monitor machine progress (or loss) and see the goings and comings, still utterly depressing. After ten minutes or so I decided to count wheel chairs, giving up around eighteen after I decided I may had counted one or two twice. I just couldn't take the looks of desperation.

Pat was down slightly but so much more up than the wheelchairs who had taken to watching. I felt somewhat aware of a possible shakedown but it never materialized. The second hour came and went. The AC was still not particularly blowing and could in no way compete with the overcrowded room and the 100 plus degrees outside. It was becoming a tad brutal.

I decided to walk down to the bar for a pair of margaritas but could only be served one. Casino policy. At this I opted to give it away as I was the mobile one here. Pat was up $150 and woofed down the drink with passion.

I took my perch back at the column and began to count the new crop of wheelchairs, twenty two counting two huvarounds. The last time I saw so many was on a VA Hospital visit. It was just plain damn weird. Two of the floor men circled me occasionally checking out whatever my action was. I did not show my hand as I stared straight ahead and ignored them. There were no Mexicans there I began to realize and probably 70% black. I was now reduced to guessing racial and demographic percentages. Pat was now down to $100 over $20. It was time to go. Nothing could be gained by giving it all back and besides leaving now we would be back in town before dark, if that made any difference. It sounded good and this suited me.

After some discussion a stop at Zack's bar for a quick couple once in could be a great way to round off the day with all its excitement. The drive back was fast and pleasant as this is my favorite time of day. The sunset dead ahead was a natural wonder. Just at dark I was sitting on my stool at the bar sipping my first draft. Not great. Either the beer was stale or the glass skunky. (A result of being stored wet) I would see if the second was an improvement but it was a little worse than before, perhaps a psychological reaction. I kept thinking about wheelchairs and penny slots. I know with this here Obama in the White House we are supposed to be shitting in tall cotton but I'm not seeing it. Every year or two I go to the Delta and remember each time why I don't go back. It's a curse on that area.

I sit and study the sports monitors, sip my stale beer and think about that. The DJ is playing all fifties music for some stupid reason and it seems to make the beer taste worse if that is possible. "Let's get out of here…I've had enough". God bless this great land!

Drunk driving…

I would certainly never glorify or encourage the practice of drunk driving. Let me say that up front. I have seen firsthand the potential aftermath of a novice (a person unprepared) or who cannot hold their liquor. There are hundreds of factors that can contribute to disaster. Many types of drink have totally different altering effects and there is always the mood of the partier to take into account. I did an experiment back in the eighties with some friends to test my theory. One single night I would consume large quantities of a particular type of liquor in a safe, controlled environment and gage my reactions. It was pretty startling. Jack Daniels, as expected caused me to be overly surly and aggressively mean. Vodka had me crying uncontrollably about the death of John Wayne, Freddy Mercury and saving the whales. Different types of rums caused me to be friendly but much disoriented. Scotch and Irish whisky made me projectile vomit while cheaper stuff like Yukon Jack just made me silly. Southern Comfort, to which I am no stranger , saw no discernible change. Beer, the tried and true, allowed me the best option to maintain, keep my wits and awareness while still enjoying the "buzz". I always, as far back as I can remember drank for effect. Taste and all that bullshit is only a delivery system and were always secondary. Several altering occurrences have also served to forge my opinion about if it must be done the importance to "maintain". In 1982, while sitting dead in traffic in a turning lane I was rear ended by a drunk driver. The guy was an older man who was nine times the legal limit at two o'clock on a Saturday afternoon. He was driving a late model tank which destroyed my car and was able to drive away until other motorists forced him over and apprehended him for police to collect. He acted like he didn't know it had happened and perhaps this is true. My car and I did not fare as well. I had at the time a restored 1964 ½ red Mustang hardtop and the rear end accident compressed the oversized gas tank to four inched wide. Lucky it was empty as I was in the process of turning left into the Kroger Store parking lot to cash a check for gas. Upon impact the back of my seat broke off and I suffered torn ligaments in my lower back and ass. It took a year or so to be really ok.

I had certainly drank and driven prior to this incident but couldn't really compare myself to the caliber of this guy. I don't remember what ever happened to him. The next huge deal was on an emotion and mixed shot drink fueled night when I lost control and planted a sports car into my neighbor's brick house, totaling my pride and joy. The low profile of the Porsche hit the high curb just so shearing off the front wheels and dislodging the engine into the flowerbed. The dirt slowed the vehicle so no real damage was done to the brick home, whose occupants were on vacation. My face "spidered" the windshield but broke neither clean. A mason fruit jar in the back of the car filled with two worm mescal flew past my head on impact and shattered on the inside windshield coating it with thick yellow liquid. It was a disaster.

Not only was the car a total loss but I received a hospital visit and the subsequent loss and embarrassment. In addition I had three hundred dollars in cash in my pocket (to pay house painters the next day) which was lifted on the scene by first responder neighborhood thugs. This was a game changer. I knew and recognized the downward spiral and turned back. I did not replace my car for five years for several reasons. One, I couldn't afford insurance. Two, I was trying to teach myself a lesson. Another part of the turn was I enrolled at the local university and earned a degree at night. I caught rides everywhere or rode public transportation which was not easy in my town at the time. I always continued to drink but rarely drank other than beer, always keeping one foot in reality. I have had lapses but nothing remotely in the realm of that night. I was lucky and I know it.

When drinking and driving its very important not to be or feel aggressive.

It can never lead to good things. The best thing is to have music that sets the proper mood and is enjoyable and uplifting. For some reason some of the best drunk driving music is by the Foo Fighters. Dave Grohl has a voice that lends itself to "leans" into curves and slingshot moves when required. The range of music is perfect with a proper balance of slower delicate acoustic ballads and hard driving rock tunes. It's all over the place which is desirable. Early Bob Dylan is also a favorite on any given day but not so much if recorded after 1985. Morphine is another band with such highs and lows, perfect for intoxicated driving. It was such a fucking shame the singer died so young. Heart exploded on stage in Switzerland I think, or maybe Austria. I'm not sure. Kiss is not good driving music. I have most certainly done this in the seventies but it was like once the makeup comes off it can never go back on sayeth the clown. Have you seen Mini-Kiss? It's a midget group in makeup I would love to see at the State Fair, again though not great drunk driving music. I love him but Neil Young is not good DD music. Bob Seger however is great. I still think it's somehow based on the highs and lows. The whole point is this is your own personal movie, the windshield is your screen. Things are happening in real time and the music is the backdrop of your experience. Some rides have a better sound system than others. Mine at the moment is I think the best I've ever had. Maybe I'm just at an age where I really enjoy it. I can appreciate it. Buy the ticket and enjoy the ride. I think Hunter Thompson said that…or was it Horatio Alger? Sharks patrol these waters…swim like a MF, quoting Morphine.

Trust...

    Trust is a complicated proposition, but you know that. Most people would assume when exploring or attempting to examine the concept of trust you would rely on romantic experience or some type of human contact at the very least. I in younger days have most certainly lied and been lied to in the area of love. I am no stranger to this. Romance, however is not the pure example of trust I have witnessed. Romance has too many complications. Too many ends and outs. Neither is business a good example although I take great pride in the fact I am well respected in the business community as a person trustworthy and with a measure of integrity in my dealings. This is not a pure example either. Business changes with the weather. It is like water in the hands.

    I have thought about an example for almost five years now and I think about it often, I'm not exactly sure why. One fall day I sat on a sailboat in its slip. This particular slip had a great unencumbered view of a major portion of the lake including a turn on race days. This particular day I was without crew and opted to pull out my oversized folding chair (the kind developed by Russian scientists after the cold war) and sat perched low in the cockpit with my picturesque view. Shoes were off (stocking feet) and book and beer in hand. Temperature was around 55 so I wore a sweater. Wind blew from the north at about ten to fifteen miles an hour as it often will that time of year. The sky was endless. If the wind was that high in the marina you could bet it was in the twenty plus range on the main lake. After a bit I noticed a boat about twenty four plus feet (formidable) coming in full sail. This is part of the fun of this vantage point watching the boats coming and going. Almost a harbor master if you will.

As most know sailing requires some instruction and preparation. With this the next step is to actually go out and do it. Only feeling with your hands the reactions and complexities of the wind can you actually achieve the next step which is a genuine love of the sport. On occasion the instruction step is skipped and people try and learn by trial and error. Fall is no season here for this. Most winds are blowing over the mountains from the north traveling the approximate five miles across open water to the marina on the south side at a pretty good clip. This makes it difficult even for the experienced to come in or out of a slip with the small 9 horsepower engines which are standard. Protocol dictates that sails are secured prior to the NO-WAKE zone buoy so that controlled access and order is maintained coming into the traffic area of the marina. This is common sense. The boat launch is near with a myriad of experienced and fishing boats of all types. Come in slow and steady. Show no fear.

The boat I spied was coming hard in full sail, jib and main. I pulled out my binoculars and could see only a single passenger. I assumed he was coming in as quickly as possible for whatever reason and went back to my book. He was a mile or so out and running with the wind. Maybe five minutes later I glanced up when rocked by a wind driven wave and noticed the guy was still on course. He was coming hard into the marina still under full sail. I took a deep sip and wondered what in the fuck he was doing.

Once past the no wake zone he veered to the left toward the boat launch and just out of my sight on the outside of the rocky point built for marina protection. I figured he had dropped sail there near the gas pump or launch, waiting with some interest knowing there were no slips to house a boat of that size in that particular area. It never occurred to me he might be out of control, his course seemed so planned and direct. I had a quick thought of that Duran Duran guy, Simon I think, capsizing that forty footer on its ocean maiden voyage.

Maybe a minute or so later he reemerged into sight traveling the other direction, still under full sail. He was now being hit broadside by the wind, heeling wildly and picking up speed. I was becoming concerned. He was either an expert and was attempting to sail into his slip or was in serious trouble. Either option was not good in these conditions. As he veered toward my row I put my beer down and leaned forward in my seat. Both the main and jib sails were still up, locked and full. He began to tac and was once again broadside as the slip walkways run east and west. I was still concerned. As he was sailing in at the turn a gust hit him and he was T-boned into the back of a twenty six foot boat breaking the motor mount and I could only assume damaging the offending boat. The wind had the craft trapped and scraping across to the next boat causing similar damage. Luckily I was on the up wind side from him and in no immediate danger. He was not attempting to lower his sails in the least. He was at this time close enough for me to notice he was a middle aged black man tightly bound in a regulation life jacket. He was sporting a yellow ball cap. He looked embarrassed and he was alone. He could feel eyes on him watching his inexperience and the damage he was causing. My thoughts were first that I felt bad for him. I had certainly had my share of early on bad decisions on the water but nothing like this. I had seen him a couple of times cleaning that boat like a proud papa and I was pretty sure at some point we had spoken.

This type of thing can haunt a guy and cause him to give up on the water, his boat and more important his dream. I really was sad for him. As he came closer I realized his problem. He was hanging on terrified and was unable to drop sail and maintain control at the same time being alone. His inexperience had not told him to turn into the wind earlier. He hit his third boat.

This boat rebound him back into the channel and he approached my position. It was about then I noticed the dog on the bow. At first I wasn't sure it was real. It was a terrier of some type (possible Scotty mix) and was tan in color. Its most unusual feature was its master-matching life jacket, no doubt a custom job. The dog stood at attention pointing forward seemingly unaffected by the fracas, the man not so much. "Drop you sails!" I heard someone on the dock shout. The wind was letting up somewhat in the protection of the marina and he was able to steer a little clearer although still under sail. He was about twenty feet away. As he came on me the dog and I made eye contact. In an instant he glanced over his shoulder at his captain and back at me with a look of calm defiance, unaware of the danger. That was the most pure example of trust I had ever witnessed. He knew his captain and master would get him home. Failure was not an option. This made me feel even worse and my heart sank for them both. Slipping on my shoes I proceeded down the dock following along in case help was needed.

The wind gratefully was dying here. Erratically he turned the corner too hot into his slip and abruptly stopped. The jar caused the little dog to stumble but he quickly regained his footing and looked back at his master with almost a grin. I helped tie him off and jumped aboard helping drop the sails. As I went by I petted the dog. "Are you ok?" I asked the captain to which he quietly said fine and looked away. At the bait shop I could see the owner operator and his man coming down to discuss the damage no doubt. I excused myself and remember thinking about that dog and the level of blind trust he/she could have in a man in impossible circumstances. I started to tear up for them both (a totally sissy move) so I grabbed a fresh beer. I knew I'd never see them again. His boat was gone the next week. They talked about it up at the bait shop for near a month.

Good dog.

The Stalker

Anyone worth his or her salt should have a stalker at one time or another. Not a prank caller, peeper or otherwise annoyance guy but a full blown, gonna kill and eat you kind a guy. I've had one of the latter for almost twenty five years, which either makes him a non-focused shitty stalker or it's more of a cat and mouse kind of deal. I came to have my stalker much by accident as I am neither famous nor terribly in the public eye, much preferring the under the radar approach.

To start at the beginning I first met my future stalker in 1977. He was just a kid and I met him when I came over to pick up his older sister who I was taking to see the first run of Smokey and the Bandit at the local theater. The date went fine but there was no follow up for whatever reason. Not uncommon for me in 1977. The boy was less than memorable. Flash forward maybe ten years. I was working at a large architectural firm and in walks the boy. No longer a kid he had graduated from the local vo-tech school with one of those quick degrees in manual drafting. This was the pre-computer drafting era and there was a revolving door for drafters (the workhorses of the operation) who came in and made their mark or didn't. He did OK. He had worked manual labor in a mining operation just out of school and knew enough to prefer the indoor conveniences of an office environment.

I didn't give him a lot of thought. I saw him occasionally but nothing regular. After a few years I did begin to notice a slightly dark turn. Very subtle at first, he became a little loud and sometimes verbally abusive. I paid it not much mind as I was deep into my own "party" related issues, being the late eighties and early nineties. Regardless my helper, "Stacker" and I were not in the taking shit business whether we had a past connection or not. These exchanges were pretty harmless and seemed to level him out a tad. Several more years went by. About 1992 a line was inadvertently crossed. Knowing nothing or caring about his personal life a joking hand gesture we had recently adopted had been taken personal. I think we had seen it on television.

When someone was speaking you didn't respect or refused to hear you rolled your eyes and did simulated masturbation with your right hand. Just a couple of strokes, innocent enough and funny the first several hundred times. Of course, when we saw we could get a rise from him we escalated a bit. Not out of malice but probably daytime boredom coupled with the fact we were annoying young people. I'm not sure which more at this point.

He was becoming loud and heated more and more daily. After about a month of this my helper and I were called to my bosses' office. We were shown chairs and the door closed behind us. Behind the desk was the boss, two other seats were occupied by the stalker and his supervisor. The guy was near tears. Immediately we were grilled on exactly why we were attacking the young man with our taunts. It was explained to us that just out of High School an accident on the job had badly injured the youth and the method of our taunts served to remind him of this fact. He didn't know how we had found out and why we were making such fun of him.

Of course the revelation made us feel like shit. We explained emphatically what our joke had meant and that he was certainly not our sole target, a fact we could absolutely verify as virtually everyone was annoyed. After some more convincing all seemed satisfied. We were instructed to NEVER make the gesture again in the office or we would be terminated. No problem. It was old hat by now anyway.

Some time passed and all seemed level again. Around this time the guy took the aggressive. It was as if he had figured out we wanted to keep our jobs more than mess with him thus more or less tying our hands in his mind. I first noticed the smell of Jack Daniels mid morning as he would pass by and occasionally drop in our area to cast aspersions. We minded our own business and soldered on. He escalated. At this time a large group of us were in the habit of going after work to a local pool hall, drink beer and play shuffleboard. One Friday night he showed up, uninvited, which was our instruction, walked over and tipped my full beer pitcher on the floor. He stood there, surveyed this, laughed and hit the door out. Again my job was worth more than retaliation so we took it. He had us where he wanted us and knew it. Then the phone calls started. He would call late sometimes in a drunken stupor and cuss from one end to the other about what a lying bastard I was about what I had no clue. If I hung up he would call right back. Sometimes ten, twenty times a night, at least three or four days a week. Then nothing. As soon as I kinda forgot about him the calls would start. This went on for eight years.

In 1999 I left the firm and as no fault of his, changed my home phone number. I soon forgot about him again. Every six months or so he would somehow retrieve my number and call drunk. After my departure I understand he fell on more hard times. His drinking had apparently become a problem at work as witnessed by slow starts and absences. The firm was a sink or swim type of operation with a long line of hungry individuals looking for one to stumble and an individual to be overtaken. Liking you as a person was not top priority.

A year or two passed before his supervisor found drugs in his desk drawer, or so I heard. I didn't believe this but anything is possible I suppose. It just didn't pass the smell test. The calls continued after I had changed my number twice. His tone by now had changed and when I would actually take time to listen he talked of castration and a good "killin" as he put it. At this point I began to record and save some of his calls not so much to prosecute but as a pointing finger upon any sudden and unfortunate demise. I would forget and he would return, and so it went.

Once or twice his obviously bat shit crazy sister of my earlier acquaintance would call and accuse me of all his ills. I called the cops but they could do nothing with the loose laws concerning these matters on the books. He would have to do harm for them to act. This was America "dammit" and he had the right to harass and extract his pound for whatever injustice real or imagined I had supposed on him. I moved and he followed. If he couldn't find me he would call and drunkenly abuse my family. Truly insane levels. Through a mutual friend I learned last month that he had finally lost his current job. Now he has all day without the distraction of a job to drink whiskey and make plans. Six months had passed and his lack of motivation and skills combined with his substance abuse issues had found him on disability. More time to drink and search the internet. People never realized exactly why I chose to operate off the grid and under the radar these many years. Nothing sinister on my part. No illegal activities. I was just tired. The bastard won! I "gots" me one fine stalker as some say in Arkansas.

A Bad Idea

The weekend was here. I had paid very close attention to the long range weather forecast starting about Wednesday because any further out is really a crap shoot here. It had not looked great and had not really changed since then. Wind was going to be a huge factor I think. The weekend before we had been all packed up, eaten and ready to go sail when the phone rang just as I got the check. Five minutes later and we were in route. It was Dylan stuck at the Shell Station on Markham Street (at the pump) in my yellow work truck. All had been good up to that point. He had stopped in for a coke and some gas after which at the turn of the ignition key… nothing. We were about five or six minutes away up in the Heights and hoping for the "quick fix" we were headed that way.

About two weeks before along with a head gasket on the passenger side I had had Alec at the garage replace the negative battery cable. It had been working loose causing the same symptom of total power loss. The other quick thing was to deactivate the anti-theft system which also disabled power to the starter. Checking and marking those two off my list I moved on to attempt a jump start assuming the battery the culprit.

The jump did nothing but cause a traffic jam of sorts at the pumps. Next move was to jam the transmission into neutral and push it out of the business area and to a dead spot. This accomplished I pulled the battery and went a mile or so to Sears and had it checked.

Battery good. I felt my sailing day slipping away, slowly. Once back and with the battery in I decided the only move left was a tow downtown. I cut everybody loose, made some calls and after two more hours and an altercation with a passing bum (I was sitting in my car with the window down, looking at facebook on my cell phone when a young bum who had pissed himself walked up and wanted to borrow my phone to make a call. I said fuck no…I don't have one and besides I never loan my phone for several reasons. I went on to explain not least of which I didn't want random strange calls coming in as my number goes viral. He called me a dick and said "I see it right there in your hand" to which I answered "No you don't ". I suggested the helpful Shell employees would hook him up and he shuffled off looking back at me in disgust.) I was leading my truck on a trailer through deserted downtown to the garage parking lot. So close but no sailing this day.

ONE WEEK LATER…

As I said wind was still not looking safe.

There was a lake wind advisory until Monday showing gusts up to 45mph and beyond. That's land speed which can easily translate to 15 to 20 more mph on the open water. The wind was a part of some frontal action and blowing South by southwest. This was also a cause for concern as with the marina on the south shore the wind would only intensify the further out and north you traveled. Not great. Saturday AM came and first thing I turned the television to channel "101" to catch the wind speed on the constant weather forecast. SSW at 7. A glimmer of hope? Maybe the front had stalled? It could be days before the foretold catastrophe. I decided to go eat early and monitor things on the smart phone. A great new restaurant had opened up the street a few weeks earlier with great food and even better prices. The parking lot was packed from open to close with us lucky enough to only have a thirty minute wait for early dinner a week before.

We would show up at 11am opening and still stand in line. Once in and seated (5 minutes) I ordered the half-pound cheeseburger, asking for medium cooking temperature. After a short bit the unsure waitress came back and informed me the kitchen was unable to complete my request as it would be a hazard to my health. "Whatever" I replied and was soon munching on an "Ok" burger. Checking the weather again I read SSW at 8. I perked up and we discussed our options. We could be on or close to the water in 30 minutes and I really couldn't see it changing that much. The sun was finally breaking the clouds. "Let's go for it" I paid the check for the inexpensive lunch and westward we went. I took Highway 10 to allow a quick liquor store stop which included 9 of the wide mouth beers, a six of baby size beers and a gallon of rum. (Not sure why I got the baby beers) This load was topped off by three bags of "Imperial Ice". I never really understood what that implied as I never regarded my ice as "regal". Off again I checked things. SSW at 8. Flags along the road fluttered listless.

The plan was if this continued we would traverse the lake with the south breeze; hide behind an island from the sure to eventually come wind, fish and drink, motor back. It was a sound plan. If we were uncomfortable in the mean time since we had provisions we would stay put secure in the slip and fish off the boat. I would finish the book I was reading. Another sensible option. As we topped the hill we could see racing in progress on the lake and our confidence soared. SSW at 10. Very manageable and still blowing the right direction. We could sail across, racing boats to our east. We cast off quickly with nothing more to discuss, time was essential. With a little extra effort we hoisted the main sail, set the breaks and let god push us due north. The wind would pick up and die periodically so we were quite comfortable as I unscrewed the cap off my first beverage. I drank deep.

The sky was becoming a little overcast now but nothing was forecast other than wind. We sailed north. Two thirds of the way I noticed all the much smaller racing vessels turning in unison and heading for the yacht club. I thought this a little odd as I hadn't heard a horn but paid it no mind. Wind was maybe twelve and we were making good way. Soon we had passed Big Island and began to enter the mouth of the cove which was to be our afternoon refuge. The wind had shifted a few times but was basically due south.

The island which was our destination was now in sight, maybe a quarter to half a mile. The wind picked up a little but still not terrible. I rationalized this due to the fact we had three plus miles of open water between us and land on which wind could build up speed, maybe now fifteen mph. We were coming up to the island and I prepared to swing port close to the rock bluffs and find a dead zone. On the open water of this lake you can always spot winds as they shift or accelerate and you can adjust accordingly. In this situation I had my back to the main lake as I leisurely eased into my turn. Pat was below putting together some tackle. At the exact moment I was out of position the first gust hit. It was at least fifty mph and hit at near broadside. Everything on the port side interior crashed against Pat and to the floor as we heeled over. Water was lapping at the rail near my foot, the sound of a sudden water rush over my right shoulder. I held the tiller firm as we lurched toward the craggy rock bluff, now flying by. I knew the drop off was a shear thirty feet there so I was only concerned with correcting the vessel. I was also concerned as Pat lay on the floor.

Almost as suddenly the boat righted itself and headed from the bluff. It was so quick that I had over corrected exposing the other side of the boat to what may come. What came was a second less powerful gust which crashed everything else (a full bar) into the floor. Pat knew this was serious as I threw a half full beer onto the deck to allow both hands free for the tiller. In an instant there we were, shaken, in dead calm behind the protection of the peak of the mountain top island.

Checking everything we could the only visible loss was a few CD's broken (Dark Side of the Moon) and a hunk torn out of the meat of my hand. I had caught my breath. As quickly as we could the sail was dropped, secured and the anchor set. The wind was back to its moderate rate and we could hardly tell anything had happened from that vantage point. I popped another beer. The stereo still worked but in the crash a large dirt dobber nest was dislodged from deep in a speaker. I tossed it in the drink. We mainly sat still a minute and breathed. I began to realize this had been a mistake and mentally prepared for the fact we had to get back. The wind had steadied and moderated to about sixteen miles an hour so I was feeling better. I popped yet another beer out of the cube cooler. After finishing my book and the fact the fish weren't biting I decided not to tempt fate. Quickly preparing everything we were underway as the motor started first try and we headed south. I gave myself and hour to cross before the November night would drop temperatures to uncomfortable levels in an instant.

    We were making good time and I had three beers left. I wanted a shot of rum but would abstain. We were not in yet. The wind was dying and correspondingly confidence soared. We would live to tell the tale as they say. It was all so quick that I never really feared (stupidly) for our safety but was more bothered by the fact that for shallow reasons I had put the boat in harm's way. I am the boats steward and protector and it was wrong. I had learned and will never forget…always live to sail another day. I unscrewed the cap on my last beer and toasted the full moon, tight in the slip.

Endgame

I really couldn't decide. I had already been to one NCAA college game this season which by my nature should satisfy my desires for three to five years... but here I sat. By all accounts this shouldn't even be that much of a game but it was the last home game this year in Little Rock, Arkansas. A warm snap had made this November day unseasonably comfortable. I would have to decide by Friday. There were several options even now with all being driven by some offhand comments of Mexican George about never having been to a college game. The game I had gone to earlier in the season was on a free pair of great seats behind the home bench which raised the expectation bar pretty high. I called George Thursday night and filled him in on the options as they presently were.

One: I could pick him up at noon; go to a tailgate party at the Budweiser corporate bus. Have free beer and watch the game on satellite in the parking lot. Maybe go in the game or not, throwing all to fate.

Two: Secure tickets somehow and go to game.

Three: Pick him up at noon, go to my house, drink my beer and watch game on TV.

Four: Disregard 1,2,3. Blow whole thing off and go sailing. Listen to game on radio. Drink beer.

Even with this level of disorganization we had solid options. He whined a little and I knew the "blow off" option 4 was not going to fly so I resigned myself to the fact. Friday morning one of my co-workers informed me he had changed his mind about going and had two choice seats available. I had always been schooled in paying less or at face value and was a little shocked they were going for $55 each. "Must be good seats?" I reasoned. They were season tickets belonging to an ex-players mother. He was not sure where in the stadium they were but couldn't see them as bad. Keep in mind my last trip was row B on the 40 yard line. It would take something special to melt my butter. I did the quick math in my head ($110) and swallowed hard. I thought of Mexican George again and agreed.

My co-worker and I were both off at 1PM that day so we agreed I would call later and hook up for the exchange. I had a few things going on and was in no real hurry for the transaction. I ran up to the bank and cashed a check for the money, two bills, one hundred and one ten. The cash was set and I drove a few blocks over to my buddy Robert Berry's 7th Street Tattoo to observe an install on a friend. Things went well although when I questioned if it was really finished the tat artist became a little shitty. I left well enough alone. We were finished there about 3:30 and I headed up to US Pizza on Kavanaugh for some beer and salad. I hadn't eaten lunch yet and as I suspected this hit the spot. As I am prone to do, I stayed behind for more beer after everyone else's departure. Beer there is almost frozen like I like it and besides I really had nowhere to go until fiveish, when I would do the ticket exchange. After a few I was feeling pretty good, made the call and was soon heading over to one of the black churches on 12th Street.

The lot was empty save for one car I recognized by the huge scrape down the entire passenger side. The tickets were still attached to page six of the full color, spiral bound season ticket holders season brochure. As I had those in my hand I was informed the tickets were ten dollars more each so I owed an additional twenty spot? I bit my tongue. This was almost pissing me off but I remembered it was for George. I took a complementary tour of the church to be polite and was soon on my way up 12th street toward the lights of University Avenue. Sitting at the light on University I considered turning quick left to go to Zack's for a nightcap. I thought better of it realizing I had just paid $110 for something I halfheartedly wanted. I had spent enough cash today. After a couple of beers at the house and a good dog petting I turned in for whatever was up the next day. I was up pretty early with the intention of eating lunch and getting the lay of things. Once my head cleared I decided to check out the section and row and see how we had done on the seating. THE FIRST THING to catch my eye was "END ZONE". I bristled. The next thing was row 46, section 19. Fumbling through the brochure I located the stadium seating chart and had to take a chair. Section 19 was a much ignored small pie shaped area in the southwest corner, nosebleed high. I was really irritated but blamed myself for not asking more questions. Water under the bridge.

I headed up to the Heights to circumvent the stadium. Traffic was already of epic proportions as the sea of tailgate parties on the golf course had been in full swing since 8am. It was now about 11:30 and the "amateurs" were out in full force. Cheers was our destination where as I walked in I saw and spoke to an old friend of mine from Springdale who was on the game officiating crew. He was in charge of TV timeouts as the game was being televised on CBS network, which I by this time wished I'd be watching. On the way I scoped out some hidden potential parking on the old Bennigan's lot across from the mall. It was open as I suspected but I didn't know for how long. Maybe we would be lucky.

At lunch the roast beef was good and the salty chips went perfect with un-sweet iced tea. After sifting through the complimentary "Times" newspaper I was as prepared as I could be. We took another shortcut back and I followed suit to avoid the other side and get to the freeway. The detour added maybe five minutes but nowhere near what sitting in traffic would have done. It took about fifteen minutes more and I was in George's front yard. I joked about his lack of school colors as he was dressed in brown, white and blue. Our school was red and white. I also pointed out the only close thing I had was a red and white "lifeguard" hoodie from Huntington Beach California which I was sporting. We were pretty pathetic as fans but we didn't really give a shit. His excitement faded a tad as I informed him of the stadium "no smoking policy" and college ban on beer sales. He equated it with an "airplane" ride and decided it would be ok. As suspected we spotted one parking spot left as we came in the back way. I snaked in, locked up and we hit the proverbial trail. Being sober made the now several hours ahead "party "revelers seem particularly stupid ...all the over the top preparation we spied and the details of the camps. The walk had put us there about 45 minutes before kickoff. George informed me he was in need of a bathroom so we opted to go on in, never passing up on a restroom opportunity being one of my mottos. I was not feeling warm and fuzzy as we entered the lowly gate 5.

It could have also been the fact we had passed through the "POLO" version of tailgating at the stadium press box elevator door area in route. The pastel sweaters tied loosely around necks attached to tortoise shell executive style be speckled fat faces. They didn't even know. And we, a bummy looking fucker who had more or less just rolled out of bed and his Mexican sidekick. I'm not judging, I'm just saying. Either way it was a class stratum we had just passed through and I was a tad off my game. Our gate had two pathetic lines, our restroom was small and cramped. The cleanly dressed man in the restroom line in front of me held a probably four year old girl who smiled sweetly at me. She had stick on red pigs on her face. I never understood or was comfortable with this practice of bringing a young female into a room of mostly drunk pissing men but I guess it couldn't be helped. I smiled at her and took my turn, after which George followed me up the walk to our "Wuthering Heights". It may have been my sobriety but I immediately held a distinct disliking for the folks on my row...just something about them.

The seats were numbered on the backless aluminum bleacher faces and allotted each ticket holder about a foot and a half of real estate. Squeezing in I was pleased the two rows (about six seats) immediately in front of us were vacant. I secretly hoped they would stay that way. Time passed toward kickoff and they stayed open. Today was looking up. At about two minutes till kick off the "posse" arrived. The leader, was a clean cut fairly ordinary fellow with the exception of his "new money" gold chains dangling down the front of his pig shirt. He had a matching visor and a freshly cut shock of hair reached skyward. His two kids followed, a boy of twelve (a little fat kid) and a girl of fourteen with a mouthful of braces, both texted constantly. The man was obviously bringing some employees to a game. I envisioned him owning a carwash or maybe a trucking operation. His guests filed in and ran the gambit. One redneck, one prepster, one black guy, etc. the final two grabbed the two seats in front of us. The guy directly in front of me was probably in his fifties and in desperate need of an eye patch. Due to an injury he had a protruding, milked over white eyeball and old and faded tattoos peaking out of his otherwise normal neckline. He smelled horrible but I couldn't exactly place what it was. I gagged as his buddy helped him to his seat. At first I thought him totally blind but it was only partial. His buddy to his right looked even more like a pirate. He had long dark hair but was in the forty to fifty year old range. A cheap oversized hoop earring and a red headband tied like aunt Jamima. His razorback jacket was tied around his waist eight year old style and when he turned and smiled I noticed his four front teeth were missing. He stank also. It was a strange smell like the pair had bathed in cinnamon in order to mask who knows what. I was holding my breath and feeling a little claustrophobic.

About the same time a reasonably attractive, highly intoxicated twenty something chick slid past us with a younger brother in tow. She parked it to the left of George. From the very beginning she talked (and slurred). George at first was polite and she took this as acceptance and continued. When he would look away to watch the action she would elbow him back to her reality and continue. He rolled his eyes at me. At least she wasn't a fragrance wafting up at me. The blind guy at one point early lit up a cigarette to which his pirate friend pointed out the policy. He chased the quick "cut short" smoke with a good snort of the Crown Royal pint he just opened. The pirate took a hit and passed back. A few minutes later they washed down some white pills they passed around, still stinking.

This was not fun.

Then came the high fives. As they got more fucked up they began to demand high fives from all around at the slightest good fortune. We indulged a while until I learned to ignore or conveniently be looking the other way. "One eye" lit up again. Sorry...he had forgotten. The girl was now telling George about her college roommate. He rolled his eyes at me again. First down high fives. Shot of Crown. Then came the dancing. I know I'm old fashioned but I have absolutely no concept of why a traditional southern university whose fight song thirty years earlier was "Dixie" would feel compelled to play the most vile loud rap music over the PA at breaks. It just didn't fit. What was more disturbing was watching the predominately older white crowd trying jerkily to move to it. I was embarrassed for them. I know they were having fun but hell man? The worst was the boss, the leader. He gyrated his ass and bobbed his visor to the point I thought he would lose it. His crew followed suit. The little girl in the second quarter noticed the one eye had wet himself. It had no effect on the stench. They laughed at him. He just smiled. We all high fived.

   The game dragged on due to all the TV timeouts making it without a doubt one of the longest afternoons in my life. The halftime show only served to enrage me. The girl was now telling George about bicycling in her neighborhood. I wanted to high five but now was not the time. The pair took another shot and a pill. I would not hang around for the outcome. At the beginning of the fourth quarter the Arkansas Razorbacks scored again and the game was firmly in hand. "Let's get out of here and beat the traffic…go to Zack's…I need a beer". As the crowd stood for the extra point we saw the light and without word to our friends hit the aisle. Cutting across the vacating golf course soon we were at the car. After some more neighborhood back road maneuvers we sat on our favorite stools at Zack's. Grabbing a trivia box we were soon joined by Pat. Beer and rum flowed only interrupted by grilled cheese and fries. The game had just finished on TV. Trivia was going great in part due to the fact that I was playing alone. At the end of my first round my game box screen went blank. "Great". it was a great cap for the day's events. "Get in the damn car" I told George.

Fear and Loathing Revisited…

Around 10am I got a text. I was surprised to get a west coast text that early and even more surprised to see who from. "Ready to come home and regroup". It was short and sweet but I got the message clear. It was going on three years since Mexican George and I had dropped my daughter Amber off at that Long Beach I-Hop. Since then she had done quite well not that I was surprised. She had decided about a year in, that the quiet and safety I appreciated in downtown Long Beach was not quite her speed and had opted for the faster pace of Eagle Rock closer to downtown LA. She complained the neighborhood bars she frequented were too heavily populated with older stoner hippie beach types, and she was probably right.

Her career in fashion had launched well after a little slow start due to the recession. Money was not her problem. She had been thrust a bit too quickly into the deep corporate waters. She was responsible for overseeing Chinese manufacturing operations for a label supplying clothing for several major US department store chains. She enjoyed the challenge of the work but it was taking its toll.

Her friends she had developed worked in various career arenas all the way from dog walker to television post production. Her friends were great but she had made the comment to me several times that her friends were like islands. They all had money and opportunities but there was something non-permanent about them all. Not so much a loyalty thing but maybe just the vibe that LA gives a young person. Regardless, she had made the decision and was walking away from her great job and apartment. I know Ambo well enough to not question too hard. We had discussed it in theory but I wasn't sure things would progress this quickly to a state of action. Besides, I would get a road trip out west with a mission attached.

My first call was to George. He is always game for the road but regretted to inform me he would have to sit this one out. Seems he was working a lot of overtime painting rocket launchers for the military with us winding down one war and ramping up another. I couldn't and didn't blame him. Make hay while the sun shines.

My second call for a companion was to Dylan. He was also always up for an adventure and readily agreed even while short on the details which were in the formative stage. I had a few weeks to study things and figure out the best course of action. The yellow truck once again out and back was the first thought but June was no good time in the Mojave for a vehicle with no AC. My compressor had gone out several years before and any long trips were at more convenient weather times. I knew for a fact we couldn't make the southern version on I-10 and would have to time the I-40 route with evening travel preferred. It could be 125 degrees easy in the desert and the engine would not stand for that. This was a concern. The final straw on old yellar was repair cost. I had called Alec at the repair center up the road and priced a compressor. The age and scarcity of the item had pushed the part alone at well over a $1000. That would probably end up $1300 before we drove a mile just to MAYBE be functional. This fact plus the estimation of 14 miles per gallon of gas at $3.85 to $4 per gallon made it a no go option. When I did the math it looked more and more like a flight out and truck rental trip back may be the ticket. Amber would need help packing and Dylan's current girlfriend, who also wanted to see Los Angeles could fly out a few days early. Dylan and I would get out of town late Thursday after work. The truck situation based on my experience would and should be a Penske one way rental using the smallest box truck available. She didn't have that much furniture with a sofa and mattress being the largest items. This would also be the best bet on gas costs. Dylan's GF would also share driving duties in Amber's car which also had to make the trip. All seemed to be falling into place. Other than some flight changes things were scheduled and the plan set into motion. Dylan and I as it turned out would be leaving Little Rock at 7am through Denver and arriving at LAX at 1pm. This would work out fine and require one less hotel night. The one way truck would be picked up in Pasadena just off the freeway which was convenient. Hotel arrangements were made around the corner on Colorado Street from Amb's place also being convenient. The 16ft truck should fit nicely at the hotel overnight for the next day's loading and departure. With a 1pm arrival we should have plenty of time to get picked up at the airport and get to Pasadena before 4:30. This was the deadline on the truck pickup. Weather all the way west was clear so shouldn't be an issue.

The flight out was spectacular. Security was light and the sky went forever. Denver was a welcome change from flights heading several hours east to Charlotte or Atlanta for the connection west. I never understood that in regard to fuel. The layover was tolerable and we grabbed a quick bite. Other than Dylan's nicotine addiction all seemed well. On the final leg of the trip we were granted the extreme pleasure of flying over the Grand Canyon at what seemed about 10k feet. I've flown many times west but I have never had this view. The one or two times I may have I was always on the wrong side or wrong seat. This was perfect. After a cat nap and "Everyone Loves Raymond" episode on in-flight TV we were touching down. LAX hadn't changed. We made our way down to baggage carousel 7 and had bags in hand rather quickly as we had both packed light. Summer will allow that. Amber was calling as she had been monitoring our progress on her I-phone and saw we were a little early. She had parked in the deck across from the main terminal. It wasn't long and we were all together again as we followed her down and across the six lanes and cab stands. Dylan stopped to smoke. I was in the rear but as we reached the deck I could sense some slight indecision. Not long after I figured out she couldn't remember where in the massive parking structure she had come out. No one raised a stink and even laughed as we dragged the luggage the entire length twice, finally finding the car right where she had left it. "What happened?" I asked her upon arrival. Virtually every panel of the small Nissan was dented with an additional one long tire tread mark up the entire passenger side. "LA Freeway" was her only defense and I let it go. I would have time later to mess with her about it. We made Pasadena in good time and I was a little disappointed in the size and scope of the truck rental operation. It was a storefront and obviously a midtown drop off. I and an elderly Chinese man had interrupted the one young black attendants Subway sandwich. I was more compassionate than the Chinaman, perhaps because of my southern upbringing. I was also reminded of my dad's old saying "If you ever want to get busy... try and eat a sandwich". I think the man was in a real hurry and there were some language barrier issues. After some wrangling we were doing the pre-trip truck inspection. All seemed in order except size. "This is a 24ft truck?" I quizzed the dude. Confused he went back to the office. This nine foot truck difference would greatly affect fuel cost. I had not counted on this. Upon further investigation it was determined that the home office had emailed me of the substitution that mid morning. An email I would not have received in flight. I was pissed a little but not totally shaken.

The 24ft truck would not fit in front of the apartment as it would also not in any spaces at the hotel. This was a problem. Sometimes doing your homework in these matters is a fucking bitch when things deviate to this level. I called Penske and complained. It didn't take long to determine the substitution was necessary as there was nothing in LA available for one way in the size I required. If I wanted to wait until Tuesday, (the day to be getting home), something "may" be available. I hung up the phone. Licking our wounds a little we decided a neighborhood beer may sooth things. That's about when trip phase two was hatched. It had always been in the back of my mind to not haul ass back with a slight detour off I-40 up to Vegas on the return.

This concept totally erased all frustration with airport parking and truck rental issues. It was agreed. If loading the truck mid-morning it was entirely possible we could be on the strip before dark. The day in LA was sunny and pleasant as it always is more or less. We snacked on Danish before beginning. The move was not the worst I'd seen. We had three flights of stairs which were on the outside, unlike the narrow claustrophobic stairs in one of Amber's Chicago moves. The move was uneventful save for the need to guard items loaded. We hadn't thought much about it until the third passerby offered to help for twenty or so…always eyeing the load. Not threatened but just cautious, we left the truck, locked and loaded, and piled into Ambers car and headed to Hollywood for her friends goodbye lunch. We stayed probably too long but the food was good, bathroom handy and I could tell she needed this. I would not push. These people we had met to dine with had been her support, her life line. Her holiday guests…her late night party. It was hard for her but I knew in this day of easily staying in touch I was confident it would be no problem. We all hugged goodbye, strangers and familiars and made our way back to the truck.

The lock was in place and gas full. Away we went with Amber following behind as she often does. This Saturday traffic was really not bad traveling out past Big Bear and east. Clouds loomed ahead and I saw a hint of lightning. The truck held the road well like I knew it would. After ten minutes or so on the LA freeways I got the feel for the size and became comfortable. I searched the radio for NPR. Once we were on the open road at the switch near Bakersfield it was old hat.

The clouds were much closer but seemed to be moving with us east. We were just about in the desert and the sky was becoming blessedly overcast, holding temperatures down. In a switch of luck we caught the rain and it traveled all the way across the summer sand. Not a hard rain but pleasant and cool. The turn to Vegas was ahead and the rain followed. This could not have been ordered. The non-straining truck engine cruised along conserving fuel on the downhill sides.

We stopped for gas at two convenient stops, once when ants poured out of the truck vents and up my legs, as if the appropriate temperature had awakened their slumber. We would find out later this infestation was becoming a problem for rentals coming out of the greater southwest. Thirty minutes or so and this was just a strange memory. The rain shielded and accompanied us all the way to the southwest mountain range protecting Vegas, where it fell apart and went away like an old friend. There's no way in hell we could have envisioned 80 degrees across the Mojave in June and I felt fortunate again. Vegas lights were in sight. I had called ahead and reserved rooms at the usual Motel 6 on Old Industrial so it was no worries. Being curious what the recession would look like here I was reminded of Hunter Thompson's snap shot of Vegas as a barometer for America's health and made it a point to see for myself in this time of Obama. The high speed burn had definitely been light and on the wussy side. As a result of a lack of tourist and general road travelers I had noticed for the first time ever average and below desert fuel prices in conjunction with actual hotel rate discounts. Very unusual indeed. This led me to the conclusion that Vegas traffic would be light as well. Coming in on I-15 I began to believe my suspicions correct. Suddenly, traffic picked up steadily and I was a little confused, maybe construction traffic. As I approached my exit onto Tropicana I saw I was totally wrong, general traffic bumper to bumper. Apparently every person with two nickels (pardon me?) had a similar idea. I was blown away.

The truck cruised past the In and Out Burger and the corner hooker one stop and into the hotel lot. This time of day it was no problem finding what would be the vehicles home for the next two days where I had convinced everyone to stay. Not a hard sell considering I was paying. Unlocking the back and surveying the load shift I jerked out the appropriate bags, tossed them in the room and we hit the strip.

Wall to wall. As is customary we inched up Las Vegas Boulevard to the Harley Café to eat and park in the confines of the deck and strike out on foot, with the "people". The crowds blew me away as we made our way down toward the glamour palaces of Paris and the Bellagio. These never really change and were of no real interest to me, losing twenty in five minutes at the former. I couldn't truly see how "America" felt in these establishments.

The COPS TV show was being filmed on the streets just ahead. Wide eyed, drugged out youths wanting to break and run, cops high fiveing and posing as if hunters of big game, piles of weed and pills on closed car trunks. Hot camera lights in alleys between casino properties. The Mexican's pointed laughing. We were in the midst of a hot game of snap cards, as usual racking up points as if the only takers, a fresh tall can of Miller every two blocks. The atmosphere was festive and alive, almost breathing. There was no recession here. Fuck no!

Once past a few of the nicer properties and the Bally's pedestrian bridge we came to shit row, this being the string of three blocks of lesser establishments. You would find no high end shows here. The bridge was more populated than usual with Mexican bottled water salesmen and musicians, an old large blood stain at the escalator head. There was no telling how long people had tracked through. Were there body parts inside the mechanics? We would never know. You would think the city would hose it away... maybe in the fall. The first casino was the one decorated with shamrocks where I've taken many pictures over the years with the door greeter dwarf dressed like a lucky leprechaun, top hat and all...or the cage girls. Cheap drinks and shows. My kind of place.

The first sign of trouble was literally a sign. The downward side of the bridge escalator almost brushes against the cheap backlit marquee announcing whatever special. (I've often wondered how they built the bridge so close). For as long as I could remember the main advertisement was for the 24 hour, $1 draft Miller special. This had changed. Draft was now $2 with the addition of a $1 margarita. This said several things to me as clues to the state of our economy. First they had increased 200% the price of beer. This would not affect the amount of required small change by the bar as one is the same as two to a blind bat. It's all fewer than five. Obviously this was just a move to earn a little more cash. Most wouldn't even notice the difference especially in contrast to the five dollar and up beers at "respectable" joints. They were only a hook to get you in the door anyway.

I heard the wafts of a mariachi band in the distance. The addition of the margarita was done to counter the added dollar but to also attract the before unaddressed female crowd. If you have ever had a one dollar margarita then you know they are no threat, alcohol light. It would take several of the small translucent cups to even get near the edge, at least for a semi-pro. I ordered five. The line moved fairly quickly as it was just add ice and pour. We scoped out a nearby table to sit a moment and survey our options.

Looking around it occurred to me there had been nowhere near this many bodies in the swankier clubs. The place was surprisingly packed. I gulped down the third of five when I saw a college kid buy a solid shot of Cuervo for three bucks. If I did this and replaced the three watered down versions I could combine everything into a decent size drink for six singles. I still heard Mexican music somewhere, I think over near the restroom where it was usually found. Near us was a really shitty rock cover band in matching cummerbunds laying down what sounded like song after song of Journey material. It was less than magical. More people poured in. the clientele outfits were predominantly 70's to early 80's with a spattering of hip-hop, hat backward horseshit kids. They were out of place and uncomfortable which pleased me immensely. The only thing drawing them in was the cheap drinks as advertised. Get one and get out, back to the Strip. There was not a single gaming spot open. The poker tables displayed almost as much neck hanging gold and metallic teeth as chips in play. It was much more animated and fun to see than the Poker Challenge on cable. These assholes were real and I was proud to see them. Everyone wore the emotion shielding sunglasses, some mirror…some standard green, most all aviator style with the occasional Elvis. The crowd over my left shoulder squealed at one of the four craps tables. This was the action polar opposite to the sloth-like movements on the poker felt. I couldn't believe how many people; regular people by day in other lives, crowded around the tables attempting a modest or better reward.

My drink idea worked great and I could feel a different edge to my beer buzz. The midget was off break and at the door, coaxing passersby's to check out the action. I often wondered if he worked on some sort of commission basis. Surely the "eye in the sky" could give some sort of an accounting of his conquests? The band was now droning on a Billy Joel medley. It was weak. I had sixty in cash so I opted to spend another six bucks on the shot and backup, to get around the corner a tad more before switching back to beer. Not able to take much more we decided to dive in and get me at some slots. I'm not sure why I thought they would be less crowded but I was wrong. After circling at least 30 minutes I found a reasonable facsimile to one of the machines I favor, .25 cent.

Winning was slow coming and my initial twenty spot was down to twelve. The cocktail waitresses avoided me like dog shit on a shoe. Was I too normal? Was there not enough bling? What the fuck is "bling" anyway? I decided the only way to get a drink was to sacrifice the twenty, get to zero and go get one my damn self. A foolish notion but at this point the tequila was in firm control. I hit the bar at a trot and kicked back the shot straight…no banter. It was no worries as I wasn't driving. "Oh wait, yes I was?". Well not far anyway, maybe a mile or two to the other side of I-15. "Where was the car?" After a minute or so I remembered it was at the Harley deck six or seven l-o-n-g blocks away. It was no matter because I had a great buzz, a pocket full of primo snap cards and I was right here with the "real" Americans…for the most part. It wasn't like I was checking green cards and passports or anything. I wasn't judging but they could be spotted past the real "real" Americans. Everyone here was gaudy and loud as they should be… Rome burns and here are the people, spectacle and drink in hand. Wallowing in it, oblivious to headlines or even what time of day it is, artificial air to go with fake boobs on the fifty plus aged tired waitresses. I breathed deep in the over oxygenated air and cigar smoke.

It felt great and I knew what today was all about in this country. It's all about where you're at. There are no real ideals like in the sixties and early seventies. In the mean time we were found to be mortal. Our bodies are breaking down from abuse but due to technology seem to look even better. Our heroes are dying, one at a time. Hunter Thompson killed himself to remain in control for god sakes and of what? The inevitable? People were scared but in the "party" collective they were untouchable. Everyone was playing his or her part. In this period of history everyone is a character. Everyone has a cell phone (tracking they're every move if necessary.) Everyone was texting. What was wrong with talking to who was with you or near? Why text your BFF in Iowa? You are here, right now in the "real America", standing on thirty year old carpet. It's our priorities I suppose. You can see it in our wall paper and light fixtures. This all swarmed over me in an instant of clarity. I had glimpsed that which I seek as they would say in the Bible. It would have to be processed, but for now I would have to hit the streets and get out of this fucking freak show. There must be more America outside, maybe redemption of sorts, I wasn't sure. What I did know as is my right I really wanted to pay more than full retail price for a drink in a commemorative keepsake glass. It was the liquor talking to be sure.

In that regard we shoved our way into Buffet's Margaritaville, a chain bar with a gift shop as large as the bar proper, a live action show (sorta) every half hour. Miraculously (which has happened before) some bar seats opened which we leaped into. The drinks were real and much more potent and I ordered the most colorful thing I could find, blue caracal I think.

This was America too, but different, this was all totally fake. I love "Buffet" but he has sold this crowd on his imaginary lifestyle. For whatever brief time there you are his bud. Pick up a towel, shot glass and license plate on your way out bitches. This is not real at all and you can tell by all the nervous cutting looks the customers give each other, looking for some level of validation. Never really finding it. I've seen this same look on the streets of large cities all over this country. Everyone is looking for a dad to tell them this is the right move. They never find him so head down they walk forward.

After blowing twenty on my plastic and not feeling particularly good about it we made our way back out to only see COPS again filming in the parking lot next to the all night karaoke margarita breakfast bar. That was the problem with all this. There was no underbelly. There was no bottom. As we passed I instinctively grabbed more snap cards and stuffed them into my cargo shorts pockets with the others. The ultimate tourist fuck. We were feeling no pain now and lumbered back toward the bridge. I tried to convince Dylan to run up and act like he knew one of the young men in handcuffs and hit him square in the face while all were on camera. Worst case was he would be on TV and also arrested. Best case National TV debut. He declined. One A&P stop for a six pack and I'm emptying several hundred snap cards on the hotel dresser. Thank god we are leaving in the morning. I seen all I can sees this trip and I can't sees no more as Popeye the Sailor would mumble.

Next morning I felt surprisingly well as I eased the truck down Tropicana to avoid Monday AM traffic and hit the highway near the airport backside toward Hoover Dam. I vaguely recalled getting a half gallon of whole milk at the whore one stop which was evidenced by our trash. The atmosphere was sparkling without a cloud in the sky. Heat was no longer a factor I think. In my side mirror I saw peaking around me Amber smiling in the little dented and permanently bird shit stained car, wearing white Jackie Onassis sunglasses. To my right Dylan snored and drooled against the inside window. We were Americans and we were in America, heading home east into the brilliant sun.

S. Ray Jackson lives and works in the United States of America which he considers his playground and home...